CONTENTS

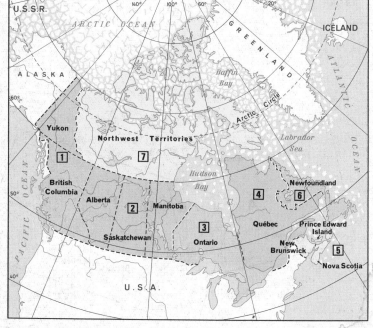

PRINCIPAL SIGHTS

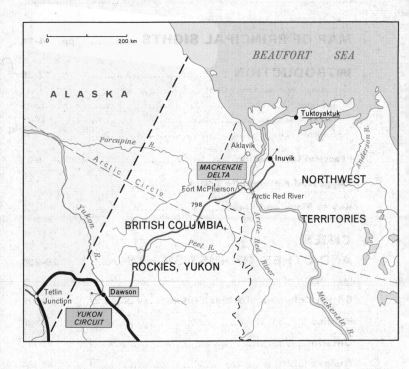

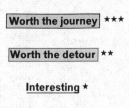

Worth the journey ★★★

Worth the detour ★★

Interesting ★

Cities and other tourist sights
described in the guide are indicated in black.
Consult the index for the page reference.

Map Symbols

●   City described

▲   Miscellaneous sights

▬   Route described

   Trans-Canada Highway

798   Distance in kilometres

   Regular ferry service

   Railway

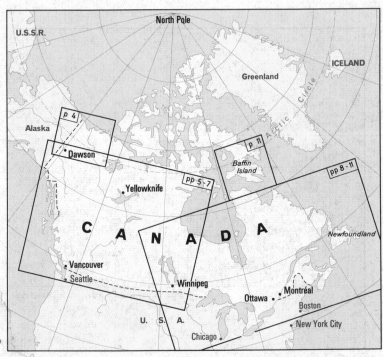

Arctic
Bathurst Inlet
Circ

GREAT BEAR LAKE

Burnside R.

Back R.

NORTHWEST TERR

Lac la Martre

Theton R.

YELLOWKNIFE

Fort Simpson

346

ahanni Butte

289

GREAT SLAVE LAKE

t Liard

Slave River

Wood Buffalo
National Park

LAKE ATHABASCA

660

ALASKA
HIGHWAY

Peace River

t Nelson

PRAIR

Fort St-John

508

591

Athabasca River

R

wson
Creek

715

EDMONTON

North Saskatchewan R.

Prince Albert
National Park

Jasper

527

OO

761

ROCKY MOUNTAIN
PARKS

299

The Battlefords

Saskatoon

Monashees
and Selkirks

Lake Louise

Drumheller

on R.

1057

Revelstoke

Banff

619

Saskatchewan R.

Dinosaur
Provincial Park

Okanagan
Valley

CALGARY

Penticton

Fort Steele

THE KOOTENAYS

Fort
Macleod

762

South Saskatchewan R.

Prairie Wildlife
Centre

Osoyoos

Kootenay R.

Columbia R.

Lethbridge

Cardston

Mo

Cypress Hills

Waterton Lakes
National Park

U. S. A.

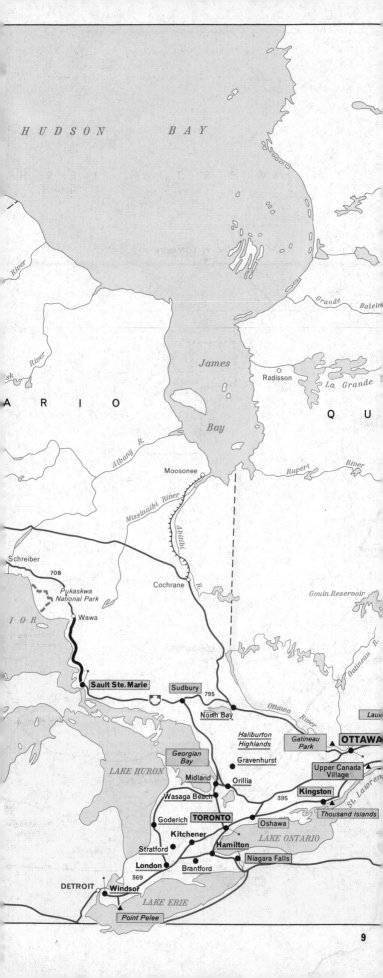

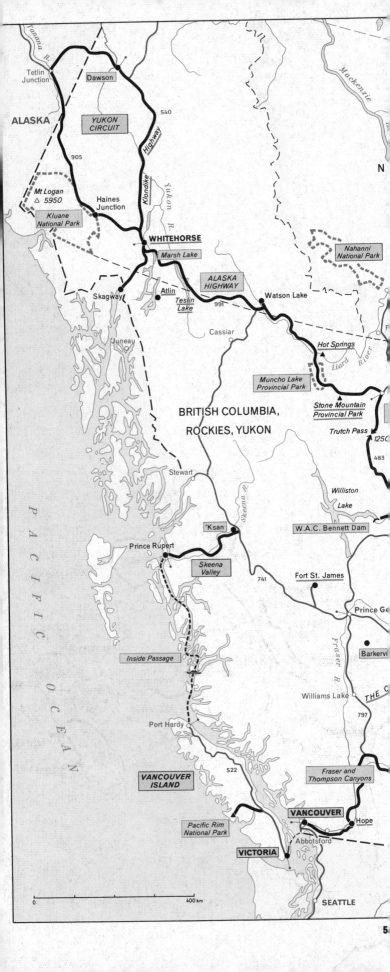

ALASKA

Tanana R.

Tetlin
Junction

Dawson

Mackenzie

*YUKON
CIRCUIT*

540

Highway

905

Klondike

Yukon R.

Mt Logan
△ 5950

*Kluane
National Park*

Haines
Junction

WHITEHORSE

*Nahanni
National Park*

Marsh Lake

N

*ALASKA
HIGHWAY*

Skagway

Atlin

*Teslin
Lake*

991

Watson Lake

Juneau

Cassiar

Hot Springs

Liard River

*Muncho Lake
Provincial Park*

BRITISH COLUMBIA,

ROCKIES, YUKON

*Stone Mountain
Provincial Park*

Trutch Pass

1250

483

Stewart

*Williston
Lake*

Skeena R.

W.A.C. Bennett Dam

'Ksan

Prince Rupert

*Skeena
Valley*

741

Fort St. James

P
A
C
I
F
I
C

Prince Ge

Barkervi

Fraser R.

THE C

Williams Lake

O
C
E
A
N

Inside Passage

797

Port Hardy

*VANCOUVER
ISLAND*

522

*Fraser and
Thompson Canyons*

VANCOUVER

Hope

*Pacific Rim
National Park*

Abbotsford

VICTORIA

0   400 km

SEATTLE

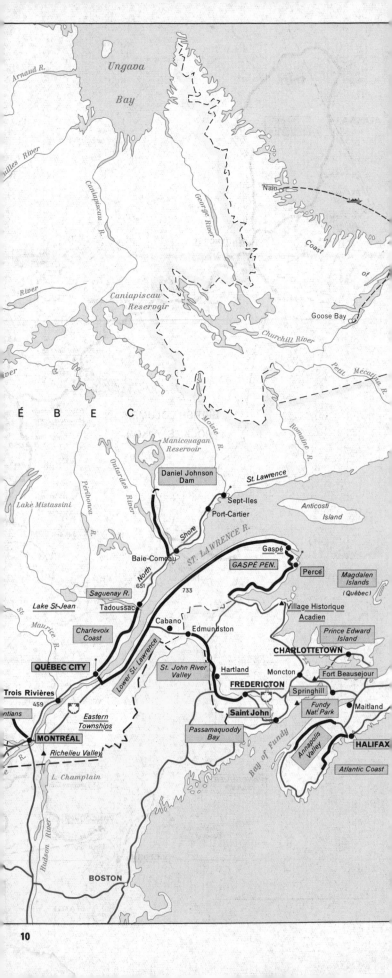

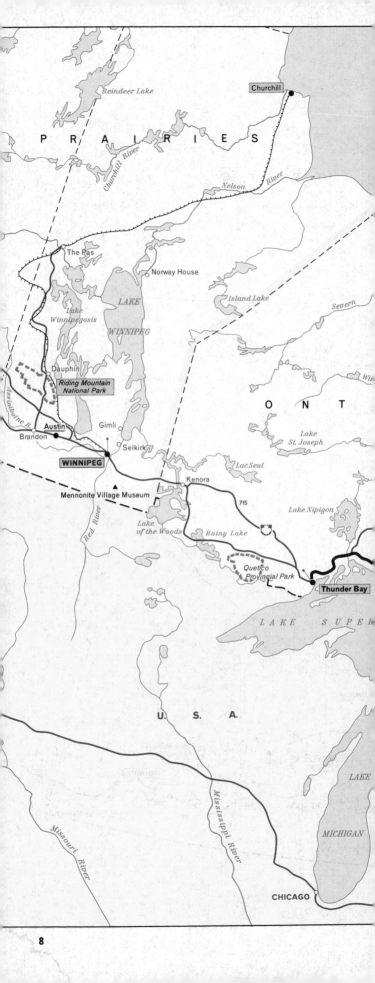

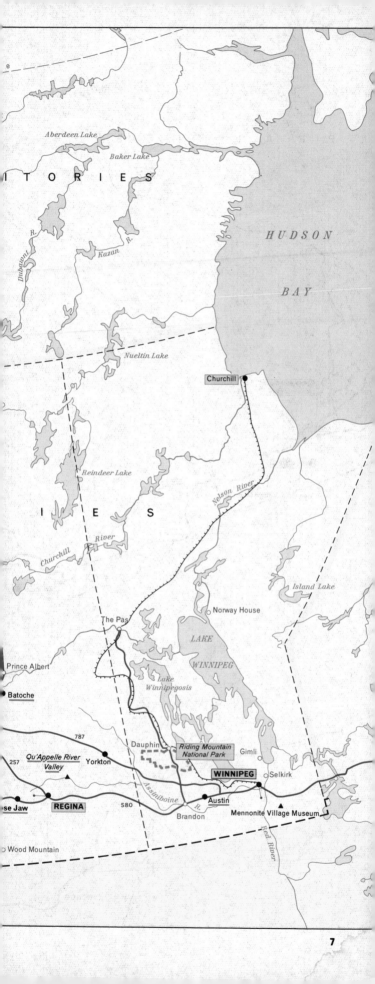

– slow down when another vehicle approaches – stones thrown up when passing or overtaking other vehicles at high speeds can crack windshields.

Distances along the Alaska Highway are marked by kilometre posts and places are referred to by their distance from Dawson Creek. For example, Watson Lake is at km 1 017 - mile 632. The majority of tourists stay in the campgrounds provided by the governments of the Yukon and British Columbia. There are, however, motels and other forms of accommodation available.

From Dawson Creek to Fort Nelson – *483 km - 300 miles*

The Alaska Highway begins at **Dawson Creek** (Pop 11 373) in the valley of the Peace River. The rural nature of this region is immediately striking. The river itself is crossed at **Taylor** which sits on a vast natural gas and oil field. Gas processing plants can be seen along the highway and oil pipelines run beneath fields of crops all the way to **Fort St. John.**

Excursion to W.A.C. Bennett Dam★★. – *234 km - 145 miles Rtn – about 1/2 day. Take Hwy 29 W 11 km - 7 miles N of Fort St. John to Hudson's Hope, then Dam Access Road.*

The road follows the valley of the Peace River for many miles climbing above it at times and giving fine **views★** of the flat-topped hills and fertile fields. The little community of **Hudson's Hope** was the site of one of Simon Fraser's trading posts and was also the place where Alexander Mackenzie began his portage around the Peace River canyon on his epic trek to the west coast *(p. 31).* From the community, the dam access road winds steeply into the mountains with views of snowcapped peaks ahead.

Tourist Lookout★★. – *22 km - 14 miles from Hudson's Hope ; follow signs to restaurant.*

Perched on a shelf overlooking the reservoir, this lookout provides an excellent view of the enormous earthfilled dam. Built between 1963 and 1967 across the upper end of a canyon on the Peace River, it has created a reservoir, **Williston Lake,** 362 km - 225 miles long, encompassing part of the valleys of the Parsnip and Finlay rivers which meet in the Rocky Mountain Trench and flow out eastward as the Peace River. The dam itself (183 m - 600 ft high and 2 km - 1 1/4 miles across) was constructed of glacial moraine deposited during the last Ice Age 6.5 km - 4 miles away in the old valley of the Peace River. After the Ice Age the river cut itself a new channel – the aforementioned canyon. So the material which once blocked the course of the river about 15 000 years ago was used to reblock it in the 1960s. At the present time the project generates over 2 700 000 kw of electricity or more than 30 % of the total electrical requirements for the province of British Columbia.

Gordon M. Schrum Generating Station★. – *Guided tours daily mid May - mid Oct ; weekdays only rest of year ; time : 1 hr ;* ☎ *(604) 783-5211.*

The tour starts from the reception centre on the sixth floor of the Control Building - the blue structure shaped like a transformer. It consists of a film *(25 min)* on the history of the site and building of the dam ; a visit to the control room where operators monitor the entire power operation, a visit to the generator chamber 152 m - 500 ft underground hewn out of solid rock ; and a visit to the manifold chamber where water is seen surging from the turbines into the tailrace discharge tunnel.

West Side Lookout★. – *3 km - 2 miles across dam.* Good views of Williston Lake and the spillway are obtained from this viewpoint. Part of the canyon of the Peace River is visible with the reservoir of the smaller **Peace Canyon Dam** *(visitor centre open same times as Schrum Generating Station)* downstream.

After the junction with Highway 29, the Alaska Highway passes through flattish and heavily wooded country, which gradually becomes more mountainous. At km 314 - mile 195, the route reaches the summit of **Trutch Pass** where there is a fine **view★** of the Rockies across the Minaker River Valley. These views continue through heavy forest until the road reaches **Fort Nelson** (Pop 3 724), a lumber centre and base for oil and gas exploration. The Liard Highway to Fort Simpson, NWT, via Fort Liard commences at this point offering access to **Nahanni National Park** *(p. 234).*

From Fort Nelson to Whitehorse★★ – *991 km - 616 miles*

After leaving Fort Nelson the Alaska Highway turns west and many sweeping views of mountains are obtained as the road traverses the end of the Rocky Mountains. The country is very open and during the first part of the drive the mountains are largely flat-topped, more akin to the ''Mesa'' mountains of the Southern Rockies in the United States than to the pointed peaks of the Banff-Jasper area. Further on the mountains are snowcapped.

Stone Mountain Provincial Park★. – *Km 627 - mile 389.* This park is named for a mountain to the north of the highway. It is a rocky and barren area resembling a stone quarry, the mountains being more rugged than previously. The highlight of the park is **Summit Lake★**, a lovely green-coloured stretch of water lying beside the highway. After leaving the lake the road passes through the rocky gorge of Macdonald Creek.

(after photo by Canadian Government office of Tourism)

Dall Sheep

Muncho Lake Provincial Park★★. – *Km 688 - mile 427.* This park is one of the most beautiful parts of the drive. At first the road follows the valley of the Toad River, a wide, rocky and rather desolate area softened only by the pale green colour of the river. The view ahead opens up, and more and more mountains come into view, many snowcapped. This is an area where Stone sheep can often be seen licking the salt off the road bed. **Muncho Lake★★** itself is reached 46 km - 29 miles after entering the park. It is a beautiful aquamarine colour which is supposedly caused by copper oxide leaking into the lake. The surrounding folded mountains rising over 2 000 m - 7 000 ft are perfectly reflected in it.

ALASKA HIGHWAY★★

At km 788 - mile 490, the first view of the mighty **Liard River** is obtained. This river rises in the Yukon, flows south into British Columbia and finally north again into the Northwest Territories to join the Mackenzie. Its valley marks the northern limit of the Rocky Mountains. The Alaska Highway follows this wild and turbulent river for approximately 240 km - 150 miles providing some good views.

Liard River Hot Springs Park★. – *Km 799 - mile 496. Take side road on right to parking area, follow boardwalk. Changing Rooms provided.* This small park consists of a large and hot (37 °C - 100° F) sulphur pool in natural surroundings, deep enough to swim in.

At km 947 - mile 588 the Alaska Highway crosses the 60th Parallel entering the Yukon Territory. British Columbia is not yet left behind, however, as the highway crosses and recrosses the border many times. Fine views of the **Cassiar Mountains** are obtained along this road.

Watson Lake. – *Pop 748. Km 1 017 - mile 632. Yukon Government Visitor Reception Centre.* Watson Lake is the transportation and communications centre for the southern Yukon. It is famous for its collection of **signposts**. In 1942 a homesick soldier, employed building the highway, erected a sign on which was the name of his hometown, and its direction. Tourists have kept up this tradition and there are now more than 1 300 signs from all over the continent.

At km 1 044 - mile 649, Route 37, the **Stewart-Cassiar Highway,** joins the Alaska Highway from the south. Winding 800 km - 500 miles through western British Columbia, this road provides an alternative route to the Yukon. After this junction the Alaska Highway begins to cross the Cassiar Mountains. There are good views of snowcapped peaks on both sides of the road.

At km 1 162 - mile 722, a height of land is crossed which marks the divide between two great river systems (Mackenzie and Yukon) emptying respectively into Arctic and Pacific Oceans.

Teslin Lake★. – *Km 1 290 - mile 802.* The name of this stretch of water means long lake in the local Indian dialect. The highway crosses Nisutlin Bay or arm, and hugs the shore of this long narrow lake for about 48 km - 30 miles. The views of the mountains and lake are good and they are frequently bordered by clusters of **fireweed,** the purple flower common all over the Yukon and British Columbia which has been adopted as the emblem of the Yukon. At the head of the lake the road crosses the Teslin River by a high bridge - a remnant of the days when river steamers carried all the traffic in this area and needed clearance under bridges.

Excursion to Atlin★. – *At km 1 392 - mile 865, Jake's Corner,* take road south for 98 km - 61 miles. An old gold mining town, the small community of Atlin in British Columbia has a pretty **site★** overlooking mountains and the lake of the same name.

Marsh Lake★★. – *Km 1 408 - mile 875.* This beautiful blue-green lake surrounded by mountains is really an arm of the much larger **Tagish Lake** to the south and thus part of the Yukon River system. Because of its proximity to Whitehorse, this lake is not as deserted as the others passed on the highway and many houses can be seen along its edge. The road follows the lake for about 16 km - 10 miles with many lovely viewpoints. At the end of the lake the road crosses the **Yukon River** at a dam.

At km 1 445 - mile 898, there is a good **view★** from above of the steep white cliffs and clear green water of the fabled Yukon River which rises only 24 km - 15 miles from the Pacific and meanders nearly 3 200 km - 2 000 miles crossing the Arctic Circle before it finally jettisons its waters into that same ocean.

Whitehorse★. – *Km 1 474 - mile 916. Description p. 67.*
    The Alaska Highway is on a plateau above the Yukon River. Below it on river level invisible from the highway sits this city, the capital of the Yukon. At km 1 462 - mile 909 there is a plaque noting the crossing of the 135th Meridien - Whitehorse is further west not only of Vancouver but of the whole of Vancouver Island and the Queen Charlotte Islands.

From Whitehorse to Alaska Border★★ – *491 km - 305 miles, described in* *opposite direction p. 72*

The CARIBOO ★ British Columbia
Map pp. 5-6

The Cariboo is the name given to the country in the valley of the Fraser north of Cache Creek *(map p. 32)*. It is part of the central plateau of British Columbia, a vast rolling plain of low arid hills, lakes and sagebrush, bounded to the east by the Cariboo Mountains, from which the area gets its name, and to the west by the Coast Mountains.

    Opened up by the fur traders, the Cariboo first reached prominence with the Gold Rush of 1861 which led to the building of the Cariboo Wagon Road. Once the gold was gone, the miners left and farmers moved in. Today, the main activity is cattle rearing and some of the biggest ranches of Canada are found in this region. The centre of the area is **Williams Lake** which holds an annual stampede in the first week of July considered the premier rodeo of the province. Cowboys come from all over North America to vie for trophies. The biggest stockyards of British Columbia are also located in Williams Lake. The region is a popular tourist area known for its sports fishing, game hunting, dude ranches and other traditional features of ''Western'' living, and for the restored gold rush centre of Barkerville.

The Cariboo Gold Rush. – Gold was first found in this area in 1859 by prospectors who had made their way from California to the lower Fraser and then north following the gold trail. By 1861, large quantities were being extracted from the upper part of Williams Creek when **Billy Barker,** a Cornish sailor who jumped ship at Victoria to try his luck, hit pay dirt in its lower reaches. Within 48 hours he had taken out $ 1 000 worth of gold.

(after photo by B. C. Provincial Archives)

Mule Train on the Cariboo Wagon Road

For ten years the area boomed and towns such as Barkerville (named for Billy), Camerontown and Richfield sprang up. To facilitate transportation to this area, the government decided to build a wagon road to Barkerville from the lower Fraser. This first Cariboo Road was constructed 1862-65 partly by the Royal Engineers and partly by private contractors. Following the wild rocky canyon of the Fraser it was something of an engineering achievement. The present Cariboo Highway, 97, follows the same route.

The gold in the Cariboo did not last long and ten years after the first discovery the towns of the area were almost deserted. In Williams Creek alone $ 50 000 000 worth of gold was found. Barkerville itself was inhabited until 1958 when the provincial government decided to restore it to its former splendour as a centennial project.

■ BARKERVILLE HISTORIC PARK★★

90 km - 56 miles E of Quesnel (Hwy 97) by Hwy 26. Open daily ; meals in summer only ; ☎ (604) 994-3209.

Barkerville is reached by an attractive **drive**★ into the Cariboo Mountains passing **Cottonwood House** *(28 km - 17 miles, open daily June-Sept)* one of the few remaining roadhouses on the Cariboo Wagon Road, and **Wells**, a mining community. The old gold mining centre has a fine **site**★ in the valley of Williams Creek surrounded by mountains.

The first place to visit is the **museum** *(open daily except weekends in winter)* where there are interesting displays on the town, methods of mining, the gold rush and its importance to the province. There are also slide shows *(shown regularly in summer months, off-season ask at Information Desk).*

The restored buildings of Barkerville include all the things one would expect to find in a mining community : stores, hotels, saloons, an assay office, etc. Note especially **St. Saviour's Anglican Church,** a rather unusually-shaped structure of whipsawn timber and square nails *(services twice daily except Tues and Wed July and Aug)* ; the Chinese section at the far end of the street with its **Chinese Freemasons' Hall** (the Chinese followed the other gold rushers from California north but tended to keep within their own community and not mix) ; **Billy Barker's claim ;** the dance hall with its shows of the type the miners watched *(regularly in July and Aug ; $ 5.50)* and the Richfield Courthouse *(1.6 km - 1 mile walk up Williams Creek)* where a dramatized sketch of **Judge Baillie Begbie** is performed *(daily except Wed, July and Aug).* Judge Begbie was the famous Cariboo judge who enforced law and order in an unruly community. Visitors can also pan for gold in the Eldorado Mine *($ 2.50).*

FORT ST. JAMES ★ British Columbia

Map p. 5 - *66 km - 41 miles N of Yellowhead Hwy 16 by Hwy 27 - Pop 2 284*

In a lovely setting beside Stuart Lake, the town of Fort St. James is one of the oldest settlements in British Columbia. In 1806, Simon Fraser *(p. 31)* founded a trading post which became the chief Hudson's Bay Company post in New Caledonia after 1821. It remained in operation until 1971.

Fort St. James National Park★. *– Beside lake in town. Open daily mid May - mid Oct ; guided tours, about 1 1/2 hrs ;* ☎ *(604) 996-7191.*

The park comprises five Hudson's Bay Company buildings dating from 1884-89 restored to their late 19th century state by the Federal Government. Of note are the **Men's House** with its meticulously restored furnishings, the **Fish Cache** built off the ground with its displays of dried fish and pork, and the dove-tailed log **General Warehouse** with its fur store. The Interpretive Centre has displays on the fort's history.

To find the description of a point of interest which you already know by name, consult the **index** p. 237.

FRASER and THOMPSON Canyons ★★ British Columbia

Map p. 5 – 480 km - 298 miles by Trans-Canada Highway – allow 1 1/2 days – Local map p. 42

Between Vancouver and Shuswap Lake the Trans-Canada Highway follows the deep valleys cut by two of the wildest rivers in the province through the rocky Coast Mountains and the dry hilly scrubland of central British Columbia.

The Taming of an Impossible Route. – The Fraser was first seen by white men in 1793 when Alexander Mackenzie followed part of its northern course on his epic journey to the Pacific at Bella Coola *(p. 31)*. His fellow partner in the North West Company, Simon Fraser, descended and reascended its entire length in 1808 thinking it was the Columbia. "We had to pass where no man should venture" was his description of the canyon which he traversed on foot along rock ledges and down ladders slung over rockfaces by the Indians. He gave his name to the river and that of David Thompson, the geographer and another North Westerner, to its major tributary.

The Fraser was much too wild for use as a fur-trading route so little activity was seen on it until gold was discovered at **Hill's Bar** near Yale in 1858. A rush began and before long every bar, bend and tributary was being searched for gold. Much was found but the major strike was made in the Cariboo further north *(p. 36)*. The problem was how to get there. Steamboats could mount the river as far as Yale, after that the river was much too turbulent (one or two boats were winched through Hell's Gate but a permanent water route was impossible). The land route was little better as Fraser had found. To resolve this problem the government of British Columbia (created 1858) decided to construct a road, and the famous Cariboo Wagon Road was built (see Cariboo above). The part through the Fraser Canyon took two years to construct and was something of an engineering miracle.

Later in the century, the Fraser Canyon and that of the Thompson were again selected as the route for a major transportation venture - the Canadian Pacific Railway *(p. 16)*. The same construction problems were encountered and finally overcome. This century has seen this once near impassable route become a major transportation artery with the building along it of a second railway and the Trans-Canada Highway.

From Vancouver to Hope★ – 141 km - 88 miles

The Trans-Canada Highway heads east from Vancouver *(p. 54)* along the wide valley of the Lower Fraser River. Rich black soil deposited by the river over aeons of time supports luxurious vegetation, tall trees, dairy cows, hay fields and market gardens. The valley is flanked by mountains – the Cascades to the south and Coast ranges to the north.

Hope★. – Pop 3 205. The mountains close in around this community as the valley narrows and swings northwards. The wildness and unpredictability of the region was well demonstrated by the **Hope Slide** of 1965. One January day a vast amount of rock from Johnson Peak *(21 km - 13 miles E by Rte 3)* slid into the valley, filling a lake and forcing its waters up the other side. Route 3 had to be rebuilt more than 45 m - 148 ft above its original level.

Manning Provincial Park★. – 26 km - 16 miles E of Hope by Rte 3. Hiking, canoeing, winter sports ; camping, accommodation ; ☎ (604) 840-8833.

After entering the park, Route 3 traverses an area called **Rhododendron Flats,** where these wild plants flower in profusion in mid–June, and crosses **Allison Pass** (alt 1 341 m – 4 400 ft). In the **Park Nature House★** *(68 km – 42 miles from Hope, beside Manning Park Lodge ; open daily except April, Oct and Nov)* the three different vegetation zones of the park are explained – the western slopes covered with the damp, dense growth of coastal British Columbia, the central area reflecting the transitional zone, and the eastern part with its dry and arid sagebrush country so typical of the interior of the province.

From Hope to Lytton★★ (Fraser Canyon) – 109 km - 68 miles

After Hope, the mountains close in abruptly and the farmland is left behind. The river changes into a rushing torrent and the road is perched on rocky ledges often high above it, sometimes at river level.

Yale★. – Pop 239. This little community surrounded by high and impressive cliffs was once a town of 20 000. During the gold rush, it was the end of river navigation and the beginning of the Cariboo Wagon Road. Hill's Bar is located just to the south.

North of Yale, the most spectacular part of the **canyon★★** begins. The cliffs are sheer, the valley narrow, tunnels are frequent and the river below seethes along, around and over rocks. Just after Spuzzum, the road crosses the river and continues on the east side.

Hell's Gate★. – The canyon here is 180 m - 600 ft deep but the river is only 36 m - 120 ft wide and it rushes past at 7.5 m - 25 ft a second. It was once wider but during the construction of the Canadian National Railway in 1914, a rockslide occurred narrowing the gap. This made passage upstream almost impossible for the salmon whose spawning grounds are in the streams and lakes around Shuswap Lake. A sharp decline in the Pacific salmon fishery occurred until finally fish "ways" were constructed in 1944-46 to enable the salmon to bypass the turbulent water.

An **airtram** *(open daily March - Oct ; $5.50 ; cafeteria, gift shop ; ☎ (604) 867-9277)* descends the 150 m - 500 ft to river level where the canyon and the incredible speed of the water can be appreciated. There are displays on the salmon and the fish ladders as well as a film *(20 mins)*. The fishways are visible in the river but salmon are never seen due to the muddy water.

The Pacific Salmon. – Every summer and autumn British Columbia's five salmon species – sockeye, pink, coho, spring and chum, leave the ocean and swim far inland up the province's rivers and streams to spawn. In none are their numbers greater than in the Fraser where they travel as much as 48 km - 30 miles a day. Soon after spawning they die. Their offspring remain in fresh water for about two years before heading for the ocean where they stay another two to five years until they reach maturity. Then their epic return journey to their spawning grounds occurs.

After Hell's Gate, the canyon becomes less dark and formidable and there are more trees on its rocky slopes. From **Jackass Mountain** there is a fine **view**★ of the canyon from high above the river, and at Cisco Creek two bridges can be seen as the railways switch sides.

Lytton.- Pop 428. This community regularly registers the highest temperatures in Canada and the vegetation is more of the sagebrush type of central British Columbia rather than the green pine trees of the lower Fraser Canyon. At this point the clear blue waters of the Thompson surge into the muddy brown Fraser making a streak visible for a short distance downstream before they are swallowed up.

From Lytton to Shuswap Lake★★ (Thompson Canyon) – *230 km - 143 miles*

The Trans-Canada Highway and the two railways leave the valley of the Fraser and turn east along the Thompson passing through a dry, treeless and steep-sided **canyon**★★. The road winds and weaves along making sharp bends. Just before Spences Bridge, where the road crosses the river, the remains of a great landslide which occurred in 1905 can be seen.

Then the Thompson **valley**★ gradually widens out into an arid, semi-desert area where scrub vegetation and sagebrush predominate. Occasionally, there is some cultivation of the terraces above the river but only due to irrigation. The remains of one such attempt can be seen 17 km - 11 miles after Cache Creek at a place once called **Walhachin** (abundance of the earth). Between 1907 and 1914 a group of young British aristocrats built irrigation flumes to carry water to their fields and for a while the area flourished. The First World War ended the experiment as most of the men left to fight and were killed. Odd bits of flume and withered apple trees are all that now remain.

Just before Savona, the Thompson widens to form **Kamloops Lake.** From the Trans-Canada there are some pleasant **views**★ of this blue lake set in its rocky arid hills. Again irrigation is bringing some of the land under cultivation. The Trans-Canada bypasses **Kamloops**, an industrial city (Pop 64 048), and follows the south branch of the Thompson to its headwaters in **Shuswap Lake.** Here the country changes from dry bareness to verdant green with sparkling waters. Many salmon spawn in this region after their long swim up the turbulent Fraser and Thompson, and it is a popular resort area.

In the peak summer season, you may have difficulty finding hotel accommodation. We advise you to make reservations in advance.

The KOOTENAYS ★ British Columbia

Map p. 6

The southeast corner of British Columbia is known as the Kootenays because of the river of the same name which winds its way through it. A major tributary of the Columbia, the Kootenay River rises in the Rockies, traverses the National Park named for it *(p. 45)*, misses the headwaters of the Columbia by a mile at Canal Flats, flows south into the United States, loops and returns to Canada to form Kootenay Lake, and finally joins the Columbia at Castlegar.

The Kootenays are an area of mountains, beautiful lakes and lush valleys. The valley around **Creston** at the southern end of Kootenay Lake, for example, is full of grainfields, orchards and other fruitbearing plants. They are also an area of great mineral wealth past and present. The **Crowsnest Pass** region has some of the largest soft coal deposits in North America. Further west, copper, lead, zinc and silver are mined and processed in the huge smelter at **Trail.**

Gold in the Wild Horse Valley. – The first settlers in the region came seeking gold. A hectic rush to the area occurred in 1864 when nuggets were found in the valley of the Wild Horse River, a tributary of the Kootenay. A certain John Galbraith set up a ferry service across the Kootenay at its junction with the Wild Horse and the settlement which grew up around it took the name of Galbraith's Ferry. A road was pushed through the mountains to the site from the capital of British Columbia, then New Westminster, by a young English engineer, **Edgar Dewdney.** To this day this road (Route 3) bears his name.

After the gold rush petered out, settlers increasingly turned their energies to farming and ranching leading to land claim disputes with the Kootenay Indians. A detachment of North West Mounted Police was sent to the area under the command of the famous Mountie, **Sam Steele.** He restored peace and order to the settlement around the ferry which changed its name to Fort Steele to honour him and to mark the first posting of the police west of the Rockies.

■ FORT STEELE PROVINCIAL PARK★

16 km - 10 miles NE of Cranbrook by Route 95. Open daily May - Oct ; tearoom ; ☎ *(604) 489-3351.*

The town of Fort Steele flourished in the early 1890s as the centre of a mining boom which brought prosperity to the Kootenays. Its death knell was sounded when the railway over the Crowsnest Pass bypassed the town going to Cranbrook instead. In 1961, the provincial government took over the practically deserted townsite and restored it to represent a typical Kootenay town of the turn-of-the-century era.

Today, with its fine **site**★ at the foot of the Rockies, Fort Steele lives again. Among the many restored buildings, the **museum** set in an old hotel, is the most interesting with excellent displays on the history of the region. The North West Mounted Police barracks can also be visited. Live entertainment is provided in the **Wild Horse Theatre** *(daily July and Aug except Fri ; $4.00).* An old steam locomotive gives rides *(20 min, $3.00)* and there are tours of the site by stagecoach *($2.00).* Overlooking the Kootenay River stands a large wooden water wheel once used to haul water out of the mines.

MONASHEES and SELKIRKS ★★ British Columbia

Map p. 6 - 219 km - 136 miles by Trans-Canada Highway – allow 6 hrs - Local map below

Part of the Columbia Mountain System, the Monashee and Selkirk Ranges are located in southeastern British Columbia between the central plateau and the Rockies. Beginning as rolling hills in the west, they soon develop sharp ridges, deep valleys and pyramid peaks, the results of heavy glaciation, especially in the Selkirks of Glacier National Park where many valley glaciers still exist. The Trans-Canada Highway crosses the two ranges by an often spectacular route through Eagle and Rogers' Passes.

Eagle Pass★. – 71 km - 44 miles from Sicamous to Revelstoke.

This pass through the Monashee Mountains (*Monashee* is a Gaelic word meaning mountain of peace) was discovered by **Walter Moberly** in 1865. Its name derives from the story that Moberly fired his gun at an eagle's nest and watched the birds fly away up a valley. He followed them and discovered the pass, which was later the chosen route for the Canadian Pacific Railway as well as the Trans-Canada Highway.

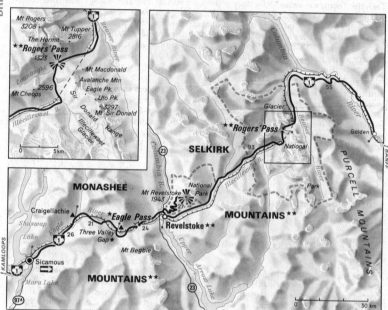

From the small resort town of **Sicamous** (Pop 1 057) set on the narrows between Shuswap and Mara Lakes, the Trans-Canada begins to climb up the valley of the Eagle River. After 26 km - 16 miles it reaches **Craigellachie**. On November 7th 1885, the last spike of the Canadian Pacific Railway *(p. 16)* linking east and west was driven here *(there is a plaque beside the railway tracks off the road on the right)*. Craigellachie is a Gaelic word which refers to the rallying point of the Grant clan in Scotland, a symbol well known to the Banffshire-born directors of the Railway.

The road climbs more steeply and the valley narrows before it reaches **Three Valley Gap★** *(47 km - 29 miles)* which has a lovely **site★** beside Three Valley Lake edged with sheer red cliffs. Soon afterwards the top of the pass is reached *(55 km - 34 miles)* and the road begins a steep descent to the Columbia in the narrow valley of Tonakwatla Creek.

Revelstoke★★. – Pop 5 544.

Set on the east bank of the Columbia River at its junction with the Illecillewaet, this small town has a lovely **site★** surrounded by mountains – the Selkirks to the east and the Monashees to the west. It is named for **Lord Revelstoke,** the head of the London banking firm of Barings which stepped in to aid financially the Canadian Pacific Railway Company in 1885 when it seemed the railway might never be completed. It is a popular winter and summer sports centre due to the excellent facilities in **Mount Revelstoke National Park** including the Nels Nelson Ski Jump. The park is famous for its timbered slopes, alpine meadows and sparkling lakes.

Mount Revelstoke National Park Highway★★. – 26 km - 16 miles of gravel road not suitable for trailers, 45 min to ascend. Begins on Trans-Canada Hwy 1.5 km - 1 mile E of Revelstoke turnoff.

This road ascends the southwest face of Mount Revelstoke in a series of switchbacks. After 5.6 km - 3 1/2 miles there is a **viewpoint★** of the town of Revelstoke. It is seen spread out below on the Columbia with the Monashees behind it, dominated by the snow-capped twin peaks of **Mount Begbie**. A little to the east of the town, the valley of Tonakwatla Creek can be seen cutting its way through the mountains.

At the summit the **view★★** is more to the north. The Columbia in its steep-walled valley can be seen and the glaciated mountains of the Clachnacudainn Range with their jagged peaks and bare slopes. There is a lookout tower, with displays naming the peaks visible, a short distance from the parking area. The vegetation has completely changed. Instead of the red cedars, hemlocks and spruce of the lower slopes, there are only stunted and wind-pruned firs.

Paths at the summit descend into the **alpine meadows** where in summer there is a profusion of multi-coloured wild flowers : Indian paintbrush (red), lupines (blue), arnica (yellow) and valerian (white).

Rogers' Pass★★. – *148 km - 92 miles from Revelstoke to Golden.*

After crossing the Rockies by the Kicking Horse Pass *(p. 47)*, it was planned that the Canadian Pacific Railway should follow the Columbia River loop *(map p. 30)* because the Selkirks were considered an impenetrable barrier. In 1881, however, a determined surveyor, **Major Rogers,** followed the Illecillewaet River into these same mountains and discovered the pass named after him. The railway was routed this way as it saved about 240 km - 150 miles.

The Avalanche Problem. – From the beginning, however, there were problems with the pass because of the incredibly high snowfall in the Selkirks (an annual average of 940 cm - 370 ins though 1 841.5 cm - 725 ins were recorded in the winter of 1966-67) and the danger of avalanches down the sheer slopes of the very steep mountains bordering the pass. These slopes have been worn so smooth by previous slides that nothing blocks the path of new ones. Miles of snowsheds were constructed over the railway but the battle with the elements every winter proved too costly for Canadian Pacific and so in 1916 the Connaught Tunnel was constructed through Mount Macdonald to avoid the most hazardous area.

(courtesy Canadian Broadcasting Corporation)

Early Canadian Pacific Railway Locomotive

For the next forty years that section of Rogers' Pass remained untouched by man. In 1959, however, after surveys had been carried out, the decision was made to build the Trans-Canada through the pass using some of the original railway roadbed. The route was completed in 1962 after having been the most expensive and difficult part of the Trans-Canada to construct. Against the winter avalanches an elaborate defence and warning system is in place. Concrete snowsheds deflect slides over the road, rubble barriers divert and break-up dangerous falls and a howitzer is used to lob shells into areas where snow is building up to trigger avalanches before they become too big to contain. Careful watch is kept on snow build-up by men stationed high in the mountains to decide when the howitzer should be fired.

In summer, travel along this road offers no problems. In winter, the instructions given by Park wardens must be followed. The road may be temporarily closed when the gun is being fired.

The Road★★. – The Trans-Canada Highway follows the high walled valley of the Illecillewaet River into the Selkirks and very soon passes through snowsheds which provide winter protection for the road. After 48 km - 30 miles, it enters **Glacier National Park** *(for admission to National Parks see p. 21. Hiking, climbing, camping ; ☏ (604) 837-6274).* Ahead the four pointed peaks of the **Sir Donald Range** can be seen. From left to right they are Avalanche Mountain, Eagle Peak, Uto Peak and the great slanting slab of Mount Sir Donald itself. To the north the steep pyramidal form of **Mount Cheops** is also visible. There are views to the south of glaciers across the rocky and bounding Illecillewaet River.

The road swings around the Napoleon Spur of Mount Cheops to reach the summit of the pass *(72 km - 45 miles)*, where a double arch commemorates the completion of the Trans-Canada Highway in 1962. The **view**★ includes the slide scarred peaks of **Mount Tupper** and **The Hermit** to the north, the Asulkan Ridge and snowfields including the Illecillewaet Neve to the east as well as the peaks of the Sir Donald Range and Mount Cheops.

The road begins its steep descent between the bare slopes of Mount Tupper and The Hermit to the north and the looming form of **Mount Macdonald** to the south. It passes through a series of reinforced concrete snowsheds and swings into the valley of the Beaver River, a tributary of the Columbia which separates the spiky, jagged Selkirks from the more rounded Purcell Mountains. The railway appears above the road to the west. Then, the road leaves the park, crosses the Columbia at Donald and follows the river south to **Golden** in the Rocky Mountain Trench.

OKANAGAN Valley ★★ British Columbia

Map p. 6 – *Local map p. 42*

The Okanagan Valley of south central British Columbia consists of a large lake – Okanagan, several smaller lakes and the river of the same name (south of the United States border it is spelt Okanogan). It is an area of low rainfall, arid hills, and sagebrush. Yet it is an important fruit growing and wine making region. Intensive use of lake water for irrigation combined with a huge amount of sunshine have made the growing of apples, peaches, plums, grapes, cherries, apricots and pears possible. The sandy beaches and beautiful lakes have also made it a popular resort area.

From Osoyoos to Vernon *177 km - 110 miles by Route 97 - allow 6 hours.*

Osoyoos★. – Pop 2 738. This small community lies on narrows in the middle of **Osoyoos Lake** which spans the international border. It is surrounded by arid hills and semi-desert country where sagebrush, greasewood and cactus thrive – a sharp contrast to the green orchards on the lake shore. **Anarchist Mountain** (6 km - 4 miles E on Rte 3) provides a fine **viewpoint**★★ of the area.

BRITISH COLUMBIA, ROCKIES, YUKON

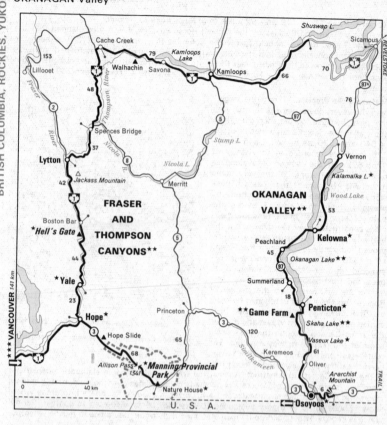

Route 97 to Penticton★★.
Route 97 follows the Okanagan River to **Oliver** through orchards and past fruit stands. As it approaches **Vaseux Lake★**, the scenery is impressive with huge rocks and barren slopes. The hills surrounding **Lake Skaha★★** on the contrary are sandy and covered with sagebrush and small trees. They contrast perfectly with the blue waters of this lovely lake.

Okanagan Game Farm★★.
– 8 km - 5 miles S of Penticton. Open daily 8am – dusk ; $4.50 ; ☎ (604) 497-5405.

This pleasant zoo overlooking Lake Skaha is set among the low rolling hills and scrub vegetation so typical of the whole area. A circular drive *(5 km - 3 miles)* enables visitors to view the great variety of animals from all parts of the world.

Penticton★.
– Pop 23 181. A corruption of the Salish Indian word *Pen-tak-tin* meaning a place to stay for ever, Penticton has a pleasant **site★** on narrows between Lake Okanagan and Lake Skaha surrounded by rolling hills. It is a tourist resort with attractive beaches and parks on both lakes. Beside Lake Okanagan lies the *SS Sicamous*, a sternwheeler once used on the lake and now beached.

Route 97 to Kelowna★★.
– After leaving Penticton, Route 97 runs closely beside **Lake Okanagan★★** offering many lovely views. Near Summerland, there are steep white cliffs beside the lake and then the road passes through terraces of orchards and vineyards supported by irrigation. The contrast between the blue of the lake, the green of the orchards, and the bare semi-desert of sagebrush, rock and dry soil hills makes the route very attractive.

Then the road follows the bend of the lake where, according to local Indian legend, the monster **Ogopogo** lives. Like his name Ogopogo is supposed to look the same viewed from either end, but the descriptions of him are as many and varied as the people who claim to have spotted him. After Peachland the road climbs up above the lake and then leaves it temporarily to pass through the orchards before Kelowna.

Kelowna★.
– Pop 59 196. Route 97 crosses the narrows of Lake Okanagan to enter this town by a floating bridge, part of which can be raised to allow boats to pass. The town with its attractive **site★** was founded by **Father Pandosy,** an Oblate priest, who set up a mission in 1859 and encouraged the settlers who followed him to cultivate the land. Today Kelowna is the marketing centre for the Okanagan and it is famous for its **International Regatta** held in August.

Route 97 to Vernon.
– After Kelowna, the road skirts Wood Lake and then winds along beside **Kalamalka Lake★** where the rolling hills descend directly into the water. They are still rocky but greener than further south. This change continues as the fruit-growing area is left behind and north of Vernon (Pop 19 987) cattle raising becomes the predominant form of agriculture.

The majority of sights described in this guide are closed on Christmas Day.
Sometimes they close for other holidays (see list p. 21).
We suggest you telephone in advance to avoid disappointment.

Map p. 6

The Rocky Mountains are the most easterly range of the **Western Cordillera.** In Canada they stretch from the United States border in a northwesterly direction for about 1 550 km - 900 miles terminating in the broad plain of the Liard River just south of the Yukon boundary. In the east they are bounded by the interior plains and in the west by the **Rocky Mountain Trench,** one of the longest continuous valleys in the world (map pp. 48-49). They constitute the **Continental Divide** from the border to about 240 km - 150 miles north of the Yellowhead Pass. After that they are crossed by the Peace River. Over most of their length they are rugged with numerous peaks exceeding 3 000 m - 10 000 ft. The highest is **Mount Robson** (alt 3 954 m - 12 972 ft).

The major Rocky Mountain Parks - **Banff, Jasper, Yoho** and **Kootenay National Parks** and **Mount Robson Provincial Park** - are situated next to each other in the southern part of the Canadian Rockies. Together they cover more than 22 274 sq km - 8 600 sq miles which make them among the largest areas of mountain parkland in the world, their individual boundaries being merely administrative. They are traversed east to west by the Trans-Canada Highway, the Yellowhead Highway and the Banff to Windermere Highway. They are connected north to south by the Icefields Parkway. Much of this area is therefore accessible by automobile, though a huge trail system is maintained for those visitors who prefer to see the mountains on foot. Waterton Lakes National Park (p. 66) is situated apart from the other parks in the southwest corner of Alberta.

Scenery and Wildlife. – The Rocky Mountain Parks offer a magnificent variety of scenery from towering peaks, mighty glaciers, crashing waterfalls, wild streams and narrow canyons to multi-hued lakes, gentle rivers, open wooded valleys and flower-strewn meadows. The difference in elevation between valleys and peaks causes a marked change in vegetation equivalent to a trip north from the Canadian Prairies to the high Arctic. The valleys have a relatively dense vegetation of Douglas fir, lodgepole pine, white spruce and aspen which gradually gives way to alpine firs, larches and Engelman spruce on the mountain slopes. Approaching the tree-line (alt 2 200 m - 7 200 ft), the trees become wizened and deformed giving way to low shrubs, mosses and lichens and finally to bare rock, ice and snow. The fauna of the mountains is no less varied, from tiny chipmonks and squirrels to black and grizzly bears, elk, mule deer, moose, big horn sheep and mountain goats. Many different birds can be seen, one of the most common being the grey jay or whisky jack, a notorious camp robber.

Practical Information. – Detailed maps and all other information are available from the Park Information Centres : Banff - in townsite (☎ (403) 762-4256), Jasper - in townsite (☎ (403) 852-4401), Yoho - in Field (☎ (604) 343-6324), Kootenay - in Radium Hot Springs (☎ (604) 347-9505 (July and Aug) (604) 347-9615 rest of year), Mount Robson - from Provincial Parks Office in Victoria – (☎ (604) 387-1696). For admission regulations for the four National Parks see p. 21. Entry to Mount Robson Provincial Park is free.

The most popular time to visit the Parks is July and August, but their fame has made them crowded in these months so some visitors prefer June or September. Activities include golf (courses at Banff and Jasper), horseback riding and swimming (hot springs at Banff, Miette and Radium) in addition to hiking and climbing. In winter both alpine and cross-country skiing are popular.

Weather. – In any mountain range climatic conditions can vary from year to year and change rapidly from day to day. Banff townsite for example registers temperatures between 6°-23°C - 43°-73°F in July. Thus warm clothes are advised for any visitor. The higher the elevation, the colder and windier it can get despite the sun. Lake Louise which is more than 300 m - 1 000 ft higher than Banff has an average annual mean temperature of 0°C - 32°F ! Visitors should also be prepared for sudden showers.

Accommodation and Other Facilities. – A full range of hotels, motels, chalets, stores, service stations, etc, is available in Banff and Jasper townsites. Limited facilities are available in Lake Louise village, Radium Hot Springs, and Miette Hot Springs. There are also lodges and rental chalets at various locations. Details can be obtained from Park Information Centres, the Chambers of Commerce for Banff and Jasper or the appropriate provincial governments (p. 33). The National Parks system maintains numerous campgrounds - details from Park offices and at Park gates. Campgrounds are popular in high season, so arrive in good time ; reservations are advisable for hotels, etc, gas stations are widely spaced so fill-up at each occasion.

Hiking Trails. – Only short walks are described in this guide though some of the most popular hiking areas are indicated. For full details of the trail system, ask at the Park Information Centres where detailed topographical maps can be bought, or at the Chambers of Commerce.

☐ BANFF TOWNSITE AND AREA★★ – Local map p. 44

Banff townsite (Pop 4 208) is the centre for Banff National Park. It lies in the broad valley of the Bow River between the present course of this river and its ancient course, the latter now being followed by the Canadian Pacific Railway and the Trans-Canada Highway. At an altitude of 1 380 m - 4 534 ft, the townsite is surrounded by high peaks. The most distinctive are **Cascade** to the north, a massive layered and slightly tilted peak, and **Mount Rundle** to the southwest, an equally imposing mountain which looks like a sloping writing-desk rising steadily on its southwest face to drop away sharply to the northeast. The Bow River has cut its new channel through part of the ridge of Rundle leaving a lump by itself immediately to the east of the townsite. This is **Tunnel Mountain,** named because the Canadian Pacific Railway Company thought they would have to build their railway straight through it (somehow the early engineering studies missed the broad valley to the north where the line now runs). Also visible from the townsite are **Mount Norquay** to the northwest with grassy ski runs descending its slopes and **Sulphur Mountain** to the south so named because of a fault in the rock strata along its base from which the hot springs seep which first brought Banff to prominence.

ROCKY MOUNTAIN Parks★★★

The Growth of Siding 29. –The hot mineral springs were first noted by **Sir James Hector** of the Palliser Expedition in 1858 just before he became the first white man to cross the Kicking Horse Pass. This pass became the route for the railway through the Rockies and in 1883, Siding 29 was constructed near the mineral springs. Canadian Pacific President, **George Stephen,** felt the siding needed a more romantic name and so he called it Banff after his native Banffshire in Scotland. Soon trips were being organized to the springs from the station and the tourist invasion of the Rockies began. In 1885 the Canadian Government declared the 26 sq km - 10 sq mile area around the springs a National Park in order to preserve it for ever. One thing led to another, the railway constructed the **Banff Springs Hotel,** one of the great resort hotels of North America, Swiss guides were imported to take visitors into the mountains, cars were admitted to the park after a bitter fight to keep them out, and in the 1920s the first winter sports facilities were constructed. Since then the number of visitors for both winter and summer activities has grown rapidly. Today, more than three million people visit Banff annually. Some of these visitors study at the **Banff Centre,** part of the University of Alberta, which has become one of the best known art schools in North America.

BANFF TOWNSITE AND AREA

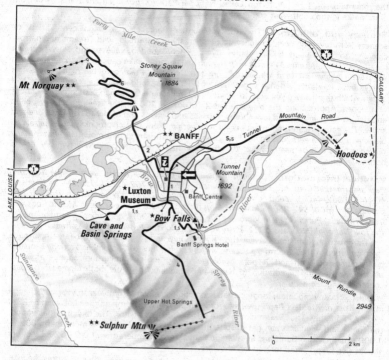

Sights time : 1/2 day

The **view**★ down Banff Avenue from the Park Administration Building is worth noting. The townsite is dominated by the massive bulk of Mount Cascade.

Sulphur Mountain★★. – *Access by gondola daily March - mid Nov, weekends only rest of year ; 8 min to ascend ; $6.00 ; restaurant ;* ☎ *(403) 762-2523.*

From the summit ridge of Sulphur Mountain (alt 2 286 m - 7 500 ft), there is a splendid **view**★★ of the whole area. To the east and north the valley of the Bow River is spread out below curving around Tunnel Mountain. The steep southeast face of this mountain shows clearly how the river cut through the ridge of **Mount Rundle,** the sloping face of which is visible across the valley of the Spray River which joins the Bow near the Banff Springs Hotel, the large turreted building. Behind Tunnel Mountain the blue of Lake Minnewanka can be seen surrounded by high mountains. A little to the west of Tunnel Mountain stands the huge bulk of **Cascade** with another small lump, Stoney Squaw, below it, and next to them Norquay with its ski slopes. From the other side of the observatory the view looks west towards the inverted V-shaped mountains of the **Sundance Range** and the Bow River Valley heading northwest to Lake Louise.

Mount Norquay★★. – *Access by chairlift daily mid June – mid Sept ; ski centre in winter ; $4.50 ; 10 min to ascend ; cafeteria ;* ☎ *(403) 762-4421.*

A well-graded switchback road climbs the side of Stoney Squaw Mountain with increasingly good views. From the top of the chairlift (alt 2 133 m - 7 000 ft) the **view**★★ looks south and east over the Bow Valley and the townsite. The tilted writing desk form of **Mount Rundle** dominates the view rising from the Spray River Valley on the right and the Bow River Valley on the left. Behind the Bow rise the peaks of the Fairholme Range and directly below the tea house Stoney Squaw Mountain can be seen with the road winding up it. Next to Stoney Squaw, and dominating the view northeast is the huge bulk of **Cascade.**

Bow Falls★. – At the foot of the Banff Springs Hotel and just before its confluence with the Spray, the Bow River tumbles over these falls. The bedrock beside them is steeply tilted and layered. There is a view down the river to the Fairholme Mountains.

Luxton Museum★. – *Open daily ; $2.00 ;* ☎ *(403) 762-2388.*

Housed in a replica of a fur-trading fort this small museum, part of the Glenbow-Alberta Institute *(p. 79)*, displays local Indian artifacts, relics of the fur trade and life-size dioramas of Indian ceremonies, dances, hunting and daily life.

Hoodoos★. – There is a **view★** of these weirdly shaped pillars, which stand beside the Bow River, from Tunnel Mountain Road. They can also be approached on a **nature trail** *(1 km - 1/2 mile ; begins on Tunnel Mountain Rd 2.25 km - 1.4 miles from Trans-Canada Hwy).* While the rest of the valley was eroded away, the gravel and silt of these shapes was cemented together with lime, and so they have been left standing by themselves. Behind them across the river the bulk of Mount Rundle rises, its sandwich formation of layers of limestone and shale very obvious from this angle.

Cave and Basin Springs. – These famous springs caused the creation of Banff, the first of Canada's National Parks. The facility is at present undergoing reconstruction. It will reopen in time to celebrate Parks Canada's centennial in 1985. A second set of hot springs (Upper Hot Springs) is located near the Sulphur Mountain gondola *(open daily).*

Excursions Map. p. 49

Johnston Canyon★★. – *28 km - 17 miles by Trans-Canada Hwy and Rte 1A. Time : falls 1 1/2 hrs on foot Rtn ; Ink Pots 4 hrs Rtn.*

A pathway follows the wooded valley of Johnston Creek which gradually becomes a narrow and deep canyon. The **lower falls★★** *(about 1 km - 1/2 mile)* drop into a pool and immediately descend to a second and larger pool. The waterfall and first pool can be viewed close-up by entering a tunnel pierced through the rock. The **upper falls★★** *(1.6 km - 1 mile further on)* are equally impressive. The path continues to an open meadow beyond the canyon where seven cold springs, called the Ink Pots because of the colour of their water, can be seen *(3.2 km - 2 miles further on).*

Trans-Canada Highway to Lake Louise★. – *59 km - 37 miles.* The Trans-Canada follows the valley of the Bow River with fine **views** of the mountains surrounding Banff. After the turn-off to the Sunshine Village Ski Centre, the jagged summits of the Sawback Range are seen on the right looking like a series of inverted V's. Beyond them the southeast face of **Castle Mountain** can be seen. This bulky turreted peak, one of the most distinctive shapes in the Rockies, dominates the drive for many miles. The rock layers are horizontal so that weathering has created a series of towers and battlements which have given the mountain its name. It is the first of a series of downfolded mountains which run north alongside the Icefields Parkway. They are known as the **Castle Mountain Syncline** because of the distinctive downward bend in the rock.

For the remainder of the drive to Lake Louise, the mountains of the Continental Divide are seen on the left dominated by **Mount Temple** (alt 3 543 m - 11 626 ft), one of the highest peaks in the park. It is easily recognized by its horizontal layers of quartzites and limestones which give it a "rippling" look.

② KOOTENAY NATIONAL PARK

From Eisenhower Junction to Radium Hot Springs – *105 km - 65 miles by Rte 93 (Banff-Windermere Highway) – allow 3 hrs - map p. 49.*

The Banff - Windermere Highway traverses this park by an often picturesque **route★**. From the junction with the Trans-Canada Highway, it climbs steeply to the summit of the

Vermilion Pass (el 1 650 m - 5 416 ft) which marks the boundary of the park. On the way up, look back at the castellated peaks of **Castle Mountain** with its distinctive downfolded strata. The effects of the forest fire which ravaged the Vermilion Pass area in 1968 are still very evident.

Marble Canyon★. – *17 km - 11 miles from junction ; trail of 800 m - 1/2 mile ; 35 min Rtn.* The blue waters of Tokumm Creek rush through a narrow canyon just before joining the Vermilion River. Outcroppings of white dolomite can be seen at several places in the canyon

Castle Mountain

but they are especially obvious near the waterfall at the end. Paths follow the top of the canyon and cross it by several bridges. Note the rounded potholes created by the water and the piece of stone which has formed a natural bridge.

Paint Pots★. – *20 km - 12 miles from junction ; trail of 1.2 km - 3/4 mile ; 40 min Rtn.* A trail follows the Vermilion River then crosses an orange–red creek bed, the "ochre beds", to arrive at three small pools. These pools, the paint pots, are actually cold mineral springs containing a significant quantity of iron which has stained the clays of the region red and yellow. For hundreds of years Indians from both sides of the Divide came to this spot to collect the ochre clay from which they made a paint to decorate themselves, their teepees and their clothing. After its discovery by the white man, the ochre was mined for a short time and taken to Calgary to be used as a base for paint.

ROCKY MOUNTAIN Parks★★★

Route 93 continues beside the Vermilion River until it joins the Kootenay in a wide and wooded valley. Turning west from the Kootenay the road crosses **Sinclair Pass** (el 1 486 m - 4 875 ft).

Sinclair Valley★. – This is the most attractive part of the drive. Sinclair Creek tumbles along beside the road dropping fairly rapidly. The road passes between steep red cliffs called the **Iron Gates** because the rock has been stained by iron oxides. After 103 km – 64 miles the road reaches **Radium Hot Springs** with its Aquacourt (*bathing facilities, open daily ; $1.25).* The temperature of these springs ranges from 35 ° - 47 °C - 95 ° - 117 °F depending on the season and the spring.

Immediately after the Aquacourt and before the Park gate, the road is caught for a short distance (15 m - 16 yd) between steep rock walls eroded by the waters of Sinclair Creek. So sheer are the cliffs of **Sinclair Canyon★** that the road was constructed on top of the creek.

③ LAKE LOUISE AND AREA★★★

This is the most famous, the most visited and the most photographed area of the Canadian Rockies. The region spans the Continental Divide with sights in both Banff and Yoho National Parks. A small locality, **Lake Louise Village,** is situated just off the Trans-Canada Highway.

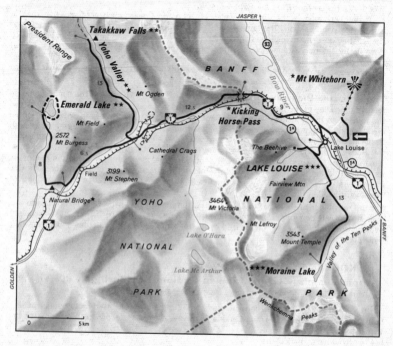

Lake Louise★★★. – *4 km - 2.5 miles from Trans-Canada Hwy ; refreshments ; accommodation.*
Set in a hanging valley above the wide valley of the Bow (alt 1 731 m - 5 680 ft), the beautiful green waters of Lake Louise are framed by the mountains of the Continental Divide. Known to the Stony Indians as "the lake of the little fishes", Lake Louise was first viewed by a white man in 1882 when **Tom Wilson,** a survey packer for the railway, was guided there by the Indians. He called it Emerald Lake because of its colour but it was soon renamed Lake Louise in honour of Princess Louise, daughter of Queen Victoria and wife of Lord Lorne, Governor-General of Canada. With the completion of the railway line it quickly became an essential stopping place for visitors crossing the Rockies by train and it attracted mountaineers from all over the world to attempt to climb the sheer and dangerous peaks surrounding it. The present massive hotel, **Chateau Lake Louise,** was constructed in 1924 to replace an older structure destroyed by fire, and roads soon connected Lake Louise to the outside world.

From the Chateau, the lake appears smaller than it is in reality (2.4 km - 1 1/2 miles × 1.2 km - 3/4 mile). At the far end, a high ridge of ice and snow dominates the view. This is **Mount Victoria** (alt 3 464 m - 11 365 ft) whose peak in the ridge may not be very prominent but whose glacier stands out clearly both in reality and in its reflection in the water. To the left of Victoria, a steep rocky cliff rises out of the lake to form **Fairview Mountain** and to the right lies the **Beehive** so named because of its rounded shape. By walking along the edge of the lake on its north side for a short distance, **Mount Lefroy** can be seen on the left of Victoria. This massive pyramidal peak also spawns a glacier which feeds the lake. The colour of Lake Louise, which varies between an emerald green and a bluish-green depending on the light, is caused by a fine silt in the glacial meltwater which feeds the lake. This silt stays suspended in the water reflecting the green rays of the spectrum. The lake itself exists because of glacial action 10 000 or more years ago. The Victoria glacier once stretched to the present site of the Chateau. When it retreated it left a huge mound of debris (moraine) which almost completely dammed the valley and therefore formed the lake. The Chateau is built on this moraine.

Many pleasant hikes can be made in this area, and two tea houses can be visited (*details available from the hotel).*

Moraine Lake★★★. – The **road★★** to Moraine Lake climbs up above the Bow Valley as it heads south. For a while the view is dominated by the ice-capped dome of **Mount Temple.** Then the road swings around Temple for views of its eastern face towering above the road. Ahead a series of very pointed peaks spotted with glaciers can be seen. These are the **Wenkchemna** or **Ten Peaks** (*wenkchemna* is the Stony Indian word for ten) and they form part of the Continental Divide.

Small and narrow, **Moraine Lake★★★,** one of the loveliest lakes of the Canadian Rockies, stands right below the Wenkchemna Peaks whose sheer sides and glaciers are reflected in its blue waters. The visitor arrives at the northern end of the lake where a large rock pile blocks the valley and has created the lake. The origin of this rock pile is uncertain. Some authorities maintain it is a moraine, thus the name of the lake. Others think that it was the result of a landslide on the **Tower of Babel,** the sheer boulder-shaped peak behind the pile. The best view of the lake is obtained by following the path around the rock pile. Another pleasant path follows the edge of the lake.

Mount Whitehorn★. – *Access by gondola daily mid June – Labour Day ; $5.00 ; time to ascend : 20 min ; refreshments ;* ☎ *(403) 522-3555.*

From the top of this gondola lift there is a fine panoramic view of the mountains across the Bow Valley : to the south the Wenkchemna Peaks and Mount Temple, to the west Mount Victoria with Lake Louise at its foot, and to the north the mountains surrounding Kicking Horse Pass.

Kicking Horse Pass★. – The summit of this pass marks the beginning of Yoho National Park which is renowned among mountaineers for its high and treacherous peaks. The pass itself got its name from an incident which befell Sir James Hector of the Palliser Expedition (*p. 73*) when he crossed it in 1858. A pack-horse kicked him and knocked him unconscious. His Indian companions nearly buried him thinking him dead.

The **descent★★** from the pass into the narrow valley of the Kicking Horse River is impressive. When the railway was built in 1884 (*p. 16*) the grade on the descent to **Field** was as steep as 4.5 % in places. This resulted in several accidents when trains ran out of control. The "big hill" as it was called also required four locomotives to haul a train up. Thus in 1909 two **spiral tunnels** were built to reduce the grade. They are in the shape of a figure of eight. Trains curve around on themselves in descent, or ascent, one half of the eight being inside **Mount Ogden** north of the road, the other half inside **Cathedral Crags** to the south. Nine kilometres - 5 miles from the summit, there is a **view★** of the Mount Ogden tunnel.

The Yoho Valley★★. – *Access road of 13 km - 8 miles with switchbacks ; no trailers allowed.*

This attractive **road★★** winds up the Yoho Valley between Mount Field and Mount Ogden with views back of **Mount Stephen,** a bulky peak with a series of ridges in its face which catch the snow, and Cathedral Crags. After climbing steeply via two switchbacks, the road passes below the avalanche–ridden slopes of Mount Wapta. Ahead, snow-clad **Yoho Peak** and its glacier can be seen.

Takakkaw Falls★★. – These falls at the end of the road can be viewed from a distance or approached on foot (*15 min Rtn*). A huge jet of water pours over the edge of a sheer cliff to fall a total of 384 m - 1 260 ft to the valley floor. Coming from the meltwaters of the Daly Glacier, Takakkaw – meaning Wow ! in the local Indian dialect – actually falls in two stages : an upper stage of about 60 m – 200 ft and a lower one of about 300 m - 1 000 ft. It is one of the highest waterfalls in Canada (Della Falls on Vancouver Island drop a total of 442 m - 1 450 ft but in three stages).

Emerald Lake★★. – *Refreshments (summer only).*

Shortly after taking the access road, there is a viewpoint of a **natural bridge★.** The blue waters of the Kicking Horse River have cut a channel beneath a piece of limestone which was once a waterfall. The **site★** is very fine with Mount Stephen standing over the river to the east and the mountains of the Van Horne Range visible downstream.

At the end of the road, beautiful green **Emerald Lake★★** lies at the foot of the President Range. It was first viewed by Tom Wilson in 1882. He called it Emerald Lake as he had previously called Lake Louise, but this time the name stuck. The meltwaters from the glaciers of the President Range give the lake its colour (*p. 46*). Rugged **Michael Peak** can be seen across the lake and reflected in it. To the southwest of the lodge, which is reached by a bridge, stands **Mount Burgess,** with its very distinctive flat peak slightly indented at the top and its second peak, a pointed spike, rising next to it. A pleasant **trail★** (5 km - 3 miles) encircles the lake.

After the turnoff to Emerald Lake, the Trans-Canada Highway follows the Kicking Horse River in its steep descent to join the Columbia at Golden in the Rocky Mountain Trench. There are many fine views along this route.

④ ICEFIELDS PARKWAY★★★

233 km - 145 miles – we strongly recommend that visitors allow at least one day for this drive to be able to fully appreciate it - there are frequent pull-offs for viewpoints.

The Icefields Parkway was built expressly to display the splendour of the Rockies to visitors and it is closed to commercial traffic. It runs in a northwesterly direction from Lake Louise paralleling the Continental Divide and following in turn the valleys of five rivers (the Bow, Mistaya, North Saskatchewan, Sunwapta and Athabasca) to join the Yellowhead Highway at Jasper Townsite. The snowcapped peaks of the Continental Divide march along on the west of the highway with many glaciers visible from the road. To the east for much of the route a series of downfolded mountains, the Castle Mountain Syncline (*p. 45*), rise steeply. The Parkway crosses two passes, the Bow and the Sunwapta, rising nearly 2 200 m - 7 000 ft above sea level.

After leaving the Trans-Canada, the Parkway quickly climbs with fine views of the Waputik Range. After about 17 km - 11 miles it approaches **Hector Lake★** set below these mountains and Bow Peak, with Mount Hector to the east.

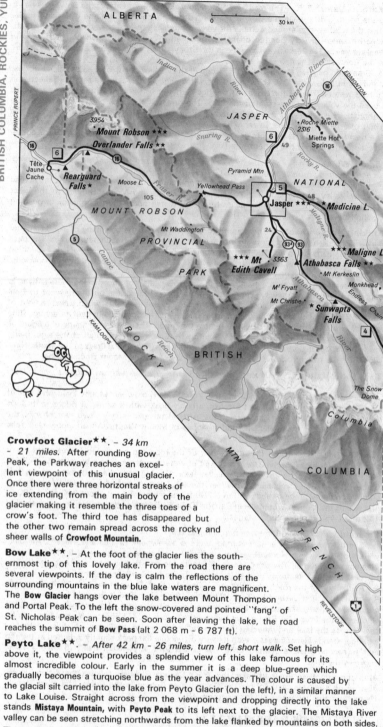

ALBERTA

0   30 km

JASPER

PRINCE RUPERT

16

6

3954

Mount Robson ★★★

Overlander Falls ★★

Tête Jaune Cache

16

Snaring R.

Yellowhead Pass

Roche Miette 2316

Miette Hot Springs

49

6

Rearguard Falls ★

Moose L.

Fraser R.

Pyramid Mtn

NATIONAL

5

Jasper ★★★

48

Medicine L.

105

5

Mt Waddington

PROVINCIAL

24

93A 93

Maligne R.

★★★ *Maligne L.*

★★★ *Mt Edith Cavell*

PARK

3363

Athabasca Falls ★★

Mt Kerkeslin

MOUNT ROBSON

Canoe

KAMLOOPS

Reach

BRITISH

R O C K Y

Mt Fryatt

Mt Christie

Athabasca

★ *Sunwapta Falls*

Monkhead

Endless Chain

4

River

The Snow Dome

Columbia

COLUMBIA

M T N

T R E N C H

REVELSTOKE

Crowfoot Glacier ★★. – *34 km - 21 miles.* After rounding Bow Peak, the Parkway reaches an excellent viewpoint of this unusual glacier. Once there were three horizontal streaks of ice extending from the main body of the glacier making it resemble the three toes of a crow's foot. The third toe has disappeared but the other two remain spread across the rocky and sheer walls of **Crowfoot Mountain.**

Bow Lake ★★. – At the foot of the glacier lies the southernmost tip of this lovely lake. From the road there are several viewpoints. If the day is calm the reflections of the surrounding mountains in the blue lake waters are magnificent. The **Bow Glacier** hangs over the lake between Mount Thompson and Portal Peak. To the left the snow-covered and pointed "fang" of St. Nicholas Peak can be seen. Soon after leaving the lake, the road reaches the summit of **Bow Pass** (alt 2 068 m - 6 787 ft).

Peyto Lake ★★. – *After 42 km - 26 miles, turn left, short walk.* Set high above it, the viewpoint provides a splendid view of this lake famous for its almost incredible colour. Early in the summer it is a deep blue-green which gradually becomes a turquoise blue as the year advances. The colour is caused by the glacial silt carried into the lake from Peyto Glacier (on the left), in a similar manner to Lake Louise. Straight across from the viewpoint and dropping directly into the lake stands **Mistaya Mountain,** with **Peyto Peak** to its left next to the glacier. The Mistaya River valley can be seen stretching northwards from the lake flanked by mountains on both sides.

The road enters the valley of the Mistaya River which runs through a series of lakes. Across **Upper Waterfowl Lake** *(56 km - 35 miles)*, there is a fine **view** ★ of rugged snow-encrusted Howse Peak and the distinctive pyramid shape of Mount Chephren.

Mistaya Canyon ★. – *72 km - 45 miles, follow trail into valley for 400 m - 1/4 mile.*
The Mistaya River has cut a narrow gorge through the limestone with rounded and smooth, almost sculptured sides.

On the Parkway Mount Murchison rises to the east and ahead the steep cliffs of **Mount Wilson** loom above the road. Both these mountains are part of the Castle Mountain Syncline. The road drops down into the valley of the North Saskatchewan River and crosses it. After 77 km - 48 miles there is a **viewpoint** ★ beside the Park Information Office *(trail through trees)* of the valley of the Howse River, a tributary of the North Saskatchewan. This river which rises on the Continental Divide was the route across the Rockies followed by many early explorers including David Thompson *(p. 31)* when he set up the first trading post west of the mountains in 1807. To the east of the river, **Mount Sarbach** dominates the view with the Kaufman Peaks and the slanting pyramid form of **Mount Chephren** visible beyond ; on the other side of the Howse, snowy **Mount Outram** rises with Mount Forbes poking its head out to the right.

After the junction with the David Thompson Highway, the road runs below the massive cliffs of Mount Wilson with views of first Survey Peak and Mount Erasmus to the west and then the snowcapped peak of **Mount Amery** which somewhat resembles a layer-cake. Across the distinctive stony flats of the North Saskatchewan River twin summits resembling small castles **(The Castlelets)** come into view between Mount Amery and the next bulky peak, **Mount Saskatchewan,** which resembles it in appearance.

The road passes below the sheer cliffs at the base of **Cirrus Mountain** which rise 610 m - 2 000 ft to the right. Parker's Ridge and Nigel Peak are visible ahead - two more examples of the syncline. The Parkway climbs steeply in what is known as the "big bend" gaining 430 m - 1 400 ft very quickly. At the top *(114 km - 71 miles)* there is a spectacular **view**★★ of the valley of the North Saskatchewan and the road below. The streams which cascade down the sheer cliffs of Cirrus Mountain have given it the name of the **Weeping Wall** – the amount of water depends on the season and temperature.

Parker's Ridge Trail★★. – 119 km - 74 miles. A trail *(3 km - 2 miles, easy winding stages)* climbs to the top of the ridge from whence there is a fine **view**★★ of the **North Saskatchewan Glacier** which looks like a vast ice divided highway charging down the valley because a line of moraine divides it into two parts. It is a tongue of the Columbia Icefield *(p. 50).* The ridge itself is covered with tiny alpine flowers in summer - blue forget-me-not, red and white heather, violet vetch and pink moss campion.

The Parkway reaches the summit of **Sunwapta Pass** and enters Jasper National Park with views ahead of Mount Athabasca and the other peaks surrounding the Columbia Icefield.

ROCKY MOUNTAIN Parks★★★

Athabasca Glacier★★★. – *127 km - 79 miles.* This glacier is part of the vast **Columbia Icefield,** the largest icefield in the Rockies covering an area of 310 sq km - 120 sq miles and spawning nine major glaciers, the waters of which flow into three oceans – Atlantic, Pacific and Arctic. From beside the **Columbia Icefield Chalet** *(off road on right)* there is an impressive **view★★★** of two of these glaciers. Straight ahead, the mighty Athabasca Glacier plunges more than 7 km - 4 1/2 miles down the valley between the flattish-topped snowcapped **Snow Dome** and the pointed **Mount Athabasca,** its toe close to the Icefields Parkway. In its descent, it flows over three cliffs giving it the look of coming down stairs. To the right the smaller **Dome Glacier** descends the valley between the Snow Dome and **Mount Kitchener** – a peak with a thick layer of ice on top known as a "cap" glacier.

Close to the Chalet there is an **Information Centre** with displays on the Columbia Icefield and a slideshow *(10 min).* On the other side of the road, visitors can park and walk right up to the edge of the ice as it melts to form Sunwapta Lake. The glacier is in retreat at present and its previous lengths are marked on the moraine.

Snowcoach Trip on the Glacier★★. – *Access by very steep road up glacial moraine not suitable for caravans or trailers, or by shuttle bus from the ticket office beside the Columbia Icefields Chalet. Daily June - Sept if weather conditions permit ; 45 min ; $10.00 ; Note – occasionally long queues in July and Aug around noon ;* ☏ *(403) 762-2241.*

These large machines travel up the glacier to a point where they are on top of about 300 m - 1 000 ft of ice. This is an impressive experience and visitors can descend, walk about and sample the glacial melt water. There are fine views of the surrounding mountains and smaller glaciers. Crevasses and mill holes (deep circular holes) are sometimes seen at close quarters.

After leaving the Athabasca Glacier, the road begins a spectacular **descent★★** between the cliffs of **Mount Wilcox** and the canyon of the Sunwapta River below Mount Kitchener. After 135 km - 85 miles, **Tangle Creek** is seen on the right dropping over a series of limestone steps, and shortly afterwards there is a fine **view★** of the **Stutfield Glacier,** another tongue of the Columbia Icefield, hanging above the valley. Tangle Ridge rises steeply above the road to the east and, across the broad flats of the Sunwapta River, **Diadem Peak** can be seen with the collection of small glaciers clinging to its sides which have given it its name. The wildly tilted **Endless Chain Ridge** comes into view ahead on the right, and the Sir Winston Churchill Range on the left.

Sunwapta Falls★. – *After 177 km - 110 miles, take side road 400 m - 1/4 mile.*

The Sunwapta River circles a tiny tree-covered island, plunges over a cliff and sharply changes direction cutting a deep and narrow canyon. A path follows the canyon to a second waterfall *(3/4 hr on foot Rtn).*

The Sunwapta River joins the Athabasca shortly after the falls and the Parkway continues in the valley of this mighty river to Jasper. This impressive valley is at first dominated by the distinctive off-centre peak of **Mount Christie** and the three peaks of **Mount Fryatt.** To the northwest the snowcapped summit of **Mount Edith Cavell,** known as the queen of the range *(p. 51),* slowly takes over the view while **Mount Kerkeslin,** the final peak of the Castle Mountain Syncline, rises steeply above the Parkway to the east.

Athabasca Falls★★. – *After 200 km - 124 miles, turn left on Route 93A for 500 m - 1/3 mile.*

The blue waters of the Athabasca roar over a narrow lip around a pinnacle rock and drop 22 m - 75 ft. The layered rock on either side of the falls is quartzite. The river then thunders down a short canyon, the edges of which have been rounded and worn smooth by the water. Above the falls Mount Kerkeslin rises, slightly red in colour from quartzite. The same layering is visible in this mountain as in the rock beside the falls.

As the Parkway approaches Jasper townsite, **The Whistlers** can be seen to the west with its tramway *(p. 51).* Straight ahead **Pyramid Mountain** rises and to the east the pinnacled peak of **Mount Tekarra** can be seen.

⑤ JASPER TOWNSITE AND AREA★★★

Jasper townsite (Pop 3 269) has a fine site in the wide valley of the Athabasca River at its confluence with the Miette, which is also the junction of the Yellowhead Highway and the Icefields Parkway *(see above).* It is on the main line of the Canadian National Railway and serves as the centre of Jasper National Park. It is surrounded by small and very beautiful lakes – **Pyramid Lake, Patricia Lake, Lake Edith** and **Lake Beauvert,** the latter being well known because the exclusive **Jasper Park Lodge** is located on its shores.

Beyond the valley, the main ranges of the Rockies rise. From the townsite, snow-covered **Mount Edith Cavell** (3 363 m - 11 033 ft) to the south is among the most prominent, with the rugged south face of **Pyramid Mountain** to the north coming a close second. The Maligne Range can be seen to the southeast, the sawtooth peaks of the Colin Range lie next to them to the north, and to the west the view extends up the Miette Valley to the mountains of the Continental Divide.

(after photo by National Museums of Canada)

Black Bear

The Growth of Jasper. – In the early 19th century the Athabasca River and Pass were an important fur trade route across the Rockies. A supply post was set up about 35 km - 22 miles from the present townsite by Jasper Hawes of the North West Company. Although later moved to the junction of the Athabasca and Miette Rivers, the name Jasper remained. In the 1860s, the townsite was visited by a group of people seeking an overland route to the Cariboo gold fields (p. 36). They were known as the **Overlanders** because most of the other gold seekers preferred the sea voyage to Vancouver.

Apart from them, visitors were few until the National Park was created in 1907 with the planning of a second trans-continental railway which would cross the Rockies via the Yellowhead Pass (p. 52). After its construction, Jasper budgeoned as a tourist centre and today it ranks second to Banff as Canada's major visitor destination in the Rockies.

Excursions

The Whistlers★★. – *Access by tramway daily mid April - mid Oct ; $6.50 ; time to ascend 7 min ; restaurant, refreshments ; ☎ (403) 852-3093.*

This tramway ascends more than 900 m - 3 000 ft to the summit ridge of The Whistlers (alt 2 286 m - 7 500 ft) which is so-called because the hoary marmots which live on the ridge have a long shrill whistle. From the upper terminal, one of the best **panoramas★★** of the Rockies is obtained. To the northeast lies the townsite in the broad Athabasca Valley with the lakes standing out clearly. To the west lie the peaks surrounding the Yellowhead Pass. Note especially the bulky peak of **Yellowhead Mountain** itself and beyond it, if visibility is good, the great white pyramid of **Mount Robson.**

From the top of the ridge *(climb of 180 m - 600 ft – hiking shoes necessary)* there is a view south of Mount Edith Cavell and the downfolded northern face of Mount Kerkeslin. The typical alpine terrain can be appreciated on the ridge with numerous tiny flowers blossoming as soon as the snow melts.

Mount Edith Cavell★★★. – *27 km - 17 miles S by Icefields Parkway, 93A and access road. Final 14.5 km - 9 miles have sharp turns ; allow 1/2 hr.*

The narrow and winding access road to the base of Mount Edith Cavell climbs up the Astoria River valley with fine views of the surrounding mountains. Shortly before the end it leaves the river and there is a view up the valley of the mountains of the Continental Divide.

At the end of the road, the vast snow-clad peak of Cavell looms over the parking area. It was called *La Montagne de la Grande Traverse* by the fur traders as they struggled up the Whirlpool River to cross the Rockies by the Athabasca Pass. But it was renamed after the First World War to honour the heroic British nurse shot by the Germans in Belgium for aiding allied partisans.

The Angel Glacier★★★. – From the parking area, a trail *(40 min Rtn)* crosses the rubble strewn valley floor to reach the foot of this striking glacier. The two horizontal pieces on either side near the top resemble outstretched wings and have thus given the glacier its name. Visitors can return by the same route or by following the tiny stream of glacial meltwater.

Another fine view of Mount Edith Cavell can be obtained from beside tiny **Cavell Lake★★** *(return along access road about 1.5 km - 1 mile and follow Tonquin Valley trail for about 400 m - 1/4 mile)*. This lovely green lake is fed by streams coming from the Angel Glacier, the fine silt particles in the water giving it its colour.

The Maligne Valley★★★. – *48 km - 30 miles by Yellowhead Hwy and Maligne Valley Rd – about 5 hrs Rtn including visits.*

Maligne Canyon★★. – *10 km - 6 miles.* The most spectacular and the longest of the gorges to be seen in the Rockies, this great gash carved out of the limestone is as much as 50 m - 166 ft deep and less than 3 m - 10 ft wide in places. A path follows the top of the canyon crossing and recrossing it by a series of bridges. There are several waterfalls. In places the walls have been worn smooth by the water and potholes or deep depressions have been created by boulders being swirled around in the current. Elsewhere, vegetation clings to the sides of the canyon.

Medicine Lake★. – *24 km - 15 miles.* This lovely lake is hemmed in by the sawtooth peaks of the Colin Range to the north and the Maligne Range to the south. Full of water in the summer, it shrinks later in the year, when run-off from melting snow decreases, and sometimes almost completely disappears. The stream bed west of the lake is barren and dry however most of the year. The lake drains through sink holes in the limestone bedrock and resurfaces as a series of springs in Maligne Canyon and other places such as Lake Beauvert. The road follows the edge of the lake for 6.4 km - 4 miles with several good viewpoints.

ROCKY MOUNTAIN Parks★★★

Maligne Lake★★★. – *Refreshments*. The road stops at the northern end of this long (22.5 km - 14 miles) and narrow glacial lake. Named "Sore-foot" Lake in 1875 by the surveyor Henry MacLeod, who was the first white man to see it, Maligne means wicked or malignant. Despite its name this lake, set against a backdrop of snowcapped peaks which plunge straight into it, is among the most beautiful in the Rockies. From the road the twin peaks of **Mounts Unwin** and **Charlton** on the west side are the most prominent. However, the mountains at the southern end are much finer and they can only be appreciated by taking the boat trip or canoeing down the lake.

Boat Trip★★★. – *Daily June - Sept ; $15.00 ; about 2 hrs ;* ☎ *(403) 852-3370.*

As the boat goes down the lake, the colour of the water changes from green to deep turquoise blue. This colour is caused by the

Maligne Lake

glacial silt in the water *(p. 46)*. Just after the Samson Narrows, where a stream has deposited alluvial debris and nearly cut the lake in two, is tiny **Spirit Island**. The **view★★★** of this tree-covered islet framed by Mounts Mary Vaux, Brazeau, Warren and Monkhead is among the most photographed in the Rockies.

⑥ YELLOWHEAD HIGHWAY ACROSS THE ROCKIES★★

From Tête Jaune Cache to east gate Jasper Park – *154 km - 96 miles – allow 3 hours.*

The Yellowhead Highway, Route 16, is named after a blonde Iroquois fur trader called Tête-Jaune (Yellowhead) who set up a cache near the Fraser River in what is now Mount Robson Provincial Park. Later the pass through the Rockies between the Miette and Fraser Rivers became known as the Yellowhead Pass, and more recently the name has been adopted for a road running across the Rockies to the Pacific at Prince Rupert *(see below)*.

Leaving the Cariboo Mountains behind at Tête Jaune Cache, the Yellowhead Highway follows the Fraser River into the Rockies.

Rearguard Falls★. – *3.2 km - 2 miles – walk of about 25 min Rtn.* The waters of the Fraser pour over low falls, almost big rocky rapids, and make a turn around a layered piece of rock. Note the incredible amount of water already in this river so near to its source and 1 300 km - 800 miles from the sea.

Mount Robson★★★. – *Viewpoint after 16 km - 10 miles.* On entering Mount Robson Provincial Park this mountain, the highest peak in the Canadian Rockies, is directly ahead. The origin of its name is uncertain but it may be named after a fur trader called Robson who in the 1820s returned to Jasper House with news of a "big hill" he had seen. This "hill" stands 3 954 m - 12 972 ft above sea level, 3 000 m - 10 000 ft of them directly in front of the viewpoint. It is rare to see so much of a mountain exposed. Robson is a huge bulky peak on which the snow collects in horizontal bands giving it a stripped look. Unfortunately it is often seen with its head in the clouds due to weather conditions, which also continue to make it a challenge to mountaineers. To the left of Robson, **Cinnamon Peak** can be seen and to the right stand the mountains of the **Rainbow Range.**

Overlander Falls★★. – *18 km - 11 miles – walk of about 1/2 hr Rtn.* Named for the Overlanders *(p. 51)* these falls drop over a fairly wide area into a whirlpool which the water leaves by a narrow channel into a canyon. The colour of the Fraser River is a lovely blue-green and the walk to the falls pleasant.

The Yellowhead Highway skirts Moose Lake, at the eastern end of which the bulk of **Mount Waddington** can be seen. Soon **Mount Fitzwilliam** comes into view to the left of Waddington. Fitzwilliam is an irregular pyramid shape resembling a cake with a burnt top. To the left a vast turreted mountain becomes visible, known as the Seven Sisters of the Yellowhead or **Yellowhead Mountain.** The road follows Yellowhead Lake and reaches the summit of the pass after 77 km - 48 miles. *(Put watches forward 1 hour).* After the pass the road follows the narrow valley of the Miette River to Jasper townsite (105 km - 65 miles).

After Jasper, the character of the road changes completely. It follows the wide glacial trough cut out by the Athabasca River. Steep cliffs rise from either side almost devoid of vegetation. The jagged peaks of the Colin Range rise steeply to the east and then up ahead a sheer cliff comes into **view★★** which juts up above the valley like the prow of a ship. This is the **Roche Miette** (Miette's rock) named for a voyageur who climbed it and sat on the edge smoking a pipe. After the Roche Miette, a road turns off to **Miette Hot Springs** *(17.5 km - 11 miles by winding and rough road).* These springs are the hottest in the Rockies (54° C - 129° F) and are noted for their calcium content.

The Skeena, "River of Mists", rises deep in the mountains of central British Columbia. It runs south to Hazelton and then west to the coast cutting a huge cleft through the Coast Mountains. This cleft was an important trade route for Indian tribes of the interior. After the arrival of the white man the river was used by sternwheelers until the railway was completed in 1912. Now the Yellowhead Highway follows the valley from Hazelton to Prince Rupert.

Prince Rupert. – Pop 16 197. *Served by B.C. ferries - see below, and Alaska Marine Highway from Skagway daily in summer ; less frequently rest of year ; for information contact Alaska Marine Highway, Pouch R, Juneau, Alaska 99811 or ☎ Prince Rupert (604) 627-1744.*

This city on Kaien Island near the mouth of the Skeena was named for the soldier-explorer cousin of Charles II of England who was the first governor of the Hudson's Bay Company. It was the winning entry in a competition held in 1906 to name the western terminus of the Grand Truck Pacific Railway. Located just south of the Alaskan panhandle, Prince Rupert is an important port exporting grain, minerals, lumber and fish products. It has a large fishing fleet which catches halibut, salmon, herring, cod, sole and crab.

Inside Passage★★. – *Prince Rupert to Port Hardy year round ; time - overnight ; for schedules and information contact B.C. Ferry Office, 818 Broughton St, Victoria, B.C. V8W 1E4 ☎ (604) 669-1211.*

This ferry trip follows part of a sheltered waterway which stretches from Puget Sound, Washington, to Skagway, Alaska. Weaving in and out of islands and passing deep fjords, the boat trip enables visitors to appreciate the wildly indented nature of the West Coast where the mountains covered with dark, damp rain forest of fir, cedar and hemlock plunge directly into the water. The weather is variable, sometimes shrouding everything with mist, occasionally bright and clear. The highlight of the cruise is the passage through narrow Grenville Channel.

Museum of Northern British Columbia★. – *On 1st Ave at MacBride St. Open daily except weekends in winter ; ☎ (604) 624-3207.*

(after photo by Otto Nelson, Denver Art Museum)

Chilkat Blanket

This small museum has a fine collection of Haida, Coast Tsimshian, Tlingit, Nishga and Gitksan exhibits especially carvings in wood and argillite. Note the fine wooden "talking" stick which Chief Shakes took with him to England to meet Queen Victoria. He was so overcome by the occasion he was completely unable to speak, so the story goes.

Outside the museum, Indian carvers can sometimes be seen at work in the totem pole carving shed, and Haida and Tsimshian poles are on display.

From Prince Rupert to Kitwanga★★. – *245 km - 152 miles by Rte 16 – allow 3 hours.*

The Yellowhead Highway follows the Skeena to New Hazelton, crisscrossing with the railway on the north bank for the first section to **Terrace,** then bridging the river to continue on the south side. There are splendid views of snowcapped mountains rising to 2 000 m - 6 000 ft for the entire trip. The road follows the river closely giving views of this wide and deep piece of water full of islands. After Terrace, where the valley widens out briefly, the road winds through the Nass Ranges. The **Seven Sisters,** a series of pointed snow-covered peaks, can be seen to the east and then the south. There is a particularly fine **viewpoint★** of them about 90 km - 56 miles from Terrace.

Indian Villages★★. – *Map p. 54.* The Indian peoples of the Skeena River and its tributaries - the Gitksan, are the most easterly penetration of the North West Coast Indian culture (p. 30). Like the coastal tribes, the Gitksan did not cultivate the land but lived on fish, mainly salmon, and other wildlife. Their life was one of ritual, full of ceremonies, customs and laws. Having no written language, great feasts or **potlatchs** were held to solemnize all agreements such as marriage, land exchange, etc. At these feasts gifts were exchanged, songs were sung and dances performed. In such an atmosphere art flourished especially the carving of very intricate and beautiful designs in wood. Chief among these were **Totem Poles,** sort of family crests depicting animals connected with the ancestors of the family involved (p. 57).

With the arrival of white settlers in this area in the 1870s, the life of the Gitksan changed. Instead of spending the long winters carving, they trapped the animals whose furs the white man desired. Missionaries tried to destroy what to them was a heathen culture – totems were pulled down and the potlatch was banned. The rich culture of the North West Coast Indians was dying everywhere. The Gitksan preserved their way of life better than most but even so little remained by the 1950s. At this time the Indians of the Hazelton area decided to try to preserve what was left by teaching the old skills to their young people. A replica of an Indian village of 1870 was built and called **'Ksan,** the Indian name for the Skeena river. In the village master craftsmen are trained. Their work has become much in demand and 'Ksan has become an important tourist attraction, the centre of a region where many signs of Indian culture can be found but which is particularly well-known for its stands of totem poles.

SKEENA Valley ★★★

Kitwanga★. – This little village has a fine stand of **totem poles★** in their original locations close to the river. Some of the poles have animals or birds perched on the top. The Seven Sisters provide an attractive backdrop.

Kitwancool★. – *18 km - 11 miles N of Kitwanga on Hwy 37.* This Indian village has the best existing stand of **totem poles★**. Note especially the one with the hole near the bottom, known as the "Hole in the Sky" totem.

Kispiox★. – *19 km – 12 miles N of New Hazelton.* This village lies at the junction of Skeena and Kispiox Rivers in a splendid **site★** below Mount Rocher Deboule. A group of finely carved **totems★** can be found in a park near the Kispiox River.

'Ksan★★. – *7 km – 4 1/2 miles from New Hazelton. Guided tours daily May - mid Oct, 9 am - 6 pm; $3.00;* ☎ *(604) 842-5544.*

INDIAN VILLAGES

This reconstructed Gitksan village has a fine **site★** at the confluence of Bulkley and Skeena Rivers with rugged Mount Rocher Deboule towering 2 400 m - 8 000 ft above it. It consists of cedar long houses, totem poles, a salmon smoke house, dugout canoes, etc.

The **guided tours** start from the **Today House of the Arts** where articles made in the village can be bought. They are conducted by Gitksan Indian women who give a splendid description of their culture and way of life, and they are the only means of entering the buildings. The **Frog House of the Distant Past** presents Gitksan life before European contact, the **Wolf House of the Grandfathers** shows some of the changes which came about with the arrival of white traders. The latter house is also used for performances of the **'Ksan Dancers** *(Fri eves in July and Aug).* The **Fireweed House of Treasures** and the larger **North West National Exhibition Centre** display Gitksan artifacts such as finely decorated clothes and carved masks. At the end of the tour, the **Carving House of All Time** can be visited if the 'Ksan carvers and engravers are at work.

VANCOUVER ★★★ British Columbia

Map p. 5 – Metro Pop 1 268 183 – Tourist Office ☎ (604) 682-2222

This famous city has a magnificent **site★★★** on a peninsula protruding into Georgia Strait between Burrard Inlet and the delta of the Fraser River. In addition to having water on three sides, Vancouver is almost surrounded by mountains. To the north, the Coast Mountains rise steeply, the most prominent peaks being **Hollyburn Mountain,** the twin summits of **The Lions, Grouse Mountain** with its ski slopes, and **Mount Seymour** to the east. To the west across Georgia Strait lie the mountains of Vancouver Island and away to the southeast rise the Cascade Range topped by the snow-clad peak of **Mount Baker** in Washington State.

Unlike most of the rest of Canada, Vancouver does not spend a third of the year under snow. Despite the existence of this substance in great quantities in the surrounding mountains, providing superb skiing, Vancouver itself rarely receives any. Instead it has a high rainfall compared with the rest of the country (152 cm - 60 ins a year). July and August are the sunniest months but even at that time a light rain and mist may shroud the mountains making them all but invisible from the city.

(after photo by Tourism British Columbia)

Aerial View of Vancouver

Early History. – The shores of Georgia Strait were the preserve of the Coast Salish Indians until 1791 when the Spanish Captain **José Maria Narvaez** entered their waters. A year later Captain **George Vancouver** explored Burrard Inlet as part of his survey of the whole coast for the British navy. The site of Vancouver was again seen in 1808 by **Simon Fraser**, this time from the land side at the end of his famous descent of the river which bears his name (p. 31). But the site aroused little interest, being bypassed by the Fraser River gold-rushers, until three young Englishmen opened a brickworks in 1862 on land stretching over much of the present downtown. For pouring their life savings into what is today reputed to be the most densely populated square mile in Canada, they received the epithet "the three greenhorns"! Despite this, others followed them and the 1860s saw the opening of saw-mills on both sides of the inlet to cut up the rich and dense timber growth. In 1867 one **John Deighton** opened a saloon near the present day intersection of Carrall and Water Streets to provide liquid refreshment for the men working at the nearby sawmills and lumber camps. The community which grew up around this saloon became known as Gastown but was later changed to **Granville** when a townsite was laid out by government surveyors in 1869.

The Coming of the Railway. – The location of the terminus of the Canadian Pacific Railway (p. 16) was a matter of controversy for some time. When a decision was finally taken to route the railway down the Fraser Valley to Burrard Inlet, land prices skyrocketed at Port Moody, a tiny settlement at its head (plan p. 58). This factor and the lack of space at Port Moody caused **William Van Horne** in 1884 to extend the line further down the Inlet to the site of Granville. Overnight a city was born. At its official incorporation in 1886 it was baptised Vancouver, the choice of Van Horne. Almost immediately afterwards the communi-ty was wiped out by fire but it had recovered sufficiently to welcome the first Trans-Canada passenger train in 1887.

Vancouver Today. – In the one hundred years since its founding Vancouver has grown from strength to strength. The population of the metropolitan area is now more than one million making it the third largest agglomeration in Canada after Toronto and Montréal. It is the financial, commercial and industrial centre of British Columbia and its major port. In-deed, it is the most important port on the North American west coast. Bulk loads of grain and potash from the Prairies, and of lumber, logs, coal, sulphur and other minerals in interior British Columbia arrive by train and are exported chiefly to Japan and other countries bordering the Pacific Ocean. Vancouver is also important as a centre for forestry industries and fishing.

Vancouver's population is very cosmopolitan. Although the bulk of its original inhab-itants came from either the British Isles or the United States, it has drawn immigrants from the Orient in great numbers (p. 57) as well as from Germany and Italy.

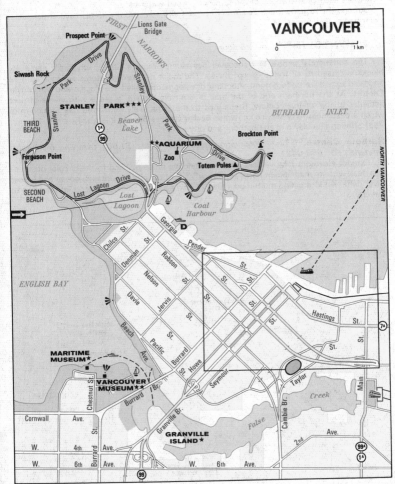

VANCOUVER ★★★

■ STANLEY PARK★★★ Plan p. 55

Vancouver's outstanding attraction is this 405 ha - 1 000 acre park which has a magnificent **site**★★★ at the end of a peninsula which almost closes Burrard Inlet at **First Narrows.** Washed on three sides by the waters of the Inlet it has splendid views of the North Shore Mountains, the peaks of Vancouver Island, the city and the port.

Stanley Park was created in 1886 when the young city of Vancouver (one month old) decided to ask Ottawa to give them the peninsula, which had been a military reserve, for use as a public park. The idea of having a woodland park was rather an advanced one in 1886 because at that time Vancouver consisted of almost nothing but forest ! However Ottawa agreed and the Governor-General **Lord Stanley** dedicated it.

Scenic Drive★★★. – *10 km - 6 miles - about 1 hr.*

This drive begins and ends at Georgia Street circling the park in an anticlockwise direction. It follows the edge of Coal Harbour with views of the yacht clubs, port and city as far as **Brockton Point** with its fine panorama of the Inlet and North Shore Mountains. Just before the Point is a display of brightly painted **totem poles** the work of the West Coast Indians. Several of the poles have thunderbirds at the top and the two shorter house poles have human figures clasped by grizzly bears at the bottom. The road continues to **Prospect Point** where shipping passing through First Narrows in and out of the port can be observed. Then the road is inland but paths lead to the sea wall near **Siwash Rock** which stands cut off from the rest of the peninsula. From Ferguson Point there are views of Third Beach, the Point Grey Peninsula where the University of British Columbia is situated, and the mountains on Vancouver Island. The road continues past Second Beach, various sports facilities and Lost Lagoon.

Aquarium★★. – *Open daily ; $4.50 ; shows at fixed times - check on arrival ; bookstore ;* ☎ *682-1118 or 685-3364.*

This famous aquarium is known for its performing **killer whales,** huge mammals distinguished by their black and white colouring and their dorsal fin. It was in this aquarium that the first killer whale ever held in captivity was trained to perform for the public, a feat quickly copied by many other institutions up and down the coast. After the shows, visitors can watch these animals below water level by means of windows in the side of the tank.

In a separate pool, there are several white or **Beluga whales,** which also give regular performances for visitors. In addition, there are performing dolphins, harbour seals and an interesting pool of sea otters.

Indoors, the aquarium is divided into two parts. The **MacMillan Tropical Gallery** features turtles, crocodiles, electric and moray eels, piranhas, sharks, etc. The **B.C. Hall of Fishes** displays the wide variety of marine life which exists off the coasts of the province while the **Rufe Gibbs Hall** has specimens of the province's fresh water fish.

Around the Aquarium is a **Zoo** *(free of access and admission)* with displays of penguins, polar bears, flamingoes, etc.

■ DOWNTOWN★★ *time : 5 hours*

The commercial centre of Vancouver lies along Granville Street, which for about six blocks is closed to all traffic except buses. The major department stores are located here and also extensive underground shopping developments called the Pacific and Vancouver Centres. At the northern end of the mall is Granville Square, a plaza with views of port activities at the wharves below. Steps lead to the attractively renovated Rail Station from which a passenger ferry service known as **Seabus** crosses Burrard Inlet *(daily, every 15 min ; 75¢)* offering fine views of the harbour and city.

Harbour Centre★★★. – *Observation deck open daily ; $1.50 ; revolving restaurant, cafeteria ;* ☎ *689-0421.*

Exterior elevators take visitors up this distinctive office building to the circular observation deck with its magnificent panoramic **view**★★★ of the city, mountains, ocean and Fraser River delta. An interesting multi-media **film** *(25 min ; $1.75)* provides a good introduction to the city.

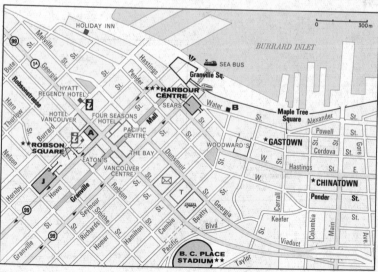

Robson Square★★. – This complex which stretches from Nelson Street almost to Georgia houses all the offices of the Provincial Government in Vancouver. Designed by Arthur Erickson *(p. 59)* and opened in 1979, it has revolutionized the downtown core.

A seven storey law court building **(J)** with a spectacular slanted glass roof *(between Smithe and Nelson Streets)* complements a series of terraced gardens with waterfalls and plants on top of offices *(between Smithe and Robson)*. A plaza under Robson Street contains outdoor cafes, a skating rink and an exhibition area. The Old Court House *(Georgia Street)* houses the **Vancouver Art Gallery (A)** *(open daily except Mon; $2.00;* ☎ *682-5621).*

Nearby is **Robsonstrasse** *(Robson Street between Burrard and Bute)* so called for its original German residents. Today it houses a collection of small boutiques, restaurants, delicatessens and butchers in the European tradition.

B.C. Place Stadium★★. – *Guided tours daily (event schedule permitting) from N side of Terry Fox Plaza; 1 hr; $2.75;* ☎ *661-3664.*

Resembling a circus "Big Top" or an enormous quilted marshmallow, Vancouver's stadium is the largest air-supported domed amphitheatre in the world at present. Designed by Phillips Barratt, it opened in 1983. The teflon and fibre glass roof is inflated by enormous fans and held in place by steel cables. The roof also contains heating elements to melt snow in winter, is self-cleaning with the aid of Vancouver's rainfall, and translucent so that artificial lighting is rarely required. The stadium seats up to 60 000 with no interior supports. A glass-enclosed concourse on its upper level offers a panoramic view of the city.

The stadium is part of a redevelopment project called B.C. Place which will consist of a commercial complex, homes and hotels in addition to the 1986 World Exposition.

Gastown★. – This attractive area of the city combines restored buildings of the late 19th century and modern buildings constructed especially to blend with their surroundings. It is Vancouver's "Yorkville" *(p. 137)*, and like Yorkville, Gastown has not always been so chic. In the 1860s the owners of the sawmills on Burrard Inlet had strict rules against the consumption of alcohol on their premises. Thus thirsty mill hands had to walk the 19 km - 12 miles to New Westminster until an enterprising Englishman decided to alter the situation. John Deighton, nicknamed **Gassy Jack** because of his garrulousness, arrived at the edge of mill property with a barrel of whisky. He enticed the mill hands to build him a saloon rewarding them with the whisky. Soon he was doing a lively trade and the settlement which grew up around his saloon took his name – Gassy's town or Gastown.

Over the years the character of the area has changed several times. Today, its centre is **Maple Tree Square,** where a statue of Gassy Jack stands. **Water Street** is the most attractive of the surrounding streets with its gaslights and shops. On the corner of Cambie stands an interesting **Steam Clock (B).** Powered by a steam engine, the mechanism actually works by gravity and the clock "hoots" out the hour, half hour or quarter hour.

Chinatown★. – *Pender St between Carrall St and Gore Ave.* This colourful quarter is the centre of Vancouver's large Chinese community. There are many restaurants and shops selling oriental foods and other wares, and most of the signs are in Chinese. This is a particularly lively area during the Chinese New Year *(between January 21st and February 19th)* with street parades complete with dragons.

Chinese Canadians are mainly descendants of fortune-seekers who left China in the mid 19th century. The first of these went to California in search of gold, later moving north after the gold in the Fraser Valley. Then, thousands of Coolies were imported to work on the Canadian Pacific Railway because they would work for very little. Those who came never had any intention of staying, they simply wished to amass a fortune and return home to live a life of luxury. Thus they did not change their traditional way of life and made no attempt to join in the community. Wherever they went little Chinatowns sprang up, and with them racial hatred. They were very unpopular with white workers especially with organized labour as they would work for practically nothing. (Needless to say they never earned enough to return to China.) Several times white mobs rampaged through Vancouver's Chinatown destroying property. Chinese immigration was halted and discrimination rife.

This situation changed after the Second World War when immigration was once more allowed and all Chinese Canadians were given the vote. Today the Chinese community is very vibrant supplying recruits for every profession and job in the city, and it is also numerous being second in size only to that of San Francisco in North America.

Harbour Tour★(D). – *Plan p. 55. Departs wharf at foot of Denman St. daily May - Sept; $9.00; 1 1/4 hr;* ☎ *687-9558.*

This boat trip by sternwheeler makes a pleasant excursion enabling visitors to see Vancouver's busy port with fine views of the city and mountains.

■ SIGHTS OUTSIDE DOWNTOWN

U.B.C. Museum of Anthropology★★★. – *Plan p. 58. Open afternoons daily, closed Mon; $2.00;* ☎ *228-5087.*

The University of British Columbia has a large campus at the end of the Point Grey Peninsula overlooking Georgia Strait and the mountains of Vancouver Island. Well known for its site, and for its research facilities in agriculture, forestry and oceanography, the university is also famous for its collection of West Coast Indian Art.

The **museum building★★** itself, opened in 1976, is an architectural masterpiece, the work of Arthur Erickson *(p. 59)*. A glass and concrete structure, it admirably complements its site. A ramp flanked by exhibits leads down into the **Great Hall ★★** whose glass walls rise 14 m - 45 ft around the magnificent collection of Haida and Kwagiutl totem poles and other large wood carvings. The trees, sea, sky and mountains visible through the glass walls give visitors the impression of seeing the poles in their original surroundings and not in a museum.

Totem Poles. – These columns of cedar wood carved with designs of birds, animals, humans and mythological creatures are not solely works of art. Each carving is a sign or crest of a family or clan. They are similar to coats-of-arms or heraldic emblems. Their purpose was varied – sometimes they were functional serving as house corner posts, sometimes they

VANCOUVER AND VICINITY

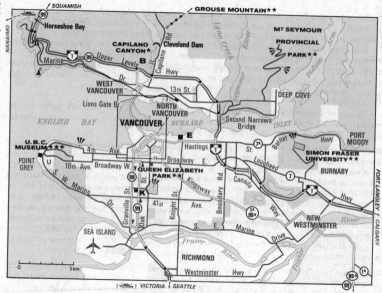

were decorative serving as the entrance to a house (a hole was made at the bottom of the pole), sometimes they were memorials to dead relatives, and sometimes they were actually part of the grave. Whatever their purpose, they represent an art form unique to the Northwest Pacific Coast Indians. The golden age of carving was between 1850 and 1900 after the introduction of metal carving implements by the white man. In recent years there has been a revival in the art as the Indians seek to recreate their traditions. In fact the poles and other carvings in the museum grounds are copies of older carvings now decayed.

Among the many fine carvings in the Great Hall, note the grizzly bear clutching a human figure ; the large sea wolf which has captured three killer whales – one in his mouth, a second beneath his front feet, and a third in his tail ; and the splendid row of potlatch bowls on wheels with a creature at each end with a spoon in its mouth.

In contrast to the massive sculpture in the Great Hall, the carvings in the **Masterpiece Gallery**★★ are tiny and very intricate, illustrating the artistic genius of the Pacific Coast peoples. Glass floor-to-ceiling cases, which allow viewing from all angles, contain pieces carved in silver, gold, argillite, horn, bone, ivory, stone and wood. The designs are the same in miniature as those on the monumental sculpture elsewhere.

Most of the rest of the museum is devoted to "visible storage" galleries. The university's worldwide collections from ancient times to today are on display – a unique idea which allows visitors to view works normally inaccessible. The pieces are catalogued by region and civilization. The museum also has galleries for changing or visiting exhibitions.

The North Shore★★.
– The mountains descend quite steeply towards Burrard Inlet on its north side and they are cut not only by deep fjords – Indian Arm and Howe Sound – but by the deep valleys or canyons of several small rivers or creeks – Capilano, Lynn and Seymour being the best known. The houses on the north shore are for the most part expensive and often cling to the mountain slopes with fine views of the inlet and city.

Mount Seymour Provincial Park★★. – *31 km - 19 miles from downtown by Second Narrows Bridge, Dollarton Hwy and Mt. Seymour Parkway ; open daily ;* ☎ *929-1291.*

From the park entrance a road climbs steeply to the Deep Cove Lookout *(8 km - 5 miles)* from which there is a **view**★★ to the east. The peak of Mount Baker in Washington State can often be seen above the clouds. The village of Deep Cove, Indian Arm and Simon Fraser University in Burnaby are visible nearer at hand. From just below the ski centre *(13 km - 8 miles)*, there is a fine **view**★★ of the city with Vancouver Island in the distance on clear days. A **chair ride** takes visitors to the top of the mountain *(July and Aug, afternoons only, weather permitting ; $4.00).*

Grouse Mountain★★. – *13 km - 8 miles from downtown by Lions Gate Bridge, Capilano Rd and Nancy Greene Way. Access by skyride daily (for skiers in winter) ; $6.00 ; restaurant ; snack-bar ;* ☎ *984-0661.*

This aerial tramway rises to an elevation of 1 100 m - 3 700 ft offering a splendid **view**★★ of the city as it ascends and a panorama embracing Vancouver Island, the Fraser delta and Burrard Inlet from the top on clear days.

Capilano Canyon★. – This deep canyon can be appreciated by visiting the narrow pedestrian **suspension bridge**★ *(B) (9 km - 6 miles from downtown by Lions Gate Bridge and Capilano Rd. Open daily ; $2.75 ; snack-bar ;* ☎ *985-7474)* which hangs 70 m - 230 ft above the river. Built in 1899, it is 137 m - 450 ft long and it sways as you walk across it. On the far side is a pleasant glade of Douglas Firs and Western Red Cedars.

A little further along Capilano Road is **Capilano Canyon Park** where there are pleasant walks and views of the canyon from below. At the northern end of the park *(access from Nancy Greene Way)* is the Cleveland Dam and Capilano Lake, a reservoir of drinking water for the city of Vancouver. Across the lake there is a **view**★ of the double peak of The Lions.

Queen Elizabeth Park★★.
– *West 23rd Ave and Cambie St. Restaurant, picnic areas.*

This beautiful park lies at the geographical centre of Vancouver and on its highest point (150 m - 500 ft). There are extraordinary **views**★★★ in clear weather of the city and mountains by day and night including the fine snowcapped peak of Mount Baker of the Cascades more than 110 km - 70 miles away. The road from the entrance climbs through an arboretum to the **Bloedel Floral Conservatory**★, a triodetic dome structure of glass and aluminum. Inside *(open daily, $2.00)* there are examples of tropical and desert vegetation much enlivened by a number of colourful tropical birds flying free. The other attraction of the park is the lovely **Sunken Gardens**★★. Paths weave among the flowers to a waterfall and bridge from which there are views of the gardens and city.

Simon Fraser University★★. – *Gaglardi Way, Burnaby. Guided tours daily in July and Aug, Sun only rest of year ; 1 hr ; charge for parking ;* ☎ 291-3111.

This architecturally famous not to mention controversial university has a lovely site on Burnaby Mountain with views of the North Shore Mountains. It is a unique ensemble of inter-connected buildings constructed along the tree-lined, partially covered pedestrian Mall and around the large Academic Quadrangle with its pond. The harmony of these otherwise rather harsh concrete structures comes from the fact that they were designed as a unit and did not grow up gradually with additions being appended hither and thither - as at so many universities. The architects were two natives of Vancouver, **Arthur Erickson** and **Geoffrey Massey**. Following the success of Simon Fraser, Erickson has designed several other interesting structures ; among them the U.B.C. Museum of Anthropology *(p. 57)*, Robson Square *(p. 57)* and Roy Thomson Hall in Toronto *(p. 131)*.

Since its opening in 1965 Simon Fraser has achieved a reputation for the avant-garde. It operates year-round on a trimester system, each term being independent so that students can study continuously or take only one or two terms a year.

Vancouver Museum★★. – *Plan p. 55. In Vanier Park. Open daily ; $2.50 ; cafeteria, gift shop ;* ☎ 736-4431.

The buildings of the museum surround the distinctive conical dome of the **MacMillan Planetarium** *(shows daily except Mon)*, which has become a Vancouver landmark since its opening in 1968. At the front entrance, there is a huge stainless steel **crab**★ in an ornamental pool, the work of sculptor George Norris. It represents the crab which traditionally guards the harbour in Indian legend. There is an excellent **view**★★ of the city and North Shore Mountains from the parking area or from the terrace of the museum cafeteria.

The museum provides an interesting introduction to the Vancouver area. The **Indian galleries** cover all aspects of the lives of the West Coast tribes. The artifacts on display, especially those of the Lipsett Collection, show an extraordinary artistic finesse ; note the tiny woven baskets of cedar, the argillite carvings and the masks. One of the masks has two faces - the first, an animal, opening to reveal the second, human, reflecting the union between these two lifeforms. There are also interesting displays on whaling (note the large Nootka canoe) and the multitude of uses for the wood of the cedar tree.

In the **Historical galleries**, the history of the Vancouver area from the first arrival of Europeans is traced. A Hudson Bay Company trading store has been recreated along with the steerage quarters on an immigrant ship. The birth of Vancouver as a lumber village is shown with its growth after the arrival of the "Iron Horse". A series of room reconstructions of the 1910 era illustrate the city's rapid growth into a metropolis.

In the **Southam Observatory** *(opening times vary and depend on weather conditions)*, visitors can look through the giant telescope at sun, moon, planets, stars, etc.

Maritime Museum★. – *Plan p. 55. In Vanier Park. Open daily ; $1.50 ;* ☎ 736-4431.

Ship models and other artifacts illustrate the maritime history of Vancouver and British Columbia. There are displays on shipbuilding, the working of a grain elevator, and the recreated wheel house of a tug. Outside, historic vessels are often moored at the marina.

The highlight of the collection is however the **St. Roch**★, a Royal Canadian Mounted Police patrol ship which navigated the Northwest Passage in both directions in the 1940s. This 31.5 m - 104 ft wooden vessel has been completely restored with authentic items in all the cabins *(guided tours every 1/2 hr ; 20 min ; National Historic Park)*.

The Northwest Passage. – A sea route between Atlantic and Pacific Oceans around the north of the American continent was the quest of explorers for centuries after it became obvious that America was a continent and not an adjunct of Asia. Among the many unsuccessful attempts were those of Martin Frobisher in 1576, Henry Hudson in 1610 and Sir John Franklin in 1845. All were halted by ice and extreme conditions sometimes resulting in the loss of the entire crew. Finally, the Norwegian **Roald Amundsen** navigated a passage between the Canadian mainland and the Arctic islands in 1903-6.

After Amundsen's voyage, various countries became interested in claiming these Arctic areas as their own. Thus in 1940 the Canadian Government determined to assert its sovereignty over the northland. The best means of doing this was to send a ship through the passage. The Royal Canadian Mounted Police vessel *St. Roch* under Captain Henry Larsen was the chosen vehicle. The *St. Roch* left Vancouver in June 1940 and, after being frozen in several times, reached Halifax in October 1942. The return trip was a little faster. Larsen left Halifax in July 1944 and arrived in Vancouver in October of the same year. He had covered the 7 295 nautical miles of ice-strewn water in 86 days ! Not only was the *St. Roch* the first ship to navigate the passage both ways but it was the first ship to do it east-west in one season.

Since the voyages of the *St. Roch*, other ships have made the passage. It is still a hazardous and tricky undertaking.

Vanterm★ (E). – *At N end of Clark Drive take overpass to Visitor Parking Lot. Open Mon – Fri 9-12am, 1-4pm ; guided tours Sun June - Aug, 1,2, and 3pm ;* ☎ 666-6129.

This enormous container-handling complex can be viewed from an observation lounge which overlooks loading and unloading activities on ships, trucks and trains - to a backdrop of the North Shore mountains.

Granville Island★. – *Plan p. 55. Accessible by car from the Granville Bridge and West 4th Ave ; by False Creek ferry from beside the Vancouver Aquatic Centre on Beach Ave, or by ferry from Maritime Museum.*

This one-time industrial area under the Granville Bridge has been renovated to house restaurants, art galleries, boutiques, theatres, hotel and residences, in addition to some surviving industry. Its highlight is the **Public Market**★ *(open Tues - Sun 10am - 6pm)* where stalls of fresh produce vie for position with the products of Vancouver's many ethnic groups.

VANCOUVER★★★

Van Dusen Botanical Garden (K). – *On 37th Ave at Oak St. Open daily ; $3.00 ; refreshments, gift shop ;* ☎ *266-7194.*

This garden offers fine displays of plants in geographical as well as botanical arrangements. There are areas devoted to Southern Hemisphere, Mediterranean, and Sino-Himalayan vegetation in addition to a Rosaceae, a magnolia garden and a Rhododendron walk. MacMillan-Bloedel Place offers a series of displays on the province's forests.

EXCURSIONS

Howe Sound★★★. – This deep fjord which extends about 48 km - 30 miles into the mountains of British Columbia provides some of the province's most spectacular coastal scenery. It can be admired by train, boat, or road. The **Royal Hudson 2860,** a huge steam engine which once pulled trains across Canada, makes regular trips to Squamish from the B.C. Rail Station in North Vancouver *(mid May - Labour Day, Wed - Sun ; all day excursion, leaves North Vancouver 10.30 am ; $10.00 ;* ☎ *987-5211 for reservations).*

A spectacular alternative for the return trip is the voyage aboard the **MV Britannia** *(mid May - Labour Day Sun, Wed, Fri ; $34 including train fare ;* ☎ *as above).* The views of both sides of the fjord are excellent and the boat goes right into Vancouver harbour.

By car *(66 km - 41 miles, allow 3 hrs),* travellers follow Route 99, a road hacked out of the almost sheer cliffs with incredible **views★★★** of the mountains and the blue-green waters of the Sound between Horseshoe Bay and Squamish.

B.C. Museum of Mining★★. – *53 km - 33 miles from Vancouver in Britannia Beach. Open daily May - Labour Day, weekends in Sept ; $4.50 ; snack bar ;* ☎ *688-8735.*

Set in an abandoned copper mine, this museum provides a fascinating introduction to mining. An interesting film traces the history of the industry from the early gold rushes to today's hard rock mining with particular emphasis on the copper found at Britannia Beach. This is followed by a **guided tour** *(1 hr)* by train of one of the mining tunnels with demonstrations of equipment, and a walk through the old copper smelting plant.

Shannon Falls★★. – *60 km - 37 miles. Park open daily, picnic area.*

These impressive falls cascade 198 m -.650 ft over a cliff in pleasant surroundings.

Squamish. – *Pop 10 272. 66 km - 41 miles.* This lumber centre has a fine site at the foot of snowcapped peaks including Mount Garibaldi (alt 2 678 m - 8 786 ft).

Fort Langley National Historic Park★. – *56 km - 35 miles SE of Vancouver by Trans-Canada Hwy and Glover St or Rte 7 and ferry. Open daily ; $1.00 ;* ☎ *888-4424.*

Fort Langley was one of a network of trading posts established by the Hudson's Bay Company in British Columbia in the early 19th century. The fur trade was the predominant occupation though a large farm was operated, and salmon were caught and packaged for trade.

Today, the restored buildings of the wooden-palisaded fort can be visited. The warehouse has a fine collection of **furs★** and the trading goods once given in exchange for them. In the Big House, the quarters of the resident Hudson's Bay Company officials can be seen, and on the second floor there is a **display★** on the history of the fort, the fur trade and colonization of the Pacific Coast.

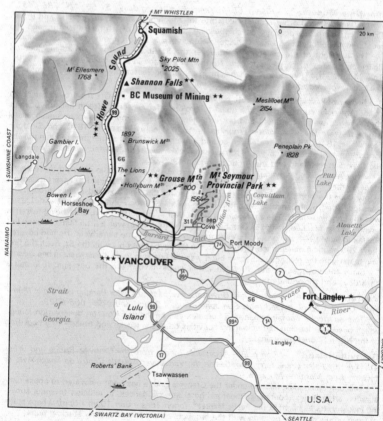

VANCOUVER Island ★★★ British Columbia

Map p. 5 - *Local map below*

Access. – Vancouver Island is served by seven ferry services :

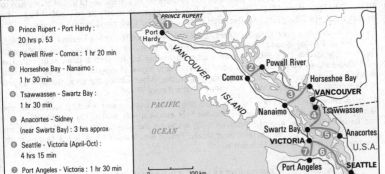

1. Prince Rupert - Port Hardy :
   20 hrs p. 53
2. Powell River - Comox : 1 hr 20 min
3. Horseshoe Bay - Nanaimo :
   1 hr 30 min
4. Tsawwassen - Swartz Bay :
   1 hr 30 min
5. Anacortes - Sidney
   (near Swartz Bay) : 3 hrs approx
6. Seattle - Victoria (April-Oct) :
   4 hrs 15 min
7. Port Angeles - Victoria : 1 hr 30 min

With an area of more than 32 000 sq km - 12 000 sq miles, Vancouver Island is the largest of the islands off the Pacific Coast of North America. Mountains rise over 2 100 m – 7 000 ft to form the central core. The west coast is deeply indented by inlets or fjords which almost dissect the island, the east coast is gently sloping with wide beaches in the south but more mountainous further north. The climate is very temperate all over the island but rainfall varies greatly : Victoria in the southeast receives 68 cm - 27 ins annually whereas Zeballos *(map p. 30)* on the west coast receives 648 cm - 255 ins. This high rainfall causes dense forest growth and not surprisingly the island's major industry is logging with saw mills and pulp mills located in many places. The population is mainly concentrated in the southeast corner around Victoria and along the shores of the Strait of Georgia. Because of this, there are few major roads but a number of logging tracks crisscross the island *(open to public travel outside working hours)*.

■ VICTORIA★★★. – *Description p. 63*

■ From Parksville to Pacific Rim★★

154 km - 96 miles by Route 4 – allow 2 hours, 4 1/2 hours including visits – Local map p. 62.

This winding route traverses the mountain backbone of the island through fine scenery. Some parts are wild and untouched by man, others are the scene of great activity particularly in the logging industry.

Englishman Falls★. – *5 km - 3 miles from Parksville turn left for 8 km - 5 miles.*

The Englishman River tumbles over two sets of falls. The upper ones are narrow and deep dropping into a gorge. A path bridges the river and follows it to the lower falls *(3/4 hr Rtn)* through a dense forest of high trees, ferns and moss covered rocks. The lower falls are twin jets dropping around a rock into a deep pool.

Route 4 leaves the plain behind and begins to enter the mountains.

Little Qualicum Falls★. – *21 km - 13 miles from Parksville, turn right to parking area.*

The Little Qualicum River descends over two sets of falls connected by a gorge. The lower falls are small but the walk to the upper falls *(1/2 hr Rtn)* though the forest is pleasant with views of the canyon. The **upper falls★** are on two levels with a pool between them.

Route 4 follows the south side of **Cameron Lake** with occasional views of it through the trees.

Cathedral Grove★★. – *30 km - 19 miles from Parksville, part of MacMillan Park. Parking beside highway.*

Cathedral Grove as the name suggests contains some of the original tall trees of the island. Elsewhere, the Douglas firs have been cut for their

Cathedral Grove

wood but fortunately this grove was preserved by the MacMillan Bloedel Paper Company and donated to the province. A walk *(3/4 hr)* under these giants is impressive but more particularly for those who have not seen the Redwoods of California. Many of them rise to 60 m - 200 ft or more. One is 3 m - 9 1/2 ft in diameter and nearly 76 m - 250 ft high. The largest trees are 800 years old. Between them grow Red Cedar and Hemlock trees.

Route 4 descends to and bypasses **Port Alberni** which is situated at the head of Alberni Inlet. This arm of Barkley Sound reaches within 19 km - 12 miles as the crow flies of the east coast of the island. Port Alberni is an important lumber centre with a large pulp mill. The road then follows **Sproat Lake** with good views. Many signs of logging activity will be seen along the road from cut areas to huge logging trucks. After leaving the lake, Route 4 begins to climb Klitsa Mountain along the valley of the Taylor River.

After reaching the height of land, the road begins its twisting and winding descent to the Pacific along the Kennedy River with **views★** of snowcapped peaks. The river widens out into **Kennedy Lake,** the largest stretch of fresh water on the island. The road follows it rising above it and dipping to water level alternately. Pacific Rim National Park is reached near the junction with the Tofino to Ucluelet road.

FROM PARKSVILLE TO PACIFIC RIM

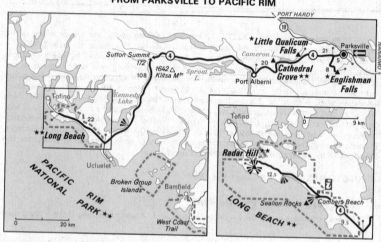

■ PACIFIC RIM NATIONAL PARK★★

Open daily ; camping, accommodation ; Park Information Centre ☎ (604) 726-7721.

Situated on the rugged west coast of Vancouver Island, Pacific Rim National Park is a long narrow strip of rocky islands and headlands stretching intermittently for about 130 km - 80 miles between Port Renfrew and Tofino. It is made up of the 72 km - 45 mile **West Coast Trail** for backpackers between Port Renfrew and Bamfield *(each end is accessible by road)*, about a hundred islands and rocky islets in Barkley Sound known as the **Broken Group Islands** *(access by private boat or by MV Lady Rose from Port Alberni ; for details ☎ 723-8313)* and famous **Long Beach.**

Long Beach★★. – This 11 km - 7 mile curve of sand and rocky points is pounded by the surf and backed by a dense rain forest and mountains rising to 1 200 m - 4 000 ft. Breakers come crashing in off the Pacific carrying huge drift logs which are deposited all over the beach one day and are carried away again the next. The power of these waves is immense, the variation in the sand level can be as great as 1.8 m - 6 ft between winter and summer in one year. At low tide the beach is nearly 1 km - 1/2 mile wide and a variety of creatures can be seen in the tidal pools among the rocks. Offshore, sealions bask on the rocks and Pacific gray whales are often spotted. Numerous birds make the beach and forest their home and many more visit it seasonally. The heavy rainfall and moderate temperatures of this coast have produced the dense rain forest where Sitka spruce flourishes and red cedar and hemlock also grow.

There are several points of access to Long Beach. Paths weave through the high trees and mossy, ferny rain forest with views of beach and ocean. From Combers Beach, the **Sealion Rocks** can be seen offshore *(binoculars advisable).* Visitors also enjoy the exceptional surfing and swimming. The water, however, is cold (10°C - 50°F) and can be extremely dangerous. Attention must be paid to tides and currents *(for information contact Park Information Centre).*

Radar Hill★★. – *22 km - 14 miles from Ucluelet junction. Take road to left which climbs 1.6 km - 1 mile to viewpoint.*

From this point above the forest a splendid overall **view★★** of the area is obtained *(telescope).* The mountains behind the park can be seen as well as the wild and rocky coastline.

Free road maps are available from all the provincial governments.
The addresses can be found in the regional introductions.

VICTORIA ★★★ British Columbia

Map p. 5 - Metro Pop 233 481 - Tourist Office ☎ (604) 382-2127

Victoria, the capital of British Columbia, occupies the southeast tip of Vancouver Island facing the **Juan de Fuca Strait** and both the **Olympic** and **Cascade Mountains** in Washington State. It is famous for its beautiful gardens (both private and public), for its elegance and gentility, and for being "a piece of the old empire" as its residents are largely of British stock. It makes a strange contrast with the rest of Vancouver Island which is largely untamed forest and rugged mountains pounded by raging seas. Victoria is certainly Canada's "gentlest" city with its annual rainfall of 68 cm - 27 ins and large amount of sunshine. This climate and scenery have made Victoria a popular tourist destination. Indeed Stephen Leacock (p. 115) wrote of it, "If I had known of this place before I would have been born here".

From Trading Post to Gracious Capital. – The Hudson's Bay Company (p. 74) built a trading post on the site of Victoria when it became clear that their previous Pacific headquarters would be declared in the United States (p. 31). They named the new post Victoria after the Queen. This post grew in the 1850s and 60s during the various gold rushes to British Columbia (pp. 36 and 38) as it became an important provisioning and outfitting centre. In 1849, it was declared the capital of the Crown Colony of Vancouver Island and later of the whole of British Columbia when the island was united with the mainland (except for the years 1866-68 when New Westminster was the capital). It became a centre of gracious living and avoided industrial development when the Canadian Pacific Railway was terminated at Vancouver (though trains do cross to the island by ferry). That city grew as a major commercial centre delegating more restricted economic development to Victoria but enabling it to maintain much of its quiet charm. The Canadian Forces have their Pacific Naval base at **Esquimalt** (map p. 65). Otherwise, Victoria residents are mainly employed in government services or tourism. A large percentage of them do not work, however, as Victoria with its pleasant climate is a favourite retirement place.

■ DOWNTOWN★★ time : 1 day

The centre of Victoria is situated along Government Street, which is the main shopping area, and around the James Bay part of the harbour where the ferries from Port Angeles and Seattle dock. There is an intriguing collection of little squares and alleys housing elegant shops, restaurants and sidewalk cafes - Nootka Court, Trounce Alley, Bastion Square and a little further north Market Square where a collection of older buildings have been renovated to house shops around courtyard gardens.

British Columbia Provincial Museum★★★. – *Open daily ; free ; guided tours 1 hr ; tearoom ; gift shop ;* ☎ *387-3701.*

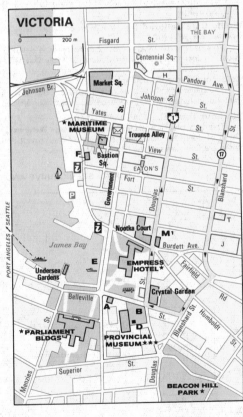

The provincial museum stands in a group of striking modern buildings called Heritage Court. Also housing the provincial archives, this court has almost an Arabic flavour with its narrow columns and arches on the ground floor. In front of it stands the **Netherlands Carillon Tower (A)**, an open-sided 27 m - 88 ft tower containing 62 bells given to the province by Canadians of Dutch origin (*carillon concerts are given Sun all year and Wed in summer*).

At the north end of the museum there is an arcade called the **Glass House**, which houses a collection of totem poles from all over the province.

In the main entrance hall there is an interesting carved cedar representation of a **Nootka Whaling Expedition.** Eight life-size men in a canoe are shown harpooning a whale. Also in the hall are a Cowichan Indian Welcome Figure and a handcarved reproduction of the province.

The second floor is devoted to the **natural history** of British Columbia. At present, it consists of a series of spectacular dioramas of the coastal forest and seashore regions of the province including animal, bird and fish life. When it is complete, there will be dioramas of all the natural regions - mountains, valleys, interior drylands, etc.

The third floor deals with British Columbia's **human history**. Visitors walk backwards through time starting with the province today. Highlights of this are the reconstruction of a turn-of-the-century street complete with shops, hotel, movie house and station ; very vivid recreations of a sawmill, fish-packing plant, farmyard and mine to show the development of these industries ; and, in the section explaining the discovery of British Columbia by Europeans, a reconstruction of part of George Vancouver's ship, the *Discovery*.

The **Indian History Gallery** contains an extensive and fine collection of Indian art. This is arranged in striking dioramas to explain the way of life before the arrival of white settlers and the changes which occurred after contact, such as smallpox epidemics, the banning of the potlatch ceremony and the problems concerning land settlement. Note especially the totem poles and the reconstruction of the house of an Indian chief.

Parliament Buildings★. – *Plan p. 63.* Set back from James Bay on the south side behind gardens stands a long squat grey stone building with a dome at its centre. Designed by Francis Rattenbury of Victoria and built between 1894 and 1898, "the buildings" as they are known locally house the British Columbia legislature and government offices. A bronze statue of Queen Victoria stands in front of them and on top of the dome there is a gilt statue of Captain George Vancouver. The entrance is through the highly decorated arch below the dome *(guided tours of the interior daily except weekends in winter ; 1/2 hr ;* ☎ *387-3046).* On summer evenings the buildings are illuminated by thousands of tiny lights making them look like something out of The Arabian Nights.

Empress Hotel★. – *Plan p. 63.* Also designed by Francis Rattenbury and built by the Canadian Pacific Railway in 1905, this enormous turreted ivy-covered hotel is one of the landmarks of Victoria. For many years "tea at the Empress" was considered an essential part of gracious living. Tea (high tea) is still served at the Empress *(daily ; reservations advised ;* ☎ *384-8111)* while musicians play, but it is now more of a tourist attraction than a facet of gracious living.

Thunderbird Park★ (B) . – *Plan p. 63.* This small park has a fine collection of totem poles and other Indian carvings. They are faithful copies of original works, many executed by Chief Mungo Martin a famous carver. As each carving decays it is copied and replaced *(carvers can sometimes be seen at work).*

Next to Thunderbird Park stands a white clapboard building, **Helmcken House (D),** *(open daily except Mon, and Tues in winter ; guided tours 15 min)* which was built in 1858.

Maritime Museum★. – *Plan p. 63.* Open daily ; $2.00 ; ☎ 385-4222.

A lighthouse beacon stands in front of the cream and orange law court building which houses this museum. There are displays on West Coast explorers, model ships and all kinds of marine paraphernalia. Of special interest are the *Tilikum,* a converted Indian dugout canoe which sailed from Victoria to England 1901-04, and the *Trekka,* a 6m - 20 ft sailing boat built in Victoria which sailed around the world 1955-59, the smallest boat ever to undertake such a voyage.

Emily Carr Gallery★ (F) . – *Plan p. 63. Open daily in summer, closed Sun and Mon in winter ;* ☎ *387-3080.*

This gallery run by the Provincial Archives is devoted to one of Canada's greatest and most original painters, British Columbian **Emily Carr** (1871-1945). Her portrayals of West Coast landscapes and Indian villages are striking, and examples can be found in most major collections across the country.

The gallery exhibits, on a rotating basis, original works by Miss Carr and other related material including letters, manuscripts, newspaper articles and photographs.

Harbour Tour (E). – *Plan p. 63. Daily May - Sept, 1 1/4 hr ; $7.00 ;* ☎ *383-6824.*

This is a pleasant excursion up the **Gorge Waterway,** around the harbour and into the Strait of Juan de Fuca. Much evidence of the province's logging industry will be seen and there are fine views of the Olympic Mountains.

VICTORIA - SCENIC DRIVE AND OAK BAY

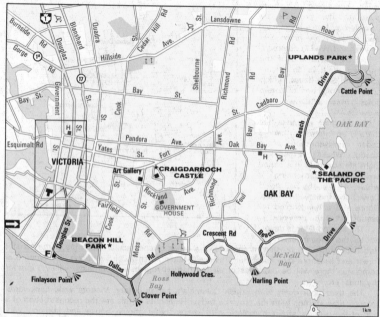

Crystal Garden. – *Plan p. 63. Open daily ; $3.50 ; tea served ;* ☎ *381-1213.*

This huge glass house was once the scene of orchestral concerts, art exhibits and a large underglass sea water swimming pool. Today, it houses a tropical garden filled with exotic birds and plants. It is also a pleasant place to take tea.

Undersea Gardens. – *Plan p. 63. Open daily ; $4.00 ;* ☎ *382-5717.*

This structure which stands in the inner harbour enables visitors to descend under the water to see fish in aquariums. During the shows *(every hour),* a frogman brings various species : small shark, octopus, etc, close to the glass walls for spectators to view.

Classic Car Museum (M1). – *Plan p. 63. Open daily ; $3.50 ;* ☎ *382-7118.*

Over 40 cars, many of historic interest, are on display.

■ SCENIC DRIVE★★ *Plan p. 64*

13 km - 8 miles. Leave from Thunderbird Park and take Douglas St S. Time : 1 hr not including visit.

This beautiful drive enables visitors to appreciate Victoria's fine site on the Strait of Juan de Fuca surrounded by mountains, and some of the lovely gardens maintained by its inhabitants.

The drive skirts **Beacon Hill Park★**, a large and pleasant park full of flowers, and passes a plaque **(F)** marking km - mile 0 of the **Trans-Canada Highway.** This highway was constructed after the Second World War to connect the ten provinces. It was completed in 1962 when the section through Rogers' Pass *(p. 41)* was finished. The Trans-Canada stretches for nearly 8 000 km - 5 000 miles to St. John's, Newfoundland *(p. 225).*

From Finlayson Point and Clover Point, there are fine **views★★** of the Olympic Mountains. The Scenic Drive then enters the municipality of **Oak Bay.** This wealthy suburb of Victoria is entirely residential with large houses, beautiful gardens, fine views and a very English population.

From Harling Point, there is a fine view of the rocky coastline and of many houses perched along the coast. Gonzales Bay is visible directly below on the right and the Trial Islands can be seen offshore to the left. The drive continues around McNeill Bay with several viewpoints and reaches the Oak Bay golf course on Gonzales Point. This is one of the most attractive golf courses on the continent with its **views★★** of the sea, the San Juan Islands and if the day is clear the high snow-clad peaks of the Cascades dominated by Mount Baker.

Sealand of the Pacific★. – *Beside Oak Bay Marina. Open daily ; $4.50 ; restaurant ;* ☎ *598-3373.*

Built on the edge of Oak Bay, Sealand is a collection of aquariums using bay water. The larger marine animals, Californian and Steller Sealions, and killer whales perform regularly for visitors *(shows every hour, about 15 min).*

The drive then passes through **Uplands Park★**, a pleasant part of Oak Bay with lovely homes and gardens. From **Cattle Point**, there are views of the coast.

■ ADDITIONAL SIGHTS

Craigdarroch Castle★. – *Plan p. 64 ; 1050 Joan Cres. Open daily ; $2.00 ;* ☎ *592-5323.*

Built in the 1880s by Robert Dunsmuir, a Scot who made a fortune from coal, this huge stone mansion has towers, turrets and a carved carriage entrance *(porte cochère).* Once it stood in 11 ha - 27 acres of gardens and was a centre for Victoria's smart society - one of the Dunsmuir sons was both Premier of the province and later Lieutenant-Governor. Now it is owned by the City of Victoria and it is being restored to its former grandeur. Note the wood panelled hall and massive oak staircase. On the third floor there is an enormous dance hall and from the top of the tower, there is a fine view of Victoria.

Fort Rodd Hill★. – *13.5 km - 8 1/2 miles W by Rtes 1, 1A and Ocean Blvd. National Historic Park. Open daily ;* ☎ *388-1601.*

Set in 18 ha - 44 acres of land at the southwest corner

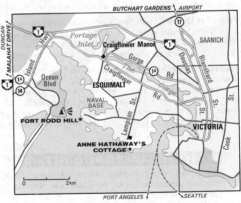

VICTORIA - WEST AND ESQUIMALT

of Esquimalt harbour, Fort Rodd Hill contains the remains of three coast artillery gun batteries built to protect the approaches to the naval base at Esquimalt. They were in operation until 1956. There are also displays on the coastal defences of this area. From beside Fishgard Lighthouse, there are fine **views★** of the Juan de Fuca Strait, Olympic Mountains and the naval base at Esquimalt.

Anne Hathaway's Cottage★. – *429 Lampson St. Esquimalt, part of Olde England Inn. Open daily ; $3.75 ; guided tours 1/2 hr ; restaurant in inn ;* ☎ *388-4353.*

This is an exact replica of the home of Anne Hathaway (the wife of William Shakespeare) in Stratford, England. It is a black and white half-timbered building with a thatched roof. Inside there are ten rooms of period furniture, note especially the wooden panelling on the ground floor. Surrounding it is an attractive English "old world" garden.

VICTORIA★★★

Art Gallery. – *Plan p. 64 ; 1040 Moss St. Open daily except Hols and Mon in winter ; $2.00 ; cafe, gallery shop ;* ☎ *384-4101.*

The nucleus of the gallery is a Victorian mansion built in 1890. Several modern additions have been made but the house remains the most interesting part with its fascinating dolls' house on the second floor and its Japanese garden. The gallery is known for its collection of Asian art which is shown in regularly changing exhibitions.

Craigflower Manor. – *110 Island Highway. Open daily except Hols, Mon all year and Tues in winter ;* ☎ *387-3067.*

This Georgian-style clapboard house was constructed in 1856 by Kenneth McKenzie, bailiff for the Puget Sound Agricultural Company, the first organization to develop the island for farming purposes. It was one of the earliest buildings in Victoria and it was partially fortified in case of Indian attack (note the studded oak door and heavy wooden shutters). Most of the manor is original and un-changed ; it contains period furnishings.

EXCURSIONS

The Butchart Gardens★★★. – *21 km - 13 miles N by Rte 17 and Keating Rd or by 17A (quieter). Open daily 9 am – dusk, until 11 pm in summer ; $6.00 ; tea house ; restaurant ;* ☎ *652-4422.*

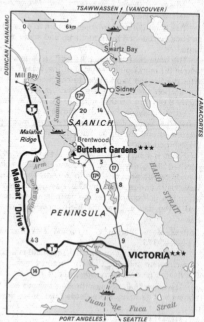

These internationally famous gardens were started in 1904 by Mrs. Jennie Butchart, the wife of a cement factory owner. The ugly hole made by the lime quarry (for the cement) offended Mrs. Butchart and she decided to create something beautiful from it. Still operated by the family, the gardens have now been considerably expanded to cover about 14 ha - 35 acres maintained by a small army of gardeners in summer.

The floral showpiece is the beautiful **Sunken Garden★★★** with its green lawns, trees and exquisite flower arrangements making the whole area a whirl of colour. It is set in a huge hole, the sides of which are covered with ivy. It is best viewed from above or from the Rock Island at its centre. Paths weave down into it through a rockery. The flowers change season to season but the effect is always the same.

The other gardens include the **Ross Fountain** with continually changing water displays in a rocky pool, the **Concert Lawn** *(concerts and shows summer eves),* the **Rose Garden★** full of blooms on both sides and overhead *(should be viewed in summer),* the dark and secluded **Japanese Garden★** with its lacquered bridges and summerhouse, and the formal **Italian Garden★** with its star-shaped lily pond and statues. On summer evenings all the gardens can be viewed by artificial lighting giving an entirely different perspective.

Malahat Drive★. – *Begins 16 km - 10 miles along Trans-Canada Hwy.*

This attractive stretch of road crosses Malahat Ridge with fine **views★★** of Finlayson Arm, Saanich Inlet, the Gulf Islands and the mainland. If the day is clear, the peak of Mount Baker of the Cascade Range is visible through the trees.

British Columbia Forest Museum★. – *65 km - 40 miles N by Hwy 1 just after Duncan. Open daily May - mid Sept ; $3.50 ; snack bar, picnic sites ;* ☎ *748-9389.*

Covering 40 ha - 100 acres, this museum provides some background to British Columbia's most important industry, forestry. Visitors can walk through the forest of Douglas fir trees, visit a log museum which has displays on the evolution of logging techniques, see a reconstructed logging camp, and ride the narrow-gauge steam railway.

WATERTON LAKES National Park ★★ Alberta

Map p. 6 - Hiking, boating, horseback riding, biking, golf, swimming, winter sports ; camping, accommodation ; admission see National Parks p. 21 ; map available at Park gate ; ☎ *(403) 859-2262.*

This lovely park in the southwest corner of Alberta forms an International Peace Park with the larger Glacier National Park in Montana. It has been described as the place "where the prairies meet the mountains" because in the park the gently rolling hills of the plains which rarely rise over 1 200 m - 4 000 ft meet a vertical rock wall towering another 1 200 m - 4 000 ft or more above them. These mountains were once part of an inland sea, the underlying sediment of which was thrust up and sculptured by erosion and glaciation into sharp peaks, narrow ridges and inter-locked U-shaped valleys. Between them the three Waterton Lakes lie in a deep glacial trough.

The mountains of Waterton were once a Blackfoot Indian stronghold. The first definitely recorded white man to visit the area was Thomas Blakiston of the Palliser Expedition *(p. 73)* who explored the area in 1858, and named the three lakes for an 18th century English naturalist, **Charles Waterton.** Oil was discovered a few decades later but it never proved profitable. The area was made into a National Park in 1895.

Waterton Townsite. – Built on delta materials deposited by Cameron Creek, Waterton has a lovely **site★★** at the point where the Upper Lake narrows into the Bosporus Strait which separates it from the Middle Lake. Behind the townsite and a little to the south the flat face of **Mount Richards** can be distinguished. Beside it stands **Mount Bertha** marked by pale green streaks down its otherwise dark green surface. These were caused by snow slides sweeping the trees off the mountain side. Across the lake stands **Vimy Peak** and Ridge. The Upper Lake stretches south into Montana separating the mountains of the Lewis and Clark Ranges which rise steeply above it. In summer **tour boats** make trips down the lake to the United States Ranger Station at the southern end (*daily mid July - mid Sept ; 1 1/2 - 2 hrs ; $5.00).* Behind the townsite, **Cameron Falls** can be seen dropping over a layered cliff. The valley of the creek behind it was left hanging when valley glaciers deepened the trough now occupied by Upper Waterton Lake.

Cameron Lake★★. – *17 km - 10 1/2 miles from townsite by Akamina Hwy.*
Before reaching the lake, the Akamina Highway passes the site of the first oil well in Western Canada. The **lake★★** itself is set immediately below the Continental Divide and, like Upper Waterton, it spans the international boundary. Dominating the view across the lake are, to the left, **Mount Custer** with the **Herbst Glacier,** and to the right, **Forum Peak.**

Red Rock Canyon★. – *19 km - 12 miles from townsite, turn left at Blakiston Creek.*
The drive to this little canyon offers fine **views★** of the surrounding mountains. A **nature trail** follows the narrow canyon (*2 km - 1 1/4 miles),* the colour of which is due to iron compounds in the rock which oxidized when first exposed to the air to form hematite.

Buffalo Paddock★. – *400 m - 1/4 mile from Park entrance. Auto circuit 3 km - 2 miles.*
A small herd of buffalo occupy a large enclosure on a fine **site★** with Bellevue Mountain and Mount Galway as a backdrop.

YUKON Circuit ★★★ Yukon - Alaska

Map p. 5 - *About 1 450 km - 900 miles ; allow 1 week ; road conditions see pp. 34-35 ; gas stations infrequent - fill-up at each opportunity - Local map below*

This is an exciting and scenically spectacular trip to one of the true faraway places of the globe. The legendary name "Yukon" conjures up pictures of mighty rivers, high mountains, deserted valleys, long winters, the midnight sun... and of course gold.

Home of the Klondike. – On August 17th, 1896, **George Carmack** and his Indian friends, Skookum Jim and Tagish Charlie, found gold on **Bonanza Creek,** a tiny stream emptying into the bigger **Klondike River,** itself a tributary of the mighty Yukon. When the news of their find reached the outside world, an estimated 100 000 people left their homes from as far away as Australia and began the long and arduous trek to **Dawson,** the city which sprang up at the mouth of the Klondike. The stories of their travels are legion (*p. 68).* Many never made it, few of those who did made a fortune. Today, thousands of people follow in their footsteps, not to hunt for gold but to discover as they did the beauty of that wild land and to experience what the poet **Robert Service** called "the spell of the Yukon".

■ WHITEHORSE★

Pop 14 814 - Tourist Office ☎ (403) 667-5340

The capital of the Yukon, Whitehorse is a modern city with all the amenities of a southern centre. It is situated on a flat piece of land on the west side of a big bend in the Yukon River immediately below sharp cliffs. These rise to another plateau where the airport is situated and across which the Alaska Highway passes. On the east side of the river, rather bare hills gently rise to become mountains - the **Big Salmon Range.**

Whitehorse owes its existence to the difficulty encountered by the Klondike Stampeders in negotiating Miles Canyon and the Whitehorse Rapids on the Yukon River. A tramway was constructed to carry goods around these obstacles so that the boats could be piloted through with more ease. This arrangement was changed in 1900 with the completion of the White Pass and Yukon Railway through the Coast Mountains from Skagway. The decision of the railway company to end its line at Whitehorse, and not continue it to Dawson, marks the birth of the city.

Whitehorse soon became an important centre with the transfer of passengers and goods from railway to riverboat in summer, from railway to overland stage in winter. The existence of the railway and of a small airport were important factors when the decision to build the Alaska Highway

WHITEHORSE-MILES CANYON

(*p. 34)* was made in 1942. Whitehorse became a major base for the construction and it changed overnight at a time when Dawson was declining in importance. In 1953 reflecting this, the territorial capital was moved to Whitehorse.

YUKON Circuit★★★

Today, Whitehorse is a centre for tourism as well as communications in the Yukon. It no longer has its frontier city appearance, though a few log structures still remain - in particular note the **Old Log Church** on Elliott at Third built in 1900, the **log "Skyscrapers"** on Lambert between Second and Third Avenues built after the Second World War when there was a housing shortage and still in use today, and the **log railway station** building on First Avenue at Main. In contrast to these is the striking steel and aluminum **Territorial Government Building** on Second Avenue opened in 1976. Its light and airy interior is finished in wood and features an acrylic resin mural which has the appearance of being stained glass.

Whitehorse is very proud of its past and particularly of its part in the Klondike Stampede. In February, the **Sourdough Rendezvous** is held when the whole population dresses up in costumes of '98 and dog team races are held on the frozen Yukon River.

Miles Canyon★★. – *9 km - 6 miles S by Alaska Hwy or by routes described below.*

For more than 1 km - 3/4 mile, the Yukon River passes through a narrow gorge with sheer columnar basalt walls, a greyish red in colour, which rise 9-12 m - 30-40 ft above it. These walls were created by shrinkage of volcanic lava on cooling. The deep green waters of the Yukon still flow through very fast and they swirl and eddy around Devil's Whirlpool. But the construction of the Whitehorse Power Dam downstream has very much lessened the speed and the hazards to navigation from the days of the Klondike Stampede.

Boat Trip★★. – *By MV Schwatka. Daily in summer ; 2 hrs ; $10.00 ; ☎ 668-3161.*

The tremendous force of the river and the sheer walls of the canyon are better appreciated from this level than from the viewpoints above. An interesting commentary on the historical background is given.

Canyon Road★. – *Sharp curves and steep grades.*

This road follows the edge of Schwatka Lake and climbs above the canyon with several good viewpoints. On the return journey, cross the river by the **Robert Campbell Bridge** and return to see the **Whitehorse Dam (A)** and its fishway which was built to enable the chinook salmon to circumnavigate the dam and reach their spawning grounds up-river. These salmon are near the end of a 3 200 km - 2 000 mile migration, the longest known chinook run in the world *(usually occurs in August).*

SS Klondike★. – *2nd Ave near Robert Campbell Bridge. National Historic Site. Guided tours daily June - Labour Day, 1/2 hr ; ☎ 668-2116.*

This restored sternwheeler is one of over 200 that once plied the waters of the Yukon between Whitehorse and Dawson carrying passengers and ore. The 700 km - 436 miles downstream trip to Dawson took 40 hours during which 32 cords of wood were burned. The return trip against the current took 96 hours and 112 cords of wood ! The huge boiler, engine room, cargo space and luxurious first class passenger accommodation are viewed.

MacBride Museum (M). – *1st Ave. Open daily late May - mid Sept ; $2.00 ; ☎ 667-2709.*

Situated in a log building with a sod roof built in 1967, this museum is devoted to the history of the region. Amongst other displays, there is a fine collection of **Yukon photographs★** featuring the Gold Rush and the building of both the White Pass and Yukon Railway and the Alaska Highway.

■ EXCURSION TO SKAGWAY★★★

The most scenically impressive trip in the Yukon is the traverse of the Coast Mountains to the little town of Skagway. At present, this trip can only be made by road. The passenger train service was suspended in 1982. *Contact White Pass and Yukon Railway, P.O. Box 4070, Whitehorse, Yukon Y1A 3T1 ☎ (403) 668-7611 for present status.*

Note : Skagway is in Alaska. Canadian citizens need some form of identification to enter USA. Other visitors need US visas which are available from any US consulate but not in Whitehorse.

The Trails of '98. – There were many routes to Dawson during the Gold Rush. The easiest was by sea to the mouth of the Yukon and by riverboat the 2 092 km - 1 300 miles upstream to the city of gold. But this was only for the rich. A few people tried an overland trail from Edmonton through almost impassable muskeg and bush following more or less the present day route of the Alaska Highway. The vast majority however sailed up the Pacific

THE KLONDIKE GOLD RUSH   **ROUTES TO SKAGWAY**

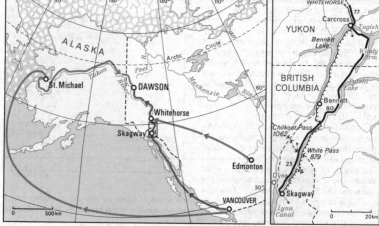

Coast to Skagway or Dyea and trudged into the Yukon across the Coast Mountains. From Skagway the trail followed the **White Pass**, a narrow and slippery climb of 879 m - 2 885 ft. More than 3 000 horses were forced along this route in 1897 most of which died before reaching the summit. Their remains were quickly mashed underfoot by the mass of humanity behind them. Dead Horse Trail as it became known was closed in the winter of 1897-98 and stampeders who insisted on continuing turned to the much more difficult **Chilkoot Pass.** Starting in Dyea this route was 183 m - 600 ft higher than the White Pass and much steeper - it climbed at an angle of 35° in places. Raw rock in summer, the route became slick ice and snow in winter and with temperatures of –50 °C - –58 °F, it was a nightmare to climb. Yet over the winter of 1897-98, 22 000 people climbed it not just once but 30 to 40 times ! The North West Mounted Police at the Canadian border insisted that anyone entering Canada have a year's supply of food and equipment due to shortages in the Territory and it took 30 to 40 trips to carry this "ton" of goods over the pass. Thus the Chilkoot was a stream of climbing humanity for the entire winter.

The trekking by foot ended at **Lake Bennett** where boats were constructed to complete the journey to Dawson. Hazards on the voyage such as Miles Canyon *(see above)* and Five Finger Rapids *(p. 70)* seemed minor after the traverse of the Chilkoot.

Today, a hiking trail is maintained over the Chilkoot Pass *(53 km - 33 miles from Skagway to Lake Bennett)*. It is still a difficult trip and is recommended for experienced hikers only.

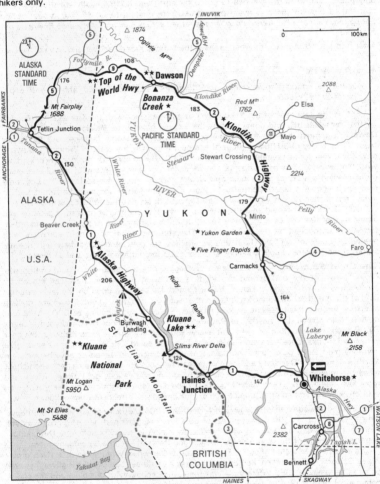

The Road to Skagway★★★. - *180 km - 112 miles by Alaska Hwy and Klondike Hwy (Rte 2) ; about 3 hrs ; section after Carcross open May - Oct only ; frontier open 8 am - 12 pm.*

Heading south from Whitehorse, Route 2 passes through forest gradually entering the mountains with views of snowcapped peaks ahead. At **Carcross,** the scenery changes dramatically as the road follows the shores of **Tagish Lake, Windy Arm** and then **Tutshi Lake.** The sight is awe-inspiring with the mountains rising sheerly from the blue waters of the lakes. After leaving Tutshi Lake, the road begins the traverse of the White Pass with another change in scenery. The landscape in the pass is desolate almost lunar, treeless with lichen-covered rocks, and then the steep descent to Skagway on the coast begins. Views of the **Taiya Inlet** of the Lynn Canal far below make this descent quite frightening at times.

The little community of Skagway (Pop 768) has a lovely **site★** surrounded by snow-capped peaks. In the days of the stampede it was home to a notorious character called **Soapy Smith** a con artist *par excellence* who succeeded in divesting many of the greenhorn gold rushers of their money. There are many mementos of him in the town today. Ferries run south to Prince Rupert, and Seattle, Washington, by the famous Inside Passage. This "marine highway" is a favoured return route for visitors to Alaska and the Yukon *(p. 53).*

BRITISH COLUMBIA, ROCKIES, YUKON

■ KLONDIKE HIGHWAY★

From Whitehorse to Dawson – *540 km - 335 miles by Rte 2 - allow 1 day - Local map p. 69*

The Klondike Highway skirts Lake Laberge and passes through hilly and largely deserted country before rejoining the river at **Carmacks** *(178 km - 111 miles)*, named for the discoverer of Klondike gold. After 196 km - 122 miles, a series of tiny flower-pot islands can be seen. These have split the river into five fast-flowing channels, known as **Five Finger Rapids★**. A hazard to navigation even today, these rapids caused problems during the Stampede and riverboats had to be winched through the narrowest channel by cable. About 15 km - 9 miles further on another series of small islands known as the **Yukon Garden★** can be seen.

Leaving the Yukon valley, the Klondike Highway crosses the central plateau and bridges the Pelly and the Stewart, two big tributaries of the Yukon. After 483 km - 300 miles, there is a **viewpoint** of the valley of the Klondike River from above, with the Ogilvie Mountains to the northeast. The road then follows the Klondike but the river is not always visible because of the great mounds of tailings left by the dredges.

After 494 km - 307 miles, there is a junction with the **Dempster Highway** which goes to Inuvik in the Mackenzie Delta *(p. 234)* across the Ogilvie and Richardson Mountains. It is the only public road in North America to go so far north and it is generally constructed of fill material to prevent the underlying permafrost from melting *(open all year except during Spring break-up and Fall freeze-up when the ferries across Peel and Mackenzie Rivers do not function)*.

After 538 km - 334 miles, the road crosses the famous Klondike River and enters Dawson.

■ DAWSON★★

Visitor Reception Centre, Front and King Sts ; open daily mid May - mid Sept ; ☎ (403) 993-5566

Set on the east bank of the Yukon River at its confluence with the Klondike, surrounded by the **Moosehide Hills** and dominated by the scarred face of the **Midnight Dome,** the city of Dawson is almost invisible from many angles as its two-storey buildings are hidden by trees. Once a city of 30 000 or more, the largest Canadian city west of Winnipeg, Dawson now has a year-round population of less than 1 000. This is swelled considerably in summer with the arrival of summer residents and thousands of tourists. Many of the old buildings remain telling a story of a grandeur and wealth seen nowhere else so far north, but some now lurch sideways due to permafrost action. The Canadian Government has embarked on a vast restoration project which will return Dawson to some of its former splendour.

One of the most remarkable things about Dawson in summer is its lush vegetation and abundance of flowers. Less than 300 km - 200 miles south of the Arctic Circle, situated on fertile soil untouched by the last Ice Age, Dawson enjoys hot and bright summers with nearly 24 hours of sunlight. Fruit and vegetables are cultivated in gardens and flowers sprout through cracks in old buildings and alongside the unpaved boardwalked streets.

The Great Stampede. – Dawson's history begins with the discovery of gold on Bonanza Creek. News of the find spread like wildfire and soon the whole area was staked by prospectors already in the Yukon. A trader named **Joe Ladue** stopped on the level swampland at the mouth of the Klondike. Instead of staking a claim, he laid out a townsite, making a fortune through this foresight as soon lots were selling for as much as $5 000 a front foot on the main street. The heyday of Dawson was underway. Prices were skyhigh – eggs $1.00 each, nails $8.00 a pound – but everything was available – Paris fashions, the best wines and foods. There were more saloons than a man could visit in a night and drinks were normally paid for in gold dust. Entertainment was as rich and varied as anywhere else in North America. But Dawson had one unique feature – despite being the biggest and richest of all the mining boom towns which sprang up during the various gold rushes, it was the most law-abiding. The North West Mounted Police maintained tight control. Everything was shut on Sundays and no one carried a gun except the police. Offenders were run out of town.

Decline. – Dawson's heyday was short-lived. By 1904 the rich placer fields were beginning to peter out – $100 million worth of gold had been shipped out. The gold was still there but complicated machinery was needed to exploit it. Many people left. The glamour departed. The age of the giant dredges began and Dawson became a company town.

Its preeminence lasted until the Second World War when Whitehorse took over, growing as Dawson shrank and connected to the outside world by road (Alaska Highway) as well as by rail and air. In 1953 Whitehorse was made the capital. With this blow and the end of commercial gold mining in 1966, Dawson would have been doomed to become a ghost town were it not for the tourist boom which is reviving the city. People still make a living mining the creeks but little gold is found in comparison with the $22 million worth of 1900.

Festivities. – There are two important dates for tourists in Dawson. The first is June 21st when the midnight sun barely dips down behind the Ogilvie Mountains. The second is the third weekend in August when the anniversary of Discovery Day is celebrated with a parade, raft races on the Klondike River and other merrymaking.

Sights *time : 1 day*

Midnight Dome★★. – *8 km - 5 miles by King St – very steep road.*

So-called because of the abundance of sun on June 21st, the Midnight Dome rises 884 m - 2 900 ft behind the townsite. The **view★★** is splendid. Below lies Dawson at the junction of the Yukon and Klondike Rivers – the Yukon weaving its way south to north, wide and muddy, the Klondike making a clear streak as it enters which is soon absorbed. Bonanza Creek can be seen entering the Klondike and the devastation of the whole area wrought by the dredges is evident. There are mountains in all directions. The Ogilvies to the north are particularly impressive.

The Town★★. – *Tours should start at the Visitor Reception Centre (p. 70) where films and displays form a good introduction to the visit.*

Dawson is a fascinating city to wander around as there are many interesting houses, shops and churches to admire. On Front Street stands the distinctive little **Anglican Church of St. Paul.** A brown and cream clapboard building, St. Paul's was built in 1902 with money collected from the miners in the creeks.

A little further along the street is the **Canadian Bank of Commerce,** an ornate cream-coloured building covered with a pressed tin facade made to imitate stone. It is famous for having employed the poet Robert Service *(see below).* Inside, mementos such as the words "Gold Dust Teller" over one of the windows remain. On the second floor is the **Gold Room**

(open daily June - mid Sept.; guided tours 20 min). Here the gold was washed, weighed and melted into bars. Scales, a smelting furnace and assay instruments are on display.

Next to the bank is the **SS Keno** *(guided tours daily June - mid Sept ; 30 min),* a stern-wheeler once used to transport silver, lead and zinc from the mines in the Mayo district. It was moved to Dawson in 1961. The tour includes a visit to the engine room, passenger cabins and pilot house at the top, from which a good **view★** of the Yukon River is obtained.

(after photo by Tourism Yukon)

A Sternwheeler

Not far from the *SS Keno* on King Street stands the **Palace Grand Theatre** *(guided tours daily June - mid Sept ; 45 min),* a pinewood structure with one of the most elaborate false fronts in Dawson. Built in 1899 by "Arizona Charlie" Meadows, it played host to a variety of entertainment from wild west shows to opera. A vaudeville show called "Gaslight Follies" plays nightly *(8 pm except Tues, in summer).*

On the other side of the street stands a grey clapboard building with a squat tower. This was the **Federal Building.** Now restored, it houses a copy of the original 1901 Post Office *(limited service daily in summer).* Around the corner on Queen Street is **Diamond Tooth Gertie's Gambling Hall.** This establishment named for one of the more notorious ladies of Dawson houses the only legalised casino in Canada *(open 8 pm - 2 am every night except Sun, in summer ; proceeds go to the reconstruction of Dawson).*

At the other end of town an elegant white clapboard structure once the Administrative Building houses the **Dawson City Museum** *(open daily June - mid Sept ; $2.00).* Inside a large collection of Gold Rush memorabilia is on display. There are also natural history exhibits and audio-visual presentations on the area.

Behind the museum on 8th Avenue stands a small log cabin with a pair of moose horns over the door. Once this cabin belonged to the "poet of the Yukon", **Robert Service** (1874-1958), who arrived in Dawson shortly after the Gold Rush. His works, in particular *Songs of a Sourdough,* vividly recreate the atmosphere of the times. There are regular outdoor **recitals** of his poems in the summer months *(10 am and 4 pm daily, 1/2 hr).*

Just along the street is the home of another writer who spent some time in Dawson during its heyday : the American author **Jack London** (1876-1916). This tiny trappers' cabin was moved from Henderson Creek nearby where London spent the winter of 1897. There are also **recitals** of his works in the summer months *(1 pm daily, about 1 hr).* His stories of the North, *Call of the Wild, White Fang* and *Burning Daylight,* are among his best known works.

Bonanza Creek★. – *22 km - 14 miles by Klondike Hwy and Bonanza Creek Road.*

The drive along Bonanza Creek is characterized by the huge piles of tailings left behind by the dredges. The claims are numbered below and above the discovery claim. Thus 16 BD means sixteen claims below discovery, 6 AD means six claims above discovery. There are many remnants of mining equipment to be seen but the biggest example is **No 4 dredge** on Claim 17 BD *(open daily June - mid Sept).* This is an enormous wooden hulled, bucket-line dredge. It has four basic parts : a barge for flotation ; a series of steel buckets to excavate the gravel in front of the barge and to deliver it to the housing built on the barge ; the housing itself where the gravel was washed with water and the gold recovered ; and a conveyor or stocker to disgorge the barren gravel behind the barge making the tailings. On the other side of the road, a **photo exhibit** *(open daily June - mid Sept)* explains methods of mining.

On Claims 13 and 14 BD, **Poverty Bar,** and on Claim 33, you can try your luck panning for gold *(daily ; $5.00 ; pans provided).* This can also be done on Claim 6 AD *(no charge ; but you must provide your own pan).*

(after photo by Tourism British Columbia)

Panning for Gold

YUKON Circuit★★★

After passing **Cheechako Hill** on the left ("Cheechakos" are people who have not seen the Yukon River freeze-up in the fall and break-up in the Spring ; "Sourdoughs" are people who have ; "Outside" is anywhere not in the Yukon), **Discovery Claim** itself is reached *(14.5 km - 9 miles from junction with Klondike Hwy)*. Only a plaque marks the place where the Klondike Stampede began. A little further on *(19 km - 12 miles from junction)* Eldorado Creek joins Bonanza. Some of the richest claims were located on Eldorado, and the community at the junction, Grand Forks, was once a thriving place - nothing remains today.

■ FROM DAWSON TO WHITEHORSE★★

905 km - 562 miles by Alaska and Alaska Highway – allow 2-3 days – Local map p. 69

Top of the World Highway★★. *- 108 km - 67 miles to Alaska border, road closed in winter. US Customs open 9 am - 9 pm daily, you can not enter Alaska if they are shut.*

Route 9 is called Top of the World Highway because for most of its length it runs along on top of ridges above the tree-line with splendid views in all directions. It leaves Dawson by the ferry across the Yukon River *(24 hours a day May - Oct)* which at this point is a vast and muddy stream due to the earth brought in by its major tributaries, the Pelly, the White and the Stewart, and a far cry from the sparkling green waters of Miles Canyon. The road then climbs for about 5 km - 3 miles to a **viewpoint★**. This gives a different perspective of the city and rivers from that seen from the Midnight Dome. After 14 km - 9 miles, there is another **viewpoint** of the Ogilvie Mountains and the valley of the Yukon. After this the road follows the ridge tops for 90 km - 50 miles and can be seen winding up and down for miles ahead. There are ever-changing views of peaks in all directions. *At the Alaska border put watches back 2 hours.*

The Route in Alaska. *- 306 km - 190 miles.* Route 9 joins the Taylor Highway, US Route 5, after 22.5 km - 14 miles and heads south along the valley of the Fortymile River. Gold was found here shortly before the great Klondike discovery. At Tetlin Junction, take the Alaska Highway south to the Canadian border. *Put watches forward 2 hours.*

Alaska Highway★★. *– 491 km - 305 miles from Alaska border to Whitehorse. Along the length of the Alaska Highway there are posts indicating the km from Dawson Creek, B.C. where it begins (p. 35). Thus the km-miles in this section are given in descending order to conform with these posts.*

After crossing the Canadian border *(km 1 965 - mile 1 221)* the highway passes through flattish muskeg country and then bridges first the White and then the Donjek Rivers full of glacial silt. Looking up the course of the latter *(km 1 810 - mile 1 125)*, there is a **view** of the Icefield Ranges of the St. Elias Mountains *(see below)*, one of the rare occasions when these high peaks are visible from the highway.

Kluane Lake★★. – Just before Burwash Landing *(km 1 759 - mile 1 093)* the road approaches this huge mountain lake following it for 64 km - 40 miles with some excellent **views★★**. The highest and largest of the Yukon's lakes, Kluane is ringed by mountains and fed by glaciers. To the south and west lie the **Kluane Ranges,** to the north and east the Ruby Range. All of them are reflected in the icy blue waters of this lake, the surface of which can change from a rippling mirror to a heaving mass of waves in a very short period.

In Burwash Landing, the Kluane Historical Society has a pleasant little **museum★** in a six-sided log building *(open daily in summer ; $1.00)*. It features a diorama of the animals to be seen in this area and some beautifully made Indian clothes - capes, mukluks, hats, belts in skin and fur. There is also a model of the St. Elias Mountains in Kluane National Park.

Kluane National Park★★. – *Camping, hiking ; headquarters at Haines Junction ;* ☎ *(403) 634-2251.*

Entered at km 1 722 - mile 1 070, this park occupies the entire southwest corner of the Yukon including most of the St. Elias Mountains in Canada. From the Alaska Highway it is the Kluane Ranges of these mountains which can be seen. Rugged and snowcapped the Kluanes rise more than 2 500 m - 8 000 ft. Behind them and largely invisible from the highway are the **Icefield Ranges.** Separated from the Kluanes by a narrow trough called the Duke Depression, these ranges contain the highest mountains in Canada with many peaks exceeding 4 500 m - 15 000 ft. Best known are **Mount Logan** (alt 5 950 m - 19 520 ft) and **Mount St. Elias** (alt 5 488 m - 18 008 ft). Mount Logan is second only to **Mount McKinley** (alt 6 193 m - 20 320 ft) in Alaska as the highest point on the continent. Below these peaks forming their base is an ice-covered plateau 2 500 - 3 000 m - 8 000 - 10 000 ft high from which many glaciers radiate. This plateau and the high peaks above it are not easily accessible. *Arrangements for expeditions to the interior of the park must be made in advance with park authorities. However, aircraft trips can be arranged at the Arctic Institute on Kluane Lake* (☎ *(403) 841-4561), in Haines Junction, or with Glacier Air Tours,* ☎ *(403) 633-3792.*

At km 1 707 - mile 1 061, the Alaska Highway passes **Sheep Mountain,** a rocky and barren peak so named for the white Dall Sheep *(illustration p. 35)* which make it their home and can sometimes be seen on its slopes *(more frequently in winter than in summer when they move to higher pastures)*. A path leads some of the way up the mountain for a splendid **view★★** of Kluane Lake and the **Slims River Delta.** This river carrying glacial silt from the Kaskawalsh Glacier makes a sandy streak for some way out into the blue of the lake until it is finally absorbed. The Alaska Highway crosses this large delta km 1 707 - 2 - mile 1 061 - 58.

Haines Junction. – *km 1 635 - mile 1 016.* This community has a fine **site★** at the foot of the Auriol Range. The Haines Road (Route 3) goes south paralleling Kluane National Park for a while and then crossing the Chilkat Pass before entering Alaska and reaching the town of Haines on the Lynn Canal.

About 13 km - 8 miles after the junction on the Alaska Highway, there is a **view★**, if the day is clear, of two white pinnacles protruding above the Auriol and Kluane Ranges up the valley of the Dezadeash River - Mounts Hubbard and Kennedy of the Icefield Ranges. Travellers in the other direction have fine **views★** of mountains along most of this part of the route.

The Alaska Highway continues to Whitehorse (km 1 474 - mile 916) with views of the Coast Mountains to the south most of the way.

PRAIRIES

Manitoba, Saskatchewan and Alberta, known collectively as the Prairie provinces, are often declared flat and monotonous by visitors who drive non-stop from Ontario to Banff and find the journey long. But no one who spends a little time exploring this vast region of nearly 1 963 000 sq km - 758 000 sq miles ever comes away with this impression. There is something awe-inspiring about the wide open spaces, the extent of cultivation and the lack of population (just over four million people). The countryside is an ever-changing rainbow of colours. The wheat which is green in the spring turns to gold before the harvest. Flax has a small blue or white flower, rapeseed a yellow one. Beside the railway tracks rise the tall **grain elevators** – the "cathedrals of the plains", painted in brilliant colours. Yet among all this evidence of man's handiwork, wildlife survives. Wild ducks and other birds are frequently seen on Prairie **sloughs** (small ponds) and ground squirrels (gophers) are a common sight along the roadside. And despite the seemingly endless plain, there are variations. Rivers have cut deep valleys into the soft soil and in some of these **badlands** – the weird lunar landscape of another age, can be seen *(pp. 83 and 84)*.

The inhabitants of this vast land represent an amazing mélange of ethnic groups and cultures and each maintains its identity perhaps because of the distances between communities. From afar, villages with their onion-domed churches rise like mirages from the wheat fields. And above everything is a vast blue sky decorated with puffy white clouds, sometimes black on the horizon as a storm approaches. Prairie sunsets are a sight not to be missed and night-time skies are so full of stars that it is rarely dark.

WHAT ARE THE PRAIRIES ?

The idea that the word prairie is synonymous with endless fields stretching to the horizon is a recent phenomenon. In fact the word is of French origin and means a meadow. It was given to the large area of natural grassland which existed in the centre of the North American continent before the arrival of the white man. This grassland, characterized by its flatness and lack of trees, was an area where the buffalo roamed in huge herds and were hunted by the various Plains Indian tribes. Today, little of this natural grassland survives, and in Canada the term "Prairies" has come to apply to the whole of the three provinces in which it was once located, despite the fact that much of their area never was real prairie.

The Dry Southwest. – The southernmost part of Alberta and Saskatchewan is a semiarid land of short grass. In 1857, a scientific expedition led by **John Palliser,** commissioned by the British government to study the possibilities for settlement in the Prairies, decided that the southwestern corner would never be of much use for agriculture. Palliser did not foresee the widespread use of irrigation which has brought much of the region into cultivation today, nor did he fully realize the nutritional value of the native grasses which today provide adequate pasture for cattle. This region especially in the vicinity of the Cypress Hills *(p. 82)* rates second in importance to British Columbia's Cariboo for cattle raising in Canada.

The Wheat Growing Crescent. – To the north of the arid lands lies a crescent-shaped region of fertile soil and higher rainfall. Once the grass grew shoulder high and few trees blocked the view of distant horizons over the flat plain. Today, this is the wheat belt, the prairie of many people's imagination. Neat farm buildings lie in enormous fields of thriving crops, practically no land is uncultivated and there is a general air of prosperity.

The Aspen Parkland. – North of the wheat belt is another roughly crescent-shaped region where trees grow in good soil and mixed farming flourishes. This is a region of rolling parkland, a transitional zone between the prairie and the forest of the north. It is in this region that the majority of the inhabitants of the three provinces live.

The Boreal Forest and Tundra. – Nearly half of the total area of the three provinces is set directly on the Precambrian rock of the Canadian Shield. This is a wild and largely uninhabited land of lakes, trees and rocks. The few people who do call it home are involved either in the forestry industry or in mineral exploitation. Along the shores of Hudson Bay in the north of Manitoba is a small region of tundra. This is a treeless and forbidding landscape in winter but startlingly beautiful in the summer *(see Churchill p. 81)*.

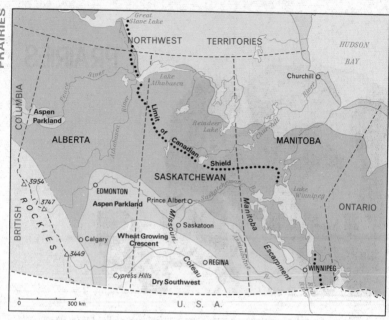

The Prairie "Steps".

– Despite their reputation the Prairies are not actually flat. Apart from the deep valleys cut by the rivers, the Prairies rise gradually from sea level at Hudson Bay to nearly 1 200 m - 4 000 ft before the Rockies are reached. This is achieved in three main steps or levels. The first Prairie step ends with the **Manitoba Escarpment** which rises to a maximum of 831 m - 2 727 ft. The second step, which contains the flattest lands, ends with the **Missouri Coteau**. This rises to a maximum of 879 m - 2 885 ft and can be seen near Moose Jaw. The third step ends with the Rockies. In addition to these steps, the Prairies are broken by numerous ranges of small hills in the north and by the Cypress Hills in the south.

Climate.

– This region experiences a climate of extremes which varies from year to year so that it is hard to find average conditions. Winter is generally long and cold, summer is short and hot, precipitation is low (380-500 mm – 15-20 ins a year) but it frequently arrives in the form of blizzards in winter and violent thunderstorms in summer, often after periods of drought. Sunshine is plentiful especially in July which is also the driest and hottest month (mean maximum for Calgary is 24 °C - 76 °F, Regina 27 °C - 81 °F, Winnipeg 27 °C - 80 °F). In the southwest, winter is alleviated by the Chinook winds which blow warm air from the Pacific through the Rockies. In a few hours, temperatures can rise by as much as 28 °C - 50 °F to 16 °C - 61 °F.

PEOPLE OF THE PRAIRIES

The Indians of the Plains.

– The Blackfoot, Assiniboine, Cree, Sarcee and Gros Ventre tribes, who were once the sole inhabitants of this vast region, lived on the buffalo and very little else. These animals were driven over cliffs or stampeded into pounds. The meat was often dried and made into **pemmican** – a nutritious mixture of pounded meat, animal fat and sometimes saskatoon berries which could be kept for up to a year. Buffalo hides were made into moccasins, leggings and tunics ; the wool was left on to make robes for the winter. Clothing was decorated with fringes and later beads. Home was a **teepee,** a conical structure with a framework of poles (some were 12 m - 40 ft long) covered with buffalo hides. The tribes were nomadic, following the buffalo herds all summer. Possessions were put on a **travois,** a structure of crossed poles pulled by a dog and later a horse (horses were in general use in the Canadian Plains by the mid-18th century). In winter the tribes dispersed. In the spring they reassembled to await the return of the buffalo and celebrate the **Sun Dance** or Medicine Lodge Dance. There was a great deal of rivalry and warfare between tribes and this became more lethal when the fur traders supplied guns. These guns also made hunting buffalo an easier matter. The result was the gradual dying out of the great herds which in turn destroyed the traditional life of their hunters.

By the 1880s the great herds were gone and white settlers arrived to cultivate and fence the once open prairie. The Indians signed treaties and moved to reservations, but a sedentary life of farming did not come easily to the one-time nomad hunters.

The Fur Traders.

– It was the fur trade which inspired the French to found the first permanent settlements in mainland Canada in the 17th century, and it was the fur trade which sent them further and further into the continent after the elusive beaver. Two fur traders, **Radisson and Groseilliers,** who were eager to cut down the long journey by canoe between Montréal and Lake Superior, suggested that it would be both quicker and cheaper to transport furs to Europe via the huge bay discovered by Henry Hudson in 1610. This scheme met with little interest in France but **Radish and Gooseberry,** as they became known, found ready listeners at the English court of Charles II. The ketch *Nonsuch* was equipped and it sailed to Hudson Bay in 1668. It returned with a rich load of furs. In 1670, Charles II granted a royal charter to the "Governor and Company of Adventurers of England trading into Hudson's Bay". The **Hudson's Bay Company** as it became known held the sole right to trade in the vast watershed which drains into the Bay, which meant most of the Prairies. Forts or factories were quickly established on its shores *(see Churchill p. 81)* and trade thrived.

The first white man to see the interior of this vast region was **Henry Kelsey** who travelled across northern Manitoba and Saskatchewan 1690-92. His contacts with the Indians threatened French supplies and so the **Sieur de la Vérendrye** established the first posts in the plains in 1730. **Anthony Henday** of the Hudson's Bay Company found the French so entrenched on the plains in 1754 when he travelled all over Alberta that he recommended the Company abandon its policy of letting the Indians bring their furs to the Bay, and establish posts in the interior as well. The fall of New France in 1759 *(p. 175)* seemed to end the threat so nothing was done.

The years at the end of the 18th century and the early 19th century, however, saw bitter rivalry between fur traders in the Prairies. The Scots who quickly established themselves in Montréal after the Conquest founded the North West Company *(p. 161)* which soon proved a ferocious competitor for the Hudson's Bay Company. Rival posts sprang up along the Prairie rivers and loads of furs were fought over. This situation finally ended in 1821 when the two companies were merged, with the Hudson's Bay having the upper hand. The fur trade remained important in the Prairies throughout the 19th century and it is still a contributor to the economy of the northern parts of all three provinces today.

The Metis and the Creation of Manitoba. – One of the offshoots of the fur trade was the creation of a new race – the Metis. These half-breed children of Indian women and the French *coureurs des bois* (and later of Scots and English traders) were mainly French-speaking and Roman Catholic although they lived the traditional life of their Indian forebears hunting the buffalo and making pemmican to sell to the fur traders. The first threat to their life-style came with the arrival of settlers along the Red River in 1812 *(p. 93)*. Conflict ensued since farms and fences could not share the prairie with wandering herds of buffalo and their hunters. But the real problem came in 1870 when the new Dominion of Canada planned to take over the vast lands of the Hudson's Bay Company. Not only did the Metis see their traditional life disappearing with the arrival of more and more settlers, but they feared for the survival of their language. When surveyors for the Dominion began marking out the long narrow strips of Metis land into neat squares, these people turned to twenty-five year old **Louis Riel** newly returned from a religious education in Montréal.

Declaring the surveys illegal as sovereignty had not yet been handed over, Riel set up his own provisional government to make sure Metis rights were recognized in the new government. Although he was supported by his own people, Riel gained no sympathy from the English Metis and other settlers particularly the many Ontarians of Irish origin who had recently moved to the area in anticipation of the Canadian takeover. This group gave Riel a lot of trouble and, after he had foiled a plot to assassinate him, he executed one of them, **Thomas Scott**. This proved to be an error which he was long to regret. Nevertheless, his plea on behalf of his people was heard and in July 1870 the new province of **Manitoba** was created (the name chosen by Riel means the spirit that speaks). Land was put aside for the Metis and both French and English were given equal status. Riel himself fled before troops arrived from the east. He was elected to Parliament several times but was unable to take his seat in Ottawa due to the anger in Ontario over the death of Scott. Eventually, he went into exile in the United States to resurface again fifteen years later *(p. 92)*.

A Human Mosaic. – Before mass immigration could occur to this vast area ceded by the Hudson's Bay Company, several matters had to be settled. Firstly, treaties had to be negotiated with the native peoples of the region. This was done by 1877 but not altogether successfully as the Northwest Rebellion of 1885 showed *(p. 92)*. Secondly, some means of enforcing law and order was required. In 1873 the **North West Mounted Police** force was created *(see Regina p. 89 and Cypress Hills p. 82)*. Thirdly, land had to be distributed. The **Dominion Lands Act** of 1872 allowed prospective homesteaders to register for a quarter section (65 ha - 160 acres). Title was given after three years if a homestead had been built and a certain amount of the land cultivated. Settlers also had an option on an additional quarter section. Finally, a means of reaching the region and more important of transporting produce to market from the region was required. This problem was resolved by the building of the **Canadian Pacific Railway** between 1881 and 1885 *(p. 16)*. In the year of its completion the population of the Prairies was about 150 000, by 1914 it was 1 1/2 million.

The prospect of free land attracted the inhabitants of an overcrowded Europe especially those who lived in the cities created by the Industrial Revolution where factory hours were long and hard. It attracted people from the eastern part of the continent which settled and where opportunities were fewer. It attracted religious refugees and groups who hoped to have the freedom to worship and live as they pleased. The Canadian government of **Sir Wilfrid Laurier** advertised all over the world : "Canada West – the last best west. Free homes for millions", etc. And the millions came from Ontario, the Maritimes, the United States, England, Scotland, Ireland, Germany, Iceland, Austria, France, Scandinavia and Russia especially the Ukraine. Mennonites, Hutterites and Doukhobors came from Russia, Orthodox Christians came from eastern Europe, Roman Catholics, Mormons, Jews and every Protestant denomination came from elsewhere. Two new provinces (**Saskatchewan** and **Alberta**) were created in 1905 to cope with the growing numbers. Since 1915 these peoples have been joined by others dispossessed in two world wars or unhappy about the political situation in their homelands. They have made the Prairies a veritable mosaic of cultures. The **population** today stands at 4.2 million (Alberta 2 237 725, Saskatchewan 968 310, Manitoba 1 026 240).

THE PRAIRIE ECONOMY

King Wheat. – Between the years 1876 and 1915, the land where the fur trade had once reigned supreme suddenly developed a wheat economy. The region where giant bluestem and needle grass thrived and prairie flowers bloomed in millions vanished under the plough. There is no more striking development in agricultural history. Three factors were responsible for this change. In 1842 David Fife, a Scots farmer living in Ontario, developed a strain of wheat which later proved ideal for cultivation on the Prairies. Called **Red Fife** for its rich red colour, it was resistant to rust and thrived in the drought-ridden short prairie season. It is the ancestor of all the strains used today. Then in 1876, the first shipment of this wheat cultivated in the Red River settlement reached Ontario.

The final factor was the building of the Canadian Pacific Railway which brought the settlers to cultivate the land and provided the means of transporting their produce to market. Loading platforms and elevators sprang up along the railway tracks, and moving grain to Thunder Bay, Vancouver, Prince Rupert and Churchill became the railway's major job. By 1915, the Prairies were unrecognizable to those who had seen them forty years before.

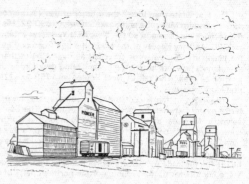

Grain Elevators

The growing of wheat has not however always flourished in this region with its changeable and unpredictable climate. The drought and hardships of the 1930s caused many farmers to abandon the land. The 1970s however saw bumper crops. Today, farmers depend a little less on wheat than previously. Oats, barley, rye, flax, rapeseed, mustard, buckwheat, peas, sunflowers and potatoes are all widely cultivated ; nevertheless 60 % of the land annually seeded to field crops is seeded to wheat. In 1983, 26.3 million metric tonnes - 29.3 million tons of wheat were produced in the western provinces, about three - quaters of which will be exported.

Cattle Country. – Although grain is by far and away the major element of prairie economy, ranching is firmly established as a secondary one. Canadian ranching began in British Columbia and spread into southern Alberta and Saskatchewan after the signing of the Indian treaties in the 1870s. The dry, short grass country turned out to be fine pasture for cattle and the Chinooks made winter grazing possible as they melted the snow exposing the grass. Slowly, as ranchers discovered that cattle were not killed by Indians or the winter and they did not run off with the buffalo, ranches increased and by the turn of the century cattle raising was second to wheat.

This southern region of Alberta and Saskatchewan (map p. 74) is still today real cowboy country. Horseback riders are a common sight among the herds and rodeos flourish in every community. The biggest cowboy event of them all is the Calgary Stampede (p. 79).

The Riches below the Earth. – The first mineral exploited in the Prairies was the **coal** found in Lethbridge in 1869 (p. 87). In the 1880s Kootenay Brown found oil in the Waterton Lakes area (p. 66) and sold it as machine grease, and the **natural gas** which underlies the whole of Medicine Hat was exploited. Coal was also found near Estevan in Saskatchewan.

Then in 1914 the **oil** of the Turner Valley was discovered (p. 79) which marked the beginning of Alberta's petroleum industry. A year later the giant zinc, **cadmium** and **copper** field at Flin Flon, Manitoba, was found. Today, mining extends over the border in Saskatchewan too. Copper was also discovered near Lynn Lake, Manitoba, and gold in the Lake Athabasca area of Saskatchewan.

The year 1947 saw the discovery of the Leduc oilfield (see Edmonton p. 85) and later of the numerous other small fields underlying Alberta. **Uranium** was found in the Beaverlodge area of Saskatchewan north of Lake Athabasca and in the 1960s the giant **nickel** field of Thompson, Manitoba, came into production and the first **potash** was mined near Esterhazy in Saskatchewan. This province's potash reserves are estimated at more than 50 billion metric tonnes – 55 billion tons which is more than a quarter of the world's total supply and, at current rates of consumption, enough to supply world needs for 2 000 years. Just as oil and natural gas underlie Alberta, potash underlies Saskatchewan in a wide arc roughly corresponding to the aspen parkland zone (see above). Saskatchewan also has **sodium sulphate** in the same regions and oil in the Lloydminster, Swift Current and Estevan areas.

Today Alberta produces 84 % of Canada's total oil production and 89 % of the country's natural gas. Saskatchewan produces about 12 % and 2 % respectively. But Alberta's oil is now supplemented by the vast reserves of the **Athabasca oil sands** which are estimated at 153 billion barrels as opposed to the 4 billion barrels of regular crude oil which remain unexploited. Two plants at Fort McMurray separate the oil from these sands commercially.

Other Resources. – In the northern regions of all three provinces the traditional industry of fur trapping still flourishes along with thriving forestry concerns. Hydro-electric power is generated in the three provinces, the biggest project being the **Gardiner Dam** on the South Saskatchewan River in central Saskatchewan.

SPORTS AND OUTDOOR ACTIVITIES

This is wonderful country for those who love the outdoors and a wide variety of activities is available. **Water sports** – boating, sailing, canoeing, water skiing and swimming, are particularly popular in all three provinces because of the number of lakes and river systems. Saskatchewan is famous for its **white water canoeing** especially along the Churchill River with its craggy gorges and treacherous rapids. Tourism Saskatchewan produces booklets (available free) on more than fifty canoe routes in the province.

The region is well endowed with provincial and national parks which offer hiking trails and campsites in summer, cross-country skiing, snowshoeing and snowmobiling in winter.

All three provinces boast good **fishing** but the northern regions of Manitoba and Saskatchewan are particularly famous with numerous fly-in lodges. Lac la Ronge in Saskatchewan is perhaps the best known region for sport fishing. Fishermen and hunters must have licenses which are available in most sporting goods stores or from the tourist offices of each province. Details of seasons, bag limits, guides, etc are also available from the tourist offices.

Finally, **farm vacations** are offered in all three provinces but Saskatchewan is especially popular. There are many **dude ranches** offering trail riding, etc in Alberta.

Special Excursions. – VIA Rail offers six night - seven day **Explorer Tours to Hudson Bay** by train from Winnipeg every week between June and mid September stopping at Thompson and Churchill *(p. 81)*. *For details contact VIA Rail, 123 Main Street, Winnipeg, Man R3C 2P8.*

In summer, the **Prairie Dog Central**, a turn-of-the-century steam train, makes weekly excursions from Winnipeg to Grosse Isle *(from CN St. James St Station, 1661 Portage Ave near St. James St ; June - Sept ; Sun at 11.30pm and 3pm ; 2 hrs Return ; ☎ (204) 284-2690).*

PRINCIPAL FESTIVALS

Month	Place	Festival
February	The Pas Man	Trappers' Festival
February	St-Boniface Man	Festival du Voyageur *(p. 95)*
February	Prince Albert Sask	Winter Festival
June	Regina Sask	Western Canada Farm Progress Show
June – July	Winnipeg Man	Red River Exhibition
July	Yorkton Sask	Saskatchewan Stampede and Exhibition
July	Winnipeg Man	Folk Festival
July	Saskatoon Sask	Pioneer Days
July	Selkirk Man	Manitoba Highland Gathering
July	Austin Man	Manitoba Threshermen's Reunion *(p. 78)*
July	Calgary Alta	Calgary Exhibition and Stampede *(p. 79)*
July	Edmonton Alta	Klondike Days *(p. 85)*
July – August	Dauphin Man	National Ukrainian Festival
July – August	Steinbach Man	Pioneer Days *(p. 96)*
July – August	Regina Sask	Buffalo Days
August	Lethbridge Alta	Whoop-up Days and Rodeo
August	Gimli Man	Icelandic Festival
August	Norway House Man	York Boat Days (3-day boat race)
August	Winnipeg Man	Folklorama *(p. 93)*
August	Brandon Man	Provincial Exhibition of Manitoba
August	Saskatoon Sask	Folkfest
November	Regina Sask	Canadian Western Agribition

PRACTICAL INFORMATION

Accommodation, Road Maps and Tourist Information. – The government of Alberta produces an annually updated **Visitors' Accommodation Guide** which lists approved hotels, motels, rental chalets and campgrounds. It also produces an **Auto Tour Guide** listing auto tours and an annually updated road' map. These are available free of charge from most tourist bureaus or from :
Travel Alberta, 10065 Jasper Ave, 14th Floor, Edmonton, Alta. T5J 0H4 ☎ 403-427-4321.

The government of Saskatchewan produces a regularly updated series of tourist publications on hotel / motel accommodation, provincial parks, campgrounds, resorts, and northern outfitters. An **Auto Tour Guide** as well as a general **Vacationer's Guide** are also available with an annually updated road map from most tourist bureaus or from :
Tourism Saskatchewan, 3211 Albert St, Regina, Sask. S4S 5W6 ☎ 306-565-2300. ☎ 800-667-3674 (toll free in province in summer)

The government of Manitoba provides a **Manitoba Vacation Guide** which lists hotels, points of interest, outfitters, campgrounds etc. This is available with a road map from tourist bureaus or from :
Travel Manitoba, 155 Carlton St, Winnipeg, Man. R3C 0V8 ☎ 204-944-3777.

Road Regulations. – All three provinces have a good paved road system but grid roads can be rough. Speed limits unless otherwise posted are :
Manitoba : 95 km - 60 mph – Saskatchewan : 100 km - 60 mph
Alberta : 100 km - 60 mph in daylight (90 km - 55 mph at night)
The wearing of seat belts is compulsory in Saskatchewan.

Time Zones. – *Map p. 20.* Alberta is on Mountain Standard Time and Manitoba is on Central Standard Time. Both advance their clocks one hour in summer. Most of Saskatchewan is on Central Standard Time all year, thus it is the same as Alberta in summer, the same as Manitoba in winter ; however, some border communities prefer to keep the same time as the neighbouring province all year.

Taxes. – Manitoba and Saskatchewan levy 5 % sales tax on all items except food. They also levy 5 % on all hotel bills. In addition Manitoba collects 5 % on restaurant bills but meals are not taxed in Saskatchewan. In Alberta there are no sales, hotel or restaurant taxes at all.

Liquor Laws. – In all three provinces liquor, wine and beer can only be publicly consumed on licensed premises. The legal drinking age is 18 in Manitoba and Alberta, 19 in Saskatchewan. In all three provinces, liquor and wine can only be purchased in government stores but beer is available for take-out in some hotels and taverns. In isolated parts of the north where no government store exists grocery stores are licensed.

BOOKS TO READ

A History of Alberta by James G. MacGregor *(Hurtig)*
Saskatchewan by Edward McCourt *(Macmillan)*
Wilderness Man - the Strange Story of Grey Owl by Lovat Dickson *(Macmillan)*
Who has seen the Wind ? by W. O. Mitchell *(Macmillan)* Fiction
Between the Red and the Rockies by Grant MacEwan *(Western Producer Prairie)*

AUSTIN ★ Manitoba

Map p. 7 – Pop 416

Set in the centre of a rich agricultural region lies the little community of Austin famous for its collection of operating antique farm machinery.

Manitoba Agricultural Museum★. – *On Hwy 34 just south of Trans-Canada. Open daily mid May - mid Oct ; $1.50 ; camping, picnic grounds ; ☎ (204) 637-2354.*

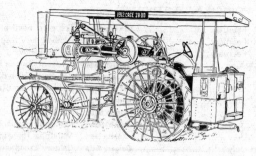

This museum has a splendid collection of "prairie giants" - steam tractors, threshing machines and the cumbersome gasoline machines which replaced them in the early part of this century. Every year at the end of July, these machines parade and demonstrate their skills in the **Manitoba Threshermen's Reunion and Stampede.** Drawing thousands of visitors from all over the continent, this festival features threshing, sheaf-tying and stooking contests and a stampede in addition to the parade of steam engines and races between them.

Steam Tractor

A **Homesteaders' Village** presents life as it was at the end of the last century when the first giant steam engines were breaking the prairie sod and bringing it under cultivation. This includes several log homes, a church and school and a large collection of pioneer artifacts in the Centennial Building.

The BATTLEFORDS ★ Saskatchewan

Map p. 6 – Pop 17 595 – Tourist Office ☎ (306) 445-6226

Surrounded by rolling country, the twin communities of **Battleford** and **North Battleford** face each other across the valley of the North Saskatchewan River at the point where the Battle River joins it from the west. Fur traders established posts on the Battleford (south) side of the river in the 18th century but it was not until 1874 that the first settlers arrived. Then events moved fast. A North West Mounted Police post was established in 1876 and the settlement was chosen as the home of the government of the Northwest Territories. A bright future seemed assured. Then the Canadian Pacific Railway Company decided to route their line through the southern plains and in 1883 Battleford lost its status as capital when the government offices were moved to Pile O'Bones Creek (later Regina). As though to add insult to injury, the settlement of Battleford was looted and burned by Poundmaker's Crees during the Northwest Rebellion of 1885 *(p. 92)* while the fearful inhabitants took refuge in the police fort.

The death knell sounded in 1903 when the Canadian Northern Railway was built along the opposite side of the river creating a new community, North Battleford, which grew as Battleford shrank. Today, the former, served by the Yellowhead Highway as well as the railway, is a distribution centre of no small importance. It has a fine **site★** overlooking the river and the older community.

Battleford National Historic Park★. – *Central Ave, Battleford. Open daily May - mid Oct ; guided tours 1 1/2 hrs ; ☎ 937-2621.*

This North West Mounted Police post was the fifth established by the police in the Northwest Territories. Enlarged after the Northwest Rebellion, it was abandoned in 1924. Today, restored, it provides insight into police life in the late 19th century. The **Commanding Officers' Residence** suggests that police officers lived reasonably comfortably. The **Officers' Quarters** are also appropriately furnished and house an office for the police. The **Guard House** and **Sick Horse Stable** can also be visited.

Just outside the palisade, a former barracks has been converted into an **Interpretive Centre** which explains the history of the fort in the context of the Northwest, and has a particularly good account of the 1885 Riel Rebellion.

Western Development Museum★. – *On Hwy 16 at junction with Rte 40 in North Battleford. Open daily except weekends and hols in winter ; $1.50 ; refreshments ; ☎ 445-8033.*

This branch of the Western Development Museum is devoted to pioneer life in the province. A large hall contains pioneer vehicles and artifacts.

Outside, an interesting **pioneer village** of the 1925 era (*closed in winter*) is set out in a curve with homes and churches reflecting the diverse origins of the peoples who settled this province. Note especially the Ukrainian Orthodox Church with its onion dome, and the thatched *dacha* displaying the handicrafts and household fittings usual to a pioneer Ukrainian home. Also featured along the boardwalked street are a cooperative general store, a police post and a railway station at which a train stands complete with first class sleeper accommodation.

Prices quoted in this guide were accurate at
the time of going to press.

CALGARY ★★ Alberta _____

Map p. 6 – Pop 592 743 – Tourist Office ☎ (403) 263-8510

Set in the foothills of the Canadian Rockies at the point where the plains cease to exist, Calgary also lies at the confluence of Bow and Elbow Rivers - two mountain torrents of clear blue water, and it has snowcapped peaks as a backdrop. This site has provided not a tourist mecca (though Calgary is rapidly developing in this direction) but Alberta's boomtown thanks to the province's vast oil wealth and its own importance as a transportation and meat-packing centre. Blessed with a pleasant climate (moderate rainfall, dry air, lots of sunshine and a moderately cold winter tempered by the warm Chinook winds), Calgary is known for its proximity to Banff and internationally famous for its Stampede.

Origins. – In 1875 a North West Mounted Police post was built at the confluence of Bow and Elbow Rivers and named Fort Calgary by Colonel MacLeod, the commander of the police in the Northwest *(p. 86)* for his home in Scotland (Calgary is derived from a Gaelic word probably meaning clear, running water). A small community grew up around the post which quickly changed in the 1880s when the Canadian Pacific Railway decided to route their railway south through Calgary and the Kicking Horse Pass rather than to Edmonton and the Yellowhead. This was a momentous decision for Calgary as it resulted in a huge influx of settlers to the lush grazing lands of the region. The Dominion Lands Act *(p. 75)* also encouraged owners of great cattle herds to move north from the United States. Thus Calgary developed rapidly into a marketing and meat-packing centre gaining the epithet of Canada's Cowtown - a title it still has not relinquished although cattle are a relatively minor part of its life today.

"Black Gold". – The discovery of oil in the Turner valley just southwest of Calgary marked the birth of Western Canada's petroleum industry. For thirty years this valley was the country's major oil producer. Then in 1947 the great discovery was made at Leduc *(p. 85)* and Calgary began a period of phenomenal growth which is still continuing thanks to the constantly increasing cost of oil from other parts of the world. Although recent oil and gas discoveries have been nearer Edmonton than Calgary, the latter has stayed predominant as the headquarters and controlling centre of the industry. Today, more than four hundred oil and gas firms work out of Calgary and the city also houses head offices of many related industries.

"The Greatest Outdoor Show on Earth". – The **Calgary Stampede**★★★, a massive ten-day event held in early July, attracts hundreds of thousands of spectators and competitors every year *(reservations should be made in advance)*. The entire population dons western garb (boots, jeans and hats) and throws itself into this festivity. There are flapjack breakfasts, street dancing and a huge parade in the city ; livestock shows and the famous **Rodeo** and **Chuckwagon Races** in the Exhibition Grounds *(plan p. 80)*. The latter were invented in Calgary and derive from the wagon races home held by cowboys after a roundup. The wagons contained all the provisions and gear necessary for life on the range and this is represented in the event. These races are without doubt the most exciting part of the Stampede. *Details of all events can be obtained from Tourist Office.*

(courtesy Lawson Graphics Pacific Limited)

The Calgary Stampede

■ **SIGHTS** time : 1 1/2 days

Calgary's downtown has undergone a revolution since the war and is still changing as the city develops. Today, the Calgary Tower *(p. 80)* is surrounded by a host of attractive glass-fronted highrise, and it has recently lost its predominance to the sloping-topped brown marble headquarters of **Petro-Canada (B)**. A pedestrian **mall** stretches for four blocks along 8th Avenue. At the western end lie the big bank blocks – the reflecting glass Royal Bank Centre, the Scotia Centre and the black towers of the Toronto Dominion Centre, all connected to one another and to The Bay and Eaton's department stores by second floor pedestrian footbridges. The Toronto Dominion Centre boasts a fine indoor "hothouse" called the **Devonian Gardens**★ **(A)** *(4th floor ; access from Eaton's or via elevator from TD Centre entrance on mall outside store hours. Open daily 9 am - 9 pm).* Sitting on top of four floors of retail shops, this garden is actually a small park covering 1 ha - 2 1/2 acres complete with fountains, stage, sculptures and a pool-cum-skating rink as well as plants and trees typical of the Calgary area.

Glenbow Museum★★. – *In same complex as Convention Centre. Open daily except Mon 10am - 6pm ; $2.00 ;* ☎ *264-8300.*

This well laid-out museum run by the Glenbow-Alberta Institute has as its focal point a large acrylic and aluminum sculpture entitled **Aurora Borealis** by James Houston which ascends the full four stories in the stairwell.

The second floor is devoted to special exhibitions of art and sculpture. Shows change regularly and range from regional to national and international topics.

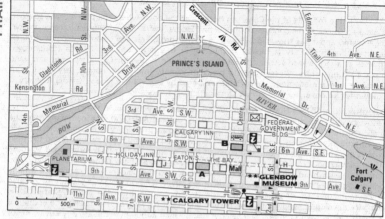

The third floor presents a history of Western Canada. There are excellent displays drawn from one of the most outstanding **Plains Indians collections★★** in the world. Note particularly the fine beadwork. There are also examples of the art of the Inuit, the Pacific Coast Tribes, and the Navajo and Pueblo Indians of the southern United States. White settlement in Alberta is traced through interesting exhibits including the fur trade, the North West Mounted Police, missionaries, the Canadian Pacific Railway, the arrival of the first farmers, ranching, the discovery of oil and Alberta life in the 1920s and 30s.

The fourth floor features a mineralogy display, an exhibit called the Crown in Canada including replicas of the Crown jewels, and an interesting section on arms and weapons tracing their development from Medieval times to the Second World War.

Calgary Tower★★. – *In Palliser Square. Observation deck open daily 7.30 am-12 pm ; (11pm Sun] ; $2.25 ; revolving restaurant ;* ☎ 266-7171.

This 191 m - 626 ft tower provides an excellent **view★★** of the city and its site. To the west the snowcapped Rocky peaks rise above the rolling, arid foothills almost devoid of trees on which the city is built. Calgary's very spread-out nature can be appreciated ; it covers the largest land area of any city in Canada (420 sq km - 162 sq miles). Immediately below the tower, the maze of railway lines indicates the importance of the city as a transportation centre.

Crescent Road Viewpoint★★. – Standing above the Bow River and Prince's Island Park, this crescent offers a fine view of the downtown buildings and, on clear days, the Rockies snowcapped to the west.

Heritage Park★. – *16 km - 10 miles from downtown. Open daily mid May - Labour Day, 10 am - 6 pm ; weekends only Sept - mid Oct ; $3.50 ; refreshments ;* ☎ 255-1182.

This park which recreates life in Alberta before our era has a fine **site★** in a recreation area overlooking Glenmore Reservoir, part of the Elbow River. A pioneer community occupies one corner. Nearby is a reconstruction of

a Hudson's Bay Company post. A turn-of-the-century town comprises homes, church, drugstore, bakery, general store, post office, newspaper office, pool hall, police post and a station complete with functioning steam train which gives tours of the site *(daily ; $1.00)*. Also beside the tracks stands a working grain elevator and on the outskirts of the town are farm buildings and a windmill. A replica of the SS Moyie, a paddle steamer once used on Kootenay Lake, gives boat trips on the reservoir *(every 35 min ; $1.50)*.

Zoo and Prehistoric Park★★. – *On St. George's Island. Parking on Memorial Drive and on Island. Open daily ; $3.50 ; snack bar ;* ☎ 265-9310.

This pleasant zoo on an island in the Bow River has a wide variety of animals from all over the world. One of the highlights is the tropical hothouse full of exotic plants, flowers and birds. The **Prehistoric Park★★** recreates Western Canada as it might have looked in the age of the dinosaurs between 230 and 60 million years ago. Life size reproductions of these giant creatures stand among mountains, volcanoes, hoodoos, swampland and Canadian Shield country along with the vegetation which might have existed in their era.

Fort Calgary. – *Open Wed - Sun, 10 am - 6 pm ;* ☎ 290-1875.

The foundations of the original North West Mounted Police post can be seen and an **Interpretive Centre** visited where the history of the city is recounted by means of displays and a slide presentation. There is a pleasant **view★** of the Bow River. Paths and a pedestrian bridge lead to St. George's Island and the Zoo.

CARDSTON Alberta _____
Map p. 6 – Pop 3 267

This small town near the Montana border is an important Mormon centre. Founded in 1887 by **Charles Ora Card,** a son-in-law of Brigham Young, it boasts one of the few Mormon temples of the world - an imposing white granite structure built 1913-23. *(Visitors' Centre open daily, films.)*

The Mormons. – This religious sect also known as the Church of Jesus Christ of the Latter Day Saints was founded in 1830 by **Joseph Smith** at Fayette, New York, after he had received a revelation in a dream. After his death, most of his followers moved to Utah under the leadership of **Brigham Young** establishing Salt Lake City in 1847. Their doctrine is based on the Bible and Smith's writings notably *The Book of Mormon.* In Canada the sect numbers about 75 000 and is largely concentrated in the Cardston region where they were pioneers in introducing irrigation systems to this semi-arid land and in cultivating sugar beet for which the region is well known.

CHURCHILL ★★ Manitoba _____
Map p. 7 – Pop 1 304

Access. – *Regular scheduled flights from Winnipeg by Pacific Western Airways (p. 19). Also accessible by VIA Rail Explorer Tours (p. 77).*

On the shores of Hudson Bay on the east side of the estuary of the wild and beautiful Churchill River lies the little town of Churchill, Canada's most northerly deep sea port. North of the tree-line, Churchill is bleak in winter, but July sees a carpet of flowers covering the tundra, beluga whales swimming in the blue waters of the bay and in the river estuary, myriad birds and scavenging **polar bears** invading the townsite, especially in October. It is a fascinating place for nature lovers and has attracted much scientific interest because it experiences some of the most amazing spectacles of the Northern Lights *(p. 229)* in the world. The National Research Council conducts research into this phenomenon every year from the Churchill Research Range near the townsite.

Churchill has also an interesting history. A fur trading post was founded at the mouth of the river in 1685 by the Hudson's Bay Company. It was named for the governor of the company, **John Churchill,** later Duke of Marlborough. It remained an important fur gathering and export centre until this century when wheat, another product of the Canadian interior, took over from it. A railway was built in 1931, a grain elevator and port facilities shortly afterwards. Although the navigation season across Hudson Bay and through the Hudson Strait *(see accompanying Map of Canada)* is only three months long *(August - October),* during this period trains arrive constantly and ships of many nations visit the townsite to take on grain.

In 1976, a **Civic Centre** was opened combining under one roof recreational and health facilities, library, high school and business offices. This low-lying complex with its **views** of the Bay is interesting to visit for its art work as well as for the idea.

Eskimo Museum★★. – *Beside Roman Catholic mission,* ☎ *(204) 675-2252. Open daily, afternoons only Sun.*

This museum houses a large and fine collection of Inuit carvings in stone, ivory and bone. Collected over forty years by the Oblate fathers, these carvings depict all aspects of life. Many refer to Inuit legends and others record the arrival of the first airplanes or snowmobiles in the north. An excellent tape recorded commentary helps explain some of the works.

Fort Prince of Wales★. – *National Historic Park across Churchill estuary from town. Access by boat mid June – mid Sept ; guided tours about 1/2 hr ; contact Parks Canada Interpretive Centre in the town,* ☎ *(204) 675-8863.*

This vast stone fortress seems an anomaly so far north, especially since it was only attacked once and then it surrendered without a shot being fired. It was constructed by the Hudson's Bay Company *(p. 74)* to protect their fur trading interests on the Bay and it took forty years (1731-71) to complete. At first it was the French who threatened these trading interests, but after the defeat of New France on the Plains of Abraham in 1759 *(p. 175),* that threat appeared to have subsided. Instead, a collection of Montréal traders (later the North West Company *p. 161)* challenged the Company's monopoly.

Thus in 1782, the great explorer Samuel Hearne *(p. 230)* who was the fort's governor, was surprised to see a French fleet preparing to attack his walls (he had not even known that England and France were again at war). There was little he could do but surrender as most of his garrison were inland making sure the Montréal traders did not take all the furs. The French commander, La Pérouse, spiked the cannon, undermined the walls and set fire to the fort.

Although Fort Prince of Wales was returned to the British soon afterwards, the Hudson's Bay Company never again used it, preferring to establish themselves further upstream.

Visit. – The Interpretive Centre *(open daily 8.00 am - 5 pm except Sun ; and Sat in winter)* offers a slide show on the fort and films which form a good introduction. The fort itself has massive stone walls nearly 12 m - 40 ft thick at their base and 5 m - 17 ft high, and forty huge cannon. Visitors can ponder how such a fortress was constructed so far north - let alone why. The boat trip to it is an excellent means of viewing the beluga whales that inhabit the estuary of the Churchill River in July and August.

Sights described in this guide are rated :

★★★ worth the journey
★★ worth the detour
★ interesting

CYPRESS HILLS ★★ Alberta-Saskatchewan

Map p. 6 – *Local map below*

Just north of the State of Montana on both sides of the Alberta-Saskatchewan boundary the plains give way to rolling forested hills cut by numerous coulees, valleys, lakes and streams. These hills rise like an island of relief in the midst of otherwise unbroken, sun-baked, short grass prairie. On their heights grow the tall straight lodge-pole pines favoured by Plains Indians for their teepees or lodges, thus the name. The trees were mistaken by early French voyageurs for the jack pines *(cyprès)* of eastern Canada. A bad translation further compounded the error and the name Cypress Hills was born – although there are no such trees within a thousand miles.

Oasis in the Desert. – In 1859 John Palliser camped for a while in the hills during his tour of the vast western domains for the British government *(p 73)*. "A perfect oasis in the desert we have travelled" was his brief description. Later settlers found the hills ideally suited for **ranching** as they contain nutritious pastures, good protection in coulees and valleys and abundant fresh water. Today, much of the private land is devoted to cattle, and cowboys are a not uncommon sight.

Not only is the scenic beauty of the hills a surprise but they are also a series of contradictions and rarities. They rise to nearly 1 500 m - 5 000 ft, the highest point in Canada between Labrador and the Rockies. A 200 sq km - 80 sq mile area of their heights was untouched by the last ice age which covered the rest of this vast area with ice 1 km - more than 1/2 mile deep. They form a divide between two great watersheds : Hudson Bay and the Caribbean. Streams flow south to the Missouri-Mississippi system and north to the South Saskatchewan River, Lake Winnipeg and the great Bay. The flora and fauna of the hills are also unexpected and the diversity is remarkable. Wild flowers and songbirds normally only associated with the Rockies flourish here, cacti grow on the dry south-facing slopes and orchids exist beside quiet ponds. Finally, an event which occurred in these hills influenced the creation of that greatest of Canadian institutions : the **Royal Canadian Mounted Police.**

HISTORICAL BACKGROUND

The Cypress Hills Massacre. – The early 1870s saw the establishment of several trading posts in the Cypress Hills by Americans from Montana. In exchange for furs, they illegally traded fire-water, a lethal brew containing all manner of things *(see Fort Whoop-up p. 87)*. During the winter of 1872-3, a band of Assiniboine Indians were camped close to two of these posts - Farwell's and Solomon's in the Cypress Hills. They were joined by a party of American wolf-hunters from Montana whose entire stock of horses had been stolen by Cree Indian raiders. Thinking the Assiniboines responsible and fired by a night's drinking, the "wolfers" attacked and destroyed the Indian camp killing about twenty people.

When news of this massacre reached Ottawa, the Prime Minister, Sir John A. Macdonald, acted fast. Already planning to create a force to keep law and order in the vast territories, he created the **North West Mounted Police** (they became the Royal Canadian Mounted Police in 1920) and dispatched them to the Northwest to stop such border incursions and end the illegal whisky trade. The men guilty of the massacre were arrested but later acquitted for lack of evidence. Despite the latter, the fact that white men were even arrested impressed the Indians with the impartiality of the new police force and helped establish their reputation.

Sitting Bull in Canada. – In 1876 a force of Sioux warriors under their great chief, Sitting Bull, exterminated an American army detachment under General **George Custer** on the Little Big Horn River in southern Montana. Fearing reprisals from the enraged Americans, Sitting Bull with nearly five thousand braves crossed into Canada. Inspector **James Walsh** of the North West Mounted Police was given the difficult task of trying to persuade the Sioux to return, and of preventing an Indian war since the Sioux were the traditional enemies of the Cree and Blackfoot tribes who inhabited this region. Riding into the huge Sioux encampment near Wood Mountain *(map p. 7 ; 350 km - 217 miles E of Fort Walsh)* with only four constables and two scouts, he informed Sitting Bull that he must obey Canadian law. This act of bravery won him the respect of the great Indian chief but nonetheless it was four years before Sitting Bull finally consented to return to the United States and life on a reservation. (His fears were not unfounded as he was killed in 1890 during an attempted arrest.)

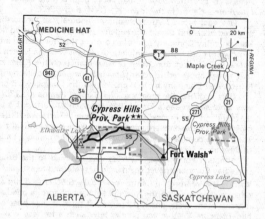

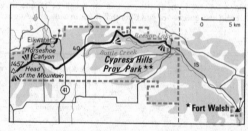

■ **SIGHTS** *time : 1/2 day*

Cypress Hills Provincial Park★★. – *Alberta. Camping, accommodation, snack-bar. Some roads are dirt and can be washed-out after heavy rain - check conditions at Park Office in Elkwater, open daily May - Aug ;* ☎ *(403) 893-3778.*

This attractive park encompasses the highest part of the Cypress Hills, several lovely lakes and some pretty routes. From Elkwater Lake, an interesting drive can be made past **Horseshoe Canyon** to **Head of the Mountain** from whence there are views south of coulees and hills as far as the Sweet Grass Hills and Bear Paw Mountains of Montana. The drive continues to Reesor Lake and the park boundary.

Fort Walsh National Historic Park★. – *Saskatchewan. Open daily mid May - mid Oct ; cafeteria, picnic sites ;* ☎ *(306) 299-4414.*

Reached by a pleasant drive from Maple Creek or from above, this North West Mounted Police post named for its builder, Inspector James Walsh, was constructed close to the site of the Cypress Hills Massacre. It served as the force's headquarters 1878-82 and as a remount station for the Royal Canadian Mounted Police 1942-68.

The visit starts in the **Reception Centre** where displays and films provide a good introduction. The fort itself *(regular guided tours 1/2 hr)* is reached by foot or by the Park bus service. The white-washed log buildings with their red roofs include barracks, stables, workshop and Commissioner's residence.

The highlight of the visit is, however, the excursion to **Farwell's Trading Post**★ *(2.5 km - 1 1/2 miles S of fort, access by Park bus service, guided tours 1/2 hr including transport).* This illegal American whisky post stands in the valley where the Cypress Hills Massacre took place near to Solomon's trading post *(not open to public).* Visitors are shown round by "Farwell" who really creates the lawless atmosphere of the times before the arrival of the police when "a man's life was worth a horse, and a horse was worth a pint of whisky".

DINOSAUR Provincial Park ★★ Alberta

Map p. 6 - 44 km - 27 miles NE of Trans-Canada Hwy at Brooks by Hwy 873 for 10 km - 6 miles, then right on Hwy 544, and left on Hwy 551. Open daily, camping, picnic area ; ☎ (403) 378-4587.

The Red Deer River has eroded a deep and sometimes wide valley across southern Alberta and other streams have dug winding courses to join it. In so doing, they have exposed rocks formed during the Cretaceous period (between 60 and 120 million years ago) and created the **Alberta Badlands,** a striking panorama of steep bluffs and fluted gullies. At this time the area was a tropical swamp inhabited by the huge reptiles known as dinosaurs. Changes in the earth's crust caused the one-time depression to be filled in and the remains of the creatures who inhabited it to be fossilized and thus preserved.

Haunt of the Dinosaurs. – The word dinosaur is derived from the Greek and it means "terrible lizard", a reference to the predatory habits and great size of some of these creatures. In fact there were many types, some were small and most were plant eaters but the biggest grew to 24 m - 80 ft in length and they weighed as much as 27 metric tonnes - 30 tons. The **Duck-billed dinosaurs** walked on their hind feet which were webbed for swimming and they had a snout resembling a duck's bill, thus their name. The **Horned dinosaurs** walked on four feet and had three horns - one over each eye and one on the nose. The **Armoured dinosaurs** had a row of bony plates on their backs and spikes on their tails as a form of protection. All of these were herbivorous, slow moving and prey to the ferocious **Flesh-eating dinosaurs** with their sharp claws and teeth, and muscular hind legs for running.

(after photo by Alberta Provincial Museum)

A Duck-Billed Dinosaur

Dinosaur bones have been found on all continents but no region is as rich as this Alberta valley. The first fossils were discovered in 1884 and since then several hundred complete skeletons have been unearthed as well as numerous bones. These are on display in many world museums including the Royal Ontario Museum *(p. 136)* and the National Museum of Natural Sciences *(p. 119).* The Red Deer valley can be appreciated in several places *(p. 84),* but its most spectacular part and the richest in fossils is Dinosaur Provincial Park. In 1979, UNESCO recognized its importance by placing it on the World Heritage List.

■ **VISIT**

Immediately on entering the park there is an excellent **viewpoint**★★ overlooking nearly 3 000 ha - 7 000 acres of badlands with the Red Deer River flowing through them. The road then descends to the valley.

A **circular drive**★ *(5 km - 3 miles)* takes the visitor through this wild and desolate almost lunar landscape where little except sagebrush flourishes. At several points short walks can be taken to see dinosaur bones preserved where they were found. Explanatory panels give details of the type of dinosaur and its size. Longer nature trails enable visitors even better to appreciate this wild terrain. But most of the park is inaccessible except by special bus tours *(1-3 hrs, daily)* or by conducted hikes *(contact Park Office for details).*

DRUMHELLER ★ Alberta

Map p. 6 – Pop 6 508 – Tourist Office ☎ (403) 823-2593 - *Local map below*

The one-time coal mining town of Drumheller lies amidst the Badlands of the Red Deer River as does Dinosaur Provincial Park *(p. 83)*. Drumheller is surrounded by fertile wheat-growing plain unbroken except by occasional oil pumps known as "donkey heads" because they bob up and down steadily. Thus, approaching the town, the wildly eroded valley nearly 120 m - 400 ft deep and about 1.5 km - 1 mile wide comes as something of a surprise.

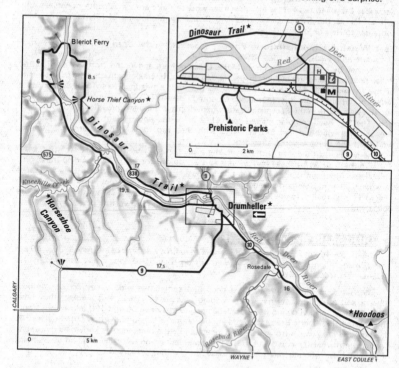

Dinosaur Museum ★ (M). – *335 1st St E with Tourist Office. Open daily April - Oct ; $1.00 ; ☎ 823-2593.*

This museum is devoted to the region's geology with examples of dinosaur fossils in which the area is rich. The most impressive is **Edmontosaurus**, a 9 m - 30 ft long, 3.5 m - 11 ft high duck-billed dinosaur with webbed feet and a strong tail for use when swimming.

Dinosaur Trail ★. – *Circular drive of 51 km - 32 miles from museum – 2 hrs. Cross river and turn left.*

This circuit is for the most part on the plain above the valley offering only occasional though good views of the Badlands. The first of these is **Horse Thief Canyon ★** with its rounded almost barren hills stretching to the river. The Trail crosses the river by the **Bleriot cable ferry** and climbs to a second fine **view ★** of the valley. The green pastures beside the river contrast strangely with the cactus-strewn bluffs and gullies immediately below.

Prehistoric Parks. – *47 km – 29 miles from beginning of Trail. Open daily April – mid Oct ; $2.50 ; refreshments, gift shop ; ☎ 823-6144.*

Authentic and lifesize models of some of the biggest dinosaurs stand among the low hills which are covered with cactus and sagebrush.

Horseshoe Canyon ★. – *18 km - 11 miles by Rte. 9.* This is one of the best views of the Badlands in the area. Paths lead through the hillocks to the river.

Hoodoos ★. – *16 km - 10 miles by Rte. 10.* These strange rock formations which look like giant mushrooms again illustrate the work of erosion in the valley. Soft rock has been worn away leaving harder pieces behind on top of pillars like hats.

EDMONTON ★★ Alberta

Map p. 6 – Pop 532 246 – Tourist Office ☎ (403) 422-5505

The city of Edmonton, capital of Alberta, spans the deep valley of the North Saskatchewan River in almost the exact centre of the province. It is a thriving metropolis, the centre of Canada's oil industry. There are more than 2 250 wells within a 40 km - 25 mile radius of the city producing about 10 % of the country's oil. It is also the centre for the development of the vast Athabasca Tar Sands to the north. The refineries and petro-chemical plants along **Refinery Row** may be the major source of Edmonton's wealth but they are not its only one. It lies in the middle of a rich agricultural area and serves as a meat-processing and grain-handling centre. It is also the major distribution centre for northern Alberta and northern Canada.

From Fur Trade Post to Provincial Capital. – By the end of the 18th century both North West and Hudson's Bay Companies had fur trading forts in the vicinity of present-day Edmonton. When the two merged in 1821, **Edmonton House** became the most important post in the far west, serving not only Alberta but the territory west of the Rockies.

Settlement grew up around it with goods arriving by York boat from York Factory *(map p. 127)* or overland from Winnipeg by Red River cart. The growing settlement suffered a relapse when the Canadian Pacific Railway Company decided to build their line through Calgary *(p. 79)* but recovered when other rail lines were built at the end of the century. People poured in especially during the Klondike Stampede of 1896-99 en route for Dawson *(p. 68)*. This was the beginning of Edmonton's development as a "gateway to the north" and one of the reasons why it was chosen as the capital of the new province of Alberta in 1905.

Donkey Head Oil Pump

Leduc. – Edmonton might have remained a quiet administrative centre had it not been for Leduc. In February 1947, oil was found 1 771 m - 5 810 ft below the ground in this small community south of Edmonton. It was the first of what proved to be a 300 million barrel oil field. In 1948 the Redwater field was found followed by many other discoveries. The great boom which occurred in 1947 has never ended.

Klondike Days. – Every year in July Edmonton celebrates its role in the great Klondike Stampede. Bedecked in costumes of the gay nineties, inhabitants and visitors parade, eat flapjack breakfasts, dance in the streets, gamble at the casino, pan for gold at the Chilkoot Mine, indulge in raft races on the river and in general "whoop it up" for about ten days.

■ **SIGHTS** *time : 1 1/2 days*

Edmonton's downtown is generally considered to be in the vicinity of Sir Winston Churchill Square and along Jasper Avenue. Around the square are a collection of fine modern buildings *(plan p. 86)*, including City Hall **(H)**, the Art Gallery, the Court House **(J)**, the attractive Centennial Library **(L)**, the Edmonton Centre with its shops, restaurants and offices, and the elegant glass and brick Citadel Theatre **(T)** which contains three stages.

Provincial Museum★★. – *Open daily ; cafeteria ; bookstore ;* ☎ *427-1730.*
This starkly modern complex occupies an attractive **site★** in a park overlooking the river beside the former residence of Alberta's Lieutenant-Governor.

Natural History. – On the ground floor to the right of the entrance are **dioramas★** of the wildlife found in the four great natural regions of the province – Grasslands, Parklands, Northern Forest and Mountains. Above these exhibits on the second floor are displays covering Alberta's geology, mineral wealth and the age of the giant dinosaurs. There are also more didactic displays on bird and mammal life and on how each species adapts to its environment.

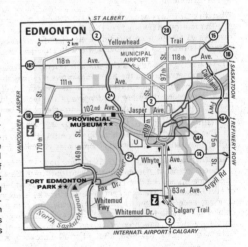

Ethnology. – On the ground floor to the left of the entrance is the **Indian Section★★** where explanations on the life of the Plains Indians in Canada can be found. There are fine examples of the exquisite bead work produced by these peoples and displays on food, clothes, shelter, transportation, recreation and religion. Above the Indian section on the second floor are the **Historical Exhibits★** where the history of white settlement in Alberta is traced with many displays evoking life in the province before our time. In particular, there is a section devoted to the various religious backgrounds of the province's population.

Fort Edmonton Park★★. – *Open daily mid May – Labour Day ; Sept - mid Oct weekends only ; $3.75 ; cafeteria ;* ☎ *436-5565.*
Set in the ravine of the North Saskatchewan River, this park is a massive undertaking to recreate the history of white settlement in Edmonton by a series of reconstructions. The Hudson's Bay Company fort of 1846 and the pre-railway village of 1885 are complete, and work is in progress on the pre-war town of about 1905. When all phases are finished, visitors will trace the development of the city back from the present day to the early fur trading settlement.

Pre-Railway Village of Edmonton. – This street is a reconstruction of Jasper Avenue in 1885 notable for its width and its boardwalks. Along it stand a series of stores selling furs, jewelry, drugs, hardware, etc. The North West Mounted Police post stands near the Dominion Land Office, and down the street the offices of the Bulletin, the local newspaper, can be visited. One interesting building is the McDougall Church. This tiny wooden structure was moved to this site from its original location in downtown Edmonton. Erected there in 1873 by the **Rev. George McDougall**, it was the first Protestant church in Alberta.

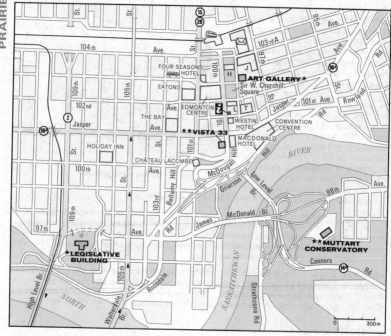

Fort Edmonton. – Inside a high palisade, the wooden buildings of the 1846 fur trading fort have been beautifully reconstructed. The most dominant structure is the "Big House", a four-storey residence with a third floor balcony from which the Chief Factor or governor of the fort, to whom it belonged, could survey his domain. Comparing its relative comfort with the quarters of the other inhabitants – in the order of 130 people, it is obvious that a rigid caste system existed with the Chief Factor at the top and the Company clerks, interpreters, artisans and labourers on various rungs of the ladder which finished with the indentured servants. The quarters of all these people have been recreated with great attention to detail as have the trade and storage rooms, the forge, stable, boatshed where York boats *(p. 96)* are under construction (a completed one can be seen on the river), and the chapel and house built for the **Rev. Robert Rundle,** the first missionary in Alberta, who spent the years 1840-48 at Fort Edmonton.

Muttart Conservatory★★. – *Open daily 11 am - 9 pm ; $2.00 ;* ☎ *428-3664.*
    The four glass pyramids of this striking architectural ensemble provide a fine setting for displays of plants from three different climatic zones – tropical, temperate and arid. One pyramid is reserved as a show house with changing displays of ornamentals.

Vista 33★★. – *In Alberta Government Telephone Tower. Open daily ; 50¢.* ☎ *425-3978.*
    This observatory on the 33rd floor offers a remarkable panoramic **view★★** of Edmonton. Immediately to the south, the river in its winding steep-sided valley can be seen. On the other three sides there are good views of the high buildings of downtown. Far to the east Refinery Row with its refineries and petro-chemical plants is visible.

Art Gallery★. – *Open daily ; $2.00 ;* ☎ *422-6223.*
    This modern building with its open central stairway has regularly changing exhibitions of high quality, sometimes visiting, sometimes compiled from the permanent collection.

Legislative Building★. – *Guided tours daily, 3/4 hr ;* ☎ *427-7362.*
    Set in pleasant gardens overlooking the North Saskatchewan River stands the yellow sandstone domed Alberta Legislative building. Opened in 1912, it occupies the original site of Fort Edmonton. The main entrance (north side) leads into an impressive hall from which a stairway ascends to the **Legislative Assembly.** The fifth floor of the dome has an interesting display on Alberta History and the Legislative Library contains a portrait of Princess Louise Caroline Alberta, daughter of Queen Victoria, wife of the Marquis of Lorne, Governor-General of Canada 1878-83, after whom the province is named.

The key on p 28 explains the symbols used on the maps and plans.

FORT MACLEOD ★ Alberta
Map p. 6 – Pop 3 139

    This small town on the Oldman River was the site chosen for the first North West Mounted Police post in the west. In October 1874 a band of weary men arrived after their long and arduous trek from Manitoba. They had been quickly trained and dispatched to the west to stop the illegal whisky trade and such border incursions as that leading to the Cypress Hills Massacre (p. 82). Under the command of **Colonel James Macleod,** they built permanent barracks on an island in the river. Today, Fort Macleod is a thriving agricultural community. Grain is grown with the aid of irrigation and cattle are raised on the ranchland of the nearby Porcupine Hills.

Fort Museum★. – *On Hwy 3 one block from centre of town. Open daily May - mid Oct ; $2.50 ; ☎ (403) 553-4703.*

This is not a reconstruction of the original police post but rather a museum of life in and around police posts during the early settlement of Alberta. Inside the wooden palisaded walls stand a number of log structures. The **Kanouse House** with its sod roof is devoted to the early settlers of the region. The **Mounted Police Building** has a maquette of the original fort and exhibits on the police. In the **Centennial Building,** a diorama and slide show *(15 mins)* on Head-Smashed-In Buffalo Jump form an excellent introduction to a visit to this site *(see below).*

In summer, students dressed in police uniforms of 1878 (red jackets, black breeches, white pith helmets) perform a musical ride *(July and Aug Wed-Sun 4 times daily).*

Head-Smashed-In Buffalo Jump. – *16 km - 10 miles W by Hwy 2 and Route 516 (Spring Point Rd). Guided tours in summer 9am - 8pm ; 45 mins.*

For over 5 000 years, buffalo were driven to their deaths over this cliff. The buffalo provided most of the necessities of life for the native Indian people - meat, hides for clothing and shelter, and bone for scrapers and needles. The 9m - 30ft deep deposits are the most extensive of any buffalo jump in North America, and their importance was recognized by UNESCO in 1981 when the jump was designated a World Heritage site. Future plans for the surrounding area include construction of a visitor centre with displays on the use of such jumps.

LETHBRIDGE ★ Alberta

Map p. 6 – Pop 54 072 – Tourist Office ☎ (403) 329-6777

This southern Alberta city faces on its western side a deep coulee cut by the Oldman River. Constructed into the side of this coulee are the striking buildings of the University of Lethbridge, and crossing it is the High Level Railway Bridge (about 1.5 km - 1 mile long and 96 m - 314 ft high). Although Lethbridge was founded in 1870 because of the discovery of coal deposits in the valley, today the city is much more important as the centre for a very productive agricultural region. Widespread irrigation and the relatively mild winters moderated by the warm chinooks *(p. 74)* have made the growing of grain and vegetables especially sugar beet very profitable. Livestock are reared, and oil and gas are also found in the area.

Nikka Yuko Centennial Garden★. – *In Henderson Lake Park on Mayor Magrath Drive. Open daily mid May - mid Oct ; $1.75 ; ☎ 328-3511.*

When Canada declared war on Japan in 1941, about 22 000 Japanese Canadians living on the west coast were placed in internment camps in central British Columbia and Alberta although in many cases they were Canadian citizens of several generations. About 6 000 Japanese ended up in Lethbridge where they chose to stay after the war. In 1967, the city of Lethbridge built this garden as a symbol of Japanese-Canadian amity (*Nikka Yuko* means Japan-Canada). It is a wonderfully serene traditional place where visitors can gain an appreciation of the Japanese concept of formality of beauty in nature. It contains five types of Japanese landscape architecture tied together by meandering paths. At its centre lies a pavilion of Japanese cypress wood which is laid out for the tea ceremony.

Fort Whoop-up★. – *In Indian Battle Park by river, access from Hwy 3. Open daily mid May - Labour Day ; $1.75 ; snack bar ; ☎ 329-0444.*

In the deep coulee of the Oldman River stands a replica of this once notorious whisky trading post. Founded by American traders from Fort Benton, Montana, this post attracted Indians from far and wide to trade buffalo skins, furs - and indeed almost anything, for a particularly lethal brew bearing little resemblance to whisky (ingredients included chewing tobacco, red peppers, Jamaican ginger, black molasses as well as alcohol). These illegal liquor forts, of which Whoop-up was the most important, sprang up all over southern Alberta and Saskatchewan in the early 1870s. The fact that they were an American encroachment on Canadian territory, in addition to the demoralizing effect they were having on the Indians, led the Canadian Government to form the North West Mounted Police *(p. 82)* to stop the trade. The force which arrived at the gates of Whoop-up in 1874 found the whisky traders fled. The founding of Fort Macleod *(p. 86)* and later Fort Calgary *(p. 80)* by the force effectively ended the illegal trade and brought law and order to the west.

The reconstructed fort flies not "Old Glory" (the American flag) but the trading flag of the original Fort Benton company. Below it, wooden buildings form a fortified enclosure. In one of the bunk houses, an interesting slide show recreates the history of the trading post and its relation to the development of the Canadian west.

MOOSE JAW ★ Saskatchewan

Map p. 7 – Pop 33 941

Rising out of the flat wheat lands of southern Saskatchewan is the province's third city, so named because the river makes a sharp turn at this point somewhat resembling the protruding jaw of a moose. An important railway junction, Moose Jaw is an industrial centre mainly handling the agricultural produce of the surrounding area - flour mills, grain elevator, stock yards - and also involved in the refining of Saskatchewan's oil wealth.

Western Development Museum★. – *At junction Trans-Canada Hwy and Hwy 2. Open daily ; $1.50 ; ☎ 693-6556.*

Housed in an imposing building, the Moose Jaw branch of this museum is devoted to transportation in Saskatchewan. The water section has displays on the *Northcote,* a steam ship used to take supplies up the South Saskatchewan River during the Riel Rebellion, and on cable ferries particularly that of Batoche. The land section has a Canadian Pacific locomotive, a reconstructed station and a 1934 Buick converted to run on rails and used as an inspection vehicle for twenty years. The land section also contains an interesting collection of automobiles. The air section features many Canadian planes including a 1927 Red Pheasant, and a gallery on the British Commonwealth Air Training Plan.

PRAIRIE WILDLIFE INTERPRETATION CENTRE ★★ Saskatchewan

*Map p. 6. 150 km - 95 miles E of Alberta border on Trans-Canada Hwy near Webb.
Open daily mid May - mid Oct 8.30am - 6pm (Sun until 9pm) ;* ☎ *(306) 674-2287.*

No one will ever consider the Prairies boring after a visit to this excellent interpretive centre. Self-guided trails through natural short grass prairie, wheatfield, pasture, coulee and past an alkali lake and slough make a fascinating introduction to this region. Displays and films in the centre and explanations by naturalists all add to the experience.

PRINCE ALBERT National Park ★ Saskatchewan

Map p. 6 - 56 km - 35 miles N of Prince Albert. Hiking, canoeing, swimming, golf, tennis, camping, winter sports ; accommodation in Waskesiu - see National Parks p 21, map available at Park information centre ; ☎ *(306) 663-5322*

This large park in the geographical centre of Saskatchewan consists of wooded hills dotted with lakes and streams. Its 3 875 sq km - 1 496 sq miles are representative of Canada's southern boreal plains, an area where the aspen forest of the south mixes with the true boreal wilderness. The variety of wildlife in the Park reflects this transition. Isolated pockets of grassland near the southern boundary support prairie animals : coyotes, badgers and ground squirrels. The northern forests are home to wolves, moose, elk, bears, beavers, otter, mink and a small herd of woodland caribou. In the extreme north, white pelicans nest on Lavallée Lake.

The **Park Nature and Information Centre** in Waskesiu (meaning place of the elk) provides an introduction to the park *(open daily May - Sept).* Roads follow both shores of Lake Waskesiu with fine views. **Boat trips** can be taken on the lake in a paddle-wheeler *(daily mid May - Sept ; 1 hr ; $4.50).*

On the southernmost edge of the park, visitors can drive around a **buffalo enclosure** where a small herd roams a prairie landscape. Hiking trails and canoe routes crisscross the park. One interesting expedition takes the visitor to the cabin and grave of the great conservationist Grey Owl *(15 km - 9 mile hike).*

Grey Owl. – Famous for his writings and lectures on the fate of the beaver and on the vanishing wilderness, this man posed as an Indian, dressed in buckskin and wore his hair long and braided. He travelled all over the North American continent and to Europe with the conservationist message, even lecturing to George VI in 1937. He worked for Parks Canada trying to re-establish beaver colonies first in Riding Mountain National Park *(p. 91)* and then in Prince Albert. At his death in 1938 he was exposed as an Englishman, **Archie Belaney,** who had taken the Indian name *Wa-sha-Quon-Asin* (the Grey Owl) about 1920. Impostor he might have been, nevertheless he is one of Canada's finest nature writers and among the first to preach the importance of preserving the wilderness and its wildlife. His most famous books are *Tales of an Empty Cabin, Pilgrims of the Wild* and *Sajo and her Beaver People.*

REGINA ★★ Saskatchewan

Map p. 7 – Pop 162 613 – Tourist Office ☎ *(306) 527-6631*

Set in the centre of an extensive, fertile, wheat-growing plain lies the city of Regina, capital of Saskatchewan. Always an important agricultural centre because of its situation on the main line of the Canadian Pacific Railway and the Trans-Canada Highway, it has of recent years become the headquarters for oil exploration in the province and for the rich potash industry.

Pile O' Bones. – Few cities have been founded in less congenial surroundings – treeless plains stretching to the horizon in all directions, a scanty water supply from a sluggish creek, soil of gumbo clay muddy in wet weather, dusty in dry... Why was this site chosen ? In the early 1880s the Canadian Pacific Railway Company decided to build their line across the southern plains, leaving the existing capital of the vast Northwest Territories high and dry at Battleford *(p. 78).* The Dominion Government thus determined to move it, and together with the railway company, chose the place where the future rail line would cross a creek long favoured by Indians and Metis for running buffalo into pounds and slaughtering them. The remains of these animals - testifying to their once great number, had acquired for the spot the Cree name *Oskana.* This was recorded by John Palliser *(p. 73)* as *Wascana* and translated as pile o'bones. The choice was very controversial, especially since the Lieutenant-Governor of the then Northwest Territories, Edgar Dewdney *(p. 39)* owned land at that place... However, chosen it was and in August 1882 when the first train arrived,

(after photo by National Museums of Canada)

Canada Goose

Princess Louise, wife of Canada's Governor-General, rechristened it Regina after her mother, **Queen Victoria.**

Queen City of the Plains. – Regina became the capital of Saskatchewan when that province was created in 1905. It immediately began to grow as immigrants poured in from all parts of the world. The initiative of these new arrivals overcame the problems of the city's site. Wascana Creek was damned to solve the water problems, thereby creating an artificial lake, the centre of a pleasant park. Trees were planted and carefully nourished, defying the notion of a treeless wilderness. Imposing public buildings were constructed and there are plans to re-organize Regina's downtown, at present cut in two by the railway tracks. Today, from 80 km - 50 miles distant, the city of Regina rises above the flat, treeless prairie like a mirage, its quiet grace testifying to its epithet, Queen City of the Plains.

The Trial of Louis Riel. – After the defeat of the Northwest Rebellion in 1885 (p. 92), the Metis leader Louis Riel (see also p. 75) was taken to Regina for trial. The court immediately became a centre of controversy. To the Québecois, Riel - a Catholic Metis who had studied for the priesthood in Montréal, was a patriot who had fought for the rights of his people. To Ontarians, he was a common rebel who had earlier got off scot free after murdering one of their number during the Red River Rebellion (p. 75). Defence counsel pleaded that Riel was insane - he had spent several years in lunatic asylums and had wished to set up a new Catholic state on the Saskatchewan with Bishop Bourget of Montréal (p. 162) as Pope. Riel himself rejected the plea and convinced the jury he was sane. But if sane he was guilty and that was the verdict brought down. Hanging was the required punishment. The Prime Minister, Sir John A. Macdonald, was inundated with petitions from both sides. The sentence was delayed while doctors studied Riel's mental health. Sir John weighed up the political consequences of hanging Riel and of not hanging him. He decided that the sentence must be carried out ; Riel lost his life on the 16th November.

Every summer **The Trial of Louis Riel★★**, a reconstruction from court transcripts by John Coulter, is acted out at Government House (Dewdney Ave W. Performances Tues, Wed, Fri, mid June - Aug ; 8.15 pm ; $3.00, tickets available from Tourist Office). This play is every bit as dramatic as the original trial, and it stirs up the same emotions.

■ **SIGHTS** time : 1 day

Museum of Natural History★★. – Open daily ; gift shop ; ☎ 565-2815.

This long low building of Manitoba Tyndall limestone houses one of the finest museums of natural history in Canada. It provides a fascinating insight into Saskatchewan and is indeed an excellent way of beginning a visit to the province. The **dioramas★★**(upper gallery) presenting each natural region with its native birds and animals are unsurpassed. They illustrate the range of terrain and wildlife in the province from the Frenchman valley and its prairie dogs, the unique environment of the Cypress Hills (p. 82), and the lovely Qu'Appelle Valley (p. 90), to Shallow Lake and its Whooping Cranes, the Saskatchewan River and its bugling elk, and the northern forests home of wolf, moose and caribou.

Wascana Centre★. – This 930 ha - 2 300 acre park is Regina's pride and joy. Formal gardens with beautiful flowers and fine trees surround the western part of artificial Wascana Lake. There are picnic spots with barbecue pits especially on **Willow Island** (access by ferry, afternoons in summer, $1.00), beaches and boating facilities. Also in the park, which can be toured by car, are the Provincial Legislative Building and the **Diefenbaker Homestead**, a three-room pioneer dwelling (open daily mid May - Labour Day, 10 am - 8 pm), the one-time home of John George Diefenbaker, Prime Minister of Canada 1957-63 (p. 92). His family moved west from Ontario and homesteaded at Borden, Saskatchewan, 1905-10, from whence this house was moved.

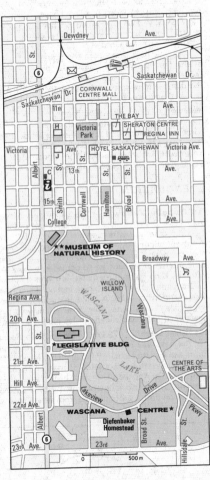

East of Wascana Parkway, the park is a bird sanctuary. Many species of waterfowl can be seen but by far and away the most common is the Canada Goose. Some of these birds are year-round residents of the Wascana Centre benefitting from free food and the warm water of the lake which is artificially kept above freezing in the winter by a power plant. There are three display ponds which can be visited (daily May-Oct). Also in this eastern section are the Saskatchewan Centre of the Arts which contains three theatres, and the campus of the University of Regina.

Legislative Building★. – Guided tours daily, 3/4 hr ; cafeteria ; ☎ 565-5357.

This graceful building of Manitoba Tyndall limestone was built in 1908-12 in the shape of a cross with a dome at its centre. It has a fine **site★** overlooking gardens and Wascana Lake. The tour visits the Legislative Chamber, Legislative Library, the Rotunda and the art galleries named after the rivers of the province. Note especially on the ground floor the fine portraits of Indian Chiefs by Edward Morris in the Assiniboine Gallery.

Royal Canadian Mounted Police Barracks★ (A). – Plan p. 90. Guided tours daily, 1/2 hr ; ☎ 359-5838.

People who know nothing else about Canada have heard of the **Mounties,** the country's federal police force. Stories about them are legion and many films have portrayed their ability to "always get their man". Created in 1873 as the **North West Mounted Police,** their job was both to formulate and to preserve law and order in the Canadian west. Faced with problems such as the illegal sale of "fire water" to Canadian Indians by American traders *(see Cypress Hills p. 82)*, the police quickly established themselves as a force to be reckoned with. They helped the various Indian tribes accept treaties and life on reservations, gave valuable aid to new settlers in the west and enforced law and order during the Klondike Stampede *(see Yukon Circuit p. 69)*. In 1920, they were united with the Dominion Police as the **Royal Canadian Mounted Police.** Today they enforce federal laws across Canada and act as the provincial police in all provinces and territories except Ontario and Québec. They are famous for their **Musical Ride,** a collection of early cavalry drills performed on horseback culminating in a rousing "charge" *(see also Ottawa p. 122).*

The Regina barracks are the scene of the first six months training for all recruits. The tour varies depending on the number of recruits and their activities of the moment.

Museum★. – *Open daily.* The history of the Mounties is illustrated through numerous artifacts, and many famous incidents are recalled such as the Great March west *(see Fort Macleod p. 86)*, Sitting Bull's years in Canada *(see Cypress Hills p. 82)*, the Northwest Rebellion *(p. 92)*, the Klondike *(p. 69)* and the voyage of the *St. Roch (see Vancouver p. 59)*. Displays also explain the work of the force today.

EXCURSION

Qu'Appelle Valley★. – This valley cuts a deep swath across the otherwise flat prairie from Lake Diefenbaker to the Manitoba border. It was carved out 12 000 years ago by meltwaters from a retreating glacier which left a wide valley with only a small stream at its midst surrounded by low, round-topped hills. Approaching the Qu'Appelle from any direction, the prairie seems endless, and then suddenly the road drops and a 2 km - mile-or-so wide stretch of verdant green comes into view. As much as 120 m - 400 ft deep in places with sparkling lakes at its midst, it makes a complete contrast to the surrounding plains.

Its name derives from Indian legend rather romanticized by the poetess Pauline Johnson *(see Brantford p. 103)*. A brave is out in his canoe, he hears his name called, *qu'appelle ?* (who calls ?) he shouts, only an echo answers him. On returning home he finds his sweetheart dead - she had called out his name moments before dying.

The Fishing Lakes★. – *73 km - 45 miles from Regina by Rte 10 – allow 1/2 day.*

The best way to appreciate the Qu'Appelle Valley is to drive alongside the river when it forms the Fishing Lakes - Pasqua, Echo, Mission and Katepwa. North of Lake Echo, there is a particularly attractive stretch of road on Route 56 leading to **Echo Valley Provincial Park★** from Fort Qu'Appelle. The park itself *(open daily mid May - Labour Day ; cars $4.00 ; camping, beach, picnic spots, snack bar)* is set between Lake Echo and Lake Pasqua with beaches on both - a good place from which to enjoy the valley.

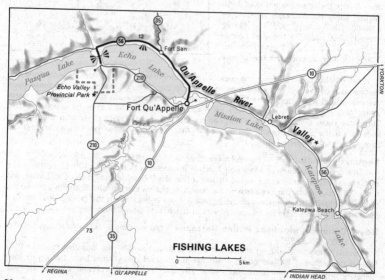

FISHING LAKES

RIDING MOUNTAIN National Park ★★ Manitoba

Map p. 7 - 97 km - 60 miles N of Brandon by Rte 10; hiking, boating, tennis, golf, winter sports, camping; accommodation in Wasagaming; admission – see National Parks p. 21, map available at Park information centre; ☎ (204) 848-2811.

This lovely park is a rolling plateau of wooded slopes and lakes standing amidst the Manitoba plain. Approached from the east and north, it rises 457 m - 1 500 ft above the surrounding countryside (756 m - 2 480 ft above sea level) and does indeed look like a mountain - or at least a hill. Early fur traders gave it the name "Riding" Mountain as it marked the place they exchanged canoe for horse to continue west. It is in fact part of the **Manitoba Escarpment** – a jagged 1 600 km - 1 000 mile long ridge which winds across North Dakota, Manitoba and Saskatchewan cut by many rivers which have made it into a series of hills rather than a continuous ridge.

The park is also a crossroads where northern, western and eastern environments and habitats meet. High areas are covered with an evergreen forest of spruce, pine, fir and tamarack. Lower areas sport a deciduous forest of hardwoods, shrubs, vines and ferns. In the west there are meadows and grassland full of wild flowers (July and August) forming some of the only true "prairie" left on the continent.

Visit. – The **Interpretive Centre ★★** (open daily mid May - Labour Day) in Wasagaming has a splendid display on the park's geological background, the different habitats and their wildlife. Films are also shown.

Near Lake Audy (47 km - 29 miles from Wasagaming), a herd of about thirty buffalo roam a large enclosure. From a viewpoint above the Audy plain, these animals can be seen in their true prairie environment. An exhibit explains how they nearly became extinct. Visitors can drive around the enclosure (4 km - 2 1/2 miles).

A fine **view★** of the Manitoba Escarpment is obtained from Route 19 (31 km - 19 miles E of Wasagaming or 5 km - 3 miles from Park east gate).

There are 29 National Parks in Canada located in a wide variety of terrain.
For general information on admission, etc, see p. 21.

SASKATOON ★ Saskatchewan

Map p. 6 – Pop 154 210 – Tourist Office ☎ (306) 242-1206

Built on both sides of the South Saskatchewan River, the city of Saskatoon occupies a naturally fine **site★** which has been enhanced by wide tree-lined streets and parkland beside the water (in particular **Kiwanis Park** with its views of bridges and the University of Saskatchewan). Saskatchewan's second city, it is a manufacturing and distribution centre set in a fertile wheat-growing area and amidst the province's vast potash reserves. The surrounding prairie landscape is a little more rolling than around Regina but it is nonetheless dominated by the "heights" of **Mount Blackstrap** (alt 91 m - 300 ft), an artificial ski hill built south of the city (40 km - 25 miles).

Temperance Town. – Founded in 1883 by Methodists from Ontario, it was the proposed capital of a temperance colony. One of the leaders of this venture, **John Lake,** selected the name Saskatoon after a small purplish berry native to the region. This teetotallers' paradise did not however attract many settlers and two decades later it numbered only 113 souls. In 1908 this changed quickly as the whole area experienced a boom with colonists arriving by the new rail lines. The German, Scandinavian, Ukrainian and British settlers transformed the city and the early temperance ideals were laid to rest. Today, they are recalled once a year in July during **Pioneer Days.**

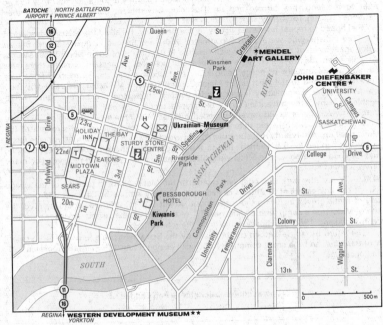

■ **SIGHTS** *time : 1/2 day – plan p. 91*

Western Development Museum★★. – *In Saskatoon Prairieland Exhibition Grounds, 8 km - 5 miles from downtown by Rte 11/16. Open daily ; $1.50 ; refreshments ;* ☎ *931-1910.*

The grand attraction of the Saskatoon branch of this museum is **Boomtown Saskatchewan,** a fascinating and authentic reconstruction of an entire street of 1910 vintage complete with its Western Pioneer Bank, garage, stores, Chinese laundry, school, church, pool hall, theatre, hotel and railway station. Along the street stand several period automobiles and horse-drawn vehicles.

Separate halls house a large collection of automobiles and agricultural equipment including steam tractors.

Mendel Art Gallery★. – *Open daily 10 am - 10 pm ; gift shop ;* ☎ *664-9610.*

This attractive modern gallery overlooking the river is named for **Fred Mendel,** a wealthy Saskatoon meat-packer of German origin who launched the idea of an art gallery and spent much of his time and money setting it up. The permanent collection includes works by the Group of Seven *(p. 139),* Emily Carr and David Milne in the Canadian section, Feininger, Chagall, Utrillo and Pissarro in the European section. The gallery also displays visiting exhibitions. At one end there is an attractive conservatory of exotic flowers and plants.

John Diefenbaker Centre★. – *In University of Saskatchewan. Open daily ;* ☎ *343-3427.*

On his death in 1979, **John Diefenbaker,** the former Canadian Prime Minister, left all his papers to the University of Saskatchewan. They have been assembled to form a veritable shrine to this man who was a legend in his own time. A lawyer by training and well known for his defence of the "little man", Diefenbaker entered politics and became a strong proponent of Western Canadian ideas in the Conservative Party. Elected leader of the party in 1956, he was Prime Minister of Canada 1957-63. He remained influential in federal politics until his death.

The centre features a replica of the Prime Minister's office and the Cabinet Chamber as they existed in the Diefenbaker era in addition to the displays on his life and works.

Ukrainian Museum. – *Open daily 1 pm - 4.30 pm ; except Mon, and Sat in winter ; $1.00 ; gift shop ;* ☎ *244-3800.*

This museum has displays of traditional costumes, tapestries, wood-inlaid objects, pioneer tools and many other items illustrating the heritage of the Ukrainian peoples who have played such a large role in the settlement of the Prairies.

EXCURSION

Batoche★. – *88 km - 55 miles NE of Saskatoon by Rte 11 to Rosthern, Rte 312 E and Rte 225 N – allow 1/2 day. National Historic Park ; open daily May - Oct ;* ☎ *423-6100.*

This quiet and beautiful spot on the banks of the South Saskatchewan River was the site of the last stand of the Metis in 1885.

The Northwest Rebellion. – The seeds of this uprising, the last armed conflict on Canadian soil, were sown in Manitoba's Red River Valley early in the 19th century when the Metis learned that the land did not necessarily belong to the men born and living on it. This led to Louis Riel's Provisional Government of 1869, the creation of the province of Manitoba and the putting aside of 567 000 ha - 1.4 million acres of land for Metis settlement *(p. 75).* Unfortunately, the Metis, left leaderless when Riel was banished for five years, were prey to land speculators who bought their land for a fraction of its worth. Many moved northwest to the valley of the South Saskatchewan River hoping to lead their traditional lives of buffalo hunting, etc and avoid survey groups and white settlers. But all the buffalo were gone and the march of "progress" and settlement caught them up. They found again that they had no right to the land they farmed and the Dominion Government consistently ignored their petitions. Thus in 1884 they sent for Louis Riel.

Riel hoped to repeat his earlier victory on the Red River. He allied the Metis with some of the Cree Indians who were also discontented with the changes in their lifestyle. But an unfortunate incident at **Duck Lake,** which resulted in the deaths of some North West Mounted Policemen, destroyed all hope of a peaceful solution. In eastern Canada there was outrage at the thought of police being killed by lawless rebels, and a military force was quickly dispatched to the west under Major-General **Frederick Middleton.** Restrained by Riel, the Metis under their military leader **Gabriel Dumont,** an experienced buffalo hunter, were unable to harass the advancing army by guerilla tactics. Instead they made a stand at Batoche which never could have succeeded against Middleton's overwhelming numbers. Nevertheless, it was a heroic defence which lasted four days due to the strength of the Metis position. Afterwards Riel surrendered and was taken to Regina for trial. He was found guilty and hanged *(p. 89).* Dumont fled to the United States though he was later pardoned and returned to Batoche. The Metis were offered the land title they had requested so many times without success.

Visit. – Today, the park is a poignant tribute to the Metis. Nothing remains of the village except the tiny **church of St-Antoine de Padoue,** the **rectory** with its bullet holes and a cemetery of Metis graves including that of Dumont. About 500 m - 500 yds south by road, the site of Middleton's camp with its fine **view★★** of the river can be visited. A visitor reception centre *(opening 1985)* will house exhibits on the rebellion.

The return trip to Saskatoon can be made by the St-Laurent cable ferry *(3 km - 2 miles N of Batoche),* and the small community of Duck Lake on Route 11 where the rebellion had its beginnings.

WINNIPEG ★★★ Manitoba

Map p. 7 – Pop 564 473 – Tourist Office ☎ (204) 943-1970 or 944-3777

Set on the banks of the Red and Assiniboine Rivers, the city of Winnipeg, capital of Manitoba, lies in the very heart of Canada and is often described as the place where "the West begins". It has for nearly a century been the traditional first stopping place for immigrants to the West but it fits this description in more ways than one. Not far east and north of the city the hilly and rocky tree-covered terrain of the Canadian Shield with its multitude of lakes gives way to the wide open fertile prairie landscape with its endless horizons (map. p. 74). This dramatic change marks more clearly than anything else the division between east and west.

Winnipeg, named for the large and shallow lake to the north which the Cree Indians called win-nipuy (murky water), indeed developed as the distribution and financial centre of the West. Although its supremacy has been challenged by Vancouver and the Alberta cities in more recent years, it retains its huge **commodity exchange** – the most important in Canada, its vast stock yards, railway yards and manufacturing industry as well as being the headquarters of the Hudson's Bay Company (p. 74).

The Red River Settlement. – In the early 19th century, Thomas Douglas, Earl of Selkirk (p. 211) obtained from the Hudson's Bay Company title to a large piece of land called **Assiniboia** covering much of present day southern Manitoba. In 1811 he began resettling some of his poverty-stricken fellow countrymen from the Highlands of Scotland in the Red River valley. The success of this colony was slow in coming however, because of the Red River's tendency to flood, plagues of grasshoppers that ate all the crops and last but not least the rivalry bordering on warfare of the great fur trading companies, the Hudson's Bay and the North West Company (p. 161). The latter allied with the Metis, who saw their traditional lifestyle disrupted by settlers (p. 75), nearly succeeded in wiping out the colony during the **Seven Oaks Massacre** of 1816 when twenty settlers were killed and the rest temporarily abandoned the settlement. However, Selkirk re-established his colony and it gradually grew in size developing as a commercial centre with brigades of carts going to and from St. Paul, Minnesota, and steamboats chugging along the Red River. For a time its connections with the United States made it seem likely that it would be annexed by that country but the Riel Rebellion and the creation of the province of Manitoba in 1870 (p. 75) prevented this.

Winnipeg Today. – The future of the community at the forks of the Red and the Assiniboine was assured when the Canadian Pacific Railway Company built their line through it and chose it as a major maintenance and repair centre. Floods of immigrants poured in by train and Winnipeg (the name was adopted at the time of the Riel Rebellion) assumed not only an outfitting role but also became a distribution centre for the entire North West. From early on its population had been a mélange of Scots, Irish, English, French, Metis and Indians. To these were added Germans, Eastern Europeans and especially Ukrainians in this century. Its skyline reflects this diversity with the domes of the Orthodox churches mixing with the spires and towers of Catholic and Protestant establishments.

Thanks to its ethnic heritage, Winnipeg is rich in its cultural institutions – the Manitoba Theatre Centre, the Symphony Orchestra, the Manitoba Opera Company and, most famous of all, the Royal Winnipeg Ballet. Every August, the city's diverse cultural

Orthodox Cathedral of the Holy Trinity

background is celebrated in **Folklorama,** a festival held in pavilions all over the city, and the Folk Festival held in July is also popular.

■ MAIN SIGHTS DOWNTOWN time : 2 days

The centre of Winnipeg has always been counted as the intersection of **Portage Avenue** and **Main Street,** the City's two principal thoroughfares wide enough, it was said, for ten Red River carts to rush along side by side. Today this corner, for long famous as being the windiest in Canada, is dominated by huge buildings which are all connected underground by an attractive shopping area, **Winnipeg Square.**

To the south of the intersection in a small park below the Fort Garry Hotel, there is a stone gateway. It is all that remains of **Upper Fort Garry,** once the local headquarters of the Hudson's Bay Company. The present day headquarters of that same company lies a block away **(A)**.

A little north of Portage and Main lies Winnipeg's **Centennial Centre,** an attractive complex enclosing concert hall, theatre, museum (p. 94) and planetarium. It is built on various levels and is connected by terrace gardens with sculptures, fountains and an outdoor cafe. Close by is the **Old Market Square** (King, Albert and Bannatyne Streets) where there are boutiques, restaurants and a weekend market. This area also has some remarkable examples of early 20th century architecture (walking tours daily in summer, ☎ museum p. 94).

Another interesting quarter for shopping and restaurants is **Osborne Village,** just south of the Assiniboine River between River and Stradbrook Avenues.

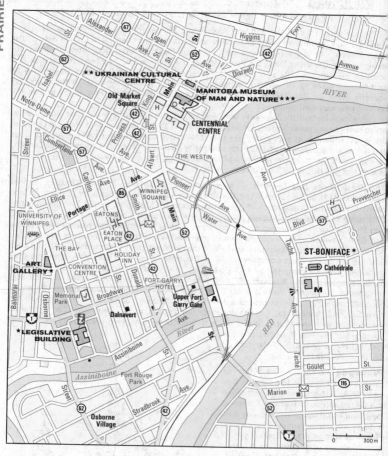

Manitoba Museum of Man and Nature★★★. *– Open daily ; mid May - mid Sept,
Mon - Sat 10am – 9pm, Sun 12am – 9pm ; shorter hours rest of year ; $2.00 ; guided tours
1 hr ; gift shop ; restaurant ; ☎ 956-2830.*

This excellent museum explains the history of mankind in Manitoba by means of fascinating dioramas, displays and audio-visual presentations. At the same time it portrays the
great natural regions of the province. Displays are constantly upgraded and increased in
number, thus the description which follows gives only a general idea of the museum.

On entering, the visitor is first struck by the magnificent diorama of a Metis hunter
closing in on a buffalo. The **Earth History Gallery** explains the geological creation of Manitoba.
Then the visitor moves into the specialized galleries.

The first of these, the **Arctic-Subarctic Gallery,** deals with the northernmost part of the
province. A polar bear is shown in the act of killing a seal, caribou are shown picking their
way along a ridge during their fall migration, artifacts and photographs illustrate the inter-
dependency of the northern residents (Caribou Inuit and Chipewyan Indians) with their environment, and there are displays on Hudson Bay marine life and the phenomenon of the
Northern Lights.

The **Boreal Forest Gallery** depicts the relationship of man and nature in this region which
covers about a third of the province. Dioramas present the area's native animals in particular
a wolf family. One impressive "walk-through" diorama shows muskeg, cliffs, a family of
moose, a waterfall and Cree Indians, one of whom is painting symbols on a rock depicting
the religious aspects of the hunt.

The **Grasslands Gallery** is devoted to the southern part of Manitoba. There are interesting
displays on the Assiniboine Indians including a full-size teepee. A log cabin and a sod hut
represent the first buildings erected by white settlers. There is an example of a **Red River
Cart,** a vehicle which screeched continuously in use as the axle joining the wheels was never
oiled because grease would quickly have been clogged by the prairie dust. The gallery also
has interesting displays on the diverse origins both geographical and religious of Manitoba's
population.

A moment in time is captured in the **Urban Gallery.** It is a fall evening in the 1920's and
Winnipeg has survived sudden growth, a world war, a depression and major labour con-
flicts. Time has been preserved in the wooden sidewalks, railway station, shops, restaurant,
rooming house, mission hall and theatre showing period movies.

The highlight of the museum is, however, the **Nonsuch**★★★ a reconstruction of the ship
which sailed from England to Hudson Bay in 1668 in search of furs. The success of this
voyage led to the setting up of the Hudson's Bay Company two years later (p. 74). The
ketch, which was built for the tricentenary of the Company in 1970, is anchored in a
reconstruction of a 17th century Thames River wharf. The wooden houses and the inn set
around the harbour make a very authentic scene.

There is also a **planetarium** *(shows several times daily ; $3.00 ; ☎ 943-3142)* and
changing exhibitions on various aspects of the province.

Ukrainian Cultural Centre ★★. – *Open daily except Mon and hols, 10 am – 4 pm, Sun 2 – 5 pm ; gift shop ;* ☎ *942-0218.*

A visit to this centre, one of the biggest of its kind outside the Ukraine, forms an interesting introduction to the life and cultural background of these people who form the largest minority group in Manitoba and whose influence on the province is very marked. The **museum**★★ *(5th floor)* features exquisite examples of Ukrainian traditional embroidery, wood carving, ceramics and beautifully painted *pysanky* (Easter eggs). The centre also houses an art gallery, library and archives.

Legislative Building★. – *Guided tours daily mid June - Labour Day ; 1/2 hr ;* ☎ *944-3700.*

This beautiful and harmonious building of Neo-Classical revival style stands in an attractive park which is also shared by the residence of Manitoba's Lieutenant-Governor. Completed in 1919, it is built of Manitoba Tyndall limestone in the form of an "H" with a dome at its centre. Above the dome stands the **Golden Boy**, a bronze gold-plated statue cast by Charles Gardet clutching a sheaf of wheat in one hand and holding a torch aloft with the other to symbolize Manitoba's glowing future. Above the building's main entrance *(north side)*, a pediment depicts Canada's motto "From Sea to Sea" – at the centre is Manitoba the keystone province joining east and west. The statues around the building and in the park represent the important figures in Manitoba history – Queen Victoria, Lord Selkirk, the explorer La Vérendrye, George Etienne Cartier, the father of Confederation responsible for the creation of Manitoba, as well as others representing the ethnic origins of the province – the Scots poet Robert Burns, the Icelandic writer Jon Sigurdsson and the Ukrainian poet Taras Shevchenko. Across Assiniboine Avenue stands a very striking modern **monument to Louis Riel** (p. 75).

The main entrance hall of the building opens onto a stairway flanked by two **bronze buffalo,** the province's emblem, also the work of Charles Gardet. The tour enables visitors to see the horseshoe shaped **Legislative Assembly Chamber** and two attractive reception rooms.

Art Gallery★. – *Open daily, closed Mon ; guided tours ; restaurant, cafeteria, gift shop ;* ☎ *786-6641.*

This unusual wedge-shaped structure designed by native Winnipeger Gustavo Da Roza contains a very beautiful art gallery. The permanent collection is large and varied. It is shown in a constantly changing series of exhibitions. The gallery is best known for its collection of Inuit art, a selection of which is always exhibited, and for the Lord and Lady Gort Collection of Gothic and Renaissance panel paintings.

The restaurant overlooks an attractive sculpture garden on the roof.

St-Boniface★. – In 1818 Fathers Provencher and Dumoulin arrived from Québec to establish a Roman Catholic mission on the banks of the Red River. They were followed by other French Canadians who made, with the largely French-speaking Metis, a numerous and lively French community. St-Boniface was incorporated into the City of Winnipeg in 1972 but it retains its distinctive French character. Every February a **Festival du Voyageur** is held celebrating the early fur traders with French Canadian food, dancing and outdoor activities.

Museum★ **(M).** – *Open daily ;* ☎ *247-4500.*

This attractive frame structure of white oak was built for the Grey Nuns in 1848 which makes it the oldest building in Winnipeg. Inside, there are scenes portraying the work of this religious order and mementos of St-Boniface residents especially Louis Riel.

Cathedral. – Six churches have stood on this site since 1818. The fifth of these was largely destroyed by fire in 1968, except for its large white stone facade. This stands immediately in front of the new cathedral which has an attractive wooden interior. In the cemetery lies the **grave of Louis Riel** and across the Red River is a **view** of downtown Winnipeg.

Dalnavert. – *Open daily except Mon, Fri and hols ; $2.00 ; guided tours 1 hr ;* ☎ *943-2835.*

This large red brick Victorian house was built in 1895 by Sir Hugh John Macdonald, only son of Sir John A. Macdonald, Canada's first Prime Minister *(p. 108)*. At the time of its construction, Dalnavert was very avant-garde with electric lighting, indoor plumbing, central hot water heating and walk-in closets. Today, beautifully restored, it reflects the life of this wealthy but philanthropic politician (Federal Member of Parliament 1891-99, Premier of Manitoba 1899-1900) who reserved part of his basement as a lodging for hobos.

■ **ADDITIONAL SIGHTS**

The Mint★. – *Trans-Canada Hwy at Hwy 59. Open weekdays ;* ☎ *257-3359.*

This branch of the Royal Canadian Mint is housed in a spectacular half-pyramid structure of rose-coloured reflecting glass. Inside there are fountains and exotic plants surrounding a coin collection and displays on the history of coinage in Canada. The process of minting coins is also viewed.

WINNIPEG★★★

Riel House. – 330 River Rd, St. Vital. National Historic Park. Open daily mid May - mid Oct ; ☎ 257-1783.

This tiny house of post on sill construction was built 1880-81 by the Riel family who lived in it until 1968. Although Louis Riel (p. 75) never actually resided there, his body lay in state in it after his execution in November 1885. It has been meticulously restored to reflect the period immediately after his death. An interpretive display on the Riel family stands outside.

Seven Oaks House. – 127 Rupertsland Ave E. Guided tours daily mid June - Labour Day, weekends mid May - mid June ; 3/4 hr ; $1.00 ; ☎ 339-7429.

This nine room log house, built 1851-53 by John Inkster, a wealthy merchant, is believed to be the oldest remaining habitable house in Manitoba. It lies in the parish of West Kildonan, part of the original Selkirk settlement, and near the site of the Seven Oaks Massacre of 1816 (p. 93). Inkster's store and post office stand beside the house. Both are furnished with period pieces.

Zoo. – In Assiniboine Park. Open daily 10 am - dusk ; refreshments ; ☎ 888-3634.

This large and pleasant zoo has a **Tropical House** home to monkeys and birds, and full of exotic plants.

EXCURSIONS

Lower Fort Garry★★. – 32 km - 20 miles N of Winnipeg by Rte 9. National Historic Park. Open daily ; $1.25 ; restaurant ; ☎ 482-6843.

Also accessible by cruises down Red River ; daily May - Oct ; $10.75 ; ☎ 669-2824 for details ; or by paddlewheeler daily July and Aug ; weekends May - Sept ; ☎ 589-4318.

This stone fort was built between 1831 and 1847 by the Hudson's Bay Company to replace their previous district headquarters, Upper Fort Garry (p. 93), which was regularly subjected to flooding. It remained an important trading post for the Company until 1911. Trading goods were transported to it from the Company's warehouse at York Factory on Hudson Bay (map p. 127) by means of a vessel called a **York boat**. These wooden hulled boats were much larger and more unwieldy than canoes but they could be sailed across lakes. There is an example of a York boat in the fort and also a Red River cart (p. 94). The fort has been restored to reflect life during its heyday in the mid 19th century.

A visit begins at the Visitor Reception Centre where an **audio-visual presentation** (20 min) forms a good introduction. The fort itself is surrounded by stone walls. At its centre stands a large and gracious stone house with high chimneys. This was built to house the offices of the governor as well as be his residence. Nearby stand the trading store and warehouse. A wide range of goods are on display, note particularly the **furloft** with its splendid collection of furs.

Mennonite Village Museum. – 61 km - 38 miles SE of Winnipeg by Hwys 1 and 12, just N of Steinbach. Open daily May - Sept ; $2.00 ; cafeteria ; ☎ 326-9661.

This village explains the life of the first Mennonites who settled in Manitoba about 1874. There is a farmhouse built in characteristic style with kitchen and stove in the centre, so that all the rooms were heated, and a barn on one end. Other buildings include a church, school and windmill. A museum displays pioneer artifacts and a map of the various Mennonite migrations. The cafeteria serves Mennonite specialities.

The Manitoba Mennonites. – There are two sets of Mennonites in Canada : the Pennsylvanian Dutch of Ontario and the Russian Mennonites of the West. Both groups are descended from the Protestant sect led by **Menno Simons** and both are extreme pacifists refusing to fight in any war. Persecuted in 17th century Europe, some fled to the United States and some to Russia. Meeting persecution again, some of the American ones moved to Ontario and the Russian ones to Manitoba. The sect numbers approximately 170 000 in Canada, 60 000 of whom live in Manitoba, 40 000 in Ontario (see Kitchener p. 110), the remainder scattered throughout the other provinces.

Train Trip to Hudson Bay. – Description p. 77.

Prairie Dog Central. – Steam train to Grosse Isle. Description p. 77.

YORKTON Saskatchewan

Map p. 7 – Pop 15 339

This city on the Yellowhead Highway was first settled by farmers from York County, Ontario. They were soon followed by a wide variety of other nationalities but especially by Ukrainians. Today, agricultural equipment is manufactured in Yorkton and there are stock-yards and poultry marketing plants.

Western Development Museum. – Hwy 16 on W side of City. Open daily ; $1.50 ; ☎ (306) 783-8361.

The Yorkton branch of this museum is devoted to the various ethnic groups who have made up the province especially the Yorkton area. There are interesting displays on the local Indian tribes, on the Metis, and dioramas of various pioneer homes – Ukrainian, German, Swedish, English and American. In addition there is a collection of antique steam and gas traction engines, and a display on Saskatchewan inventions.

ONTARIO

Ontario is Canada's heartland industrially, economically, politically and culturally. It is the country's most populous province (8.6 million inhabitants) and its richest. It encompasses a wide variety of scenery, stretching as it does from the Great Lakes in the south to Hudson Bay in the north. The vast majority of its natural beauty spots are connected with water, not surprisingly in a province which has nearly 200 000 sq km - 70 000 sq miles of lakes. Indeed, the name *Ontario* derives from an Iroquois Indian word meaning shining waters.

DESCRIPTION

A Land Shaped by Glaciers. – When the last ice age which covered much of North America receded about 10 000 years ago, it left the region which is now Ontario scarred, marked and completely reshaped. Great holes had been gouged out of the earth which gradually filled with water, and over much of the land the geological core of the continent was revealed. These Precambrian rocks (beween 600 million and 3 billion years old), known as the **Canadian Shield,** are still today exposed over a large part of the province. Only in the extreme south and in the north are they covered with sedimentary deposits which allow a landscape other than one of rock, water and trees precariously clinging to the rocks, so typical of the Shield.

The Great Lakes. – These vast expanses of fresh water are one of the most extraordinary legacies of the glaciers. **Lake Superior,** the biggest, deepest and coldest of the lakes, was created before the Ice Ages by a fault in the Canadian Shield but the other four (Lakes **Huron, Michigan, Erie** and **Ontario**) were formed by erosion of the original sediment over millions of years. With each advance and retreat of the glaciers, their basins were reshaped. At one time, they drained south to the Gulf of Mexico. Today, their waters flow northeast down the St. Lawrence to the Atlantic. All but one of them (Michigan) border Ontario giving the province a freshwater shoreline of 3 800 km - 2 360 miles and in great measure determining its climate.

The North. – Ontario is often divided into two by a line from the Ottawa River to Georgian Bay via Lake Nipissing *(map p. 98).* The large region to the north of this line, always referred to as "Northern Ontario", is very sparsely populated except around the exploited mineral deposits in which the area is rich *(p. 100).* The land rarely rises above 460 m - 1 500 ft except for a few rocky ridges near Lake Superior. It is an unproductive region agriculturally although there are a few farms in the clay belt between Lake Timiskaming and Cochrane. The region does however provide a large harvest of wood for the pulp and paper mills and its many lakes make it a sportsman's paradise.

The South. – The smaller region south of the Ottawa River - Georgian Bay dividing line is the most densely populated and industrial part of Canada especially the area at the western end of Lake Ontario which is known as the **Golden Horseshoe** *(see Toronto, p. 130).* Approximately a third of the region lies directly on the Canadian Shield. This is the picturesque rocky, tree-covered terrain full of lakes which the **Group of Seven** made so famous *(p. 139).* This section of the Shield cuts the rest of southern Ontario into two. East of it lies a small agricultural triangle in the forks of the Ottawa and St. Lawrence Rivers. To the west, are the fertile farmlands of the **Niagara Peninsula** and the region called southwestern Ontario. Once this was hardwood forest where maple, beech, walnut, elm and ash trees flourished. But today these have been replaced by intensive agriculture in Canada's most southerly region and thus most favourable climatically.

Climate. – There are wide variations in the climate of this region. Northern Ontario experiences long, bright but cold winters and sunny summers with hot days and cool nights. In the south, the winters are less severe due to the moderating influence of the Great Lakes. The summers are also longer than in the north but much more humid, again due to the Great Lakes. The mean maximum temperatures in July are : Ottawa 27 ℃ - 80 ℉, Toronto 27 ℃ – 81 ℉, Thunder Bay 23 ℃ - 74 ℉. In January they are : Ottawa –6 ℃ – 21 ℉, Toronto

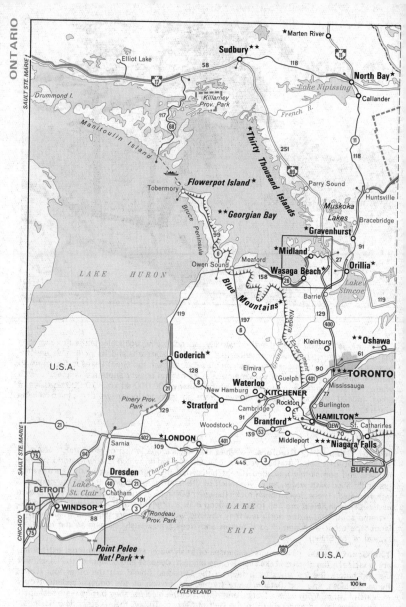

This map does not show the whole of Ontario but only the section with the most sights of tourist interest. Refer also to the Map of Principal Sights pp. 8-9.

–1 °C – 31 °F, Thunder Bay –8 °C – 17 °F (Kapuskasing away from the influence of Lake Superior registers similar July temperatures to Thunder Bay but experiences a January mean maximum of –12 °C – 10 °F).

The amount of precipitation received varies over the province (660 - 1 016 mm - 26-40 ins) but it is evenly distributed throughout the year in most regions and it includes 200-250 cm - 80-100 ins of snow in the north. July rainfall is about 100 mm - 4 ins in Ottawa and 76 mm - 3 ins in Toronto and Thunder Bay. The number of frost free days varies from 179 on the Point Pelee peninsula in the south to 60 on the shores of Hudson Bay.

HISTORICAL BACKGROUND

Before the White Man. – Northern Ontario was inhabited by Indians of the sub-Arctic culture whose subsistence lifestyle in a meagre environment was similar to that of the tribes in the Northwest Territories *(p. 230)*. The south, on the other hand, was the realm of Indians of the Algonkian and Iroquoian language groups commonly known as the **Eastern Woodlands culture** *(map p. 15)*. These tribes generally lived a fairly sedentary life in organized villages around which fields of beans, corn and squash were cultivated. No crop rotation was practised, thus every ten or so years when the land was exhausted, the village was moved to a new site. The men also hunted and fished extensively, travelling by birchbark canoe in summer, by snowshoe and toboggan in winter but they never spent long away from their palisaded villages. They lived in large rectangular huts made of a framework of poles covered with hides. These **long houses** accommodated several families, each having their own fireplace and sleeping platform (some of the Algonkian tribes built circular dome-shaped huts instead of long houses). Clothing was minimal in summer and consisted of deer skin leggings, fur robes and moccasins in winter.

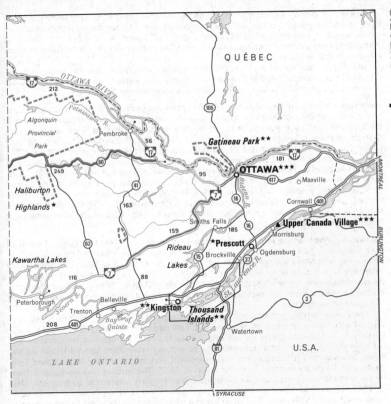

The roads outlined in green are particularly attractive to follow.

Iroquoian society was matrilineal (descent was from the mother) and the women of these tribes wielded considerable power, among other things selecting the chiefs who were men. Algonkian society, on the other hand, was patrilineal. Both groups were rich in religion and mythology. The Iroquoian **False Face Society** performed dances in elaborate masks of wood and real hair usually to frighten away disease or other evils. Many of these tribes were extremely warlike. The **Iroquois Confederacy,** which was made up of six tribes (Mohawk, Onondaga, Seneca, Cayuga, Oneida and Tuscarora), tried repeatedly to wipe out the early French settlers and succeeded in destroying the Hurons, another Iroquoian group.

Today, little remains of this way of life and most Indians live on reservations.

Part of New France. – The region that is now Ontario was criss-crossed by most of the French explorers of the 17th and 18th centuries. **Etienne Brulé** was the first to visit it *(p. 130)* but he was soon followed by **Champlain** himself *(p. 144)*, **Radisson** and **Groseilliers** in their search for a route to Hudson Bay, **Marquette** and **Jolliet** in their search for a river flowing west from Lake Superior, and **Lasalle** on his famous trip down the Mississippi. The fur trade was the main reason for this exploration and trading posts were set up all over the province. There were also two attempts at permanent settlement. In 1639, the **Jesuits** established a mission on the shores of Georgian Bay to convert the Hurons to Christianity. This only lasted until 1650 because of the fierce attacks of the Iroquois who captured and martyred five of the Jesuit fathers *(p. 104)*. Then in the early 18th century, farms were laid out on the shores of the Detroit River in the southwest of the province. At the time of the fall of New France *(p. 175)*, there were about 400 people living there.

Meanwhile, the **Hudson's Bay Company** *(p. 74)* was establishing itself in the north of the province. A post was founded at **Moosonee** on James Bay in 1673 which justly claims to be Ontario's oldest settlement *(p. 101)*. Despite these attempts, Ontario, or Upper Canada as it was known, was still very much the realm of the Indians at the time of the American Revolution.

The Arrival of the Loyalists. – When the thirteen American colonies rebelled against British rule in 1775, there were many people who refused to join the rebels. These people known as Loyalists as they remained loyal to King George III or Tories because they resisted change, may have numbered 1 1/4 million or a third of the population. As the revolutionary war ended, they found themselves very unpopular and most were forced to leave their homes and flee for their lives. Some were tarred and feathered, others were imprisoned, yet others found their land confiscated despite Washington's assurances to the British government that they would be fairly treated when the war ended. Indeed several states passed laws saying that anyone who had helped the British could neither own land nor vote.

It has been estimated that about 80 000 of these Loyalists finally settled in Canada - in Nova Scotia, New Brunswick, Prince Edward Island, the Eastern Townships of Québec *(p. 150)*, the St. Lawrence Valley and the Niagara Peninsula. They also went to England itself and the West Indies but Canada was popular because they were promised free land. Among the Loyalists in Ontario were Indians of the **Six Nations Iroquois Confederacy** who had fought for the British under their great chief, Joseph Brant *(p. 103)*. These Indians and other disbanded soldiers were known as **United Empire Loyalists** because they had actually fought for the British as opposed to the regular Loyalists who had just supported the King's cause.

The arrival of such a great number of people, one of the largest mass movements of the time, created a province of Upper Canada almost overnight. A separate administration was set up in 1791 in Niagara-on-the-Lake and then in Toronto. And, although many more immigrants have settled in Ontario since this date, the influence of the descendants of these Loyalists is still strong in Ontario today.

Meanwhile, the waters and lakes of the province were alive with the brigades of fur traders of both Hudson's Bay and North West Companies. Indeed, the latter set up its great rendezvous point at Fort William on Lake Superior *(see Thunder Bay p. 127)*.

American Invasion Repulsed. – In 1812, the Americans, infuriated by British high-handedness on the high seas, declared war and invaded Canada in the hope of taking it quickly while the British were preoccupied fighting Napoleon in Europe. They were also sure that the inhabitants would rush to join their standard. Instead they found the population of Upper Canada united in its dislike of the United States, if not in its loyalty to Britain. The war was fought mainly in Upper Canada. There was much fighting in the Niagara Peninsula where **Isaac Brock** and **Laura Secord** engraved their names in Canadian history *(p. 113)*. There were naval encounters on the Great Lakes during which Toronto was looted and burned *(p. 130)*. There was also fighting along the St. Lawrence particularly at Crysler's Farm *(p. 141)* and also in the province of Québec at Châteauguay *(p. 173)*. Battles were often indecisive but the Americans were kept out of Canada, and in Ontario at least a sense of nationhood was born.

Increased Population and Responsible Government. – Another result of the war was that the British government decided to encourage immigration to Upper Canada to bolster the population against possible future American attack. Free land was offered and, since this was a time of great economic distress in Britain, approximately 1 1/2 million people crossed the Atlantic 1820-40 for a better life in Ontario. Towns, villages and farms sprang up where there had previously just been bush and the face of the province was changed immeasurably.

These new settlers brought not only their industry but also their political ideas with them. Fresh from a struggle to promote electoral reform in England, they found Canada backward. Real political power lay not with the elected assembly but with the Governor and his council. This council was dominated by several well-connected groups known as the **Family Compact** *(p. 130)*. Opposition to this system was led by a fiery Scot, **William Lyon Mackenzie** who finally resorted to armed revolt in 1837. The uprising was quickly put down by the colonial authorities but it did persuade Britain to grant responsible government. Thus in 1841, Upper and Lower Canada were reunited in a sort of confederation with equal representation for both parts. This union led to a movement to unite all the British colonies in North America led by an Ontario politician, **John A. Macdonald** *(p. 108)* and his Québec colleague George Etienne Cartier *(p. 165)*. When this was achieved in 1867, Upper Canada officially took the name of Ontario.

Since Confederation, Ontario has grown enormously in population, drawing immigrants from all over the world. This factor added to its abundant natural resources and strategic location in relation to the rest of Canada and the United States, led to its rapid industrial development and its pre-eminence in Canada today.

RESOURCES AND INDUSTRIES

Agriculture. – Farming of various types has been practised in Ontario since earliest times and it is still an important activity today. The southern part of the province boasts some of the richest soil in Canada as well as the longest frost-free season. Dairy farming and its attendant products (cheese, butter, eggs) is the predominant activity in the southeast corner, along the shores of Lake Ontario and in the Upper Thames valley. Other livestock are raised in the Georgian Bay - Upper Grand River region. Tobacco is the predominant crop in the southwest but crops such as corn, sugar beet, soybeans and other vegetables are also grown. The section of the Niagara Peninsula on the shores of Lake Ontario sheltered by the Niagara Escarpment is Canada's most important **fruit-growing** region. Not only are peaches, cherries, strawberries and grapes grown but a **wine-making** industry thrives.

Mining. – No other province is as rich in minerals as Ontario. It is the world's largest supplier of nickel, and a major producer of gold, silver, platinum, uranium, zinc, copper, iron and a range of structural materials. Also, it is an important source of salt, gypsum, and nepheline syenite, and it produces more non-fuel minerals for commercial use than any other province.

The vast majority of these minerals come from the Canadian Shield which covers much of Ontario. The **Sudbury Basin**, the largest producing area of nickel in the world, was first discovered in 1883 during the building of the Canadian Pacific Railway *(p. 126)*. In 1982, nickel from Sudbury accounted for 71 % of Canada's total production, most of which was exported to the United States. Platinum, copper, cobalt, silver, gold, sulphur, and tellurium are also extracted from the ore.

In 1903 not long after the discovery at Sudbury, the great **silver** deposits of Cobalt were found, again during the building of a railway. This was followed by the location of the significant **gold** mines of the Porcupine - Kirkland Lake - Timmins region. Gold was also found at Red Lake to the west and iron ore at Wawa which was taken to Sault Ste. Marie for smelting. During the Second World War, the iron ore deposits of Atikokan were also developed and the end of the war saw a huge mining boom in the province. In the 1950s, the vast **Manitouwadge** field of copper, zinc and silver deposits was exploited and the uranium of Elliot Lake was tapped for the first time. In the 1960s, the Porcupine-Kirkland Lake region was revived by zinc, copper, lead and iron finds to replace the exploited gold. Most notable was the Kidd Creek copper-zinc-silver discovery, which is the richest in the world. Recent gold discoveries at Detour Lake and Hemlo continue to demonstrate the wealth of the Shield.

Not all of Ontario's minerals, however, are found in the Shield. Southwestern Ontario has produced a small amount of oil and gas since 1859. **Salt** is mined extensively at Goderich *(p. 105)*, and gypsum and a range of structural materials are found in sizable quantities. Altogether, mining is an essential base of Ontario's economy and this is reflected by the number of mining interests listed on the Toronto Stock Exchange.

Forestry, Fishing, Furs and Hydro-Electricity. – These four resources add a small but not insignificant amount to Ontario's economy. The province is still largely covered with forest despite serious depletion of this resource in the last century. Today, pulp, paper and sawn lumber are the main products and Ontario ranks third after British Columbia and Québec in the value of production. On the other hand, the province leads the rest of Canada in the value of fish taken from inland waters thanks to the Great Lakes. Fur production, the province's oldest industry, is still carried on both by trapping and fur farms.

The development of hydro power has gone hand-in-hand with the province's total growth this century especially as there is little oil, gas or coal. The harnessing of the Niagara River, the St. Lawrence and many others were essential for industrial development, and today Ontario ranks third, again after Québec and British Columbia in its exploited hydro-electric power.

Manufacturing. – Nearly 50 % of Canada's total output of finished goods comes from Ontario. It is by far and away the province's biggest industry and it is what has made Ontario Canada's industrial heart. Motor vehicles and parts rank first in production value, but also important are the production of heavy electrical machinery, agricultural implements, rubber, iron, steel and chemical goods, printing and publishing, food processing, etc. Most of this industry is concentrated in the Golden Horseshoe around Toronto and Hamilton, which is Canada's largest marketing area and which ranks high as an industrial region over the whole of North America. This is partly due to Hamilton's vast primary iron and steel industry. Other important industrial regions are : Windsor (motor vehicles), Sarnia (petro-chemicals) and Sault Ste. Marie (iron and steel).

St. Lawrence Seaway. – Cheap water transportation on this system of lakes, rivers and canals (see also Montréal, p. 170) has been of unparalleled importance to the development of Ontario. Raw materials are transported to smelters and factories, finished products are taken to markets. It is not only the sea-going nature of the system which is important. The heaviest traffic is between the Upper Lakes - the locks at Sault Ste. Marie for example are busier than the Panama Canal.

SPORTS AND OUTDOOR ACTIVITIES

Map pp. 98-99

Ontario's enormous number of lakes, its fine resorts and its scenery make it unequalled vacation land. **Georgian Bay** (p. 104), the **Muskoka Lakes** (p. 106), the **Haliburton Highlands** (p. 106), the **Kawartha Lakes** and the **Thousand Islands** area of the St.Lawrence (p. 109) all offer splendid facilities for boating, camping and outdoors activities. Two popular routes to follow by boat are the **Rideau Canal** and **Lakes** from Ottawa to Kingston, and the **Trent - Severn system** from Trenton on Lake Ontario to Georgian Bay via the Kawartha Lakes and Lake Simcoe. For details on these routes contact Ontario Travel (p. 102).

Canoeing. – All over Ontario, canoeing is a major activity. There are dozens of outfitters and a wide variety of water from calm lakes to wild, fast-flowing rivers. The best known regions are in **Algonquin Park** which has 1 600 km - 1 000 miles of canoe routes and in **Quetico Provincial Park** (map p. 8) which is similarly well endowed, and through which the Boundary Waters Fur Trade Canoe Route passes (523 km - 325 miles with 43 portages). Details of this and other routes can be obtained from Ontario Travel.

For those who would like to experience white water without the responsibility of being in their own boat, **Wilderness Tours** of Beachburg, near Pembroke, offer thrilling roller coaster rides down the rapids of the Ottawa River in large rubber rafts (May - Sept ; for details contact Box 89, Beachburg, Ontario K0J 1C0 - ☎ 582-3351 ; advance reservations required). There are also outdoors specialists who teach all season travel and survival in Ontario's northland (contact Ontario Travel).

Hiking, Fishing and Winter Sports. – There are many organized hiking trails in Ontario, the most famous of which is the **Bruce Trail**. This follows the Niagara Escarpment for 692 km - 430 miles across the southern part of the province (map pp. 98-99). A very different type of hiking is offered along the Coastal Trail of wild and remote **Pukaskwa National park** (map p. 9) on the shores of Lake Superior.

Ontario is also a fisherman's paradise especially in the north away from the bustle of the southern waterways. All non-residents must have licenses which are available from most sporting goods stores or from the *Ministry of Natural Resources, Parliament Buildings, Queen's Park, Toronto M7A 1W3.* The Ministry can also give information on seasons, catch and possession limits.

Like every other region of Canada, Ontario offers a great deal in the way of winter sports. There are a wide range of snowmobile and cross-country ski trails (details from Ontario Travel) and even a few excellent alpine ski centres (Thunder Bay, Blue Mountains area near Collingwood and Calabogie west of Ottawa) despite the general flatness of the terrain.

Special Excursions. – In July and August, the **Polar Bear Express** makes all day excursions to Moosonee on James Bay from Cochrane (daily except Fri ; map p. 9). This is an exciting train trip down the Arctic watershed across bushland and muskeg. Sufficient time is allowed to visit the Hudson's Bay Company post in Moose Factory (on an island in the Moose River) which was founded in 1673 making it one of Ontario's oldest settlements. *For details contact the Ontario Northland Transportation Commission, 805 Bay St, Toronto M5S 1Y9 - ☎ 965-4268.*

In summer, the National Capital Commission organizes **steam train excursions** from Ottawa to Wakefield, Québec (July - Oct, Wed and Sun ; all day trip from National Museum of Science and Technology p. 121 ; ☎ 992-4401).

A few recommended books are given at the
end of each regional introduction.

PRINCIPAL FESTIVALS

March	Elmira	Maple Syrup Festival
April – May	Guelph	Spring Festival of Arts and Music
May	Ottawa	Festival of Spring
May	Niagara Falls	Blossom Festival
May	New Hamburg (near Kitchener)	Mennonite Auction Relief Sale
May - Oct	Niagara-on-the-Lake	Shaw Festival (p. 114)
June - Oct	Stratford	Stratford Festival (p. 126)
June	Toronto	International Caravan (p. 131)
June – July	Windsor	International Freedom Festival
July	Ottawa	Festival Ottawa (p. 117)
July	Thunder Bay	Great Rendezvous Pageant (p. 128)
August	St. Catharines	Royal Canadian Henley Regatta
August	Brantford	Six Nations Indian Pageant (p. 103)
August	Maxville	Glengarry Highland Games
July - August	Toronto	Caribana (p. 131)
August	Ottawa	Central Canada Exhibition
August	Manitoulin Island	Wikwemikong Indian Pow-Wow
August	Sudbury	Rockhound Festival (p. 127)
Aug - Sept	Toronto	Canadian National Exhibition (p. 131)
September	St. Catharines	Niagara Grape and Wine Festival
Sept - Oct	Muskoka Lakes Region	Muskoka Cavalcade of Colour
October	Kitchener - Waterloo	Oktoberfest (p. 110)
November	Toronto	Royal Agricultural Winter Fair

PRACTICAL INFORMATION

Accommodation and Road Maps. – The government of Ontario produces an annually updated guide called **Ontario Accommodation,** and also a list of campgrounds. These are available free of charge, with a regularly updated road map, from most tourist bureaus or from :

    Ontario Travel, Queen's Park, Toronto, Ontario M7A 2E1 ; ☎ (416) 965-4008.

Road Regulations. – Ontario has an excellent road system which is well maintained winter and summer. Drivers of vehicles and all passengers must wear seat belts if the vehicle is equipped with them. Speed limits unless otherwise marked are :
    highways : 100 km - 62 mph   other roads : 80 km - 50 mph

Time Zones. – Most of Ontario is on Eastern Standard Time with daylight saving of 1 hour in force in the summer. The small section of the province west of Longitude 90° is on Central Standard with Manitoba (map p. 20).

Taxes. – A sales tax of 7 % is levied on all items except foods. There is a 5 % tax on hotel bills and a 10 % tax on restaurant bills over $6.00.

Liquor Laws. – Liquor, wine and beer can only be consumed publicly on licensed premises. On Sundays, liquor and wine can only be consumed with food. Liquor and wine are available from stores of the Liquor Control Board, beer is available from Brewers' Retail outlets. Domestic wine (produced in Ontario) can be bought at retail wine stores. The legal drinking age is 19.

BOOKS TO READ

Toronto - No Mean City by Eric Arthur   *(University of Toronto Press)*

Georgian Bay - the Sixth Great Lake by James Barry   *(Clarke, Irwin)*

The Niagara Escarpment by W. Gillard and T. Tooke   *(University of Toronto Press)*

Ottawa Waterway - Gateway to a Continent by Robert Legget   *(University of Toronto Press)*

The Invasion of Canada 1812-13 by Pierre Berton   *(McClelland and Stewart)*

Roughing it in the Bush by Susannah Moodie   *(McClelland and Stewart)* First published 1852.

Sunshine Sketches of a Little Town by Stephen Leacock   *(McClelland and Stewart)* FICTION.

The Man from Glengarry by Ralph Connor   *(McClelland and Stewart)* FICTION.

BRANTFORD ★

Maps pp. 9 and 98 - Pop 74 315 - Tourist Office 77 Charlotte Street ; ☎ (519) 753-2617

This manufacturing city stands on what was once part of a grant of land in the valley of the Grand River given to the Six Nations Indians *(p. 99)* in 1784 by the British government. Led by their chief, **Joseph Brant,** these Indians had fought on the British side in the American Revolution and were thus treated like the other Loyalists at the end of the war and forced to flee from the United States. To show his personal gratitude to his Indian subjects, George III provided the money for the construction of a chapel known as **Her Majesty's Chapel of the Mohawks** (it is of course "His" if the monarch is male). This chapel is the oldest Protestant church in Ontario *(on Mohawk St, 3 km - 2 miles SE by Greenwich St. Open daily July and Aug ; weekends only April - Oct).*

White settlers purchased land from the Indians in 1830 and the present city was founded keeping the old name of the location - Brant's ford, because the chief had crossed the river there. The Indian reserve still exists to the south, though much reduced in size. It is the scene every year of the **Six Nations Indian Pageant** in which the Iroquois tribes re-enact their history and culture *(first 3 weekends of Aug).*

The Telephone City. - Brantford is also famous for being the family home of the inventor of the telephone - **Alexander Graham Bell** (1847-1922). The young Bell moved to Ontario from Scotland with his parents in 1870. Soon afterwards he took a job as a teacher of the deaf in Boston, a profession he shared with his father. It was while trying to find a means of reproducing sounds visibly for the benefit of his deaf pupils that he solved the problem of transmitting and receiving speech along an electrified wire. From this the telephone developed, an idea he conceived in Brantford in 1874 while on vacation with his parents and which he tested in Boston the next year. The first "long distance" call was also made from Brantford when Bell in Paris, Ontario *(about 11 km - 7 miles to the northwest),* picked up the voice of his father.

The invention of the telephone made Bell's fortune and enabled him to devote himself to many fields of research in addition to his work for the deaf. Much of this research was carried out at his summer home in Baddeck, Nova Scotia *(p. 195).*

■ SIGHTS *time : 3 hours*

Bell Homestead ★. - *94 Tutela Heights Rd. From downtown take Colborne St W across Grand River, turn left on Mount Pleasant St and left again on Tutela Heights Rd. Open daily mid June - Labour Day ; closed Mon rest of year ; National Historic Park ;* ☎ *756-6220.*

This pleasant white house with its covered verandah is furnished much as it would have been in Bell's day with many original pieces. There is an interesting display on his life, inventions and research.

Next door it stands a smaller clapboard structure moved to this spot from the centre of Brantford. Among other things it housed the first telephone business office in Canada. Inside there is an early telephone exchange and displays on the development of the telephone since Bell's day.

Museum of the Woodland Indian. - *In Woodland Indian Cultural and Educational Centre, 184 Mohawk St near Chapel - see above. Open daily ; 75¢ ;* ☎ *759-2650.*

This museum houses an interesting collection of artifacts depicting the way of life of the Eastern Woodland Indians *(see also p. 98)* of which group the Six Nations Indians are a part.

Chiefswood. - *11 km - 7 miles E by Hwy 54 in Chiefswood Park on Indian reservation. Guided tours mid May - Labour Day, Mon - Fri and hols ; 30 min ; 75¢ ;* ☎ *752-1329.*

This house was erected in 1853 by Chief Johnson for his English bride, Emily Howells. It was the birthplace of his daughter, the poetess **Pauline Johnson** (1861-1913). She travelled extensively in North America giving recitals of her verse in Indian costume and gaining for herself the title of "Mohawk Princess". Her collected poems **Flint and Feather** and a volume of prose **Legends of Vancouver,** a city where she lived for some years, are her best known works.

The house, furnished in 1870s style, displays the original manuscripts of some of Miss Johnson's work.

In the peak summer season, you may have difficulty finding hotel accommodation. We advise you to make reservations in advance.

DRESDEN

Map p. 98 - Pop 2 550

The country around this small manufacturing centre was first settled by black slaves who had escaped their masters in the United States and fled to freedom in British North America. Among them was **Josiah Henson** who arrived in Ontario with his family in 1830. With the aid of donations from Britain, Henson purchased land in the Dresden area, established a refuge for fugitives from slavery and founded a school to teach the children the skills their parents had never learned. Unable to write, Henson dictated the story of his life *(The Life of Josiah Henson - formerly a slave)* which was subsequently published. This manuscript so much impressed **Harriet Beecher Stowe** that she met him and used him as the model for her novel *Uncle Tom's Cabin.*

Uncle Tom's Cabin Museum ★. - *1.6 km - 1 mile W off Hwy 21. Open daily May - Oct ; $2.50 ; snack bar ; souvenir shop ;* ☎ *(519) 683-2978.*

This collection of wooden buildings includes Josiah Henson's house (Uncle Tom's Cabin), a simple church where Henson preached, a fugitive slave's house and some agricultural buildings. In the museum there are posters advertising slave sales, a ball and chain which some slaves were forced to wear to prevent their escaping, slave whips, handcuffs, clubs, etc. A recorded commentary explains the exhibits and tells Henson's story. His grave is outside.

GEORGIAN BAY ★★

Maps pp. 9 and 98 – *Local map below*

This huge bay, named for George IV of England, is almost a lake in itself cut off as it is from the rest of Lake Huron by the Bruce Peninsula and Manitoulin Island. Its eastern and northern shorelines are wild and rocky with numerous indentations and literally thousands of islands some of them mere slabs of rock with perhaps a few wind-swept pines or other hardy plants maintaining a precarious hold. This is the landscape immortalized by the Group of Seven *(p. 139)*. The western and part of the southern shores of the bay form a section of the **Niagara Escarpment,** a ridge of limestone with one gentle rolling slope and one steep escarpment which crosses Ontario from Niagara Falls, mounts the Bruce Peninsula, is submerged then surfaces again to form Manitoulin and other islands and finally peters out in Wisconsin.

As a complete contrast to these rocky shores, the coast along the western side of the Midland peninsula has long sandy stretches, especially in the region of Wasaga Beach. This variety makes Georgian Bay a popular area to visit. Many summer cottages line its shores and islands, and it is most attractive sailing and boating country. It is more than a resort area, however, as Owen Sound, Collingwood, Midland, Port McNicoll and Parry Sound are fair-sized ports with grain elevators and considerable light industry, including ship-building in Collingwood.

Huronia. – Etienne Brulé, one of Champlain's young men *(p. 130)*, visited Georgian Bay in 1610. He was soon followed along the 1 300 km - 800 mile canoe route from Québec by fur traders and the Jesuits, the latter being eager to convert the Huron Indians to Christianity. In 1639 they built a mission post called Sainte-Marie near the present site of Midland. But at this time the Hurons were suffering frequent attacks from the Iroquois tribes to the south *(p. 99)* and weakened as they were from the "white man's diseases", they were unable to resist the onslaught. Caught in the middle, several of the Jesuit fathers were killed after suffering indescribable tortures and this led to the decision to abandon Sainte-Marie in 1649. With the Jesuits back in Québec and the Hurons almost wiped out by the Iroquois, the area saw many years of peace. Then in the early 19th century warfare erupted again, this time between British and Americans over control of the Great Lakes. With peace, the present borders were established and the region has seen no fighting since.

■ HISTORICAL SIGHTS

Midland★. – Pop 12 132. This busy city on the bay is well known for its attractions of historical interest.

Sainte-Marie among the Hurons★★. – *5 km - 3 miles E on Hwy 12. Open daily mid May - mid Oct ; guided tours ; $2.00 ; suggested time for visit 1/2 day ; ☎ (705) 526-7838.*

This is a reconstruction of the mission established by the Jesuits in 1639 and destroyed by them before their retreat in 1649. An excellent **film** *(20 min)* explains the background and should be viewed before the rest of the visit. The mission itself consists of twenty two structures of squared timbers inside a wooden palisade. The chapel, forge, sawpit, carpentry shop and residences are "peopled" by students in costume re-creating 17th century life. The mission is divided into separate sections for the Jesuits, their lay workers (called *donnés*) and the Indians. A rectangular bark-covered Long House has been constructed in the Indian section and also a hospital where the Jesuits tended the sick. The **museum★★** explains Sainte-Marie in the context of its times by slide shows and excellent displays on early 17th century Europe, New France, the Jesuits as an organisation, the Hurons, etc.

★*Thirty Thousand Islands* PARRY SOUND
0   10 km
Beausoleil Island   Honey Harbour
Christian Island
★*Penetanguishene*   **Martyrs' Shrine ★**
★*Midland*   *Sainte Marie among the Hurons* ★★   Waubaushene
GEORGIAN BAY
The Blue Mountains ★
Nottawasaga Bay   Elmvale
Wasaga Beach ★
Collingwood
TORONTO   ORILLIA

Beside Sainte-Marie is the **Wye Marsh Wildlife Interpretation Centre** *(open daily mid May - mid Oct)* where nature trails, a boardwalk and an observation tower allow visitors to appreciate the life of a marsh. There are also slide and film shows, and a display hall.

Martyrs' Shrine★. – *5 km - 3 miles E of Midland on Hwy 12 near above. Open daily mid May - mid Oct, 9am - 9pm ; parking $2.00 ; cafeteria ; ☎ (705) 526-6121.*

This twin spired stone church was built in 1926 as a memorial to the eight Jesuit martyrs of New France - Jean de Brébeuf, Gabriel Lalemant, Garnier, Daniel, Chabanel, Jogues, Goupil and de la Lande, who were declared saints in 1930. They were all killed by the Iroquois 1642-49, the first five while they were missionaries at Sainte-Marie. The church has **statues** of Brébeuf and Lalemant on the front portico (the two Jesuits who suffered incredible tortures before death). It has a striking **interior** with wood panelling and a roof of sandalwood from British Columbia which is shaped like a canoe.

From the church, a path leads up the hill past the Stations of the Cross to the Lookout Tower from which there is a good **view★** of the reconstructed mission of Sainte-Marie and Georgian Bay. A panel details the long canoe trek from Québec.

Huron Indian Village★. – *In Little Lake Park on King St. Open daily mid May - mid Oct ; $1.50 ; guided tours in mid summer ; snack bar ;* ☏ *(705) 526-8757.*

This is a replica of a 17th century Huron Indian village *(see also pp. 98 and 111).* There is an introductory **film** *(15 min),* and then the visitor goes inside the wooden palisade where there are examples of the long rectangular bark-covered frame houses in which the Hurons lived communally with skins, plants and herbs hanging to dry. The Medicine Man's house, a sweat bath, storage pits and a canoe-making site can also be visited.

Beside the village in the park is the **Huronia Museum** *(open daily mid May - mid Oct ; $1.50 ;* ☏ *526-2844)* which has a collection of Indian artifacts and pioneer displays.

Penetanguishene★. – Pop 5 315. The southern entrance to this town with its large French-speaking community is guarded by two angels symbolizing the harmony between the two cultures.

Naval and Military Establishments★. – *At end of Church St. Open daily late May - Labour Day ; $1.25 ;* ☏ *(705) 549-8064.*

On a pleasant site above Penetang harbour stands this collection of whitewashed log buildings built by the British in the early 19th century. The War of 1812 persuaded the British that they needed a naval dockyard on the Upper Lakes. The chosen site also became a military base when the former garrison sites at Michilimackinac and Drummond Island *(map p. 98)* were ceded to the United States and the troops were moved to Penetanguishene in 1818. A large number of buildings have been restored and furnished with early 19th century artifacts. These include naval workshops, offices, a storehouse, residences and the original Officers' Quarters built of stone.

Wasaga Beach★. – Pop 4 705. This popular resort is well known for its 14 km - 9 mile stretch of white sand.

Nancy Island Historic Site★. – *In Wasaga Beach Provincial Park, Mosley St off Hwy 92. Open daily late May - Labour Day ; charge for parking $2.50 ; picnic sites ;* ☏ *(705) 429-2516.*

This museum stands on a small island in the Nottawasaga River near its mouth. The island was caused by silt collecting around the hull of a sunken schooner, the **Nancy.** During the War of 1812, the *Nancy* was requisitioned by British forces to act as a supply ship for British military bases. After the American victory at the naval battle of Lake Erie, the *Nancy* was the only British ship left on the Upper Lakes and so she was tracked down and sunk by the Americans while hiding in this spot on the Nottawasaga. Her hull was recovered in 1927 and is now displayed in front of the museum.

This museum and the adjacent theatre explain the history of the *Nancy* and the War of 1812. The 300 year history of Great Lakes navigation is also related by means of ship models, photographs and other displays.

■ NATURAL SIGHTS

Thirty Thousand Islands★. – An excellent means of appreciating the natural beauty of Georgian Bay and its many islands is by taking one of three different boat trips : from **Midland** town dock *(daily June - mid Oct ; reservations* ☏ *526-6701 or 5438) ;* from **Penetanguishene** town dock *(daily mid June - Labour Day ;* ☏ *549-7795) ;* and from **Parry Sound** town dock *(map p. 98 ; daily June - mid Oct ;* ☏ *746-2311).*

Flowerpot Island★. – *Map p. 98. Part of Georgian Bay Islands National Park, Box 28, Honey Harbour, Ontario POE 1EO ;* ☏ *756-2415 ; and Box 189, Tobermory, Ont NOH 2RO ;* ☏ *596-2233. Access : private boat or water taxi from Tobermory ; round trip of island 2 hrs ; $5 - $10 ; camping.*

This tiny island was at one time completely covered by the waters of Lake Huron. The effects of water erosion can be seen by the existence of caves high up in the rocks and by two islets or rock pillars just off the coast known as the **Flowerpots.** These pink and grey pillars have a limestone base which has been eroded, and a harder dolomite top. They stand 15 m - 50 ft and 11 m - 35 ft high and can be closely approached by boat or on foot from the island. The boat trip provides good views of the island and the harbours at Tobermory.

Beausoleil Island, also part of the Georgian Bay Islands National Park, can be reached from Honey Harbour *(private boat or water taxi ; $10 - $15 per car load ; parking charge ; camping).* There are walking trails and an interpretive centre *(open summer afternoons).*

The Blue Mountains★. – *35 km - 22 miles from Collingwood to Meaford by Rte 26.*

This is a pretty drive with the waters of Georgian Bay on one side of the road and the Blue Mountains, the highest part of the Niagara Escarpment, on the other. The Blue Mountain Chairlift *(11 km - 7 miles W of Collingwood on Blue Mountain Park Rd ; daily mid June - mid Oct ;* ☏ *445-0231)* ascends the ridge providing a good **view★** of Georgian Bay.

GODERICH ★

Maps pp. 9 and 98 - Pop 7 322

This town built on a bluff above **Lake Huron** at the point where the Maitland River joins it, was founded in 1828 as the terminus of the Huron Road, a right-of-way built by the **Canada Company** in the early 19th century to encourage settlement. The town has wide tree-lined streets which radiate from a central octagonal square **(Court House Square)** like the spokes of a wheel. It has a sizeable harbour and several industries including rock-salt mining.

Huron County Pioneer Museum. – *110 North St. Open daily April - Oct ; $1.50 ;* ☏ *(519) 524-9610.*

All aspects of pioneer life in the region are explained in this museum. Outside stands a stump puller used by pioneer farmers in clearing their land.

Huron Historic Jail. – *181 Victoria St. Open daily May - Labour Day, weekends Labour Day - Oct ; $1.50 ;* ☏ *(519) 524-6971.*

This unusual 150-year-old octagonal stone structure housed the county jail until 1972. The Governor's house constructed 1901 can also be visited.

GRAVENHURST ★

Maps pp. 9 and 98 - Pop 8 532

This attractive town with its tree-lined streets, elegant houses and Opera House on the main street (now a summer theatre) lies at the southern end of the **Muskoka Lakes**, Ontario's most popular vacation region. Lake Joseph, Lake Rosseau and Lake Muskoka itself, on which Gravenhurst stands, are picturesque bodies of water with indented shorelines and numerous islands. **Boat cruises** from the wharf aboard the **S.S. Segwun** enable visitors to appreciate their beauty and see some of the summer homes along their shores (daily June - mid Oct ; cruises of varying lengths ; ☎ (705) 687-5811).

Birthplace of Dr. Bethune. – Gravenhurst was also, possibly slightly incongruously, the birthplace of Norman Bethune, surgeon, inventor, advocate of socialized medicine and, last but not least, national hero of the Chinese people. Bethune was born in Gravenhurst in 1890, the son of a Presbyterian minister. He studied in Toronto then practised in Detroit where he contracted tuberculosis. Confined to a sanitorium in Saranac Lake, he learned of a little known method of treating tuberculosis by collapsing a lung. He insisted that this operation be performed on himself - and he recovered.

Between 1928 and 1936 he worked as a chest surgeon in Montréal but then, disillusioned at the lack of interest in socialized medicine in Canada, he departed for Spain to fight on the Republican side in the Civil War. There, he set up the first mobile blood transfusion unit to treat soldiers where they fell. In 1938 he went to China and worked alongside the Chinese Communists fighting the Imperial Japanese. He organized a medical service for the Chinese army but died of blood poisoning late in 1939. His unselfish service and dedication to the cause have made him a national legend and hero to the Chinese.

Bethune Memorial House★. – 235 John St. National Historic Park. Guided tours daily except hols in winter ; 20 min ; ☎ (705) 687-4261.

This plain clapboard house has ground floor furnishings typical of the 1890s. The second floor has an **interpretive display**★ on Bethune's life and importance in three languages - English, French and Chinese. This is a popular visit with Chinese diplomats.

HALIBURTON Highlands ★

Maps pp. 9 and 99

Wooded hills and lovely lakes have made the Haliburton Highlands of central Ontario a popular resort area. The small towns of Minden and Haliburton are the chief centres. One popular activity is canoeing because many of the lakes are inter-connected and the rivers flow south to the Kawartha Lakes (map p. 99). To the north is **Algonquin Park**, an impressive wilderness famous for having inspired the painter Tom Thomson (p. 139) and for its web of canoe routes.

Kanawa Canoe Museum★. – In Camp Kandalore 32 km - 20 miles N of Minden by Hwy 35. Open daily mid April - Oct, 9.30am - 5pm ; $2.00 ; ☎ (705) 489-2644.

A series of log buildings houses this fascinating and comprehensive collection of about 600 canoes of all types and construction from all over the continent. There are examples of the different craft used by the various Indian tribes - West Coast dugouts, Inuit kayaks, a Kutenal canoe from central British Columbia, a Mandan Bull boat used by the Prairie Indians to cross rivers, etc. There is a replica of a 28-foot long canot du nord developed by the early fur traders, and several finely crafted canoes made by immigrant artisans. There is even a Reed boat from Lake Titicaca in Peru, a small version of the vessel used by Thor Heyerdahl on his Ra II expedition.

*Use the **Map of Principal Sights** (pp. 4 - 11) and the **Suggested Automobile Tours** (pp. 22 - 27) to help you plan your vacation.*

HAMILTON ★

Maps pp. 9 and 98 - Metro Pop 542 095 - Tourist Office ☎ (416) 526-4222

The city of Hamilton, Canada's Pittsburgh, lies at the extreme western end of Lake Ontario. It has a fine land-locked harbour bounded on the lake side by a sandbar through which a canal has been cut to enable the ships of the Seaway to reach the port with their loads of iron ore for the huge steel mills. This sandbar is crossed by the Burlington Skyway, part of the Queen Elizabeth Way which connects Toronto with Niagara Falls. Hamilton is also set at the foot of and on top of the Niagara Escarpment (p. 104) which swings around the end of Lake Ontario at this point rising steeply to 76 m - 250 ft in the city. Known locally as the "mountain", it provides pleasant parks and views.

City Centre★. – Hamilton has a very modern downtown area (along Main St between Bay and James Sts) with many attractive buildings, in particular City Hall **(H)**, the Education Centre, the Art Gallery and Hamilton Place, a cultural centre with two theatres. A few blocks west is **Hess Village**★ (junction Hess and George Sts), a collection of attractive older homes now containing boutiques, restaurants and cafes in the Yorkville tradition (see Toronto p. 137).

Also in the vicinity is the **Hamilton Market** (York St, Tues, Thurs, Fri and Sat) one of Ontario's largest farmers' markets selling the produce of the Niagara peninsula, Canada's chief fruit growing region.

Art Gallery★. – Open daily except Mon and hols ; gift shop ; ☎ 527-6610.

This distinctive concrete structure stands across a plaza from City Hall. Its attractive interior is airy and open with wooden ceilings. Changing exhibitions from its extensive permanent collection are displayed, as well as visiting shows.

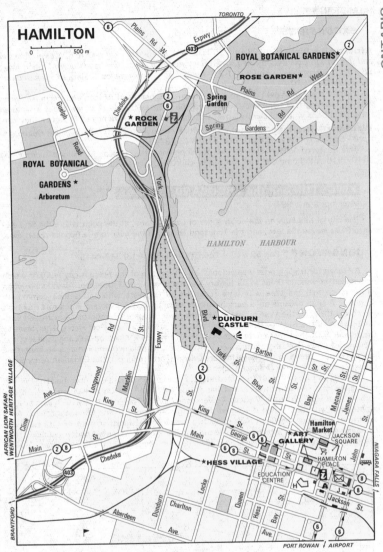

Whitehern (A). – *Guided tours afternoons daily ; about 45 mins ; $1.60 ; ☎ 522-5664.*

This Georgian style house in small but pleasant gardens surrounded by Hamilton's modern centre belonged to the McQuestern family until 1959. It reflects the life of a prosperous Ontario family between the years 1840 and 1960. The McQuesterns, who settled in Hamilton in the early 19th century, were pioneers in the heavy industry now Hamilton's lifeblood and were involved in public life inspiring such projects as the Royal Botanical Gardens and the Niagara Parkway *(p. 112)*. The house contains the original furnishings.

Dundurn Castle★. – *Open daily mid June - Labour Day, 11am - 4pm ; afternoons only rest of year ; $2.65 ; restaurant ; ☎ 522-5313.*

This grand white stone house with its Classical portico over the entrance stands on a hill overlooking Hamilton Bay. It was built 1832-35 by Sir Allan Napier MacNab - soldier, lawyer, politician and member of the Family Compact who fought against Mackenzie *(p. 130)* and who was knighted for it by Queen Victoria in 1838. He was Prime Minister of the Province of Canada 1854-56. It is a showplace of 19th century privilege and illustrates well the wealth and power of the Family Compact *(see also The Grange p. 134)*, though actually MacNab died in debt. The interior is elaborately furnished though the furnishings are not original. Of particular interest is the basement, the domain of the army of servants needed to run a house of this nature in the mid 19th century.

The house is situated in Dundurn Park from whence there is a good **view** of the bay and the city of Hamilton. The grounds are also the scene of summer theatre and many other activities.

Royal Botanical Gardens★. – *Open daily dawn to dusk ; Information Centre on Rte 2/6 where plan available ; seasonal highlights ; ☎ 527-1158.*

These gardens occupy 800 ha - 2 000 acres of land at the western tip of Lake Ontario. Much of this area is natural parkland with nature trails, but there are several feature gardens worth visiting *(car required)*. Across the road from the Information Centre is the **Rock Garden★** with its water, rocks, shrubs, flowering plants and pleasant tea house *(May - Oct)*. The **Spring Garden** has fine displays of flowers *(May - Sept)* depending on the season - irises, tulips, peonies, lilies, Michaelmas daisies, etc. Further along Route 2 is the **Rose Garden★** which has magnificent displays in June and July. In the Arboretum *(return along Route 2 and turn right)*, the **Lilac Dell** is splendid in late May.

107

EXCURSIONS

African Lion Safari★. – *32 km - 20 miles NW by Hwy 8, right on Rte 52N after Rockton and left on 7th Concession Road. Open daily mid Mar - Oct, weekends only Mar and Nov ; $6.50 ; automobile circuit 1-2 hrs ; no convertibles allowed ; cafeteria ; ☎ (519) 623-2620.*

Visitors drive their own cars through various enclosures of African and North American animals roaming free. One enclosure called the Monkey Jungle contains about a hundred African baboons who will climb all over your car and steal any removable parts if they can.

Wentworth Heritage Village. – *Near Rockton on Rte 52 just before above. Open daily April - Dec except Mon ; $4.00 ; ☎ (519) 647-2874.*

This restored village shows the development of a typical agricultural community 1810-1910 with homes, stores, industries, churches, railway station, etc.

KINGSTON and the THOUSAND ISLANDS ★★

Maps pp. 9 and 99

The city of Kingston on the north shore of Lake Ontario, at the point where the St. Lawrence River leaves the lake, and the Thousand Islands in the river form a popular resort area.

■ KINGSTON★★ Pop 52 616 – Tourist Office ☎ (613) 548-4415

A French fur trading post was established on the site of the present city in 1673 which was called at various times in its history Cataraqui and Fort Frontenac. Abandoned when New France fell, the area was later resettled by Loyalists who called their community Kingston. It soon became an important British naval base and dockyard and a fort was built to protect it during the War of 1812. After the war, Kingston's importance increased with the building of the Rideau Canal *(p. 116)* and of a stone fortress, Fort Henry, equivalent to the citadel in Québec in strength. Between 1841 and 1844, Kingston was the capital of the province of Canada. Although this honour was lost, it remained and remains an important military centre, home to the **Royal Military College** (Fort Frederick), the Canadian Army Staff College and the National Defence College.

The city is pleasant with tree-lined streets, parks and attractive public buildings in the local limestone. Among these is the handsome **City Hall★**, in Confederation Park on the harbour opposite one of the Martello Towers *(see Murney Tower p. 109)*, which was built as a potential Parliament when it seemed that Kingston might become Canada's capital. Also worthy of note are the **Court House★** with a small dome similar to that of City Hall, the **Cathedral of St. George**, which is reminiscent of Christopher Wren's London churches, the **Grant Hall** building of Queen's University and some of the buildings of the Royal Military College.

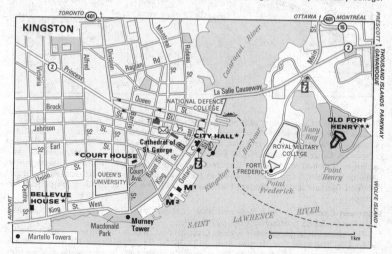

Old Fort Henry★★. – *Open daily mid May - mid Oct ; guided tour 1 hr ; $3.40 ; snack bar ; ☎ 542-7388.*

This large and immensely strong stone fortress is set on a peninsula above Lake Ontario. Built 1832-36, its main defences face inland. This was not a mistake but was done expressly so that the fort would guard the land approach to the naval dockyard at Point Frederick ; the water approaches were covered by Martello Towers built later. The fort was never attacked so it fell into decay. Restored in 1936 it is now best known for the **Fort Henry Guard,** a troop of specially recruited and trained students who recreate the life of the 19th century British soldier and give military displays. These guardsmen guide visitors around the restored quarters and storerooms of the fort, but a visit is not complete without viewing one of the military displays *(daily July and Aug)*, the **Ceremonial Retreat** if possible *(July and Aug, Wed and Sat at 7.30pm ; weather permitting)*. The Guard travels extensively giving these displays and is very professional.

Bellevue House★. – *Open daily except hols in winter ; National Historic Park ; ☎ 542-3858.*

This rather surprising Italian style villa caused quite a sensation when it was built 1838-40. Its exotic appearance contrasted strangely with Kingston's fine stone buildings and it was variously named the "Pekoe pagoda" and "Tea Caddy Castle". Its main claim to fame is that it was for a short time (1848-49) the residence of **Sir John A. Macdonald,**

Canada's first Prime Minister (1867-73, 1878-91). A Scot by birth, Macdonald spent much of his youth in Kingston and opened his first law office there in 1835. He went on to enter provincial politics and was one of the chief architects of Canadian Confederation in 1867. It was during his term in office that the Canadian Pacific Railway was built *(p. 16)*, one of his dreams. The house is furnished to reflect Macdonald's time of residence and there are exhibits and a slide show in the Visitor Centre.

Marine Museum of the Great Lakes★ (M1). – *Open daily April - mid Dec, closed Mon in Nov and Dec ; $2.25 ;* ☎ *542-2261.*

Set in old shipbuilding works beside Lake Ontario, this museum has displays on the various vessels which ply or have plied the Great Lakes – both sail and steam. An interesting shipbuilders' gallery explains different ways of constructing boats, and a special section is devoted to Kingston's shipbuilding days – it was one of the main shipbuilding centres on the Great Lakes in the 19th century. There are also audio-visual presentations and changing exhibitions on various aspects of marine life.

Murney Tower. – *Open daily July and Aug, weekends May and June ; 50¢.*

This squat stone tower in a pleasant park beside the lake is one of Kingston's Martello Towers *(see also Halifax p. 203)*. It is in good repair with fine stonework and vaulting. Inside there is a museum of pioneer life and recreated garrison living quarters.

Pump House Steam Museum (M2). – *Open daily mid June - Labour Day ; $1.50 ;* ☎ *546-4696.*

Kingston's 1849 pumping station has been restored to pay tribute to the steam age in Canada. Among many operating machines and scale models are two enormous steam pumps once used in the pump house and restored as they were in 1897.

■ THE THOUSAND ISLANDS★★

At it leaves Lake Ontario, the St. Lawrence River is literally littered with islands for about an 80 km - 50 mile stretch. Some of these islands are large and lushly forested, some are small and support just a few ragged pine trees, and yet others are mere barren boulders a few feet square. There are either 995 or 1 010 islands depending how many of these boulders are counted. All are of Precambrian rock, the remnants of the **Frontenac Axis** which links the Canadian Shield with the Adirondacks of New York State. They are

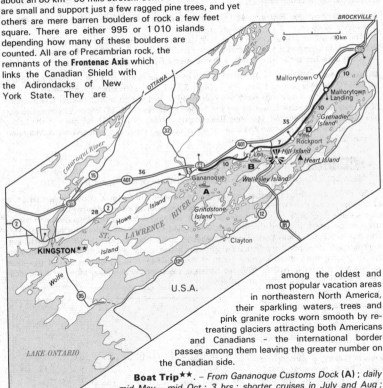

among the oldest and most popular vacation areas in northeastern North America, their sparkling waters, trees and pink granite rocks worn smooth by retreating glaciers attracting both Americans and Canadians – the international border passes among them leaving the greater number on the Canadian side.

Boat Trip★★. – *From Gananoque Customs Dock* **(A)** *; daily mid May - mid Oct ; 3 hrs ; shorter cruises in July and Aug ; refreshments ;* ☎ *382-2144. Also cruises from Rockport* **(D)** *(*☎ *382-4129), and Ivy Lea* **(B)** *(*☎ *659-2295).*

This is a very beautiful and relaxing cruise through the maze of islands. There are views of trees and rock and water, sometimes interspersed with summer homes. The latter vary from small shacks on rocky islets to the palaces of Millionaire's Row on Wellesley Island. The huge ships of the St. Lawrence Seaway, which follows the American coast, can be seen alongside private cruisers, yachts and canoes. A stop can be made at Heart Island to visit **Boldt Castle,** built by the German immigrant owner of the Waldorf Astoria Hotel at vast cost but never finished *(in USA, non-Americans must have identification to land).*

Thousand Islands Parkway★. – *Begins just E of Gananoque and stretches 37 km - 23 miles towards Brockville.*

This scenic drive follows the shore of the St. Lawrence with many fine views and frequent picnic spots. Just after the small resort town of Ivy Lea, the Thousand Islands Bridge crosses the river. The **Skydeck** on Hill Island offers a fine **view★** of the area *(take bridge to island, toll $1.50, do not enter USA ; open daily mid May - mid Oct ; $2.95).*

At Mallorytown Landing, the headquarters of the **St. Lawrence Islands National Park** can be visited *(open daily mid May - mid Oct).* Beside the Interpretive Centre, a hut encloses the remains of the wreck of the *HMS Radcliffe,* an early 19th century gun boat.

KITCHENER - WATERLOO

Maps pp. 9 and 98 – Metro Pop 287 801 - Tourist Office 67 King St E ;
☎ (519) 576-5000

These twin industrial cities in southern Ontario are attractive, orderly and clean reflecting their German heritage. They were first settled about 1800 by the Pennsylvanian Dutch or **Mennonites**, a Protestant sect much persecuted in Europe for its religious ideas and pacifism (members refused to serve in any army). Many emigrated to Pennsylvania in the 17th century, but again their pacifism got them into trouble during the American Revolution and many moved to Ontario with the Loyalists where they were granted land in the Kitchener area. Strict Mennonites live a simple frugal life as farmers. They use no modern machinery, cars or telephones. They can sometimes be seen in the country to the north and west of Kitchener - Waterloo driving along in horse-drawn buggies which display a fluorescent triangle on the back. The men wear black suits and wide hats, the women ankle-length black dresses and small bonnets. (See also Manitoba Mennonites p. 96.)

Other German-speaking people came to this area in the 19th century and the German influence remains strong. Every Fall there is an **Oktoberfest**, nine days of German food and drink, oompah-pah bands and dancing. At the Kitchener **Farmers' Market** (entrance Market Square at Frederick and Duke Sts), German specialities are for sale along with fresh fruit and produce (Sat mornings all year, Wed mornings May - Dec). Nearby, in William Lyon Mackenzie Square (Queen St) stands the **Centre in the Square** which comprises concert hall, studio theatre and art gallery (open daily except Mon ; ☎ 579-5860).

Woodside. – 528 Wellington St N. Open daily except hols in winter ; National Historic Park ; ☎ 742-5273.

This low-lying stone and brick house stands in an attractive park. Built in 1853, it was for some years the family home of **William Lyon Mackenzie King**, Prime Minister of Canada 1921-26, 1926-30, 1935-48. It has been restored to reflect the period of Mr. King's residence in the 1880s. In the basement there is a **display★** on King's life with many photographs. The influence of his grandfather, the rebel leader William Lyon Mackenzie (p. 130), is of particular note.

Joseph Schneider Haus. – 466 Queen St S. Open daily mid May - Labour Day ; Wed - Sun only rest of year ; $1.25 ; ☎ 742-7752.

This Georgian frame house was built about 1820 by Kitchener's founder, Joseph Schneider. It is restored and furnished to the period of the mid 1850's. Special events and seasonal activities reflect the family's Pennsylvania-German Mennonite roots.

Doon Pioneer Village. – About 10 km - 6 miles from centre or 3 km - 2 miles from Hwy 401 Exit 275, turn N. Open daily May - Dec ; $3.50 ; refreshments ; ☎ 893-4020.

Many authentic buildings have been removed to this site to reflect the early settlement of the region. Of special interest are : the **Gingerbread House** of 1890 Victorian vintage which has a display of dolls, the **Township Hall** with its displays on the Mennonites in the basement, and the **museum** which has interesting exhibits on the first white settlers of Waterloo County as well as on the native Indians.

LONDON ★

Maps pp. 9 and 98 – Metro Pop 283 668 – Tourist Office ☎ (519) 672-1970

In 1792, **John Graves Simcoe,** the Lieutenant-Governor of Ontario, chose the present site of London as his capital because he considered the existing administrative centre, Niagara-on-the-Lake, too close to the American border. Naming it for the British capital and calling the river on which it stood the Thames, he applied to higher authorities for approval. This was not forthcoming and York (Toronto) received the honour instead (p. 130). Nevertheless, a settlement developed on Simcoe's site which has since grown into a major industrial centre serving the rich agricultural south of the province. It is a pleasant city of tree-lined streets and attractive houses (Dundas Street is the principal shopping area), and the location of the University of Western Ontario.

Art Gallery★★. – Open afternoons daily except Mon ; $1.00 ; cafe ; gift shop ; guided tours ; ☎ 672-4580.

Set in a park overlooking the River Thames, this spectacular gallery is remarkable chiefly for its architecture. Designed by Toronto architect **Raymond Moriyama** (p. 137), and opened in 1980, it has an unusual structure of concrete barrel vaults covered by aluminum and baked enamel. Each vault contains skylights - Moriyama's answer to the difficulty of providing natural lighting for a gallery without risking damaging works of art by direct light. The result is a series of airy and spacious galleries where changing exhibitions of high quality are displayed. Selections from the permanent Canadian Collection of 18th and 19th century works are also normally on view.

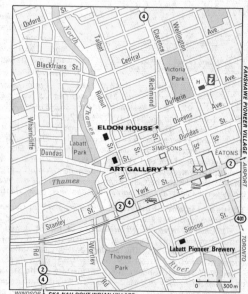

Eldon House★. – *Open afternoons daily March - Nov ; 45 mins ; $1.00 ; guided tours ;* ☎ *433-6171.*

Just north of a series of restored Georgian houses on Ridout Street stands this large and elegant white frame residence completely surrounded by a verandah. Constructed in 1834 by John Harris, a retired Royal Naval captain, it is the oldest house in London and it was for many years a centre of social and cultural activities in 19th century Southern Ontario. Its furnishings reflect a refined way of life at a time when the majority of pioneer settlers were living in log cabins. It belonged to four generations of the Harris family and then was donated to the City of London. The Library and Drawing Room are particularly fine.

Labatt Pioneer Brewery. – *Open daily June - Labour Day, 12am - 5pm ;* ☎ *673-5211.*

This small wooden structure with a shingled roof is an exact replica of the original brewery built by the Labatt Company in 1828. Inside, visitors can follow the process of making beer over a century ago and compare the output of 300 barrels a year with that of the modern brewery next door - 1 200 000 barrels a year.

EXCURSIONS

Fanshawe Pioneer Village. – *15 km - 9 miles NE in Fanshawe Park. Open daily May - Sept, weekdays Oct-Dec ; $3.00 including admission to Park ;* ☎ *451-2800.*

This reconstructed 19th century community of pre-railroad era is part of a large park beside Fanshawe Lake, a reservoir constructed to control flooding by the River Thames. The village contains several houses and shops, the Lochaber Presbyterian Church with a Gaelic bible, a fire hall, and an Orange Hall, the social centre of the community. The **Orange Order,** founded in Ireland in 1795 and named for William III (of Orange), had considerable influence in the foundation of Ontario. In the summer, costumed guides lend life to the village.

Ska-Nah-Doht Indian Village. – *32 km - 20 miles SW in Longwoods Road Conservation Area by Hwy 2. Open daily, except weekends and hols in winter ; animation in summer ; admission to park $2.50 per car ;* ☎ *264-2420.*

This is an interesting recreation of the type of village inhabited by the prehistoric Iroquois Indians in Ontario 800-1 000 years ago. These Indians cultivated the land, fished and trapped animals *(see also p. 98)*. The recreated village is surrounded by a stake palisade with a complicated entrance to make it easy to defend. Inside, the buildings and exhibits display all aspects of daily life. There are three long houses where the families lived, a primitive sauna called a sweat lodge, drying racks for smoking meat, stretching racks for hides, storage pits, a fish trap, etc. Outside the palisade, examples of the crops grown can be seen : corn, squash and beans.

The park resource centre nearby *(open daily)* has audio-visual programs and displays.

*A general picture of Canada can be found in the **Introduction** pp. 12 - 28.*

NIAGARA FALLS ★★★

Maps pp. 9 and 98 – Tourist Office ☎ (416) 356-6061 ; Niagara Parks Commission ☎ (416) 356-2241 - *Local map below*

Roughly halfway along its course from Lake Erie to Lake Ontario, the Niagara River suddenly changes its level by plunging over a cliff. In so doing it creates one of the world's great natural wonders. Niagara Falls are not only among the most famous in the world but they are also the most visited. Every year more than twelve million people travel vast distances just to view them - and they never fail to be impressed. Even **Rupert Brooke,** who as a blasé young British aristocrat visited Niagara in 1912, wrote "I was so impressed by Niagara. I had hoped not to be, but I horribly was".

(after photo by Niagara Parks Commission)

Aerial View of Niagara Falls

There are in fact two sets of falls separated by tiny Goat Island which stands at their brink. The so-called **American Falls** (because they are on the US side of the river) are 300 m - 1 000 ft wide and more than 50 m - 160 ft high. The Canadian or **Horseshoe Falls** (named for their shape) are nearly 800 m - 2 600 ft wide, about the same height, and contain 90 % of the water that is allowed to flow down the river. Thus it is these latter falls that people think of as Niagara. The volume of water in the river varies with the hour of the day and the time of year. Major power developments on both sides of the river divert up to 75 % of the water above the falls to generating stations downstream by means of canals. Also the flow of water over the falls is greater by day than by night (when more is diverted to generate the electricity needed for the night illumination of the falls !), and in winter so much water is diverted that the falls partially freeze-up, a spectacular sight. Thus, standing on the brink of the falls and watching the mighty rush of water, bear in mind how much is being diverted and what the cataract must have looked like in 1678 to **Louis Hennepin** - the first white man to view it. Hennepin heard such a mighty noise on Lake Ontario that he followed the river upstream to discover its source - the falls cannot be heard from Lake Ontario today.

The Erosion of the Falls. - The falls of the Niagara are not old in geological terms. At the end of the last Ice Age the waters of Lake Erie created an exit channel for themselves to old Lake Iroquois. The edge of Lake Iroquois was the present day **Niagara Escarpment** over which this new river plunged to the lake. Immediately this force of water began eroding the soft shale underlying rock causing the harder limestone surface rock to break off, thus creating a gorge. Today the waters of Lake Iroquois have receded to the present level of Lake Ontario and the Niagara River has cut a gorge back some 11 km - 7 miles from the edge of the escarpment at Queenston to the present position of the falls *(map p. 114)*. In another 25 000 years or so, if its progress is not arrested by man, the gorge will extend back to Lake Erie and the falls as we know them today will practically cease to exist.

The Site. - In the 19th century Niagara was a hucksters' paradise with every conceivable device being employed to separate the tourist from his money. Then the Province of Ontario and the State of New York stepped in and bought up all the land on both sides of the river adjacent to the falls. Today, beautiful parks full of flowers line the river bank. The "huckster-ism" still exists in the City of Niagara Falls (Pop 70 960) but visitors can enjoy the natural dignity of the falls themselves without being bothered. In the text which follows, we have chosen to describe only the attractions at Niagara which concern the natural beauty of the site and its history.

■ THE FALLS★★★

The falls can be viewed from the river bank level, from the water level at the bottom of the cataract and from high in the sky on top of various towers constructed especially for this purpose.

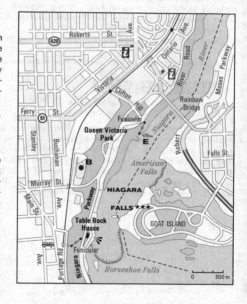

The Walk from Rainbow Bridge to Table Rock★★★. -
About 1.5 km - 1 mile.

From the Rainbow Bridge, wander along the bank beside the river passing Queen Victoria Park and its beautiful flowers *(especially fine in April when the daffodils are in bloom)*. The American Falls are viewed and then it is possible to stand on the very brink of the horseshoe at Table Rock. It is an impressive experience to watch the water dropping over the edge. In Table Rock House, elevators descend and visitors walk along **tunnels★** to see this vast curtain of water as it falls *(daily ; $3.50)*.

The Maid of the Mist★★★ (E). - *Descend funicular from River Rd (55¢). Daily mid May - mid Oct ; 1/2 hour ; $4.40 ; ☎ 358-5781.*

This is an exciting, memorable and wet boat trip *(visitors are equipped with raincoats and hoods)* right up to the foot of the cataract passing the American Falls. It is the only way to really appreciate the mighty force of the water.

The View from Above★★★. - There are three towers in Niagara Falls which provide a spectacular **view★★★** of the cataract from above. The best is the **Skylon (B)** *(Robinson St ; open daily ; $3.95 and parking charge ; revolving restaurant)*, which looks like a mini CN Tower *(p. 131)* and is ascended by exterior elevators known as the yellow bugs.

EXCURSIONS plan p. 113 then map p. 114

Niagara Parkway North★★

From the Falls to Niagara-on-the-Lake – *26 km - 16 miles – about 5 hours with visits*

The Niagara Parkway follows the river north to its junction with Lake Ontario. It is maintained by the Niagara Parks Commission with viewpoints and attractive gardens.

From the Falls, the Parkway passes under the Rainbow Bridge, through a pleasant residential area and past the Whirlpool Rapids Bridge.

Great Gorge Trip★★. – *4 km - 2 1/2 miles. Daily May - Oct ; $2.25 ;* ☎ *356-0904.*

An elevator descends to the bottom of the gorge where some of the world's most hazardous water can be seen roaring, boiling, jumping along and rising up in huge **rapids**★★. There is a boardwalk which follows the river for a short distance and along it are displayed some of the craft in which people have tried to negotiate this stretch of water - usually unsuccessfully. A small exhibition details their attempts and tells the story of the great French tight-rope walker, **Blondin,** who crossed the gorge on a wire many times 1859-60.

The rapids and gorge can be viewed from the top of the gorge but they are not nearly as impressive. After a short distance the river widens out briefly into a pool. This has been made into a foaming whirlpool by the force of the water and the rapid drop in its level.

The Whirlpool★★. – *5 km - 3 miles.*

A colourful Spanish aero car *(daily mid April - Oct ; $2.50)* crosses the gorge high above the river with excellent **views**★★ of the water as it swirls around the whirpool and the rocky gorge.

By driving another 1.5 km - 1 mile, the far side of the whirl-pool is reached. There is a **view**★ from Thompson's Point Scenic Overlook.

Niagara Glen★. – *7.5 km - 4 3/4 miles.*

There is a view of the river from above and trails to the water's edge *(15 min to descend, 30 min to ascend).*

Niagara Parks Commission School of Horticulture★ **(F).** – *9 km - 5 1/2 miles. Information Office on Parkway ; open daily in summer, dawn to dusk.*

There is a beautiful display of flowers, shrubs and trees maintained by students at this school which offers a three year course in horticulture. The **rose garden**★ is particularly fine in early June.

About 1.5 km - 1 mile from the School of Horticulture the industrial side of Niagara is reached. Across the river, the huge **Robert Moses Generating Station** can be seen, and a lit-tle further on the **Sir Adam Beck Generating Station** on the Canadian side is passed. These two stations use the water diverted from the river above the falls to generate electricity.

Just after the power stations, a large **floral clock** can be seen beside the road.

Queenston Heights★. – *12 km - 8 miles. Map p. 114. Restaurant.*

These heights are part of the Niagara Escarpment and were once the location of Niagara Falls. Today they make a pleasant park with views of the river.

At the centre of the park stands a monument to **General Sir Isaac Brock,** the Canadian military hero of the War of 1812. During the war, the heights were captured by the Americans. Brock led a charge to recapture them and was killed for his pains. The heights were however recaptured and now Brock surveys them from the top of his monument *(open daily mid May - Labour Day ; 235 narrow steps ; National Historic Site ; self-guided walking tour of battlefield available).*

Queenston★. – *14 km - 9 miles.* This village at the foot of the escarpment has attractive houses and gardens.

Laura Secord Homestead. – *Partition St. Guided tours June - Labour Day, Fri - Sun and hols ; 30 min ; 75¢ ; shop ;* ☎ *262-4851.*

In 1813 Laura Secord set out from her home in enemy-held Queenston and walked 30 km - 19 miles through the bush to warn the British of a surprise attack planned by the Americans. Forewarned, the British won a great victory at the Battle of Beaver Dams which followed. This rather plain looking house was the home of this Canadian heroine and it has been beautifully restored by the candy company named after her. An interpretive display about her stands outside.

Continuing along the Parkway, turn round to see the statue of Brock on his monument on top of the escarpment. For the rest of the drive to Niagara-on-the-Lake, there are occasional fine views of the river and several parks with picnic tables. Along the way in summer, there are stalls selling the produce of the Niagara peninsula.

Niagara-on-the-Lake★★. – *Pop 12 186.* This charming town at the northern end of the Niagara River where it joins Lake Ontario resembles a picturesque English village. Settled by Loyalists, it was the first capital of Upper Canada and was burnt down by the Americans in 1813. Rebuilt soon afterwards, it seems to have remained the same ever since. It has gracious 19th century houses with beautiful gardens, tree-lined streets and a wide and attractive main street (**Queen Street**★) with a clock tower at its centre and pleasant little shops, restaurants, tea houses, hotels and the **Niagara Apothecary,** an 1866 pharmacy *(open daily mid May - Labour Day ; noon - 6pm)* along its length.

Niagara-on-the-Lake is also a cultural centre, home to the **Shaw Festival,** a season of theatre devoted to the works of the British playwright, **George Bernard Shaw** (1856-1950). The main theatre, a brick structure with a beautiful wood interior, stands at the junction of Queen's Parade and Wellington Street. There are two other theatres in the town. *Details of the festival (daily May - Oct except Mon) can be obtained from Box 774, Niagara-on-the-Lake, Ontario LOS 1J0 ;* ☎ *468-3201.*

Fort George★. – *On River Rd near theatre. Open daily mid May - Oct ; $1.00 ; guided tours ; National Historic Park ;* ☎ *468-4257.*

Built by the British in the 1790s, this fort played a key role in the War of 1812 being alternately captured by the Americans and recaptured by the British. Restored in the 1930s, it has grassy earthworks and a wooden palisade enclosing officers' quarters, forge, powder magazine, guard house and three blockhouse barracks of 25 cm - 10 inch thick timbers housing military displays.

Welland Canal★★

From Niagara Falls, take QEW to St Catharines exiting at Glendale Ave interchange, follow Glendale Ave and cross canal by the lift bridge, turn right or left on canal service road - Government Rd.

From Niagara-on-the-Lake, take the Niagara Stone Rd (Rte 55) to its end, turn left on the south service road, right on Coon Rd to Glendale Ave, turn right and cross canal as above.

The early explorers and fur traders portaged their canoes around the falls and rapids on the Niagara River but navigation of anything bigger between Lakes Ontario and Erie was impossible until canals and locks were built in the 19th century. The present canal, part of the St. Lawrence Seaway *(p. 170),* is 45 km - 28 miles long and it crosses the Niagara Peninsula between St. Catharines and Port Colborne. It has eight locks which raise ships 99 m - 326 ft, the difference in level between the two great lakes.

Drive alongside Canal★★. – *About 14 km - 9 miles from Lake Ontario to Thorold on Government Rd.*

There are fine views of the huge ships of the Seaway negotiating seven of the eight locks of this section. Lock No. 3 *(just S of the lift bridge)* has a **viewing platform★** *(open daily May - Sept)* and information office on the Seaway. The times when ships will be passing through the lock are posted but these are fairly continuous as the canal is busy *(it takes nearly an hour for a ship to negotiate a lock).* Locks 4, 5 and 6 in Thorold raise ships up the Niagara Escarpment. They are twin-flight locks – two parallel sets of locks, so that one ship may be going up as another comes down.

Niagara Parkway South★

From the Falls to Old Fort Erie – *32 km - 20 miles - about 1 hr.*

Just above the falls the Niagara River is impressive, rushing along at 48 kmh - 30 mph with **rapids★★** as it prepares to plunge over the cliff. The Parkway crosses to **Dufferin Island** where there is a pleasant park *(open daily)* with hiking trails and streams.

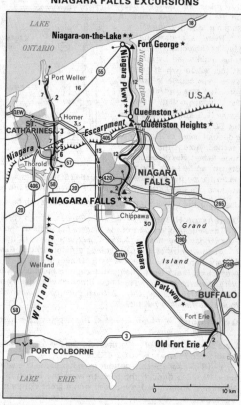

NIAGARA FALLS EXCURSIONS

It passes the large international control dam and the gates which divert water along canals to the generating stations downstream. The river slowly becomes a wide but quietly flowing stream, a complete contrast to its lower stretch. There are some pleasant views of the United States shore and Grand Island. At **Fort Erie** (Pop 24 096), the Peace Bridge crosses the river to the huge American city of **Buffalo.** There are good **views★** of the Buffalo skyline.

Old Fort Erie. – *Open daily May - mid Oct ; $2.00 ; snack bar ;* ☎ *871-0540.*

This star shaped stone fort is set at the mouth of Lake Erie. It is a reconstruction of the third fort built on this site, the first two were destroyed by storm and flood, the third by the Americans in 1814. Visitors enter by a drawbridge and can tour reconstructed officers' quarters, barracks, guard house and powder magazine. Students in early 19th century uniforms perform manœuvres and act as guides.

NORTH BAY ★

Maps pp. 9 and 98 - Pop 51 268 – Tourist Office ☎ (705) 472-8480

This pleasant resort and recreational centre on the shores of **Lake Nipissing** was on the old canoe route to the west. The La Vase portage connected the waters of Trout Lake, the Ottawa and Mattawa Rivers with Lake Nipissing, the French River and Georgian Bay. Today, these waters are used solely for recreational purposes. From the Government dock on Main Street, there are **cruises** across Lake Nipissing and down the attractive French River with several stops *(mid May - mid Sept, Sun, Wed and Fri ; more frequently in July and Aug ; 6 hrs ; $12.60 ; moonlight cruises on Fri ;* ☎ *472-4500 Ext 371).*

North Bay is also the centre of a rich fur trapping industry. Five times a year *(Jan, Mar, Apr, June and Dec)* **wild fur auctions** are given by the Ontario Fur Trappers' Association which rate among the biggest in the world. Beaver, marten and muskrat are the most popular furs.

Quints' Museum. – *10 km - 6 miles S by Hwy 11. Open daily mid May - Sept ; $1.50.*
The town of Callander just to the south of North Bay on the lake was the birthplace in 1934 of the **Dionne Quints,** the five little girls who became all the world's sweethearts. The house where they were born today displays much "quint" memorabilia.

EXCURSION

Marten River★. – *Pop 24. 64 km - 40 miles N by Hwy 11.* Just north of this little community is a small **Trappers' Museum**★ *(open daily May - Oct ; $1.00)* which tells the story of the fur trapping industry. It contains a trapper's cabin complete with equipment, pelts which can be felt and touched, a wide range of traps, and a reconstructed beaver pond containing all the Northern Ontario furbearers in their natural habitat.

ORILLIA ★

Maps pp. 9 and 98 - Pop 23 955

Set on the narrows between Lakes Simcoe and Couchiching, Orillia is a small industrial and resort centre with a reputation out of all proportion to its size. **Stephen Leacock** (1869-1944), humourist, author, Professor of Political Science at McGill University in Montréal, and possibly the best known Canadian in the literary field, spent his summers here and was inspired by it to write some of his finest works : Orillia is the model for the "Mariposa" of his famous *Sunshine Sketches of a Little Town.*

Stephen Leacock Memorial Home★. – *In Old Brewery Bay off Hwy 12B. Guided tours daily mid June - Labour Day ; 1 hr ; $1.00 ; bookstore ;* ☎ *(705) 326-9357.*
This attractive house set in pleasant grounds overlooking Brewery Bay was designed and built in 1908 by Leacock. The whimsical, nonsensical, uproarious humour of this man, who said he would rather have written *Alice in Wonderland* than the whole of the *Encyclopedia Britannica,* pervades the house, and the guides who take visitors around it.

OSHAWA ★★

Maps pp. 9 and 98 – Metro Pop 154 217 – Tourist Office : 48 Simcoe St S ; ☎ (416) 728-1683

This industrial city on the north shore of Lake Ontario is one of the main centres of Canada's automobile industry. Its name has for long been synonymous with **R.S. McLaughlin** (1871-1972) who turned his father's carriage manufacturing business into the McLaughlin Motor Company, and used an American engine in his famous **McLaughlin-Buick** motor car. In 1918 he sold his company to the General Motors Corporation of the United States but remained chairman of the Canadian Division, whose main plant is in Oshawa. McLaughlin was a great philanthropist *(pp. 137 and 140).*

Parkwood★★. – *270 Simcoe St N, 2.5 km - 1 1/2 miles N of Hwy 401. Guided tours of house and conservatory daily June - Labour Day except Mon ; Sept - Nov, April - May Tues - Fri and Sun afternoons ; closed Dec - March ; about 1 hr ; $3.00 ;* ☎ *579-1311.*
This imposing and gracious residence was built by R.S. McLaughlin in 1917 and donated by him after his death to the Oshawa General Hospital. The hospital maintains it as it was at his death and opens it to the public. A visit to Parkwood provides an insight into a style of life few have experienced or can ever hope to achieve. It is beautifully and tastefully furnished with priceless antiques from all over the world. Every room has furnishings of the finest woods and fabrics representing the work of skilled craftsmen. Carpets, ornaments, pictures - all enhance the charm and elegance.

This gem of a house - a visit unique in Canada, is set in some of the finest **gardens** *(open same as above ; $1.00)* in the eastern half of the country. Containing mature trees, manicured lawns and shrubbery, formal gardens, statuary and fountains, they are a delight to wander in. A visit is further enhanced by a stop at the pleasant **tea house** *(light lunches, English teas, June - Labour Day)* set beside a long pool with fountains.

Canadian Automotive Museum★. – *99 Simcoe St S, about 1.5 km - 1 mile N of Hwy 401. Open daily ; $2.50 ;* ☎ *576-1222.*
This interesting museum is much more than just a display of cars. The history of the automobile industry in Canada is explained by means of photographs, illustrations, models, etc, and of course by actual examples. About 70 vehicles in beautiful condition are on display mainly from the 1898-1930 period. Among them note the 1903 Redpath Messenger built in Toronto and the only remaining example of its type, the 1912 Tudhope, the 1912 McLaughlin Buick, and the 1917 Rauch and Lang electric car.

Cullen Gardens. – *In Whitby, 5 km - 3 miles N of Hwy 401 by Hwy 12 and Taunton Rd. Open daily ; $4.00 ;* ☎ *(416) 668-6606.*
These attractive gardens combine flower beds, a rose garden, topiary, ponds and a stream with miniature reproductions of historic houses from all over Ontario.

OTTAWA ★★★

Maps pp. 9 and 99 – Pop 295 163 Metro Pop 717 978 – Tourist Office
☎ (613) 237-5150 or (613) 992-5473

The federal capital of Canada defies the image most people have of a capital city. It is not a "contrived" place created to impress visitors with the greatness of Canada, despite the fact that it almost owes its existence - at least in its present form - to its choice as capital. It lacks the mass of imposing architecture, the vistas and grandeur of other world capitals, but this is perhaps its charm. Visitors' images of it do not include vast monuments but such things as civil servants skating to work clutching briefcases, joggers along the Rideau Canal, the Sunday bicycle brigade, tulips in the spring, stalls of handicrafts around the National Arts Centre and outdoor concerts on Nepean Point.

Ottawa sits on the south bank of the **Ottawa River** at the point where the **Rideau River** joins it from the south and the **Gatineau River** from the north. It is due west of Montréal about 160 km - 100 miles upstream from the confluence of Ottawa and St. Lawrence Rivers. The Ottawa River marks the boundary between the provinces of Ontario and Québec but the area administered by the **National Capital Commission** (all federally-owned land) spans the river encompassing a large area in both provinces including the city of **Hull** in Québec (Pop 56 225).

Mounted Policeman

Philemon Wright. – There was no settlement of any kind in the Ottawa area until 1800 although the region was known to the Outaouais Indians and visited by French explorers. The first settler was an American called Philemon Wright who harnessed the **Chaudière Falls** to power a gristmill and sawmill on the Hull side of the river. He cut wood and floated the first raft of squared timber to Québec in 1807, the beginning of what was to become a vast industry.

The Rideau Canal. – The War of 1812 *(p. 100)* exposed the dangers of the St. Lawrence as a means of communicating and indeed of supplying the military in Upper Canada from Montréal. Any ship could be swept by gunfire from the United States, quite apart from the dangers posed by the rapids. Thus after the War, the **Duke of Wellington** sent men to Canada to look for a safer way. The route which was finally selected followed the Ottawa, Rideau and Cataraqui Rivers as well as a series of lakes to reach the Royal Navy base at Kingston on Lake Ontario. Construction of the canals and locks necessary to make the route navigable was entrusted to **Lieutenant-Colonel John By** of the Royal Engineers in 1826. By established his base at the present site of Ottawa and soon a thriving settlement grew up which was known as Bytown. The canal system was finished by 1832 but it cost so much that By returned to England unemployed and penniless.

Lumbertown. – The end of canal building did not mean the end of the boom for Bytown. By the mid 1830s, it had become the centre of the Ottawa valley squared timber industry. Sawmills were built on the Bytown side of the Ottawa River using the power of the Chaudière Falls - as the mills of Philemon Wright did to the north. The splendid stands of red and white pine in the valley fell victim to the new industry which, as the century wore on, concentrated more and more on sawing lumber and exporting it to the United States for the developing cities and less on floating rafts down to Québec for export to England. The Rideau Canal which never saw any military use blossomed briefly as a means of transporting this lumber south. Bytown itself became a rowdy centre for lumberjacks and rivermen skilled at negotiating the rapids (so skilled were they that the British Government specially recruited some of them to negotiate the dangerous cataracts of the Nile in order to relieve **General Gordon** at Khartoum in 1884).

The Westminster in the Wilderness. – The 1850s saw great rivalry between the major cities of Upper and Lower Canada -Montréal, Toronto, Kingston and Québec - over which should be selected as the capital of the new united Canada. Contention was so rife that the government decided to ask **Queen Victoria** to decide the issue. She picked Bytown which had hastily changed its name to Ottawa as being a more suitable title for a capital city. The choice did not please everyone – "the nearest lumber village to the north pole" wrote Torontonian **Goldwin Smith** *(p. 134)*. But the American press found that Ottawa had something in its favour – it could not be captured even by the most courageous of invaders because they would become lost in the woods trying to find it ! Despite such quips the Parliament Buildings were begun in 1859 and were complete enough by 1867 to be used for the representatives of the new Confederation, of which Ottawa was accepted as the capital, this time without demur.

Ottawa Today. – Ottawa is a city of parks, of pleasant driveways with bicycle paths used for cross-country skiing in winter. It is also a city of flowers especially in May when thousands of tulips bloom - a gift of the people of Holland whose Queen spent the war years in Ottawa. It is a city that has made the most of the factor which caused it to be created – the Rideau Canal. Flanked by tree-lined drives this waterway is a sportsman's haven : canoeing, boating, jogging, strolling, biking in summer ; and skating and cross-country skiing in winter. The waterway can be followed for its 200 km - 125 mile length to Lake Ontario through pleasant rural countryside and lovely lakes. Ottawa has other driveways which follow the Ottawa and Rideau Rivers *(p. 118)* and more are planned.

Ottawa is also the city of government. Although still a centre for forest products and indeed for the rich agricultural hinterlands to the south, today government is its major concern. Not here do the "temples of finance" rule the skyline as in Toronto and Montréal. Instead the highrise contain government departments and ministries - the most dominant, **Place du Portage** across the river in Hull, being completely government-owned.

Finally, Ottawa is a cultural centre with a fine selection of museums *(pp. 119 and 121)* and excellent music, dance and drama presentations at the **National Arts Centre.** The city is particularly lively in February during the winter festival, **Winterlude**, in May for the **Festival of Spring**, and in July when it celebrates **Festival Ottawa**. Another major event is the **Canada Canoe Festival** *(late June - early July)* which recalls the colourful past of the Ottawa River.

■ PARLIAMENT HILL AND AREA★★ *time : 1/2 day – plan p. 118*

Approached from Wellington Street, the name Parliament "Hill" seems to belie the fact. Actually Canada's Parliament stands on a bluff overlooking the Ottawa River and it must be viewed from that angle to appreciate the name. The "Hill" as it is familiarly known was purchased in 1859 from the British Military who had used it for barracks during the building of the canal. Construction began immediately on the Parliament Buildings which were occupied in 1866 though not completed until 1876. The three Gothic sandstone structures which stand there today do not all date from the mid 19th century. A disastrous fire destroyed the middle one in 1916 except for the library ; it was rebuilt in 1920. The **Peace Tower** at its centre was added in 1927 as a monument to Canadians killed during the First World War.

Today, the **Centre Block** contains the Houses of Parliament - Commons and Senate. The **East Block** with its whimsical tower, which has windows in each side designed to look like a face, and the **West Block** contain offices for Members of Parliament and Senators. Once these three buildings were sufficient to house not only Parliament but the entire civil service - a far cry from today !

Parliament Hill is "guarded" by members of the **Royal Canadian Mounted Police** (the Mounties) in their famous ceremonial dress - stetsons, red jackets, riding breeches, boots and spurs *(summer only)*. There are also regiments of Guards on the Hill in summer wearing bearskin hats, red coats and black trousers. A **Changing of the Guard★★** is performed *(daily in July and Aug weather permitting ; 10am ; 1/2 hr)* resembling the ceremony held outside Buckingham Palace *(see Michelin Green Guide to London)*.

The Canadian Parliament from Nepean Point

Centre Block★. - *Guided tours daily ; 1/2 hr ;* ☎ *996-0896.*
These tours enable visitors to enter the House of Commons, the Senate, the Library, Confederation Hall and the Hall of Honour. Separately, the Peace Tower can be ascended for a fine **view★** of the capital spread out below. Sessions of Parliament can also be attended by members of the public if the House is sitting *(weekdays except Christmas, Easter, July - Sept ;* ☎ *for details)*. Each session begins with the **Speaker's Parade** through the Hall of Honour to the Commons.

East Block★. - *Guided tours daily in July and Aug, weekends only rest of year ; 30 mins.*
The interior of this mid 19th century building has been restored to look as it did in 1870 just after Confederation. Some of the offices have been authentically furnished to represent their use by the Prime Minister of the time - Sir John A. Macdonald, his Québec colleague and fellow Father of Confederation - Sir George Etienne Cartier, the Governor-General - Lord Dufferin, and the Privy Council.

The Grounds. – In front of the Parliament Buildings is a low lying fountain called the **Centennial Flame (A)** because of the natural gas which is always burning at its centre. It symbolizes the first one hundred years of Confederation and it was lit at midnight of New Year's Eve 1966. Around the flame, the twelve shields of the Canadian provinces and territories are displayed with the dates when each entered Confederation.

The walk around the Centre Block is pleasant and there are **views★** of the river and of Hull which is fast changing from an industrial city to a federal government annex with vast office developments. A notable collection of statues graces this walk, many of them the work of the well-known Québec sculptor **Philippe Hébert.** Most of them are Canadian Prime Ministers but there is also a statue of **Queen Victoria.**

At the back of the Centre Block there is an attractive polygonal building housing the **Parliamentary Library★**, the only part of the original structure to escape the 1916 fire. It is modelled on the Reading Room of the British Museum but from the outside it looks like the chapter house of a Gothic Cathedral.

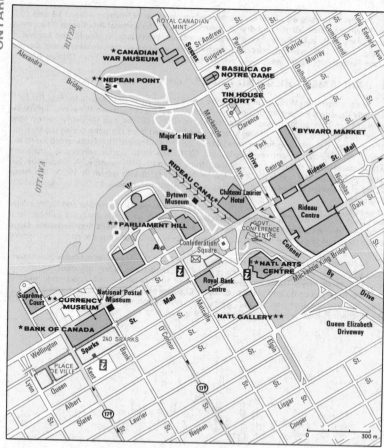

Ottawa River Boat Trip★★. – *Plan p. 120. Departs from Hull Municipal Wharf in Jacques Cartier Park - free shuttle bus service from Confederation Square. Daily mid May - mid Oct ; 1 1/2 hrs ; $6.00 ; ☏ 733-5186.*

This is an excellent trip especially in the evening light at the end of a tiring day sight seeing. The sheer size and force of the Ottawa River are impressive. There are close up views of Parliament Hill, the Rideau Falls *(p. 122)*, and the houses along Sussex Drive overlooking the river, in particular the Prime Minister's Residence. The boat descends as far as Pointe Gatineau, a pretty village on the Québec shore, where log booms can be seen in the mouth of the Gatineau River.

Rideau Canal ★. – *National Historic Park.* From Wellington Street, descend into the little gorge where the Rideau Canal begins, part of Colonel By's waterway to Lake Ontario. Eight **locks★** *(under renovation)* raise boats from the Ottawa River to the top of the cliff. Beside them stands the **Old Commissariat Building,** constructed by Colonel By in 1826-27 as a military supply depot and treasury. It now houses the **Bytown Museum** *(closed until 1985).* Across the canal stands the **Chateau Laurier,** Ottawa's most distinguished hotel, easily recognizable by its turrets and steeply pitched copper roofs in true "chateau" tradition.

There is also a **boat trip** on the Rideau Canal *(departs from Government Conference Centre ; daily mid May - mid Oct ; 1 1/4 hrs ; $5.00).*

National Arts Centre★ ; Sparks Street Mall. – Facing the canal and backing onto Confederation Square is the National Arts Centre, a complex of inter-related concrete structures built in 1969 and containing theatres, a restaurant and a charming cafe with outdoor terrace *(summer only)* beside the canal. Across the canal stands the **Rideau Centre,** a complex of shops, hotel and convention centre.

Across Confederation Square is **Sparks Street,** a pleasant pedestrian mall with trees, seats and cafe tables between the shops. Along it note the **Royal Bank Centre** and the attractive **Bank of Canada★** building designed by Arthur Erickson *(p. 59)* and opened in 1980. The original Classical style bank is now flanked by two 12-storey towers of solar-tinted glass and oxidized copper, and set within a 12-storey court. In the court are trees, shrubs, a pool and the Bank's Currency Museum *(p. 121).*

Nepean Point★★. – This point high above the river beside the Alexandra Bridge offers a splendid **view★★** of Parliament Hill, Hull and the Gatineau Hills across the river. The statue is **Samuel de Champlain** who sailed up the Ottawa River in 1613 and 1615. In summer concerts are given in the theatre below the statue.

In Major's Hill Park nearby stands the **Noon Gun (B),** a muzzle loaded ship's cannon which is fired every day *(10am on Sun so as not to interrupt church services ; loud report, do not stand too close).* On fine days it can be heard over a 22 km - 14 mile area.

Basilica of Notre Dame★. – This church with its twin spires is the Roman Catholic Cathedral built between 1841 and the 1880s. Between the steeples, note the gold leaf statue of the Madonna and Child. To the right of the basilica there is a statue of Joseph-

Eugene Guigues the first bishop of Ottawa who was responsible for the basilica's comple-tion. The very fine **woodwork**★ of the interior was carved in mahogany by Philippe Parizeau. Around the sanctuary there are niches which contain statues of the prophets, patriarchs and apostles. These were carved in wood by Philippe Hébert though they have been painted to look like stone.

Tin House Court★. – In this pleasant square with its stone houses and fountain, a strange object can be seen hanging from the wall. It is the facade of a house built by one Honoré Foisy, a tinsmith. Foisy spent his time decorating the front of his home with sheet metal, making it look like wood or stone. When his house was destroyed, the facade was moved here to preserve forever this example of the tinsmith's art.

Byward Market★. – *Daily, indoors in winter.* This colourful market which stretches for several blocks has existed since 1846. From Spring to Fall, there are stalls of flowers, fruit, vegetables, etc.

Supreme Court. – *Guided tours weekdays 9am - 5pm ; 20 min ;* ☎ *995-4330 for details of sessions.*

Created in 1875 but not "supreme" until 1949 (when appeals to the Judicial Committee of the Privy Council in England were abolished), Canada's Supreme Court occupies a build-ing with green roofs overlooking the Ottawa River. The Court itself consists of nine judges, five of whom are required for a quorum. Visitors can listen to the legal arguments if the Court is in session, and visit two other court rooms.

■ THE NATIONAL MUSEUMS★★★

Ottawa as befits the capital has a fine collection of museums and no visit would be complete without a visit to at least some of them.

National Museum of Man★★★. – *Plan p. 120. West wing of Victoria Memorial Build-ing. Open daily 10am - 5pm ; closed Mon Sept - April except statutory hols ; plan available at entrance ; snack bar ; bookstore ;* ☎ *992-3497.*

This superb museum, which traces its origins to 1842, underwent an extensive renov-ation in the early 1970s and has emerged revitalized. Dealing with man in Canada from earliest times to today, it has beautiful innovative displays and dioramas accompanied by recorded soundtracks, slide shows and films.

After introductory sections on man's evolution from other mammals and on his arrival on the North American continent *(ground floor),* the visitor reaches the displays on native Canadian cultures for which the museum is so famous. **Canada Before Cartier** looks at native pre-history and features an archaeological excavation of an ancient West Coast Indian village. **The Buffalo Hunters** *(second floor)* deals with the life of the Prairie Indians and feat-ures full scale models of a buffalo and of a teepee, as well as displays on religion, hunting and clothing.

The People of the Longhouse *(second floor)* deals with the Iroquoian tribes of the Eastern Woodlands. There is a model of a village with its long houses, examples of the famous Iroquois masks and a section on the Great Iroquois League (the Five - later Six-Nations). The life of Canada's northern dwellers, **the Inuit** *(second floor)* is explained by careful display of artifacts in dramatic diorama settings. Among them are a full size model of a kayak (canoe) and the reconstruction of the interior of an igloo.

The most fascinating of the displays, **the Children of the Raven** *(third floor),* is devoted to the life of the wealthy and artistic West Coast tribes who produced much fine carving from huge totem poles to tiny intricate trinkets. The complex social order and way of life of these peoples is explained.

The fourth floor is devoted to the arrival of the white man and his gradual settlement of the whole country. There are displays on the various heritages and traditions of the peoples who make up the Canadian population today.

National Museum of Natural Sciences★★. – *Plan p. 120. East wing of Victoria Memorial Building. Open daily 10am - 5pm ; closed Mon Sept - April ; plan available at entrance ; snack bar ; bookstore ; film shows ;* ☎ *996-3102.*

The ground floor displays of this museum deal with the geological history of our planet. There are interesting exhibits on the creation of oceans and continents particularly North America. From this, the origin of life on earth is traced. There is an outstanding display on **dinosaurs**★★ with several complete reconstructions of skeletons.

On the second floor, there are films and fine **dioramas**★★ of Canadian mammals and birds, each species being represented in its own habitat. These are very varied from the Muskox of the Northwest Territories to the Pronghorn Antelope of Saskatchewan, the Grizzly Bear of British Columbia, and the Moose of New Brunswick.

On the third and fourth floors, animal life is studied in a more general way. The evolu-tionary threads which bind all of the animals of the world together are explained and such topics as animal geography, animal behaviour and relationships with man are explored. There is also an interesting **hall of plant life** on the fourth floor.

National Gallery★★. – *Plan p. 118. Open daily 10am - 5pm ; Thurs 10am - 9pm Sept - May but closed Mon ; cafeteria ; bookstore ; auditorium ; guided tours ;* ☎ *992-4636.*

The National Gallery owns the most extensive and important collection of Canadian Art in existence. Its European works are also of very high calibre enabling the visitor to see the Canadian collection in its historical context. Since 1960, the gallery has been housed in temporary quarters. There are plans to erect a new building beside the Ottawa River.

European Art★★. – This comprehensive collection is well laid out so that the visitor wanders from one room to the next following the main lines in the development of Western Art. Among the highlights : Lucas Cranach the Elder's *Venus,* Rembrandt's *The Toilet of Esther,* El Greco's *St. Francis in Meditation with Brother Leo,* Bernini's fine marble bust of Pope Urbain VIII and Benjamin West's *Death of Wolfe* (the original of this much reproduced painting). The Impressionists are well represented and a gallery is devoted to the 20th century including works by Fernand Léger, Picasso and Gustav Klint. There are also chang-ing displays of contemporary art and sculpture.

119

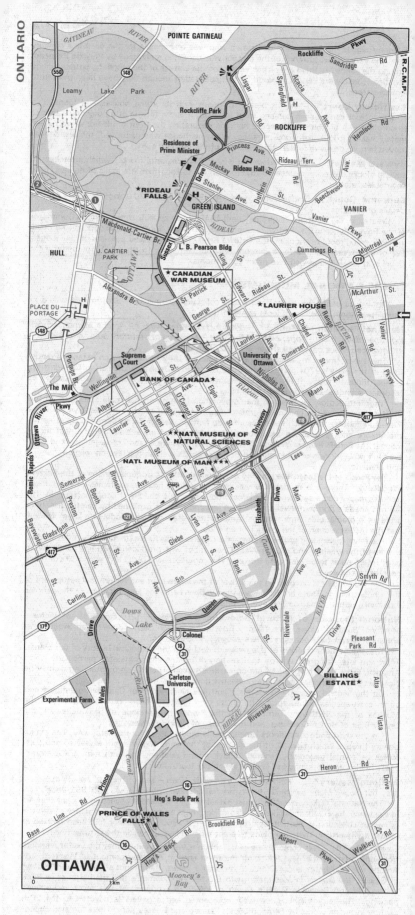

The key on p. 28 explains the symbols used on the maps and plans.

120

Canadian Art★★. – The visitor strolls through well arranged galleries following the development of Canadian art. Paul Kane and Cornelius Krieghoff are well represented but the highlight of the collection is the gallery devoted to the Group of Seven (p. 139) and to Tom Thomson, their precursor. Thomson's famous *Red Leaves* can be seen - the first of the Group of Seven type works. Among more recent works, there are paintings by Paul-Emile Borduas and Harold Town - possibly Canada's greatest living artist. Contemporary works and sculptures are displayed in changing exhibitions.

The sixth floor of the gallery is devoted to changing displays from the small but excellent **Prints and Drawings** collection. The National Gallery also often houses major visiting exhibitions from other parts of the country and the world.

National Aviation Museum★★. – *Plan p. 122. Rockcliffe Airport. Open daily 9am - 9pm ; closed Mon Sept - April ;* ☎ *993-2169.*

Well displayed in two hangars, this large and interesting collection explains the history of aviation from pioneer days to the present, with special emphasis on Canadian contributions.

There is a replica of the *Silver Dart,* the first aircraft to fly in Canada in 1909. It flew under the auspices of Alexander Graham Bell's Aerial Experiment Association at Baddeck, Nova Scotia (p. 196). There are fighters and bombers used in both World Wars - a Nieuport 17, a Sopwith Snipe, a Hawker Hurricane, a Supermaine Spitfire and a Lancaster Bomber. There are also examples of early "bush" planes with floats illustrating the importance of aviation in opening up Canada's northland.

Currency Museum★★. – *Plan p. 118. Open daily ; closed Mon Sept - April ;* ☎ *563-8914.*

This is a well designed and interesting exposé of the history of money from early China, Greece, Rome, Byzantium, Medieval and Renaissance Europe, to its introduction and use in North America. The development of Canadian money is highlighted with examples of wampum, the card money of New France, Hudson Bay Company tokens, the first banknotes, the emergence of the Bank of Canada and decimal currency.

National Museum of Science and Technology★. – *Plan p. 122. 1867 St. Laurent Blvd. Open daily 9am - 9pm ; closed Mon mid Sept - mid May ; snack bar ; gift shop ;* ☎ *998-4566.*

This museum has many displays of the do-it-yourself experiment type especially in the Physics Hall. There are sections on astronomy, meteorology and the development of electrical communications.

Transportation is dealt with in great detail - there are carriages and sleighs, street cars and trains (*excursions in summer p. 101*), and a fine collection of old **automobiles** in beautiful condition, which includes one more recent model - a 1975 Bricklin made in New Brunswick. The aircraft section of the museum is located separately at Rockcliffe Airport (*see above*).

Canadian War Museum★. – *Plan p. 118. Open daily ; closed Mon Sept - April except statutory hols ; films ; bookstore ;* ☎ *992-2774.*

The main building has exhibits on three floors tracing the history of war in Canada from the Wolfe - Montcalm debacle on the Plains of Abraham to the Korean War. There is a lifesize reconstruction of a First World War trench complete with sound effects, a diorama of the Normandy landings in 1944, and Luftwaffe Chief Hermann Goering's staff car - a huge armoured Mercedes Benz capable of reaching 135 mph (217 km).

The **annex★★** traces the development of arms and armour through the ages. Well displayed and explained, it begins with early castle warfare and ends with the aerial bombardment of our times.

Laurier House★. – *Plan p. 120. 335 Laurier Ave E. Guided tours daily except Mon and hols ; about 1/2 hr ;* ☎ *992-8142.*

This yellow brick house with a verandah pays tribute to three Canadian Prime Ministers. In 1897, **Sir Wilfrid Laurier,** Canada's first French-speaking Prime Minister 1896-1911 (*p. 157*), moved into the house. After Sir Wilfrid's death, Lady Laurier willed the house to **William Lyon Mackenzie King,** grandson of the rebel (*p. 130*) and Prime Minister 1921-26, 1926-30, 1935-48. He in his turn lived in it until his death in 1950 and willed it to the nation along with his estate in the Gatineau (*p. 123*).

The visit includes Mr. King's study, bedroom, dining and other rooms, two rooms containing Laurier memorabilia, and finally a reconstruction of the library of **Lester Bowles Pearson,** Nobel Peace Prize winner 1957 and Prime Minister 1963-68. Pearson did not live in the house, but the photographs and cartoons in his library are fascinating.

Billings Estate★. – *Plan p. 120. 2100 Cabot St. Guided tours daily mid May - Labour Day ; weekdays only rest of year ;* ☎ *563-3075.*

This attractive white clapboard house with its dormer windows is one of Ottawa's oldest houses. Built in 1828 by Braddish Billings, it was inhabited by four generations of his family before becoming the property of the City of Ottawa in 1975. The rooms are full of documents, artifacts, photographs and furniture relating to all four generations. When the weather permits, tea is served on the lawn (*weekdays, 1-4pm*).

National Postal Museum. – *Plan p. 118. Open daily except Mon in winter ; 9am - 5pm ;* ☎ *995-9904.*

Operated by the Post Office, this museum displays the thousands of stamps in the national collection. They are mounted in withdrawable metal vertical files which make them easy to view. They are accompanied by a postal history of Canada, including a reconstruction of a turn-of-the-century post office where first day covers can be bought and postcards mailed with the special museum cancellation.

*An **Autopass** is available to visitors to the National Capital Region. Valid for 3 days, it gives up to 5 hours free parking at any one time at 15 different parking areas.* ☎ *992-5473 for details.*

■ DRIVES AROUND THE CAPITAL★★

Ottawa is well known for its lovely drives beside the river, canal and north into the Gatineau Hills.

Sussex Drive and Rockcliffe★★. – *Plan p. 120. 5.5 km - 3 1/2 miles starting from Confederation Square – about 1 1/2 hrs.*

This is a pleasant drive along the river and through the prestigious residential area of Rockcliffe. It passes the Basilica of Notre Dame and the Canadian War Museum and then, immediately after the Macdonald - Cartier bridge to Hull, a modern structure of darkened glass and concrete is seen on the left. This is the **Lester B. Pearson Building** which houses the Department of External Affairs. Then the road crosses the Rideau River to Green Island passing **Ottawa City Hall (H)** which offers a pleasant **view★** of the river from its top floor *(open weekdays 9am - 3.30pm).*

Rideau Falls★. – *Park beside French Embassy* **(F)**. The Rideau River drops over a sheer cliff into the Ottawa River on both sides of Green Island. *Rideau* means curtain in French, and this is what the falls are supposed to resemble. The amount of water depends on the time of year. They are best viewed in the spring or in winter when they are frozen. The first set of falls can be crossed by a bridge to see the second set. There are good views of the Ottawa River and Hull.

Continuing along Sussex Drive, the entrance to **24 Sussex Drive,** the official residence of Canadian Prime Ministers, is seen on the left. The grey stone house is hidden among the trees. It overlooks the river and is best viewed from the water. Just around the corner is the gate to **Rideau Hall,** the official residence of the Governor-General, the head of the Canadian government *(p. 12).* Guardsmen stand at the gate *(July and Aug ; 10am - 6pm).*

The route then passes through **Rockcliffe Park** on a one-way system. There are some good views of the river on the return section but a little further on there is a covered pavilion **(K)** from which there are excellent **views★★** of Pointe Gatineau on the Québec shore, of log booms in the river and of the Gatineau Hills in the distance. The church with the steeple in Pointe Gatineau is St. François de Sales built in 1886.

Rockcliffe itself is an area of large stone houses, tree-lined streets and lovely gardens, occupied by senior civil servants and members of the diplomatic corps. The drive ends at **RCMP Division N** where the horses and men of the famous **Musical Ride** are trained *(see Regina p. 89).* When the troupe is not on tour, the horses can be seen in training *(sometimes performances are given -* ☎ *993-2723 first for information ; stables open weekdays 8.30am - 4pm ; follow signs to visitors' parking outside Administration Building).*

Rideau Canal Driveways★. – *Plan p. 120. About 9 km - 6 miles starting from Confederation Square - about 1 hr.*

This is a picturesque, green and pleasant drive especially in tulip time *(May).* The **Queen Elizabeth Driveway** follows the west bank of the canal, the **Colonel By Drive** the east bank. In all seasons the canal is a centre for sports. Soon after setting out, the University of Ottawa, Canada's only bilingual university, is passed on the left. Later on, Carleton University will also be seen. At **Dow's Lake** where the canal widens out, there are fine tulip displays in May and paddle boats can be rented. At this point the two driveways diverge, the Colonel By continuing along the canal, the Queen Elizabeth entering the **Experimental Farm,** the headquarters of the Department of Agriculture. The greenhouses, animal barns, arboretum, and ornamental gardens can be visited *(open daily,* ☎ *995-5222).*

From the Colonel By Drive, there are views of Prince of Wales Falls and the Rideau Canal locks before the drive ends at Hog's Back Road.

Prince of Wales Falls★. – *Free parking in Hog's Back Park*. After it leaves Mooney's Bay, the Rideau River drops over these falls and rushes through a small gorge. The falls are the result of a geological fault that has heaved the terrain about to expose the underlying formations and strata. They are particularly impressive in the spring thaw. The dam was built by Colonel By in 1829.

Mooney's Bay marks the end of the canal section of the Rideau Canal, as after this the river is navigable. The Bay is also one of the main recreational areas of Ottawa with a beach and picnic grounds *(access from Riverside Drive)*.

Ottawa River Parkway★. – *11 km - 7 miles starting from Confederation Square – 1 hr.*
Wellington Street passes the Parliament Buildings, the Bank of Canada *(p. 118)* and the Supreme Court *(p. 119)*. The Parkway itself begins just after the Portage Bridge to Hull. Almost immediately, there are signs on the right to **The Mill**. This old stone structure built in 1842 was once a sawmill and gristmill, and it stood near a log flume - a means by which timber could be floated downstream without being battered by the Chaudière Falls. Today, The Mill has been restored, and it houses a restaurant run by the National Capital Commission.

The drive beside the Ottawa River is green and pleasant with several lookout points for the Remic Rapids. The best view of these rapids is from **Bate Island★** *(take Champlain Bridge to Hull and exit for island)*. The parkway continues with other good viewpoints.

Gatineau Park★★. – *Circular drive of 55 km - 34 miles from Confederation Square – about 3 hrs with tea. Cross Portage Bridge to Hull, turn left on Rte 148 for just over 2 km - 1 mile, then turn right on the Gatineau Parkway.*
This large park in the Gatineau Hills, part of the Canadian Shield, is run by the federal government. Much of it is wilderness but parts are devoted to outdoor recreation of many kinds – camping, swimming, fishing, biking, alpine and cross-country skiing *(☎ 819 - 827-2020 for details)*. **Camp Fortune,** the alpine ski centre, becomes an open air theatre in summer. The Prime Minister's official summer residence is also located in the park beside Harrington Lake *(not open to public)*. The Gatineau Parkway is partially a circular route through well kept parkland with fine trees. Many hiking trails start from it and there are good picnic spots.

Champlain Lookout★★. – *26 km - 16 miles.* From this terrace there is a sweeping view of the Ottawa River and valley. The lowlands end abruptly in the Eardley Escarpment of Precambrian rock on which the terrace is built. The river meanders over the valley widening out into lakes from time to time.

Moorside★. – *35 km - 22 miles (or 13 km - 8 miles from downtown direct). Turn off parkway to Kingsmere and follow signs. Open daily mid May - mid Oct 12am - 6.30pm ; ☎ (819) 827-2364.*
This small clapboard cottage with two dormer windows in the roof was the summer home of William Lyon Mackenzie King *(p. 121)* which he willed to the nation on his death. Inside, there is a **tea house** *(light lunches)* and a small museum of Canadiana of the Gatineau area. In the grounds, there is a collection of **ruins** which Mr. King had erected. Among them are pieces of the Parliament Buildings burnt in 1916 and pieces of the British Parliament bombed in 1941. The grounds are pleasant with several walks established by Mr. King.

*To find the description of a point of interest
which you already know by name,
consult the **index** p. 237.*

POINT PELEE National Park ★★

Maps pp. 9 and 98 – *9.5 km - 6 miles from Leamington. Open daily ; admission - see National Parks p. 21 ; no cars beyond Visitors' Centre April - Sept ; transit rides to rest of park 9am - 9pm ; canoe and bike rentals ; refreshments, picnic sites ; no camping or accommodation ; guided walks ; park map available at entry ; ☎ (519) 326-3204 - Local map p. 142*

This triangular-shaped peninsula sticking down into **Lake Erie** is the southernmost tip of the Canadian mainland. It is well known to ornithologists across North America and its latitude - 42°N, that of Rome, Northern California and Sapporo, Japan, gives it a plant and animal life unique in Canada.

The peninsula took its shape 10 000 years ago when wind and lake currents deposited sand on a ridge of glacial till under the water of Lake Erie. This ridge is today covered with as much as 60 m - 200 ft of sand. This sandspit is itself covered with a lush forest of deciduous trees (there are few evergreens). White sassafras covered with vines flourishes alongside hop trees, sumac, black walnut, sycamore, shagbark hickory, hackberry and red cedar. Beneath them all kinds of plants grow including the prickly pear cactus which has a lovely yellow flower. Indeed Point Pelee is one of the few places on the continent where the true deciduous forest of eastern North America still exists.

An Ornithologists' Paradise. – However, it is the **birds** that are the major attraction of Point Pelee for most people. The shape of the peninsula jutting down into Lake Erie, and the fact that it is one of the few uncultivated areas of highly agricultural Southern Ontario, attracts birds, and two major flyways converge here. The Spring and Fall migrations can be spectacular, as many as one hundred species have been sighted in one day. More than three hundred species have been recorded in the park, with approximately a hundred of them remaining to nest. September is also the month of the southern migration of the **monarch butterfly,** and visitors can see trees completely covered with these beautiful creatures.

POINT PELEE National Park ★★

VISIT

Visitors' Centre ★★. – *Open daily*. There are excellent flora and fauna displays in this centre as well as a graphic account of the creation of the peninsula. Slide presentations and films on the park can also be seen. A nature trail *(2 km - 1 1/4 miles)* starts from the centre.

Boardwalk ★. – The marshland area between the sand bars can be toured by a boardwalk *(1 km - 2/3 mile)*. There are two lookout towers with good **views ★** over the marsh where muskrats, turtles and fish can be seen in addition to birds.

From the end of the transit ride, visitors can walk to the tip of the peninsula, an ideal place to watch birds starting off across the lake in their migration south in the Fall. The sand bar continues under the waters of the lake for miles - a hazard for shipping. The modern lighthouse offshore stands on it.

From the tip, paths lead in both directions along the park's 22 km - 14 miles of fine sandy beaches *(accessible from other places also)*.

PRESCOTT ★
Map p. 99 – Pop 4 670

This small industrial town on the St. Lawrence is the only deep water port between Montréal and Kingston. Originally settled by Loyalists, it was the chosen location for a fort to protect shipping on the St. Lawrence from American attack during the War of 1812. It was also the site in 1838 of the **Battle of the Windmill.** Rebel supporters of Mackenzie *(p. 130)* and their American sympathizers occupied a windmill on the banks of the river and were only dislodged with difficulty.

Today, relations with the United States are more cordial and an international bridge spans the river near the town.

Fort Wellington ★. – *On Hwy 2 just E of town. Open daily mid May - Oct ; National Historic Park ;* 📞 *(613) 925-2896.*

This small fort built by the British is a good example of 18th century French military engineering. It has strong earthworks better able to withstand heavy artillery attack than stone walls. Inside, there is a three storey stone **blockhouse** restored to reflect military life in the 1840s and also Officers' Quarters. One weekend in July every year the fort is the location of a historic **military pageant** performed by British and American regiments in period costume.

A little to the east of the fort *(1.5 km - 1 mile)* between Highway 2 and the river stands the famous **windmill** of battle fame. Today it is a lighthouse but there are displays on the battle and a pleasant **view** of the river *(picnic tables)*.

SAULT STE. MARIE ★★
Map p. 9 – Pop 82 697 – Tourist Office 📞 (705) 949-7152 – *Local map below*

The "Soo" as the city of Sault Ste. Marie is commonly called lies on the north side of the **St. Mary's River,** the waterway which connects Lakes Superior and Huron and forms an important link in the St. Lawrence Seaway *(p. 170)*. The river is also the international boundary and Sault Ste. Marie, Ontario, is connected to Sault Ste. Marie, Michigan, by both road and railway bridges.

The rapids in the river between these two cities were a gathering place from earliest times when the Ojibwa Indians came to catch whitefish here. Etienne Brulé *(p. 130)* visited them in 1622 as did many of the great explorers of New France : Nicolet, Radisson, Groseilliers, Marquette, Jolliet, Lasalle, the La Vérendryes, etc. In 1668 Père Marquette established a mission beside them calling it Sainte Marie du Sault *(sault* means rapids in French). The **North West Company** built the first lock and canal to bypass the rapids in 1797-98. Since then, locks of increasing size have been constructed and today the enormous ships of the Great Lakes are able to bypass the rapids by four parallel locks on the American side of the river and one on the Canadian side (the Canadian section is a heritage canal operated by Parks Canada).

These locks are the busiest section of the entire Seaway handling a yearly average of eighty ships a day (unless extreme winter conditions cause a freeze-up) which amounts to more than 90 million metric tonnes - 100 million tons of cargo annually.

Sault Ste. Marie is also an industrial city with a huge steelworks and a pulp mill. It is the "gateway" to the wild and uninhabited **Algoma** wilderness to the north, and the headquarters of the Firebirds, Ontario's aerial firefighters who control the spread of forest fires by water-bombing among other things.

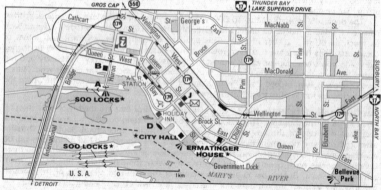

The Soo Locks★. – The vast lock system in the river can be appreciated either by driving to the base of Huron Street, where there is a **viewing platform (A)** of the Canadian lock and nearby a reconstruction of the first **lock** built by the North West Company **(B)**, or by taking a **boat trip** *(from Norgoma Dock beside Holiday Inn, mid May – mid Oct ; 2 hrs ; $9.00 ;* ☎ *253-9850)*. This boat trip goes through one of the big American locks and returns by the smaller Canadian one.

City Hall★. – Sault Ste. Marie has a pleasant riverfront area at the base of Brock Street dominated by its attractive City Hall built of copper coloured reflecting glass. Nearby stands the permanently berthed *MS Norgoma* **(D)**, the last passenger ship used on the Great Lakes *(guided tours June – mid Oct ; 30 mins ; $2.50)*.

Ermatinger House★. – *Open weekdays April – Nov, daily June – Sept ;* ☎ *949-1488.*

This attractive Georgian style stone house was built in 1814 by Charles Oakes Ermatinger, a partner in the North West Company, for his wife Charlotte, an Ojibwa princess. It has been restored to reflect this period when it stood almost alone in the region and received many eminent visitors. On the second floor, there are interesting displays on the history of Sault Ste. Marie and of the Ermatinger family.

Among the visitors was the artist **Paul Kane** (1810–1871), who made several long canoe trips across Canada sketching and making notes about the Indians of the Great Lakes, Plains and Pacific Coast regions. On his return to Toronto he wrote *Wanderings of an Artist among the Indians of North America,* which was published in 1859. His works can be seen in the Royal Ontario Museum *p. 136,* the National Gallery *p. 119,* and the Montréal Museum of Fine Arts *p. 164.*

Bellevue Park. – From this park on the river there are fine **views★** of the shipping using the locks and the bridge to the United States.

EXCURSIONS

Gros Cap★. – *26 km – 16 miles by Hwy 550.* From this headland, there is a fine **view★** of Lake Superior and the beginning of the St. Mary's River.

Train Trip to Agawa Canyon. – *183 km – 114 miles by Algoma Central Railway ; daily mid June – mid Oct, 8am – 5pm ; also snow train in Jan, Feb and Mar ; $25.50 ; refreshments ;* ☎ *254-4331 for information ; reservations can only be made 1 day in advance at the station.*

This train traverses some of the Algoma wilderness country north of Sault Ste. Marie. There is a stop-over in Agawa Canyon *(2 hrs, except in winter)* when travellers can climb to a lookout for a fine **view★** of the canyon and the Agawa River. This trip is especially popular in late September for the Fall colours.

Lake Superior Drive★★. – *230 km – 143 miles by Trans-Canada Hwy (17) to Wawa.*

This is a ruggedly beautiful drive as the road cuts through some of the oldest rock formations in the world - the Canadian Shield *(p. 97)*. For a long stretch after Batchawana Bay, the road follows the wild shore of Lake Superior with views of headlands, coves, islands, rocks and high granite bluffs all pounded by the waters of this the deepest of the Great Lakes. The drive is especially fine around **Alona Bay★** *(viewpoint after 108 km – 67 miles)* and **Agawa Bay★** *(viewpoint after 151 km – 94 miles)*. Lookouts have been built beside the road.

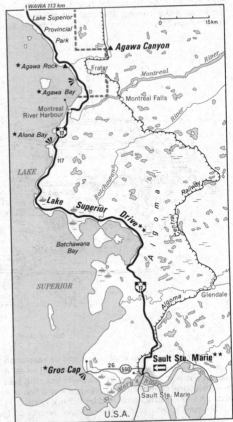

For 84 km – 52 miles, the road passes through **Lake Superior Provincial Park** *(camping, hiking, canoeing ;* ☎ *856-2284)*, a wilderness area of forested hills and cliffs rising straight out of the lake. It is also known for its Indian pictographs, primitive rock paintings often commemorating great events or related to nature. After 153 km – 95 miles, a side road leads to a parking lot from whence a rugged trail *(10 min)* descends to the lake. On a sheer rock face, called **Agawa Rock★**, rising out of the water are a series of these designs possibly several hundred years old. The **view★** of the lake is also very fine.

A few recommended books are given at the end of each regional introduction.

STRATFORD ★

Maps pp. 9 and 98 – Pop 26 262 – Tourist Office : 38 Albert St ☎ (519) 271-5140

This community is home every year to the **Shakespeare Festival** one of the major theatrical events of the English-speaking world. Every summer people travel from all over North America to Stratford for the Festival. It could be said that the Festival had its beginnings in 1830 when one William Sargint called his establishment on the Huron Road to Goderich *(p. 105)* the Shakespeare Inn. The community which grew up around it took the name of Stratford after the birthplace of the famous English dramatist and the river was named the Avon. In 1952 a local journalist, **Tom Patterson,** dreamed of creating a festival to celebrate the works of the poet in his Ontario "home". From modest beginnings one year later in a tent, the Festival has grown to its present proportions : a five month season *(June-Oct),* three theatres offering a wide variety of drama and music – though the central emphasis is still Shakespearean, and a visiting annual audience of nearly 500 000 *(for details contact Stratford Festival, P.O. Box 520, Stratford, Ontario N5A 6V2 ; ☎ 273-1600).*

Festival Theatre. – This building reflects the tent origin of the Festival. Somewhat resembling a circus "big top", it contains an apron or thrust stage surrounded on three sides by the audience. This modern development of the Elizabethan stage of Shakespeare's day was revolutionary in the 1950s (but since much copied) as it meant no elaborate scenery could be used and no member of the audience was more than 20 m - 65 ft from the stage.

The theatre is set at the edge of a pleasant park which stretches down to the River Avon, dammed at this point to form **Victoria Lake,** the home of many swans. Before evening performances in the summer, these lawns and the little island in the lake are covered with picnicking theatre-goers and at intermission the elegantly clad crowd wanders between the formal flower beds and over the beautifully manicured lawns which surround the theatre.

SUDBURY ★★

Maps pp. 9 and 98 – Metro Pop 149 923 – Tourist Office : Civic Square, West Tower, Brady St ; ☎ (705) 673-4161

Located on the largest single source of nickel in the world, Sudbury is one of the biggest and most important mining centres in Canada. Its mineral wealth (platinum, copper, cobalt, silver, gold, etc, in addition to nickel) comes from the geological formation known as the **Sudbury Basin.** This phenomenon, which is about 60 km - 37 miles long by 27 km - 17 miles wide, may have been created by a meteorite millions of years ago or it may have been the result of a huge volcanic eruption. Geological opinion is divided on the issue.

Whatever its origins, the mineral wealth of the Basin was discovered in 1883 during the construction of the Canadian Pacific Railway *(p. 16).* One **Thomas Flanagan,** a blacksmith, noticed a rust coloured patch of rock while working with a crew in a recently blasted rock cut just west of the present city. Today this discovery is commemorated by a plaque *(on Hwy 144 near the Murray Mine)* and by the fact that the city boasts the world's largest integrated nickel mining, smelting and refining complex topped by an enormous smoke stack – **Super Stack** – which rises 380 m - 1 250 ft above the surrounding countryside.

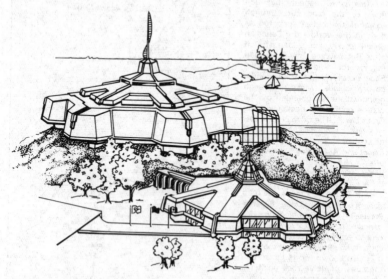

(By permission of Science North)

Science North

Despite its industrial importance and its reputation for pollution, the Sudbury region is typical Canadian Shield country with beautiful lakes, rocks and trees. In fact, a number of lakes are encompassed within city limits including **Lake Ramsey,** which has enough pickerel to supply local fishermen, and beaches just a few minutes walk from the Civic Centre. Its western end is today dominated by Science North *(p. 127).*

Sudbury is also one of the principal centres of Francophone culture in Ontario. The **Franco-Ontarians** make up about a quarter of the population of this region which they prefer to call *Le Nouvel Ontario* rather than Northern Ontario. **Laurentian University,** which serves the northeastern part of the province, is bilingual and there are a variety of other French cultural organizations and festivals.

■ **SIGHTS** *time : 1/2 day*

Science North★★. – *About 1.5 km - 1 mile S of Trans-Canada Hwy by Paris St on Ramsey Lake Rd. Opening mid 1984 - daily ; restaurant ; cafeteria ; gift shop ;* ☎ *522-3700.*

This dramatic science centre, perched on a rock outcropping on the shores of Lake Ramsey, was designed by **Raymond Moriyama** *(see also Toronto p. 137)* in association with local architects. A hexagonal exhibit building resembling a snowflake (to represent the glacial action which shaped Northern Ontario) is set over a cavern blasted out of the rock (to represent the probable creation of the Sudbury Basin by a meteor).

Visitors enter a small reception building (also hexagonal in shape) and proceed to the centre proper via a **rock tunnel**. The raw rock is exposed here as it also is in the impressive **rock cavern** (9 m - 30 ft high by 30 m - 100 ft in diameter) where an introductory film is shown. Then visitors ascend to the exhibit floors via a spiral ramp which zigzags over the **Creighton Fault**, a geological fracture within the Canadian Shield active over 2 billion years ago which has left a groove 4 m - 13 ft deep at this point. The glass walls of the ramp offer views of Lake Ramsey.

The exhibits are being developed to emphasize first-hand experience of science and northern technology. They will cover the life sciences, human performance, growth and development, computers, electro-magnetic phenomena, mechanics, astronomy and the earth sciences. Five "object" theatres will provide visitors with an overview of science and an understanding of broad concepts. A working forge will demonstrate the principles of forging, smelting, casting and alloying. Around it, there will be exhibits on the biosphere including an insect zoo, the atmosphere including an operating weather station and air quality monitoring device, and the geosphere including exhibits on continental drift, folding, fracturing, and on how mountains are formed. Scientific staff and guides will be on hand to help visitors experience and understand the exhibits.

Big Nickel Mine★★. – *On Trans-Canada Hwy just W of city. Open daily mid May - mid Oct ; underground tours $3.00 ; 1/2 hr ; protective clothing provided ; roughhouse and lapidary shop ; gift shop ; cafeteria ;* ☎ *673-5659.*

This demonstration mine run by Science North is the only authentic hard rock mine open to the public in Ontario. Visitors descend 21 m - 70 ft by miners' cage to the underground "drifts" or tunnels where the mining process (drilling, placing the explosives, blasting, mucking out, etc) is explained and demonstrated - there is even a simulated blasting sequence.

On the surface, visitors can buy pieces of ore from various Canadian mines in the roughhouse, and have them cut and polished in the lapidary shop, or watch craftsmen make jewelry, etc. The park above the mine is the site of a **Rockhound Festival** in August.

Near the mine stands the **Big Nickel**, a replica of the 1951 Canadian commemorative five cent piece. Long a Sudbury landmark, it stands 9 m - 30 ft high and is 0.6 m - 2 ft thick.

Path of Discovery. – *Twice daily late June - Labour Day ; 2 1/2 hrs ; $8.00 ;* ☎ *673-5659.*

This bus tour organized by Science North is designed to show visitors the Sudbury Basin and explain such things as its creation, the discovery of nickel, and the giant mining, smelting and refining operations of today.

THUNDER BAY ★★

Map p. 8 – Metro Pop 121 379 – Tourist Office ☎ *(807) 623-2711 - Local map below*

The city of Thunder Bay is situated almost at the centre point of Canada, yet it is among the country's largest ports (after Vancouver and Montréal). It stands on the shores of Lake Superior and it is the Canadian "lakehead" or western extremity of that vast inland waterway, the St. Lawrence Seaway *(p. 170)*. It is a clutter of rail lines transporting a wide range of commodities to the docks where the transfer to the huge ships of the Seaway takes place. Wheat from the Prairies is the most important commodity. Thunder Bay has fifteen enormous grain elevators dominating the skyline with a capacity of more than 2 million tonnes ; one of them, the **Saskatchewan Pool Terminal No. 7,** alone holds 362 650 tonnes making it one of the largest in the world.

There is also an enormous ore dock where the mineral wealth of Northern Ontario is loaded for market, and a modern coal-handling facility. This impressive port can not be appreciated from the land, a boat trip of the harbour is essential.

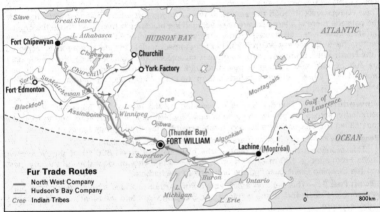

Fur Trade Routes
— North West Company
‑‑‑ Hudson's Bay Company
Cree Indian Tribes

THUNDER BAY★★

Lynchpin of the Fur Trade. – This exchange of goods and transportation at Thunder Bay is not a recent situation brought about by the construction of the St. Lawrence Seaway. Thunder Bay or rather Fort William (the communities of **Port Arthur** and **Fort William** were amalgamated in 1970 to create the city of Thunder Bay) was for many years the lynchpin of the fur trade. Every summer brigades of canoes left the widespread posts of the North West Company in the northwest and carried their year's collection of furs to Fort William. There these "wintering" partners (so named because they spent the winter in the wilds) met the Montréal partners who had made the long canoe trek through the Great Lakes with the trading goods their counterparts would need for the next year.

This **"rendezvous"** lasted about two weeks and was a time of wild celebration as well as serious discussion of trading policy and strategy against the rival Hudson's Bay Company, who were also established in the northwest and who took their furs to market by way of the great bay (*see also p. 74*). After the rendezvous, everyone returned from whence they had come, the transfer of goods completed. Fort William lost its position as the place of the great rendezvous when the two fur trading companies merged in 1821, but it remained a fur trading post until late in the century. Today, the fort has been recreated as it was at its peak and every year the rendezvous is re-enacted (*early July*).

■ **VISIT** *time : 1 day*

Harbour Cruise ★★. – *From Port Arthur marina at foot of Red River Rd (Hwy 102), daily mid May - early Oct ; 2 hrs ; $7.50 ;* ☎ *344-2512.*

This impressive and fascinating cruise is the only way to appreciate the port of Thunder Bay and the sheer size of the **elevators** (*guided tours possible weekdays in July and Aug, contact Tourist Office*) and the **lakers** that load at them. The largest of these ships may be 222 m - 728 ft by 23 m - 75 ft capable of carrying a million bushels of grain - the yield of 20 650 ha - 51 000 acres of land requiring five trains to carry it to Thunder Bay !

The ore docks, shipyards and drydock are seen as well as the Coast Guard Centre with its hovercraft used to break ice in the winter and the breakwater protecting the harbour from the storms of Lake Superior (waves can be 12 m - 40 ft high in the Fall). In the summer, however, the lake is calmer and sailboat races are held weekly in and out of the breakwater.

Old Fort William ★★. – *16 km - 10 miles by Broadway Ave. Also accessible by boat from Port Arthur marina, daily mid May - early Oct ;* ☎ *344-2512. Open daily mid May - Sept ; guided tours ; $3.00 ; restaurant ;* ☎ *577-8461.*

This is an excellent reconstruction of the fort of the great rendezvous located on the Kaministikwia River which was part of the trade route to the northwest. An essential introduction to the visit is the **film** (*20 min, every 1/2 hr*) which explains the rendezvous.

THUNDER BAY

Then visitors walk through the woods to the palisaded fort which is almost a town. Inside the palisade there is a large square of dovetailed log buildings some raised above the ground on stilts (the river still floods). Some fifty structures represent all aspects of early 19th century fur trade society. With the help of costumed guides, the life of the fort is recreated - the North West Company partners discuss business in the Council House, the warehouses are full of furs and trading goods, birchbark canoes, ships and barrels are built and repaired, etc. Other highlights include a farm, hospital, Indian encampments, living quarters and a jail.

Viewpoints ★. – Thunder Bay is surrounded by the hills of the Canadian Shield and hemmed in across the bay by the long peninsula which rears its head at its end to form the cape called the **Sleeping Giant** because of its resemblance to the prone figure of a man.

Mount McKay ★. – *At end of Mountain Rd on Indian reservation. Cars $3.00.*

This prominent flat topped peak is the highest (488 m - 1 600 ft) of the Norwester Chain. From a ledge 180 m - 600 ft up it, there is a fine **view** on clear days of the city, port and the Sleeping Giant guarding the entrance to the harbour.

Hillcrest Park ★. – This park on a cliff above Port Arthur provides a good **view** of the port, elevators, ore dock and, in the distance, the Sleeping Giant and the islands which close the harbour mouth.

EXCURSIONS

Kakabeka Falls ★★. – *29 km - 18 miles W by Trans-Canada Hwy (17). Provincial Park open daily ; camping.*

The Kaministikwia River plunges 39 m - 128 ft over a cliff round a pinnacle of rock into a narrow gorge. A bridge crosses the river to enable visitors to view the falls from both sides. These falls were the first obstacle negotiated by the fur traders of the North West Company when leaving Fort William on their return trip to the northwest.

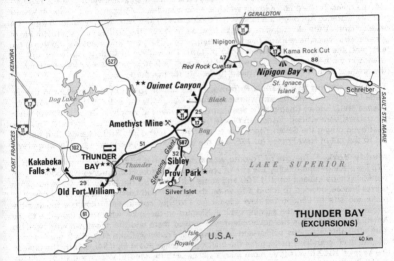

THUNDER BAY
(EXCURSIONS)

North Shore Superior ★★. – *211 km - 131 miles to Schreiber by Trans-Canada Hwy.*

This route passes several interesting features northeast of Thunder Bay.

Terry Fox Monument and Scenic Lookout. – *1 km - 1/2 mile E of Hodder Ave (plan p. 128).*

This fine bronze monument commemorates the heroic efforts of Terry Fox to raise money to fight cancer. Deprived of his right leg by the disease at age 18, he undertook a cross-Canada run in 1980 starting in Newfoundland. Two months later, he was forced to abandon his run close to this spot because of recurring cancer. He died of the disease in 1981. The monument overlooks Lake Superior.

Sibley Provincial Park ★. – *After 51 km - 32 miles take Rte 587. Camping ;* ☎ *933-4332.*

This pleasant park occupies most of the peninsula which has at its end the Sleeping Giant. There are trails, high cliffs, fine **views ★** of Lake Superior, and the remains of the village of Silver Islet. This community was formed in 1868 when a rich silver vein was discovered on the tiny islet offshore. This vertical vein yeilded $300 000 000 worth of ore before the shaft flooded at a depth of 400 m - 1 300 ft.

Amethyst Mine. – *After 56 km - 35 miles take East Loon Rd for 8 km - 5 miles. Open daily mid May - mid Oct ; $1.00 ; rock shop ;* ☎ *622-6908.*

Amethyst, a purple quartz, is found in many places along the north shore of Lake Superior. This open pit mine is a rockhound's delight as pieces of amethyst can be collected (*charge of $1.00 a lb*), or polished stones purchased.

Ouimet Canyon ★★. – *After 76 km - 47 miles take rough road for 12 km - 7 1/2 miles. Open daily mid May - mid Oct ; allow 1 hr ; caution : canyon is not fenced.*

This incredible canyon is quite a startling find in the country north of Lake Superior. Gashed out of the surface of the Canadian Shield by glaciers - or possibly a fault in the earth's crust, the canyon is 100 m - 330 ft deep, 150 m - 500 ft across and more than 1.5 km - 1 mile long. It is rocky and barren except for a few Arctic flowers which grow on its floor - the cold, sunless environment will support nothing else.

Just after the Red Rock turnoff on the Trans-Canada Highway, a cliff of layered limestone coloured red by hematite, can be seen. Called the **Red Rock Cuesta,** this unusual geological formation is nearly 210 m - 690 ft high and about 3 km - 2 miles long.

Nipigon Bay ★★. – *88 km - 55 miles from Nipigon to Schreiber.*

After crossing the Nipigon River, the Trans-Canada runs along the shore of this bay with constant **views ★★** of rocky islands covered with conifers and rocks worn smooth by the action of Lake Superior.

The **view ★★** of Kama Bay through the Kama Rock Cut (*27 km - 17 miles from Nipigon*) is particularly fine. The rock itself indicates the type of problems involved in the construction of this highway in 1960, the same met with when the Canadian Pacific Railway was built at the end of the last century (*p. 16*).

Sights described in this guide are rated :

★★★ worth the journey

★★ worth the detour

★ interesting

TORONTO ★★★

Maps pp. 9 and 98 – Metro Pop 2 998 947 – Tourist Office ☎ (416) 979-3143

Innovative, energetic, stimulating, today Toronto is the heart-beat of Canada and its largest city - it overtook Montréal in 1977. A major port thanks to the St. Lawrence Seaway, Toronto is also the hub of the **Golden Horseshoe**, the area within an arc about 160 km - 100 miles wide stretching from Oshawa to Hamilton where a huge percentage of Canada's manufacturing industry is located. The city itself is home to many head offices and has one of the busiest stock exchanges in North America.

Toronto is set on the north shore of **Lake Ontario** and it sprawls over a vast 62 178 ha - 240 sq miles. It has a fine harbour which is almost landlocked because of a series of islands in Lake Ontario. Although the land is flat beside the lake, it rises sharply about 5 km - 3-4 miles inland at the old shoreline of Lake Iroquois (p. 139). The plain is cut by a multitude of small rivers which have made ravines for themselves. The most important are the **Don** in the east and the **Humber** in the west (map p. 138). The valleys of both these rivers and the islands in the lake have been largely used for parks. In fact Toronto is singularly fortunate in the amount of land put aside or given to the city for this purpose.

Toronto during the French Regime. – The site of Toronto was important in the fur trade long before a permanent white settlement was made there. In 1615 it was visited by **Etienne Brulé**, one of Champlain's young men who travelled widely in Ontario. Soon French fur traders were visiting the site and **Fort Rouillé** was built to protect their interests. This was destroyed during the Seven Years War to prevent its falling into British hands - but the war led to the fall of New France (p. 175) and the end of French presence in the Toronto area.

Muddy York. – The site of Toronto was at first ignored by the new British rulers but in 1787 a piece of land roughly the size of present day Metropolitan Toronto was bought from the Missisauga Indians for £ 1 700 and some gifts. In 1793 the Lieutenant Governor, **John Graves Simcoe,** decided to found a town on the site. He had been frustrated in his desire to make the site of London his new capital (p. 110) but considered Toronto a much more strategic location than the existing capital, Niagara-on-the-Lake, which was too close to the American border. Thus the government was moved there and the new town was baptised **York** after the victorious soldier-son of George III, Frederick Duke of York. It grew slowly despite such grandiose projects as the building of **Yonge Street** (p. 134), and by the time of the War of 1812 it was little more than a village with the unfortunate sobriquet of "Muddy York", because its swampy site caused all the streets to be just that.

In April of 1813 the town was jolted out of its slumber by the arrival of an American fleet which rapidly proceeded to capture it and burn down the Legislature with the few other imposing buildings. In retaliation for this and for the burning of Niagara-on-the-Lake, the British attacked Washington in 1814 and burnt part of it - the smoke damage on the Presidential residence was covered up with white paint, which gave it its name.

The Family Compact. – After the war York began to grow thanks to the great waves of immigrants who came to Ontario from Britain after the Napoleonic Wars. Government of York and of the whole of Upper Canada had become concentrated in the hands of a small group of wealthy, privileged men with strong British ties who maintained an exclusive elite and appointed officials only from their own ranks. The power of this group, who were called the Family Compact, began to be challenged by some of the new arrivals. One of these, a fiery Scot named **William Lyon Mackenzie,** used his newspaper, *The Colonial Advocate,* to mount attacks on the group. In 1828 he was elected to the Legislative Assembly and became the leader of the radical wing of the Reform Party which opposed the Family Compact. He was expelled by the latter, re-elected and re-expelled five times and even declared incapable of sitting. Then in 1835 he was elected the first mayor of the City of Toronto (incorporated 1834) and he re-assumed his seat in the Legislature. This victory for the Reform Party was however short-lived as in 1836 the Assembly was dissolved by the Governor, **Sir Francis Bond Head,** and the subsequent elections saw their defeat at the polls.

Mackenzie appealed to the British Parliament but gaining no satisfaction there he turned to armed rebellion. He gathered his supporters at **Montgomery's Tavern** (near present intersection of Yonge and Eglinton Streets) when the Toronto garrison was absent in Lower Canada (p. 161) and commenced marching down Yonge Street towards the city. Some loyal citizens hurriedly got together to form a defence but quickly turned tail after a skirmish with Mackenzie's men. Unknown to them Mackenzie's troops also retreated, and the same thing happened the next day when reinforcements arrived under Colonel Allan MacNab (p. 107). This was the end of the revolt in Toronto but Mackenzie fled to the United States where he stirred up more trouble for some years.

Toronto the Good. – Despite the comic-opera touch to the revolt it had its effect as it persuaded the British Parliament to grant responsible government to the Canadian colonies. The United Province of Canada was created (p. 100) and Mackenzie was allowed to return. The other effect of the revolt was a hatred of violence and support for the government among Torontonians which lasted for a very long time. In fact by the end of the 19th century Toronto had acquired the reputation of being a bastion of Anglo-Saxon rectitude. It was immensely wealthy thanks to its growth as a major manufacturing centre but financiers, industrialists and wealthy merchants were all of one mind when it came to preserving Sunday as a day of rest and church-going, when no other form of social activity was allowed, and to believing that intemperance was a fundamental social problem. Toronto was nicknamed "The Good" and people considered it dull. **Rupert Brooke** wrote of it in 1913: "It is not squalid like Birmingham or cramped like Canton, or scattered like Edmonton or a sham like Berlin or hellish like New York or tiresome like Nice : but the depressing thing is, it will always be like it is, only bigger". Little did he know.

Toronto Today - The Urban Miracle. – As late as 1941 Toronto was 80 % Anglo-Saxon, but since the Second World War this has changed. Immigrants from all over the world have descended on this once smug and puritanical city. It has blossomed - some of the old smugness remains (Torontonians know their city is best) but none of the puritanism. Instead it is very vibrant and colourful. Italians, Germans, Ukrainians, Dutch, Poles, Scandinavians, Portuguese, Indians, Chinese, West Indians etc, have all made their home in the city and by doing so have made Toronto truly cosmopolitan and given it a stimulating mix of indigenous and imported cultural activities. The area around **Kensington Market** *(plan p. 135)* is the realm of the Portuguese community. **Chinatown** *(Dundas St from Elizabeth St to Spadina Ave)* has a completely different character. The Italian districts *(College Street west of Bathurst)* contain people and places straight from Italy. It is hard to credit the change which has taken place in Toronto. Walking along **Yorkville Avenue** in the middle of the night, a visitor could well imagine he were in London or Paris ; and **Markham Street** and **Cabbagetown** *(plan p. 132)* are other colourful areas.

The last fifteen years have seen the Toronto skyline transformed. Once dominated by the **Royal York Hotel** and the old **Bank of Commerce Building**, it now has shining glassfronted skyscrapers and the CN Tower. This rapid development caused much heartache to many people, and citizen action groups were formed to stop the destruction of residential areas for highrise and freeways. The success of these groups added to all the other advantages that Toronto has to offer have made it an exception to the trend in most North American cities - it has remained livable while supporting an ever increasing population and an industrial base to supply them with jobs. Toronto was also the first city in North America to embark on a metropolitan or tiered system of government to overcome the problems of controlling development caused by municipal boundaries created in the 19th century.

Cultural and Sports Centre. – Toronto is the centre of English language culture in Canada. It offers symphony concerts, the National Ballet of Canada, the Canadian Opera Company and a large number of lively theatre groups performing experimental works as well as more traditional pieces. It is also a great centre for almost every sport imaginable : skiing, sailing, horseback riding, etc (☎ *Sports Ontario 964-8655 for details).*

There are several events which draw visitors to the city, the **Canadian National Exhibition** (CNE) being the biggest *(held in the Exhibition Grounds for three weeks before Labour Day).* Also popular are : the **Metro International Caravan,** a festival of the culture of the various ethnic groups in the city *(late June, pavilions all over city, special buses),* the **Dragon Mall,** a Chinese celebration *(August, Elizabeth Street),* and **Caribana,** a West Indian festival of steel bands, floating night clubs in the lake, etc *(August).* For details contact the Tourist Office.

Visiting Toronto. – *The many sights of this city are listed according to the area in which they are located. We recommend organizing a visit in this way. However, visitors with little time (1-2 days) may prefer to concentrate on Toronto's world class attractions* (**CN Tower**★★★ *below,* **Royal Ontario Museum**★★★ *p. 136,* **Ontario Science Centre**★★★ *p. 137,* **Metro Toronto Zoo**★★★ *p. 138,* the **McMichael Canadian Collection**★★★ *p. 139) not forgetting that* **Niagara Falls**★★★ *p. 111, is only a 130 km - 81 mile drive away.*

Toronto has an excellent public transport system with a clean and efficient subway and streetcars in addition to buses. "Ride Guides" are available from the Tourist Office, and information can be obtained by ☎ 484-4544.

■ THE WATERFRONT AREA★★

Unless otherwise indicated see plan p. 132

The area to the south of Front Street is largely reclaimed land. At one time Front Street was just that with the lake lapping up to the houses built along it. Now railways, expressways and the port lie between it and the lake.

CN Tower★★★. – *Access from Front St – plan p. 135. Open daily, 9am - 10pm in summer (11pm Sun) 10am - 10pm in winter ; $4.00 to Sky Pod, additional $1.00 to Space Deck ; parking $2.50 ; revolving restaurant (reservations advised) ; cafeteria ; gift shops ; ☎ 360-8500.*

The tall slim concrete rocket-like structure is 553.33 m - 1 815 ft 5 ins high making it the tallest free-standing building in the world. Considered elegant by some and a monstrosity by others, it certainly enhances Toronto's skyline. It was built by Canadian National Railways (CN) not primarily as a tourist attraction, though that is what it has become. It contains a transmission mast for radio and television stations and microwave facilities for CN telecommunications.

The circular bump about two thirds of the way up is called the **Sky Pod.** Glassfronted elevators mount the outside of the tower to it in just one minute. The Pod is seven stories "thick" and has good views. But by no means miss the ascent to the **Space Deck,** 447 m - 1 465 ft above the ground. From this height the **view**★★★ is superb and it is rather akin to being in an airplane. On a clear day Niagara Falls and Buffalo 120 km - 75 miles away can be seen,

The C N Tower

but such days are rare in summer. The impression of height is reinforced as the planes from Toronto Island Airport fly past below the tower. The great number of parks and trees in Toronto is evident as is the contrast between the industrial and transportation life directly below and the placid lake and peaceful islands.

Roy Thomson Hall★★ . *Plan p. 135. Guided tours Tues, Thurs and Sat, 12.30pm ; otherwise no admission except for concerts ; ☎ 593-4822.*

This glittering circular glass-sheathed structure which opened in 1982 was designed by Arthur Erickson *(see p. 59).* The walls are made of diamond-shaped glass panels which shimmer by day and are transparent at night when lit. Not only is Roy Thomson Hall an

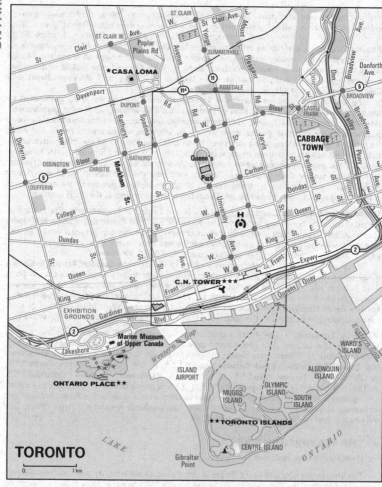

architectural triumph, but it is also a masterpiece acoustically. The concert hall itself is reached through sound-proof doors from the outer shell and everything in the interior – from the soft grey carpeting to the colourful woven banners hanging from the roof – is organized to achieve the best acoustical results (the banners can be raised or lowered to adjust the resonance of the hall).

Ontario Place★★. – *955 Lakeshore Blvd W, access from Exhibition Grounds. Open daily mid May - mid Sept; $4.00; free parking in Exhibition Grounds except during CNE, pay parking on site; restaurants, refreshments, gift shops; visit: 1/2 day;* ☎ *965-7711.*

Described by someone as looking like a "futuristic off-shore oil drilling rig", Ontario Place is a leisure complex built on man-made islands among lagoons where the people of Ontario (and elsewhere) can enjoy themselves. It has nothing of the funfair about it but is based on the idea of the Tivoli Gardens in Copenhagen.

Five metal "pods" suspended above the lake house the pavilion theatres which have all types of shows, and often excellent films on Ontario. The **Cinesphere** which looks like a giant golf ball covered with lights has a curved screen six storeys high where films are shown. The **Forum** is an outdoor concert hall with a suspended tent roof built in a hollow so that audiences can sit on the grassy slopes as well as seats to watch ballet or opera, or listen to the Toronto Symphony Orchestra or a pop concert. The **Children's Village** has a large wading pool full of water jets and games (and a huge "kid" dryer shaped like a bird).

The complex can be toured on foot or in a paddleboat. There is a marina where the **HMCS Haida**, a Canadian destroyer that saw service in the Second World War and the Korean War, is docked *(open daily mid May - mid Sept 75¢)*. Boat trips of the Toronto Islands leave from the marina.

Harbour and Islands Boat Trip★★. – *From dock at foot of Yonge St daily May - Oct; from Ontario Place daily mid May - mid Sept; and from Harbourfront daily June - Labour Day, weekends until mid Oct; 1 hr; $6.95;* ☎ *364-2412.*

These cruises offer excellent **views★★** of downtown Toronto. The docks are glimpsed and the cruise through the islands is pleasant.

Toronto Islands★★. – *Ferry from foot of Yonge St to 3 different points mid May - mid Sept, 2 points rest of year (not Centre Island); $1.50 return; no cars, pay parking lots close to ferry terminal; refreshments; bicycle rentals;* ☎ *Metro Toronto Parks Dept 947-8193.*

These islands, which are almost completely parkland, are a pleasant and popular retreat from the heat of the city in summer. A wind off the lake keeps them cool on even the most humid days. One of their chief attractions is the magnificent **views★★** of the city obtained from them, but there is also an amusement area for children, beaches on Lake Ontario, picnic spots with barbecue pits and miles of bicycle and foot paths.

Geologically, the islands are also interesting because they have not always been surrounded by water. They are formed of material eroded from Scarborough Bluffs (p. 139) and were once a peninsula. In 1853, a violent storm washed a gap through them (Eastern Gap) making them islands. The sand of which they are made is still moving. Gibraltar Point Lighthouse was once on the water's edge !

Old Fort York★. – Plan p. 135. Access by car : from Lakeshore Blvd take Strachan just before Princes' Gate entrance to Exhibition Grounds, then right on Fleet St and left on Garrison Rd (under Gardiner Expressway) ; or by Bathurst Streetcar. Open daily ; $3.00 ; refreshments ; gift shop ; ☏ 366-6127.

On a most unlikely site surrounded by railway tracks and expressways stands Old Fort York. The site is original but the surroundings have changed greatly - once the waters of Lake Ontario lapped against the walls !

Fort York was first constructed in 1793 by Governor Simcoe. It was captured along with the rest of the town by the Americans in 1813 and destroyed. Reconstructed after the war, its military importance gradually diminished as threats from the United States subsided. After 1841 a "new" fort was built to the west, of which Stanley Barracks, the present Marine Museum (see below) was part, and the old fort fell into disuse. In 1934 it was renovated for the city of Toronto's centennial and it has become a tourist attraction.

The eight buildings which date from 1813-15 have been authentically restored. The **Officers' Quarters** is the oldest surviving residential building in the city and it has been carefully furnished to show the lifestyle of the senior officers of the period. One room houses a fascinating display on the development of the role of the military surgeon and his techniques. The **Blue Barracks** contains interesting exhibits on the military history of Canada 1792-1967. The **Soldiers' Barracks** houses a display of York in 1818, a model of the fort in 1816 and a plan of Toronto today with one of the early 19th century superimposed over it to show such things as the change in the edge of the lake.

In one of the blockhouses a diorama on the Battle of York in 1813 can be viewed (13 min) and also a film on life in a British military post after the War of 1812 (20 min). Costumed soldiers conduct tours of the fort and in summer perform manœuvres.

Marine Museum of Upper Canada. – In Exhibition Grounds. Open daily ; $1.50 ; restaurant ; ☏ 595-1567.

The museum is housed in a grey limestone building, the last remaining structure of Stanley Barracks built in 1841 (see above). It concentrates on the development of shipping on the Great Lakes and St. Lawrence River. There are displays on canals, navigational aids, shipwrights' tools and other maritime subjects, as well as ship models and other marine artifacts.

Outside the museum stands the steam tug Ned Hanlan which can be boarded during the summer months.

Also on the Exhibition Grounds, hockey fans can visit the **Hockey Hall of Fame** (open daily except Mon in winter ; $2.00 ; ☏ 595-1345) where the Stanley Cup is generally on display (p. 21).

Harbourfront★. – Plan p. 135. Access from York St and Spadina Ave ; bus 77B from Union subway station ; information centre at 235 Queens Quay West ; ☏ 364-5665.

This collection of wharfs in Toronto harbour covering about 37 ha – 91 acres is gradually being renovated by the federal government to make a waterfront park. There are marinas, lakeside walkways, outdoor cafes and a variety of different cultural and recreational events.

The **York Quay Centre** contains an art gallery, craft studios and summer theatre in addition to an information centre. The **Queen's Quay Terminal** is a completely renovated building with offices, living accommodation, a range of boutiques and restaurants, and the Premiere Dance Theatre on the third floor.

Pier 4 has an antique market (Sun, indoors in winter), a marina, sailing schools and nautical stores. And more is planned.

■ THE BANKCORE★★ plan p. 135

The King and Bay Street area of Toronto could be described as Canada's Wall Street. The Stock Exchange (A) is found here beside the major branches of some of the country's leading banks. The original name of Bay Street was Bear Street, not because of the number of people who have burned their fingers on the Stock Exchange but because in early days those animals were frequently observed ! Today, peering up at the vast structures which compete amongst themselves to be the highest or the most attractive, this is difficult to imagine. The major buildings are connected underground by concourses and passage ways housing a wide variety of shops and restaurants.

Toronto Dominion Centre★. – The black reflecting glass buildings of the Toronto Dominion Centre, headquarters of the bank of the same name, were inspired by the ideas of the architect Mies van der Rohe, who was involved in the project as a consultant.

Royal Bank Plaza★. – This is the Ontario district office of the Royal Bank. Two triangular towers of gold reflecting glass flank a 40 m - 130 ft high glass-walled banking hall. Beneath them is a concourse of shops around a garden court.

Commerce Court. – This complex contains the head office of the Canadian Imperial Bank of Commerce. Like the TD Centre it consists of four buildings around a central court, the dominant structure being a 57-storey stainless-steel-clad tower designed by I. Mario Pei.

First Canadian Place. – This complex consists of two towers. One First Canadian Place (72 storeys) houses the Toronto offices of the Bank of Montréal. Two First Canadian Place (36 storeys) or the Exchange Tower houses the **Toronto Stock Exchange.** They are connected underground by a plaza of elegant shops and there is an attractive waterfall at street level. A passageway under Adelaide Street leads to **The Lanes,** a shopping development in the Richmond-Adelaide Centre which extends as far as the Sheraton Centre. This provides a pleasant enclosed means of walking to City Hall.

TORONTO ★★★

■ CITY HALL AREA ★★ *plan p. 135*

Toronto's City Hall stands in **Nathan Phillips Square** with its pool where fountains play in the summer and office workers skate in the winter. In front of it stands a large bronze sculpture by Henry Moore.

City Hall★. – The two crescent-shaped towers connected by a mushroom-like structure have been the symbol of Toronto since they were completed in 1965. Designed by Finnish architect, **Viljo Revell,** Toronto City Hall has been internationally acclaimed as an architectural masterpiece. Today, hemmed in on all sides by higher towers, City Hall has lost a little of its 1965 glamour but is nonetheless worth visiting.

The two curved towers and the mushroom-shaped central part rise from a three storey podium. This contains the "stem" of the mushroom which is the only support for the council chamber at the top. The two towers are unequal in height and are clad with concrete on one side and windows on the other. There are **guided tours** of the complex *(Mon-Fri except hols ; from main Lobby ; ☎ 947-7341).*

The previous home of the City Fathers, **Old City Hall,** stands on the east side of Nathan Phillips Square providing an interesting contrast in architectural style with its clock tower and castle-like appearance. To the south is the **Sheraton Centre,** the beginning of an underground route of shops leading to the Bankcore *(p. 133).* West of the square hidden behind trees is **Osgoode Hall,** home of the Law Society of Upper Canada. The iron fence around it on Queen Street was put up shortly after its construction in 1829 to keep cows and horses off the lawn ! Next to it between the square and University Avenue, stands the **Court House (J).** A circular building called the Rotunda protrudes from it, under which a path leads to University Avenue.

The Eaton Centre★★. – *Open Mon - Sat ; ☎ 598-2322.*

This enormous shopping complex which stretches for several blocks is enclosed by a gigantic glass and steel arched roof. Inside with its natural lighting, trees, plants and fountains, it is reminiscent of the Crystal Place built in London to house the Great Exhibition of 1851. There are shops and restaurants on three levels with offices above. The centre was developed by a consortium including the T. Eaton Company which had its beginnings on this site in 1868 and now has stores coast to coast. Shopping at Eatons and at its rival Simpsons *(connected to the Centre by a bridge across Queen Street),* which opened in 1871, is an essential part of Toronto life.

Both Eatons and Simpsons stand on **Yonge Street** one of the best known roads in Canada. It was built by Governor Simcoe in 1795 as a military road to Lake Simcoe.

Art Gallery of Ontario★★. – *Open daily except Mon, 11am - 5.30pm (until 9pm Wed and Thurs) ; $3.50 includes admission to The Grange ; free Thurs eve ; restaurant, cafeteria ; gallery shop ; ☎ 977-0414.*

Approaching the white concrete structure on Dundas Street, which houses an art collection of no small importance, it is hard to imagine that in 1900 the AGO was a gallery with no home and no collection ! Its first permanent home was The Grange, today restored to its former splendour while the gallery has moved into adjoining custom-built quarters.

Henry Moore Sculpture Centre★★. – Opened in 1974 by Moore, one of the best known living sculptors, the Centre displays more than 300 of his works including 5 large bronzes, 40 major original plasters, 43 plaster maquettes, 200 woodcuts, lithographs and etchings, and 60 drawings. Most of these were donated by the artist himself when he discovered that the AGO intended to devote a gallery to him. It is now the largest public collection of his works in the world.

Ascending the ramp to the second floor, a fine bronze *Warrior with Shield* which Moore completed in 1954 can be seen. The **Irina Moore Gallery** houses a vast collection of small things - models, casts, bronzes, sketches and etchings, but it is the **Moore Gallery** itself which is the *pièce de résistance.* In this room which was designed by Moore to use natural lighting from the ceiling, there are more than fifteen large sculptures - all plaster casts or original plasters for some of Moore's famous bronzes, an impressive collection.

The European Collection★★. – Walker Court with its important collection of sculptures (Rodin, Degas, Bourdelle, Malliol, Picasso and others) is at the centre of this fine collection which covers the Old Masters, Impressionism and early 20th century movements. It is well laid-out in small galleries through which visitors can wander *(for preference begin in Fudger Rotunda and proceed anti-clockwise).* Among the highlights are works by Peter Brueghel the Younger, Tintoretto, Rembrandt, Franz Hals, Gainsborough *(The Harvest Waggon),* Reynolds, Renoir (Le Concert), Degas, Monet, Van Gogh, Gauguin, Picasso *(Crouching Woman),* Dufy and Augustus John *(The Marchesa Casati).*

The selection from the permanent collection is changed regularly so not all of these works may be seen at the same time. Also these galleries are sometimes used for major visiting exhibitions.

The Canadian Collection★. – An extension houses this comprehensive collection with fine examples of the Group of Seven *(p. 139)* and contemporary artists.

The AGO also has several galleries devoted to changing displays and a pleasant restaurant with an outdoor terrace in summer.

The Grange★. – *Entrance through Art Gallery or from Grange Rd. Open daily except Mon 12am - 4pm (6-9pm Thurs). Admission as for Art Gallery.*

Built in 1817 by **D'Arcy Boulton Jr,** this simple but elegant Georgian house once stood on grounds which stretched from Queen to Bloor Street. It was the centre of the social and political life of Upper Canada under the Boulton family, Loyalists from New England who became leaders of the Family Compact *(p. 130).* One of the Boultons, Henry John, played a leading part in four of the five expulsions of William Lyon Mackenzie from the Legislature.

In 1875, The Grange became the home of **Goldwin Smith,** Regius Professor of History at Oxford and a well known scholar. He turned the Grange into a centre of intellectual pursuits and progressive ideas. His widow willed the house to the newly formed Art Gallery of Toronto (now of Ontario) and it became their permanent home in 1909.

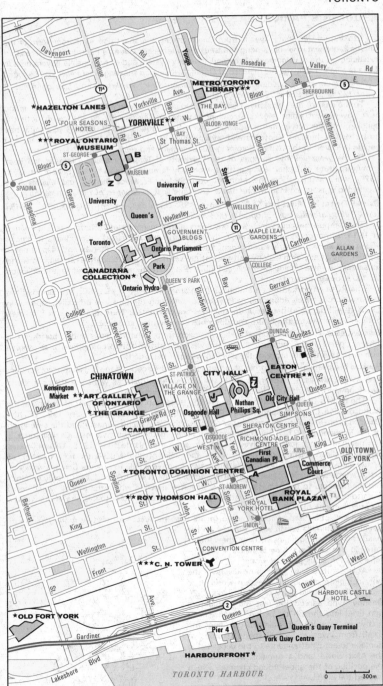

In 1973, the house was restored to its 1830s appearance. The rooms are meticulously furnished to give the aura of the Family Compact days. The basement contains kitchens typical of a gentleman's house in the 19th century. Of special interest is the beautiful curved cantilever staircase.

Campbell House★. – *Guided tours daily except weekends in winter ; $1.00 ;* ☎ *597-0227.*
This fine Georgian mansion once belonged to Sir William Campbell, chief justice of Upper Canada 1825-29. It was moved to this spot from its original location in 1972. There is an photo display detailing this move in the basement. The rest of the house is furnished with period pieces, and local history displays can be seen on the second floor.

Mackenzie House (E). – *Open daily ; $1.50 ;* ☎ *595-1567.*
This Victorian house was the last home of **William Lyon Mackenzie,** first mayor of Toronto but better known as the leader of the 1837 Revolt in Upper Canada *(p. 130).* When his rebellion failed he fled to the United States and lived in exile until 1849 when he was allowed to return to Toronto. Friends purchased this house for him and he lived in it until his death in 1861.
The house itself has been restored to the 1850 period. There are displays on Mackenzie's life and demonstrations of his hand-operated flatbed printing press on which he produced *The Colonial Advocate.*

■ **QUEEN'S PARK AREA**★★ *plan p. 135*

Looking up University Avenue from Queen Street, the squat pink sandstone form of the **Ontario Parliament** is visible among the trees and statues of Queen's Park. Inside, there is an exhibition on the development of the parliamentary system and of responsible government in Canada also a display on the minerals of Ontario with a map showing where each can be found.

Guided tours of the building *(daily June – Labour Day ; weekdays and hols only rest of year ; 1/2 hr ; ☎ 965-4028)* are available.

To the east of the Legislative Building, called simply "Queen's Park" by Ontarians, stand new government office blocks stretching across to Bay Street. To the south note the building with the curved mirror sidewall. This is the headquarters of **Ontario Hydro** and it has no furnace or heating plant. Instead energy given off by artificial lighting, equipment and people is stored in thermal reservoirs in the basement and recirculated.

To the west lies the campus of the **University of Toronto,** Canada's largest and best known institute of higher learning. It is especially famous for its Medical School where in 1921, while working on the problem of diabetes, **Frederick Banting** and **Charles Best** succeeded in isolating insulin, one of the great medical discoveries of the 20th century.

Royal Ontario Museum★★★. – *Plan p. 135. Open daily except hols ; $2.50 ; guided tours 1 hr ; cafeteria ; gift shop ;* ☎ *978-3690/92.*

This famous museum which was once part of the University of Toronto was first opened in 1914. Although independent now, the museum has maintained its academic traditions and is well known as a research organization. It consists of more than twenty departments in the fields of art, archaeology and the natural sciences – a combination rare among world museums. It also includes the McLaughlin Planetarium and the Canadiana Collection *(p. 137)* housed separately.

The ROM embarked on an ambitious program of renovation in 1980. This included the construction of much additional gallery space. Although the museum officially reopened in 1982, it will be 1990 before all the galleries are completed. Thus, the text which follows outlines the plans for the future and describes the situation at present.

Main Entrance Hall. – The domed ceiling is made from Venetian glass and it portrays the different parts of the museum. In the stairwells stand two totem poles, one three storeys high. It relates the life story of the chief to whom it belonged.

Mankind Discovering. – This forms an introduction to the scope of the museum's collections.

East Asian Galleries. – *Partially open.* In the future, these galleries will trace the continuous development of China and illustrate other East Asian cultures.

The ROM's Chinese collection is one of the largest and most important of its kind in the world outside China. It spans nearly 4 000 years from the Shang Dynasty 1523 BC (the Chinese Bronze Age) to the overthrow of the Ch'ing or Manchu Dynasty and the setting up of the Republic in 1912. The collection was mainly gathered by two men, **George Crofts,** a fur merchant and trader who lived in Tientsin and, after his death in 1925, **William Charles White,** Anglican Bishop of Honan. With the help of the Museum's first director of archaeology, **Dr. Charles Trick Currelly,** these two men were able to procure Chinese works of art at a time when such pieces were little known in the Western world. Dr. Currelly committed the museum to the acquisition of this art never knowing where the money would come from to pay for it. The money was however found and today Toronto has one of the world's great collections of Chinese Art.

The collection is particularly noted for its **tomb retinues** – exquisitely made replicas of people and animals which were buried with the dead, and other figurines such as the famous ceramic **Yen Lo Wang, King of Hades** – a magnificently ferocious piece of work.

At present, a **Ming Tomb** is on display - the only complete one in the Western world. It is reportedly the burial place of a 17C general, Zu Dashou, who served the last Ming emperors and lived into the Ch'ing period. It consists of archways, statues of animals guarding the tomb from invasion by evil spirits, statues of humans to act as attendants to the deceased in the next world, and a tumulus which marked the position of the underground chamber which housed the coffin.

Also on view is the **Bishop White Gallery** which contains three very fine Chinese temple frescoes. The largest, Maitreya Paradise, is Buddhist with a probable date of 1320. It is flanked by two Daoist frescoes from Shanxi province of about the same date. In addition, a series of large polychromed and gilded statues of Bodhisattvas of 12-14 th centuries stand in the gallery.

(after photo by Royal Ontario Museum)

Yen Lo Wang - Ming Dynasty

Earth Sciences. – *Not yet open.* These galleries will house displays on geology and mineralogy including the ROM's magnificent **gem collection**. There will also be an astronomy section attached to the Planetarium.

Life Sciences. – *Partially open.* A gallery on Darwin's theory of evolution forms an introduction to this section which contains displays on botany, living invertebrates especially arthropods, reptiles and mammals. There are some excellent **dioramas** of the wildlife of different parts of the world. Also included are interesting exhibits on invertebrate and vertebrate fossils. The highlight of the latter section is the truly magnificent display of re-assembled huge **dinosaur skeletons** in authentic settings. The skeletons come from upper cretaceous rocks exposed in the badlands of the Red Deer River valley in central Alberta which is one of the richest dinosaur collecting places in the world *(p. 83)*.

From the Collections. – This changing display features favourites from the ROM's collections such as mineral specimens, Egyptian mummies, West African masks, armour, etc.

Prehistory. – *Not yet open.*

The Mediterranean World. – *Partially open.* This series of inter-linked galleries presents a fascinating look at the development of civilization in Egypt, the Near East and the Classical World around the Mediterranean basin. Such things as the beginning of recorded history (writing), the origins of monotheism (Judaism and Christianity) and the growth of manufacturing and trade (Imperial Rome) are explained. One highlight is the **Islamic section** with its reproduction of a Middle Eastern house and bazaar.

European Galleries. – *Partially open.* This section will feature the decorated arts of Europe from the Middle Ages to the 20th century. The ROM has a fine collection of furniture, glass and ceramics which will be displayed in a series of room reconstructions. There will also be a costume gallery exhibiting the trends in fashionable Western costume from 1700 to today.

The New World and Europe/Canada. – *Not yet open.* These galleries will contain sections on various native cultures in addition to the life of early European settlers in Canada.

Discovery Gallery. – *Open varying hours, check on arrival; restricted number of people allowed inside at any one time.* Called a "hands-on" experience, this gallery contains a variety of artifacts and specimens which can be touched or closely regarded through a microscope.

Across the street from the Royal Ontario Museum, note the **George R. Gardiner Museum of Ceramic Art (B)** *(opening early 1984 ; ☎ 593-9300).*

Yorkville★★. – *Plan p. 135.* Once the hangout of drug addicts and dropouts (like Gastown in Vancouver), the name Yorkville now signifies all that is chic and stylish in Toronto. Centred on the small streets around Yorkville Avenue between Yonge Street and Avenue Road, the area plays host to numerous art galleries, good restaurants and expensive boutiques. Some of these are located in charming erstwhile Victorian houses, sometimes with modernized fronts which somehow manage to look harmonious. In summer, outdoor cafes flourish and plenty of activities go on in the street. The area is packed with the young and fashionable sipping drinks, parading, window shopping and purchasing.

On Yorkville Avenue itself, make sure not to miss **York Square** on the corner of Avenue Road. Here boutiques are grouped around an interior bricked courtyard with a large tree in the centre under which cafe tables are placed in summer. Behind it lies the elegant **Hazelton Lanes**★ and on the other side of Yorkville Avenue further down is **Cumberland Court** which provides a passage through older houses to Cumberland Street.

Metro Toronto Library★★. – *Plan p. 135. Open daily ; closed Sun in summer ; ☎ 928-5150.*

This building housing Canada's most extensive public library is another of **Raymond Moriyama's** architectural gems *(see Ontario Science Centre below and Scarborough Civic Centre p. 138, etc.).* The rather plain brick wall on Yonge Street belies the fascinating interior over which visitors marvel for so long that many leave without looking at the books ! The library has a wide open central area rising the full five floors with balconies flowing around it draped with plants. Warm orange carpeting on floors and walls, and special baffles in the ceiling, cut sound to a minimum in what might otherwise be a noisy place to work.

McLaughlin Planetarium★ **(Z)**. – *Beside main ROM building (p. 136). Shows daily except Mons not statutory hols ; $2.75 ; bookstore ; ☎ 978-8550.*

The white dome of the planetarium makes it a landmark in Toronto. It was built with money donated by automobile magnate R.S. McLaughlin *(p. 115).* Around the theatre, there is an astronomy display area.

Canadiana Collection★. – *Open daily except hols ; ☎ 978-3711/6738.*

This building and much of the collection were a gift to the Royal Ontario Museum from the philanthropist, Sir Sigmund Samuel. There are some interesting period room settings from Ontario, Québec and the Maritime Provinces. Note particularly the panelled room from the Boniface Belanger House of St-Jean-Port-Joli, Québec *(second floor).* One gallery is devoted to changing exhibitions from the museum's vast resources of Canadian watercolours, paintings and prints.

■ SIGHTS OUTSIDE DOWNTOWN

Ontario Science Centre★★★. – *Plan p. 138. 11 km - 7 miles from downtown ; 770 Don Mills Rd ; subway to Eglinton and Eglinton bus E. Open daily 10am - 6pm ; $3.00 ; parking $1.00 ; restaurant, cafeteria, snack bars, summer beer garden ; gift shop ; recommended time for visit : 1/2 day ; ☎ 429-4100.*

Built in the Don River ravine, this popular science centre, which welcomes annually more than 1 1/2 million visitors, seems to cascade down the valley. The architect, **Raymond Moriyama** *(see also Metro Toronto Library above and Scarborough Civic Centre p. 138),* designed a series of buildings on different levels connected by enclosed escalators to take advantage of the site. Opened in 1969, it is a suitable home for the Centre which has departed completely from the traditional collection of objects which usually make up science museums. Only 20 % of the exhibits are historical, the remainder are concerned with today's science.

The great attraction of the Centre and the reason why it is so popular is the high proportion of exhibits which involve action and participation. By pushing buttons, turning cranks, operating computer keyboards etc, visitors learn all about the importance of science and technology in their lives. For example the energy required to generate electricity is demonstrated by a pedal bicycle - as you pedal a bulb lights up. There are many little theatres with film or slide shows. At regular hours *(check at entrance)* demonstrations on such things as laser beams, high voltage electricity, paper making, printing, television producing, weather forecasting, etc are given.

Metro Toronto Zoo★★★. – *40 km - 25 miles NE of downtown in Scarborough ; subway to Kennedy and bus 86A. Open daily ; $3.50 ; parking $2.00 ; snack bars, picnic areas, gift shop ;* ☎ *284-0123.*

Set in the Rouge River valley and covering 287 ha - 710 acres, Metro Zoo is a new concept in zoos. The stress is not on animals in cages but rather on exhibiting and interpreting nature as a whole. This has been done by recreating natural habitats from different parts of the world. In these, the nearly 3 000 animals, birds, reptiles and amphibians can be seen. Five pavilions recreate habitats impossible to reproduce out-of-doors in Canada. Of these the **African pavilion** is the largest and the most interesting. Constructed of wood and glass, it is like being inside a vast exotic greenhouse. Brightly coloured tropical birds fly around squawking, lush vegetation covers the ground and unusual and rarely seen animals can be viewed.

The main part of the zoo is encircled by a totally undeveloped area where the North American animals can be viewed in their natural habitat. This area can only be visited by taking the domain ride *($1.00)* - a quiet air-conditioned train which glides past caribou, moose, wolves, bears, etc. The architect responsible for the zoo lay out and the various pavilions was **Raymond Moriyama** *(see Metro Toronto Library and Ontario Science Centre p. 137, and Scarborough Civic Centre below).*

Black Creek Pioneer Village★★. – *29 km - 18 miles from downtown ; 1000 Murray Ross Parkway ; subway to Jane and 35 bus N. Open daily March - Dec ; $4.00 ; restaurant, refreshments ; gift shop ;* ☎ *661-6610.*

In the early 19th century a Pennsylvania German pioneer called Daniel Stong established a prosperous farm on this site. The farm house and five other buildings are still there forming the basis of this village. Twenty-five other original buildings were moved to the site to recreate a mid 19th century Ontario community. Despite the freeways and highrise of York University which stand so close, Black Creek is a quiet and tranquil little spot seemingly untouched by time. Unlike some other pioneer villages, all the buildings seem to have grown in their places giving a harmonious and life-like atmosphere enhanced by costumed personnel.

The highlights of the village are **Roblin's Mill,** a beautiful four storey stone water mill where visitors can watch flour being ground, the **Dalziel Barn,** an enormous wooden structure which is an outstanding example of Pennsylvania German architecture in Ontario, and the **Half-Way House,** which was once one of the coach stops on the Toronto to Kingston run. Today it serves home-cooked meals, 19th century style *(make reservations on arrival in village during peak periods).*

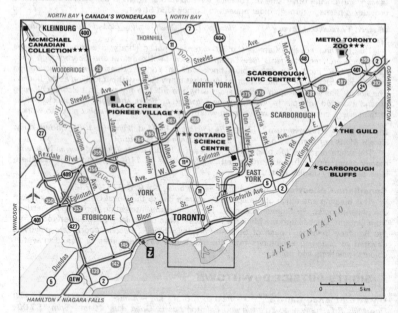

Scarborough Civic Centre★★. – *35 km - 22 miles from downtown ; 150 Borough Drive, S of Hwy 401 at McCowan Rd. Open daily 7.30am - 10pm ;* ☎ *296-7216 or 7212.*

Scarborough, the biggest and probably the wealthiest of the boroughs which make up Metropolitan Toronto, is home to one of its architectural showplaces. The Civic Centre is a gleaming white futuristic structure, designed by **Raymond Moriyama** *(see Ontario Science Centre and Metro Toronto Library p. 137)* and opened in 1973. Inside, it is a bright, light, airy and beautiful place. From an open central area rising the five storeys of the building, balconies flow around in tiers providing the office space. Trees grow in the centre beside a pool, plants hang over the balconies and there are colourful art exhibits reflecting some of Moriyama's Japanese heritage. The Council Chamber is built underground - Moriyama's solution to the problem of incorporating a large chamber into his structure without spoiling its lines.

Visitors should try to visit the Civic Centre in office hours when it is vibrant with life, and take the **guided tour** *(daily, 10am - 4pm ; 3/4 hr)* - the only way of reaching the balconies at weekends.

Outside, the Albert Campbell Square separates the Civic Centre from the adjacent shopping plaza. The square is the site of concerts, movies, art shows and other activities in the summer months.

Scarborough Bluffs★. – Scarborough was given its name by governor Simcoe's *(p. 130)* wife because the picturesque cliffs along Lake Ontario reminded her of the Yorkshire town. These cliffs, easily Toronto's most dramatic geographical feature, protrude in places rather like hoodoos and run for about 16 km - 10 miles along the lake shore. Geologically they have attracted world-wide scientific interest because the layers of sand and clay of which they are comprised provide a comprehensive record, unique in North America, of the last stages of the Great Ice Age.

Scarborough Bluffs Park ★. – *From Kingston Rd (Rte 2) turn left on Midland Ave then immediately right onto Scarborough Cres ; at end, park on Drake Cres.*

There are good views of the high sand structures standing away from the cliffs and of Bluffers Park below.

Bluffers Park ★. – *Return to Kingston Rd from above and continue east to Brimley Rd ; follow to the end.*

The road descends the cliffs emerging on an artificial peninsula which has been constructed to protect the Bluffs. This is a pleasant park on the lake.

The Guild (Spencer Clark Collection of Historic Architecture)★. – *On grounds of Guild Inn, 201 Guildwood Parkway off Kingston Rd. Open all the time ;* ☎ *261-3331.*

This unusual sculpture park near Scarborough Bluffs contains important architectural features from about 60 Toronto buildings which were demolished as the downtown core developed. Among the most striking examples are the white marble facade of the Imperial Bank of Canada (demolished 1972) and the Corinthian columns and capitals of the Bank of Toronto (demolished 1966) which have been assembled to form a Greek theatre.

This collection was the brainchild of Rosa and Spencer Clark who founded a haven for artists and craftsmen on this site in 1932 called "The Guild of All Arts". Works of sculpture, many by Guild members, also adorn the grounds.

Casa Loma ★. – *Plan p. 132. 1 Austin Terrace, subway to Dupont. Open daily ; $3.00 ; souvenir shop ;* ☎ *923-1171.*

Fairy-tale castle or stock-broker's fantasy ? This vast castellated mansion has been described as "a mixture of 17th century Scotch baronial and 20th Century Fox" ! It has 98 rooms including 38 bathrooms, a private telephone system and elevator, a pipe organ in a hall where as many as 3 000 people were entertained, a marble-floored conservatory, an oak-panelled passage which is a copy of Peacock Alley in Windsor Castle, a library for 100 000 books and a tunnel to stables, for twenty horses, through vast wine cellars.

Its creator, **Sir Henry Pellatt,** was a financier who made his money from, among other things, the exploitation of Niagara Falls for hydro-electricity. His "castle" took three years and $2 000 000 to build. But the cost of heating it and of paying the servants, both of which increased apace in the 1920s, eventually led to Casa Loma's being taken over by the City of Toronto for unpaid taxes. Since 1937 it has been run by the Kiwanis Club of Toronto who have restored it and turned it into a tourist attraction.

When visiting Casa Loma, visitors can either follow the suggested route and listen to the taped commentaries in each room *(1 1/4 hr),* or wander freely around using the plan and description available at the entrance.

Casa Loma stands on the crest of the **Davenport Ridge** and can be seen from miles away. This ridge is actually the edge of glacial **Lake Iroquois** which existed after the retreat of the last Ice Age. Its edge can be traced along or near Davenport Road between Yonge and Dufferin Streets.

EXCURSIONS

McMichael Canadian Collection★★★. – *About 40 km - 25 miles N in Kleinburg ; accessible by bus from Islington Subway Station. Open daily except Mon in winter ; 11am - 5pm ; $2.50 ; dining room ; snack bar ; gift shop ;* ☎ *893-1121.*

Housed in sprawling square-hewn log buildings amongst the trees and hills of the Humber valley stands this art gallery which contains the most important collection of the Group of Seven Canadian painters in existence.

The Group of Seven. – The most internationally famous of Canadian artists and the most original, they created the first completely Canadian School of Art. The original seven were **Lawren Harris, A.Y. Jackson, J.E.H. MacDonald, Franklin Carmichael, Arthur Lismer, Frederick Varley** and **Frank Johnston.** Johnston resigned from the Group and was replaced by A.J. Casson, and the Group also enrolled Edwin Holgate and later Lemoine Fitzgerald as an "honorary member" before its demise.

Before the First World War Harris, Jackson, MacDonald and Carmichael (and sometimes Varley) often worked together and made trips with **Tom Thomson.** The latter had been a not very accomplished commercial artist when he "discovered" Algonquin Park in Ontario *(map p. 99).* The country there so inspired him that he became a rugged outdoorsman to appreciate it and a fine landscape painter to portray it. His name is synonymous with the search for a native Canadian art expression and he was the chief inspiration for those who followed him.

The five above-mentioned artists worked together in a studio in Toronto built by Harris, an independently wealthy man of the Massey-Harris (now Massey-Ferguson) clan. Thomson generally worked in a shack in the grounds preferring this to a studio. He led several expeditions to Algonquin Park and introduced the others to its wilderness. The First World War interrupted this way of life and in 1917 the group was shattered by the death by drowning of Thomson. After the war the remaining four got together with Lismer, Varley and Johnston and formed the Group of Seven. It was a sort of defence against the criticism of their work. They held their first joint exhibition in Toronto in 1920, the first of many.

The Group of Seven "Revolution". – Until the appearance of the Group's works, Canadian artists had tried to reproduce European scenes either as background to Canadian subjects or as the entire picture. This was to change with the Group whose ideals could be explained by Jackson's words : "Only by fostering our own Canadian art shall we develop ourselves as a people". The paintings they produced showed raw Canadian nature, a fantastic contrast to the neat countryside of Europe. Critics considered that the Group was giving Canada a bad name by presenting only the "sinister and tragic" aspects - snow, muskeg, rocks, etc. Between 1920 and 1932, ten to twelve shows were held in Toronto and Montréal. Travelling shows visited the United States and the Group participated substantially in the **British Empire Exhibition** in Wembley, where the reception accorded their works was tremendous. "The foundation of what may become one of the greatest schools of landscape painting", and "the most vital paintings of the century" were two of the comments. After this reception, opinion slowly began to change in Canada. The Group officially disbanded in 1932 but some of its members formed the **Canadian Group of Painters** with other artists in the next year which had much the same aims.

The Group of Seven made the breakthrough and revolutionized Canadian art. Now their works are so well known and so accepted that it is their pictures of places like Algoma, Algonquin Park, Georgian Bay and northern Lake Superior that people envisage when they hear these names mentioned.

The McMichaels. – In 1952 Robert and Signe McMichael bought land near Kleinburg and built a home of old timbers and stone. To decorate it they bought paintings of Canada - more precisely pictures of Canada as portrayed by the Group of Seven. By 1964 their collection had become so famous that they decided to make it public. The Government of Ontario stepped in and acquired the surrounding land to preserve the setting. The McMichaels remained for many years as unpaid curators. Donations by such people as R.S. McLaughlin (*p. 115*) have swelled the collection.

VISIT

The galleries are arranged so that visitors can just ramble around looking at pictures, sketches and the Indian and Inuit art while getting glimpses of the countryside through the windows. There are many changing exhibitions on various themes thus mention of a particular work is no guarantee that it will be on show.

Much space is devoted to **Tom Thomson**, the precursor of the Group, to **A.Y. Jackson** who might be described as the "grand old man of Canadian art" (notably his *The Red Maple* which, with Thomson's *Red Leaves* in the National Gallery *p. 119*, was one of the first "Group" type works), and to **Lawren Harris**,

(McMichael Canadian Collection)

Lawren Harris "Mt Lefroy"

the life and soul of the Group and the prime leader in Canadian art for many decades (he died in 1970). Towards the end of his life Harris became an almost totally abstract painter. This trend can be seen in his magnificent *Icebergs, Davis Strait, Mount Lefroy, Pic Island* and his famous *Maligne Lake*. Examples of the work of all the members of the Group can be seen including A.J. Casson (*White Pine*) and Lionel Lemoine Fitzgerald, the Westerner who joined the Group just before its demise. He was a "pointilist" painter, a long and painstaking technique which meant he produced relatively few works.

The collection also contains works by artists encouraged or influenced by the Group of Seven though never actually attached to it. Among these are **Clarence Gagnon, Emily Carr** the colourful portrayer of West Coast landscape and the way of life of its Indians (*p. 64*), and **David Milne**.

The gallery also owns some fine examples of West Coast Indian carving. Another room is devoted to Woodland Indian prints notably the dramatic works of **Norval Morrisseau**, and there is an excellent collection of Inuit soapstone carvings and lithographs.

Outside the gallery stands the shack where Tom Thomson did most of his famous landscapes. It was moved here from the grounds of the studio in Toronto where several of the Group worked.

Niagara Falls★★★. – *130 km - 81 miles, full day trip. Description p. 111.*

Parkwood★★. – *61 km - 38 miles, half day trip* to the home of R.S. McLaughlin with its fine gardens and tea house. *Description p. 115.*

Royal Botanical Gardens★. – *70 km - 44 miles, half day trip. Description p. 107.*

Canada's Wonderland. – *In Vaughan, 30 km - 19 miles N by Hwy 400 and Rutherford Rd ; special buses from Yorkdale and York Mills subway stations, $1.75 one-way – buy tickets first. Open daily June - Sept ; weekends in May and Sept ; admission $15.95 but special books of coupons available ; parking $3.00 ; cafeterias, snack bars ;* ☏ *832-2205.*

This Disneyland of the north opened in 1981 has a series of theme areas - International Street, Medieval Faire, Grande World Exposition of 1890, the Happyland of Hanna-Barbera, International Festival etc. There is a man-made mountain which can be climbed, as well as a variety of rides, shows and shops.

UPPER CANADA VILLAGE ★★★

Maps pp. 9 and 99 – *11 km - 7 miles E of Morrisburg by Hwy 2 (exit Hwy 401 at Upper Canada Rd), in Crysler Farm Battlefield Park. Open daily mid May - mid Oct ; adults $4.40 ; recommended time for visit : 1/2 day ; restaurant, cafeteria, snack bar, gift shop ; ☎ (613) 543-2911*

This living museum of early Ontario is without equal in Canada - and is indeed one of the finest restoration projects in North America. Lying in an area settled by Loyalists after the American Revolution, the village was created when plans were made to flood a large part of the valley during the construction of the St. Lawrence Seaway *(p. 170)* and the control dam at Cornwall. Some of the older homes and buildings were moved to this site to preserve them, other structures were found elsewhere, and a community reflecting life in Upper Canada 1784-1867 was created.

Visit. – The first impression on entering this village is one of bustling activity. The visitor is transported at once to the 19th century. The "inhabitants", suitably attired, roam the streets or travel about by stage coach or other 19th century conveyance. They perform a vast variety of activities - cheese and bread making, quilting, dyeing, cabinet-making, and many farm chores. The progress in the life of the first settlers from pioneer shanties to substantial dwellings of brick and stone is excellently illustrated. Note in particular the elegant refinement of the **French-Robertson House,** the solid prosperity of the **Farm,** and the evident wealth and luxury of **Crysler Hall** with its

(after photo by St. Lawrence Parks Commission)

Stage Coach at Upper Canada Village

Greek Revival architecture. There are churches and schools, a village store, doctor's surgery and a tavern. An 1850s style meal can be eaten at **Willard's Hotel.**

The **Sawmill** and **Asselstine Factory** (where woollen cloth was produced) both operate on water power and they show the gradual trend towards industrialization evident in Ontario by 1867. Regular demonstrations are given for visitors. Museums devoted to agriculture and the importance of the St. Lawrence River explain these aspects of the life of the time. A boat trip can be taken in a **bateau** - a wooden boat of the early 19th century which was pulled along canals or rivers by a horse or horses on the bank.

Battlefield Monument. – *Beside Upper Canada Village in the park ; same hours.*

This monument commemorates the Battle of Crysler Farm in 1813 when a small force of British and Canadian troops routed a much larger American force. It stands beside the St. Lawrence River with a fine **view** over the site of the farm now flooded by the Seaway. A small museum at its base contains a graphic account of the Battle and details of the rest of the War of 1812 *(p. 100).*

Auto Wonderland. – *2 km - 1 mile W of Upper Canada Village on Hwy 2. Open daily mid May - mid Oct ; $2.50 ; ☎ (613) 537-2105.*

This collection of automobiles includes an 1898 Locomobile steam car, an 1910 International Auto Buggy high wheeler, an 1923 Durant Touring, and an 1962 Amphicar for use on road and water.

WINDSOR ★

Maps pp. 9 and 98 - Metro Pop 246 110 - Tourist Office 80 Chatham St E, ☎ (519) 255-6530 – *Local map p. 142*

The city of Windsor lies on the south side of the **Detroit River** opposite the American city of that name and connected to it by suspension bridge and tunnel. Like Detroit, Windsor is a major automobile manufacturer and industrial city. It is also a port on the St. Lawrence Seaway *(p. 170)* and the home of Hiram Walker whisky.

The Windsor - Detroit area was first settled by the French in the early 18th century. In 1701, **Antoine de la Mothe Cadillac** built a post on the north side of the Detroit River which became the headquarters of the French fur trade in the Great Lakes -Mississippi River area. It was captured by the British in 1760. After the American Revolution, the fort and town were handed over to the Americans and the Detroit River became the international border except for a brief period during the War of 1812. The town of Sandwich developed on the Canadian side but it was later engulfed by its neighbour, Windsor, which was founded in the early 1830s.

In 1838, there were several invasions across the river by the American supporters of William Lyon Mackenzie *(p. 130).* But since that time relations between the two cities have been very cordial. Every year an **International Freedom Festival** is celebrated at the beginning of July to include the national holidays of both countries : July 1st and 4th. Windsor is also Canada's busiest point of entry.

Dieppe Gardens★★. – The outstanding attraction of this park, which stretches for several blocks along the river west of the main thoroughfare *(Ouellette Street),* is its **view★★** of the Detroit skyline across the water. It is also a good place from which to watch the huge ships of the St. Lawrence Seaway.

Art Gallery★. – *445 Riverside Drive W. Open daily except Mon and hols ; gift shop ; cafeteria ;* ☎ *258-7111.*

Housed in a restored waterfront warehouse, this pleasant gallery displays changing exhibitions from its permanent collection which encompasses the Group of Seven *(p. 139),* Inuit sculpture and East Asian art. There are fine views of the river from the third floor cafeteria.

EXCURSIONS

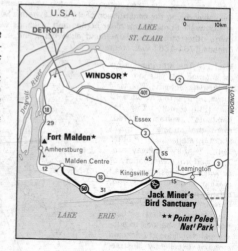

Fort Malden★. – *29 km - 18 miles S in Amherstburg. Open daily ; National Historic Park ; picnic sites ;* ☎ *736-5416.*

This fort, built by the British at the end of the 18th century when they had abandoned Detroit to the Americans, has a fine **site★** overlooking the Seaway. Some of the ramparts remain, now grass-covered, and a barracks has been restored to its 1840 state. In the **Interpretive Centre,** a slide show *(6 min)* explains the history of the fort and its part in the War of 1812 and the Rebellion of 1837-38. An example of Mackenzie's rebel flag of 1837 hangs in another room. There are other military displays in the **museum.**

Route 50. – *31 km - 19 miles from Malden Centre to Kingsville.*

This quiet road runs along the coast of Lake Erie offering vistas of the lake. It also affords the traveller opportunities to view the many birds that make their home in this marshland and to appreciate the rural nature of this area with its market gardens growing a wide variety of fruit and vegetables.

Jack Miner's Bird Sanctuary. – *On Rte 18 in Kingsville. Open daily mid Oct - mid May, except Sun ;* ☎ *733-4034.*

This sanctuary, founded by the conservationist Jack Miner (1865-1944) and one of the earliest in Canada, is a well known stopping place for geese and wildfowl on their seasonal migration. The best time to visit it is late March or late October to early November between 3.30pm and 5pm when an estimated 40 000 geese and ducks land to feed.

Point Pelee National Park★★. – *65 km - 40 miles by Rtes 3 and 33. Description p. 123.*

QUÉBEC

This huge province, which covers one sixth of Canada's total area and is more than twice the size of Texas, is first and foremost a French-speaking region. More than 80 % of its population of 6.4 million are francophone, the survivors of an empire founded in the early 17th century which once covered half the continent *(map p. 145)*. Very proud of this long tradition, the **Québécois** have their own culture and lifestyle. They have retained some of the finest French qualities - language, cuisine and a tremendous *joie de vivre,* and created a unique and attractive society in a North American milieu. About 11 % of the province's population is of British origin and these people are largely concentrated on Montréal island. The existence together of these two particular language groups has made that city unique in the world. The remainder of Québec's population are from a wide variety of ethnic origins, and again most of them live in Montréal. They also include, however, a number of Indians and Inuit who live in small settlements in the north.

VAST AND EMPTY WILDERNESS

Stretching from the United States border in the south to Cape Wolstenholme on Hudson Strait, a distance of 1 900 km - 1 200 miles, Québec is enormous and largely uninhabited. The extreme north is a forbidding land of treeless tundra underlain with permanently frozen ground, which gradually turns to forest further south. This forest covers most of the province, leaving only a tiny region in the south where the land can be cultivated. It is in this region that the population lives.

There are in fact three main physiographic regions in Québec. The vast forested area and the tundra to the north of it lie on the **Laurentian Plateau,** part of the Canadian Shield *(map p. 13)*. This plateau rises to heights of 1 190 m - 3 900 ft in Laurentides Park and 960 m - 3 150 ft at Mount Tremblant *(p. 157)*. Otherwise it is monotonous flattish land strewn with lakes. The extreme south of the province and the Gaspé peninsula, on the other hand, are part of the **Appalachian Mountains** which stretch from Alabama to Newfoundland. These reach heights of 972 m - 3 190 ft in the Eastern Townships *(p. 150)* and 1 268 m - 4 160 ft in Gaspé, and provide much arable land especially in the south. Between these two regions also in the south is the triangular wedge of the **St. Lawrence Lowlands** *(map p. 13)*, the most important region and the earliest settled.

Forests, Mines and Water Resources. – Québec's economy can be simply summed up with these three words. About half of the province's vast forest cover can be exploited. Of this, roughly three quarters is softwood suitable for making **pulp and paper.** Québec is the Canadian leader in this field producing a third of the country's total output - but when **newsprint** is taken alone the percentage rises to one half or 20 % of the world's supply. To obtain this, the province supports nearly sixty processing mills along St. Lawrence, Ottawa, St. Maurice and Saguenay Rivers and in the Eastern Townships.

As far as minerals are concerned, the province lies mainly on the Canadian Shield *(see above)*, whose age-old rocks are a great source of mineral wealth. The Abitibi and Témiscamingue regions have large deposits of **copper** (Noranda, Matagami, Chibougamau) as well as gold, silver, zinc, lead and nickel in smaller quantities. These are processed at a huge smelter in Noranda, also in Montréal and at an electrolytic zinc plant in Valleyfield. Copper is also found at Murdochville in the Gaspé.

A relatively new development is the exploitation of the **iron ore** of the Labrador Trough with mines at Gagnon in Québec *(see also Newfoundland p. 218)*. The ore is taken to the coast by train and transported to steel mills elsewhere .

It is not however only in the Shield that rich mineral deposits exist in Québec. The Eastern Townships region *(p. 150)* has vast **asbestos** supplies. The term asbestos is given to a range of fibrous silicate minerals, the most significant of which is chrysotile. Canada produces 95 % of the world's chrysotile asbestos, 80 % in Québec.

Thirdly, the province has enormous exploitable **hydro-electric resources.** The St. Lawrence, St. Maurice and Saguenay Rivers generate large amounts of electricity mainly for industrial use *(pp. 183 and 184)*. On the north shore of the St. Lawrence, the Manic-

Outardes project produces in excess of 5 1/2 million kilowatts *(p. 174)* and the huge new project on the **La Grande River** which runs into James Bay will when it is completed in 1985 have a capacity of more than 10 million kilowatts *(see also p. 147)*. All this power is vital for the province's industries - the pulp and paper mills and smelters including those which process raw materials not found in Québec. The province has become one of the major areas of the world for the production of **aluminum** with smelters located at Beauharnois on the St. Lawrence, Shawinigan on the St. Maurice and Arvida on the Saguenay *(p. 183)*.

Agriculture, Fishing and Trapping. – These three activities, the traditional supports of the economy, still thrive in the province. Trapping is important in the north, and the Gaspé peninsula and Magdalen Islands rely on fishing for survival *(pp. 152 and 159)*. Only a tiny percentage of Québec is cultivated but those regions - Montréal island, the St. Lawrence valley, parts of southern Québec and the Lake St-Jean area, produce fruit and vegetables, beef and dairy products in sufficient quantities to supply the province's population.

Climate. – One of the most surprising things about Québec is the range of its climate. Winters can be bitterly cold especially in the north though bright and sunny. Snowfall is enormous – accumulation can be as much as 1.5 m - 5 ft over the winter in much of the central interior. Then suddenly as May succeeds April, summer arrives. Spring is perhaps of two weeks duration and then the whole southern region of the province is plunged into hot weather when swimming gear replaces the mufflers of winter. Summer can also be extremely humid making air-conditioning essential in offices – just as humidification was necessary against the dryness of the winter. Unlike its sudden arrival, summer departs slowly and the Fall with its beautiful colours is a true season. Sometimes, after all the leaves have dropped in late October or early November, summer returns briefly for a last fling. This "Indian" summer is another characteristic of Québec's climate.

Montréal registers a January maximum mean of –5 °C - 23 °F with an average of 254 cm - 100 ins of snow falling over the winter. Going north up the St. Lawrence, winter becomes colder and snowier. Québec City has a January maximum mean of –7 °C - 19 °F with 315 cm - 124 ins of snow, and Sept-Iles registers –10 °C - 14 °F with 422 cm - 166 ins of snow - the heaviest recorded snowfall in eastern Canada. Away from the river to the north, less snow falls but temperatures are lower.

In July, Montréal registers maximum means of 26 °C - 79 °F, Québec City 25 °C - 77 °F and Sept-Iles 20 °C - 68 °F. Temperatures in excess of 32 °C - 90 °F are not uncommon, however, in the southern region and humidity frequently exceeds 80 %. Total annual precipitation in the south varies from 75-100 cm - 30-40 ins and is fairly evenly distributed throughout the year.

HISTORICAL BACKGROUND

Birth of New France. – When **Jacques Cartier** planted a cross at Gaspé in 1534 and claimed this new land for the King of France *(p. 153)*, it was already inhabited by Indians of the Eastern Woodlands culture *(map p. 15)* - Algonkians, Montagnais, etc, and regularly visited by Basque fishermen. Cartier himself came seeking a passage to the Orient and its riches. In the next year, he visited two Indian villages - Stadacona (site of Québec) and Hochelaga (Montréal) returning to France after a terrible winter *(p. 179)* with incredible stories of the great mineral wealth to be exploited. Crossing the Atlantic a third time in 1542, he collected up some of the minerals only to find that they were worthless when they were analysed back in France. This killed interest in the new land for a while although fishermen still came. Then in 1600, interest revived for another resource - the pelts of fur-bearing animals especially the beaver.

La Grande Hermine - Jacques Cartier's Boat

The first trading post for these furs was established by **Pierre Chauvin** at Tadoussac *(p. 183)* but it is to **Samuel de Champlain** that the honour always goes for founding New France. After trying to establish himself at Port Royal in Acadia in 1604 *(p. 191)* Champlain descended the St. Lawrence and built a *habitation* at the site of Québec City *(p. 175)*. He immediately set about making alliances with the local Indians and gathering furs to send to France.

The Iroquois "Scourge". – Very soon after establishing his *habitation*, Champlain ran up against the fierce and warlike Indians of what is now northern New England and New York State. The Algonkians enlisted Champlain's aid against the Iroquois, their traditional enemies. During a battle in 1607, Champlain walked through his allies with an arquebus and shot four Iroquois dead. When more Frenchmen appeared, the Iroquois fled. But they never forgot or forgave the French. They turned to first the Dutch in New Amsterdam (later New York) and then the English to supply them with guns, and soon they became the scourge of New France attacking the convoys of furs going to Québec and the French settlements themselves. The inhabitants of **Trois Rivières** founded in 1634, Huronia founded in 1639, and **Montréal** founded in 1642 all lived in daily fear of their raids. In 1649, the Huron Indian allies of the French were almost completely wiped out by the Iroquois and several of their French Jesuit priests were martyred (p. 104). In 1660, **Dollard des Ormeaux** saved Montréal from destruction by an act of incredible bravery. With sixteen others, he fought off a huge Iroquois warband on the Ottawa River for many days. Although he and his men were all killed, the Iroquois were so impressed by their courage that they left Montréal untouched.

After this, the King of France, realizing the daily peril in which his colonists lived, made New France a crown colony instead of a private trading enterprise, and sent regular soldiers across the Atlantic to defend it. He appointed Louis de Buade, **Comte de Frontenac,** as Governor. The latter found himself fighting both the Iroquois and the English but he success-fully defended the colony against the joint threat. His colleague, **Jean Talon,** the Intendent, to whom all the administrative functions of running the government fell, set about strengthen-ing the colony by increasing the population and giving the economy a wider base.

The Seigneurial System. – Settlement of the colony was organized according to the feudal system which existed in France until the Revolution in 1789. A *seigneurie* or piece of land was granted to a landowner or **seigneur** who swore loyalty to the King. He in turn granted parts of his land to tenant farmers **(habitants)** who paid him in various dues - produce and work on his land when required. The *seigneur* established a mill and a church, and the *habitants* also paid dues to support the church. The land was granted in long thin strips which started at the river bank so that as many people as possible had access to the water, the major means of transport. The remains of this system can still be seen today along parts of the St. Lawrence and Richelieu River valleys.

Under this system, New France slowly increased its population as more colonists ar-rived. Its growth was, however, slow compared with other European colonies on the contin-ent. In 1641, there were 500 people in New France and 40 000 elsewhere ; by 1760, New France had grown to 85 000 compared with 1 200 000 in the American colonies.

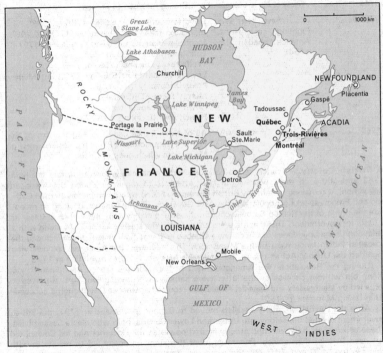

Maximum Extent of French Influence in North America

Vast Empire. – From the beginning, **coureurs des bois** (fur traders) and missionaries from New France explored wide areas of the continent. Champlain himself discovered the lake named after him, the Ottawa River, Georgian Bay, Lake Simcoe and Lake Ontario. His followers, **Etienne Brulé, Jean Nicolet, Nicolas Perrot,** etc, reached Lake Superior. In the 1650s, **Pierre Radisson** and the **Sieur de Groseilliers** travelled through the Great Lakes and north perhaps as far as Hudson Bay - they certainly knew of its existence. They planned a quicker trade route to Europe via the bay which would avoid the long canoe/portage route back to Montréal. There was no interest in this scheme in France, so they tried the English, with such success that the Hudson's Bay Company was the result (p. 74).

In 1673, **Louis Jolliet** and the Jesuit, **Jacques Marquette,** explored the Great Lakes and the Mississippi as far south as Arkansas. Following in their steps, the **Sieur de LaSalle** went down the Mississippi to the Gulf of Mexico, calling the region **Louisiana** after the French King, Louis XIV. In 1699, Louisiana was colonized by the **Sieur d'Iberville,** who was famous for his raids on Hudson Bay. Soon afterwards, the French built a series of forts along the Mississ-ippi.

The greatest explorers of them all, however, were the La Vérendrye family. Pierre Gaultier de Varennes, **Sieur de la Vérendrye,** explored much of Manitoba and Saskatchewan between 1731 and 1738 setting up a series of trading posts. His sons François and Louis-Joseph explored even further west, reaching the foot of the Rockies in present day Montana in 1742, the first white men to see this mountain range.

At its greatest extent, therefore, New France stretched from Hudson Bay to the Gulf of Mexico, and from the St. Lawrence almost to the Rockies. But it was always a trading empire with very few inhabitants, and it was thus continually threatened by the populous colonies to its south and east. It was also the victim of an increasingly corrupt administration who neglected the defence needs of the colony in order to line their own pockets. Finally, there was very little interest in France itself for the colony - *quelques arpents de neige* (a few acres of snow) as Voltaire called it.

Anglo-French Wars. - The rivalry between France and England in North America was only part of a broader struggle which took place largely in Europe but also in other parts of the world - the Caribbean, India, etc. Only the events which took place in North America and treaty terms relevant to that continent are listed here.

1689-97 .... War of the League of Augsburg	Iberville captures Hudson's Bay Company forts and Newfoundland. Iroquois raid Lachine *(p. 172)*. Phipps captures Port Royal (Acadia), but fails before Québec *(p. 175)*.
1697 .... **Treaty of Ryswick**	Acadia returned to France. Newfoundland returned to England. France keeps Hudson Bay.
1701-13 .... War of the Spanish Succession	Nicholson captures Port Royal *(p. 190)*.
1713 .... **Treaty of Utrecht**	All of Hudson Bay, peninsula Acadie, Newfoundland and the Iroquois country (south of Great Lakes) to England.
1740-48 ...... War of the Austrian Succession	Louisbourg surrenders to New Englanders *(p. 205)*.
1748 .... **Treaty of Aix-la-Chapelle**	Louisbourg returned to France
1756-63 .... **Seven Years' War** (fighting in North America began in 1754)	Deportation of the Acadians 1755 *(p. 188)*. Monckton takes Fort Beausejour 1755 *(p. 198)*. Montcalm captures and holds Ticonderoga 1757-8. Louisbourg falls 1758 *(p. 205)*. Wolfe takes Québec 1759 *(p. 175)*. Lévis wins battle at Ste-Foy 1760 but Murray holds Québec. Murray takes Montréal 1760. New France capitulates. French raid St. John's 1762 *(p. 225)*.
1763 .... **Treaty of Paris**	All of New France ceded to England except St-Pierre & Miquelon *(p. 222)* and Louisiana west of Mississippi which goes to Spain.

A British Colony. - France ceded her vast North American empire to Britain finally in 1763 and, although there were some later attempts to regain it (during the American Revolution), it remained definitively British thereafter. Faced with a completely Roman Catholic and French-speaking population, the new Governor, **Sir Guy Carleton,** decided to recognize the rights of the Roman Catholic church, the seigneurial system and French civil law as a basis for government. These rights were enshrined in the **Québec Act** of 1774 along with a definition of the boundaries of the colony - Québec as it was now called, which included the so-called Indian lands west of the Mississippi. This infuriated the American colonies who regarded the Québec Act as one of the **Intolerable Acts** which led to revolution in 1775.

During the Revolution, the Americans tried to persuade the French Canadians to join them, but without success as the latter were satisfied with the Québec Act. An invasion force led by **Montgomery** and **Benedict Arnold** was repulsed at Québec City though it succeeded in taking Montréal *(p. 160)*.

After the Revolution, many **Loyalists** moved to Québec *(p. 99)* and in 1791, the British government divided the colony into Upper and Lower Canada, both with elected assemblies. These assemblies, however, had strictly limited power as the Governor and his Council did not need to take their advice. Frustration over this situation finally led to revolts in both colonies *(pp. 130 and 161)* but the issue was further inflamed in Québec because the Governor and Council were English and the assembly was French. Although the **Patriotes,** as they were called, were defeated, full representative government was granted in the end when Upper and Lower Canada were joined in a sort of a confederation in 1841. This was the precursor of the confederation of all the British colonies in North America which came about in 1867 *(p. 209)*.

Province of Canada. - Since Confederation, Québec has grown from strength to strength always maintaining her unique separate identity, and creating a true "New France" on the North American continent.

When walking in the forest or camping by a lake :

— be careful not to start forest fires,

— leave no trace of your passage.

SPORTS AND OUTDOOR ACTIVITIES

The government of Québec produces a series of brochures on various sports activities in the province - golf, skiing (alpine and cross-country), fishing, hunting, boating, etc. These are available free of charge from the Tourist Office *(see Practical Information p. 148)*. The government also maintains an excellent system of provincial parks with good camping facilities.

Canoeing and **hiking** are the major summer activities in these parks which are in the main located in the rocky, forested, lake-strewn Canadian Shield region *(p. 143)*. Outside the parks, canoeing in Québec is restricted because so many of the river systems are used for log driving, but boating and sailing are practised on Ottawa, St. Lawrence and Richelieu Rivers. The most outstanding parks for canoeing excursions are La Mauricie National Park *(p. 184)* and La Vérendrye Provincial Park *(map p. 9)* ; for hiking - de la Gaspésie Provincial Park, Forillon *(p. 153)* and Gatineau *(p. 123)* National Parks.

(after photo, Public Archives of Canada, Ottawa C-13585)

Voyageurs running a Rapid

The major resort areas of the province are the **Laurentians** and **Eastern Townships** *(pp. 157 and 150)*. They are famous in summer for water-based activities and in winter for their alpine ski slopes. Other major alpine ski areas of the province are the Gatineau and **Mount Ste-Anne** near Québec. **Cross-country skiing**, snowshoeing and snowmobiling are practised all over the province with many organized trails.

Fishing. – Québec is renowned for its fine fishing. The salmon rivers of the Gaspé peninsula *(p. 152)* are perhaps the best known but the *ouananiche* (fresh water salmon) and trout of the interior lakes are also worthy of note. Details of licenses, seasons, limits and outfitters are available from the Tourist Office *(see below)*. It should be noted that many areas are under private lease and not open to individuals without permission. This is also true of hunting.

Special Excursion. – An impressive trip can be made to view the hydro-electric development on the rivers running into **James Bay** *(map p. 9)*, the largest construction site in the world. As it is only accessible by air, visitors must join a group for a one or two day excursion. *For details contact Nortour, 310 rue Ste-Catherine Ouest, Montréal, Qué H2X 2A1,* ☎ *(514) 875-7400 ; or Agence Marco Polo, 1117 Ste-Catherine Ouest, Montréal, Qué H3B 1H9,* ☎ *(514) 281-1481.*

PRINCIPAL FESTIVALS

The national holiday of the province of Québec is June 24th, the saint day of **John the Baptist** (St-Jean-Baptiste). Many communities arrange special celebrations during the week of the saint's day. Early April is another time of general festivity when the sap of the maple tree begins to run and **sugaring-off parties** *(parties de sucre)* are held.

February	Québec	Carnaval *(p. 176)*
February	Chicoutimi	Carnaval-Souvenir
February	Lachute – Hull	Canadian Ski Marathon
June – Labour Day	Montréal	Man and his World *(p. 169)*
June – August	Magog	Festival Orford - Jeunesses Musicales du Canada *(p. 150)*
July	Drummondville	Festival mondial de folklore
July	Québec	Summer Festival
July	Valleyfield	International Regatta
August	Péribonka – Roberval	Swimming Marathon *(p. 156)*
August	Mistassini	Blueberry Festival
September	Trois Rivières	Grand Prix Molson
September	La Tuque – Trois Rivières	International Canoe Race
September	St-Tite	Festival Western
October	Rimouski	Fall Festival

Accommodation and Road Maps. – The government of the province of Québec produces an annually updated accommodation guide called **Hébergement Québec** and a guide to campsites called **Camping Québec.** These are available free of charge with a regularly updated road map from most tourist bureaus in the province or from :

Tourisme Québec, P.O. Box 20 000, Québec, Qué G1K 7X2 ☎ (418) 643-2280 or Montréal (514) 873-2015.

Road Regulations. – The province of Québec has a good road system maintained summer and winter despite severe temperatures in winter. During the period of thaw (generally late March - April), some minor roads may be closed to heavy traffic. Speed limits unless otherwise indicated are 100 km/h - 62 mph on autoroutes, 90 km/h - 56 mph on other main roads and 50 km/h - 31 mph in built-up areas. Seat belts must be worn at all times when driving.

Language. – The official language of the province of Québec is French and all road signs and other indications are given in this language. Outside the main tourist centres (Québec, City, Montréal, etc) very little English is spoken or understood . Visitors are advised to learn a few phrases to help them find their way around these regions.

A glossary of terms used in the text or on the maps of the guide follows.

anse	cove, beach	islet	small island
autoroute	highway	jardin	garden
baie	bay	lac	lake
banque	bank	maison	house
belvédère	viewpoint	métro	subway
canton	township	mont	mount
cap	cape, headland	montagne	mountain
cathédrale	cathedral	moulin	mill
champ	field	musée	museum
château	large house	parc	park
chute(s)	waterfall	place	square
colline	hill	pointe	point (of land)
côte	shore, coast (hill)	pont	bridge
écluse	lock	porte	door, gate
église	church	rivière	river
gare	station	rocher	rock
gîte	resting place	rue	street
hôtel	hotel	salle	room (hall)
hôtel de ville	city hall	vallée	valley
île	island	ville	town

Time Zones. – Most of the province of Québec is on Eastern Standard Time with daylight saving of one hour in force in the summer months. The extreme easterly parts of the province - the coast south of Labrador, Anticosti Island and the Magdalen Islands, keep Atlantic Standard Time, which is one hour in advance of the rest of the province. Clocks in these regions are also advanced one hour in summer. For exact division see map p. 20.

Taxes. – A sales tax of 9 % is added to all purchases except clothing, furniture and food. There is no tax on hotel bills but a 10 % tax on restaurant meals over $3.25.

Liquor Laws. – In Québec, liquor, wine and beer can only be publicly consumed on licensed premises. Taverns (beer and cider) are for men only, brasseries admit both sexes. The legal drinking age is 18. The Québec Liquor Board (Société des Alcools) runs stores where a wide variety of wine and liquor is sold. Cornerstores (dépanneurs) can be licensed to sell beer, cider and certain wines (those made or bottled in the province).

BOOKS TO READ

The Beginnings of New France by Marcel Trudel   (McClelland and Stewart)

Montréal Guide - an Architectural and Historical Guide by James Wolfe and Cécile Grenier   (Libre Expression)

Two Solitudes by Hugh Maclennan   (Macmillan) FICTION

Shadows on the Rock by Willa Cather   (Random House) FICTION

The Golden Dog by William Kirby   (McClelland and Stewart) FICTION

The Tin Flute by Gabrielle Roy (translation)   (McClelland and Stewart) FICTION

Maria Chapdelaine by Louis Hémon (translation)   (Macmillan) FICTION

CABANO

Map p. 10 - Pop 3 291 - *Local map p. 183*

This lumbering centre on the Trans-Canada Highway has a pleasant **site★** beside **Lake Témiscouata**. The lake was once part of an important portage route connecting the Saint Lawrence and Saint John Rivers. In 1839 during a dispute with the state of Maine over the location of the frontier *(p. 215)*, a fort was built to protect this route.

Fort Ingall. – *2 km - 1 mile by Rte 232. Open weekdays April - mid Nov, daily mid June - Labour Day except Mon ; $1.25 ; guided tours 1 hr ;* ☎ *(418) 854-2052.*

On a fine **site★** beside the lake stands this fort with its wooden stockade and log buildings which once housed two hundred soldiers. Several structures have been rebuilt including the South Barracks where there are exhibits, the Officers' Quarters where there are displays on the history of the region and a section on Grey Owl who lived nearby for a short time *(p. 88)*, and a block house.

CHARLEVOIX Coast ★★ (Côte de Charlevoix)

Map p. 10

Between Beaupré *(see Québec p. 180)* and the Saguenay on the north bank of the St. Lawrence, there is a region of great beauty where the age old hills of the Canadian Shield plunge into the St. Lawrence. Known as the Charlevoix Coast after the Jesuit historian François Xavier de Charlevoix, much of it can be viewed by following Routes 138 and 362. These roads weave up and down sometimes at cliff top, other times at water level offering unsurpassed views of forested hills, headlands, the rocky coast, the St. Lawrence and the south shore. The river becomes a veritable arm of the sea with its tides and salt water.

From Beaupré to Baie-Ste-Catherine
173 km - 108 miles by Routes 138 and 362 – about 2 days – Local map p. 182

Route 138 swings away from the St. Lawrence and climbs steeply into the hills.

St. Anne's Falls★★ (Chutes Ste-Anne). – *4 km - 2 1/2 miles after Beaupré, access road on left. Open daily mid May - Oct ; $2.25.*

A pleasant forest walk takes visitors to the St. Anne River at a point where it drops 74 m - 243 ft in an impressive narrow fall.

After a stretch inland, Route 138 rejoins the coast at Baie-St-Paul with a splendid **view★★** as it descends.

Baie-St-Paul★. – Pop 3 961. This little town in the Gouffre valley has long been a favourite with artists. It lies in an agricultural valley which makes a fertile streak through the otherwise rocky and heavy evergreen forested hills.

On leaving the town on Route 362, a second **view★** of its site is obtained from above.

Follow Route 362, turn left at Les Eboulements.

St-Joseph-de-la-Rive★. – Pop 247. This community beside the river is known for its parchment mill (Papeterie St-Gilles) where paper is made by hand, the only enterprise of this nature in Canada. From the wharf, where the ferries leave for Ile aux Coudres, there is an excellent **view★** of the island, the bay of Baie-St-Paul and the cliffs to the north.

Ile aux Coudres★★. – Pop 1 505. *Access by ferry daily every hour on half hour ; less frequently in winter ; 15 min ; car $2.75, passengers $1.10 ;* ☎ *(418) 438-2743.*

This charming little island is named for the hazel trees *(coudriers)* which grew on it in 1535 when Jacques Cartier celebrated the first mass in Canada on its shores. Inhabited since 1728, its residents are farmers, boat builders and fishermen. They are known for their skill at negotiating the ice floes which fill the river in winter by a combination of paddling their large *canots d'hiver* and hauling them over the ice. The ferry service has now made this skill unnecessary but it is demonstrated each year at the Québec Carnival *(p. 176)*.

A circular tour of the island can be made *(24 km - 15 miles – about 2 hrs)*. When the weather is favourable, there are fine **views** of both north and south shores of the St. Lawrence especially from **l'Islet★** at the southern end and from **Pointe du bout d'en bas★★** at the northern tip. Along the coast, there are many beached and deserted boats. One of these, the schooner **Mont-St-Louis,** can be visited *(Musée des Voitures d'eau, St-Louis, open daily in summer ; $3.00)*. Two mills dating from the 18th century, one powered by water, the other by wind, *(open daily in summer, $2.00)* stand together nearby. At La Baleine, the stone **Leclerc House** (1750) can be visited *(open daily in summer ; $1.00)*.

Return to Route 362

After Les Eboulements, the road weaves up and down through very rural country.

La Malbaie. – Pop 4 030. Named Bad Bay by Champlain who anchored off it in 1608 and awoke to find his ships beached, La Malbaie includes the resort centre of Pointe-au-Pic where the massive **Manoir Richelieu** Hotel stands overlooking the river. The valley was first settled by Scots soldiers after the English Conquest who named it Murray Bay for their commander in chief. It later reverted to Champlain's name.

Continue on Route 138.

Port-au-Persil★. – This tiny natural harbour now uninhabited has fine **views★** of Ile aux Lièvres and the south shore.

Baie-des-Rochers★. – *Turn right and follow a rough road for 3 km - 2 miles, park and continue on foot.*

This is a pretty and almost deserted bay hemmed in by low hills and nearly closed to the St. Lawrence by an island.

Baie-Ste-Catherine. – Pop 209. The road descends to the Saguenay with a fine **view★** of the beginning of the fjord. *Continuous ferry service day and night to Tadoussac ; 15 min.*

149

EASTERN TOWNSHIPS ★ (Cantons de l'Est)

Map p. 10 – *Local map below*

This region hugging the American frontier in the extreme south of the province is known as the "Eastern" townships because it lies east of Montréal. After the American Revolution, the British government offered previously uninhabited land on both sides of the city to Loyalists fleeing the new United States *(p. 99)*. The western area, now in Ontario, has long since ceased to be called the Western Townships, but the term Eastern remains to confuse visitors especially those coming from Québec City.

The **Townships,** as Montréalers simply call them, are a region of great rural charm quite distinct from the rest of Québec and bearing some resemblance to New England thanks to their origins although today the population is predominantly French-speaking. In the south a series of beautiful lakes – **Brome, Memphremagog, Magog, Massawippi,** etc, fill the valleys between the low ranges of the **Appalachians** which just touch this corner of the province (Round Top in the Sutton Mountains 972m - 3 190 ft), Mount Orford 876 m - 2 875 ft). This is resort and cottage country dotted with ski hills and boat docks.

It is also a region of summer theatre. North Hatley, on Lake Massawippi, offers theatre in both French and English, and performances of the **Jeunesses Musicales du Canada** are given all summer in the music centre in Mount Orford Park *(p. 151)*.

Sherbrooke (Pop 74 075), at the confluence of St. François and Magog Rivers, is the industrial centre of the region. To the northeast lies asbestos country, a belt which extends from the community of **Asbestos** to the city of **Thetford Mines** (Pop 19 965) where a large percentage of the world's supply of this fibrous mineral is mined. To the north is the region often called the **Bois-Francs** (hardwoods) around Victoriaville where maple trees abound and sugaring-off parties *(p. 147)* are common in the spring. There are also pulp and paper mills in the Townships but the predominant impression is not one of industry but of fertile fields, neat farms and lovely views.

Magog★. – Pop 13 604. This resort has a lovely **setting★** at the northern end of long and narrow Lake Memphremagog. Mount Orford rises above the city on one side and other peaks of the Appalachian Mountains (Sugar Loaf, Owl Head, etc) are visible along the lake.

An attractive **drive★** *(23 km - 14 miles)* takes visitors to the Benedictine monastery of **St-Benoît-du-Lac** *(open daily)*, distinguished by its high tower designed by Dom Paul Bellot *(see also p. 168)*, and famous for its blue cheese, *L'Ermite*, made by the monks.

Boat Trip★. – *From town dock, daily in July and Aug ; 2 1/2 hrs ; $5-7.00 ; Sun in June ; refreshments ;* ☎ *(819) 843-8068.*

This is a pleasant cruise down this long lake with views of the surrounding mountains and the summer homes of wealthy Québeckers.

ST. LAWRENCE VALLEY – MONTRÉAL TO QUÉBEC CITY

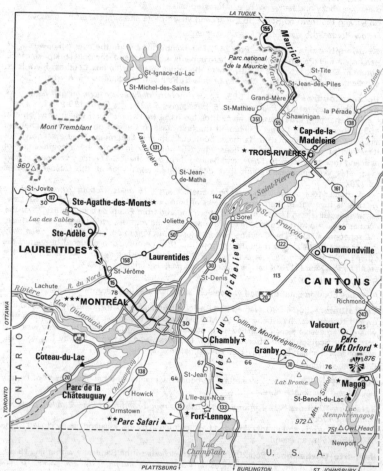

Mount Orford Park★ (Parc du Mont-Orford). – This provincial park, dominated by the peak and bordered by Lakes Orford and Stukely, offers year-round sports *(camping, swimming, boating, hiking, skiing)* as well as its cultural centre.

In summer, a **chairlift** takes visitors up Mount Orford itself *(daily in July ; weekends mid June - mid Oct ; $5.50)*. From the top of the lift, there is a **view★** south of Lake Memphremagog and Vermont. The best viewpoint, however, is obtained by following the rough path past the television aerial to the actual summit of Orford. On clear days there is a stunning **panorama★★** embracing the Sutton Mountains and Lake Brome to the southwest, the Monteregian Hills *(p. 167)* and the flat plain of the St. Lawrence to the north and west, and the heavily wooded Appalachian hills stretching off to the east.

Compton★. – Pop 728. This quiet village was the birthplace of **Louis-Stephen St-Laurent** (1882-1973), successful lawyer, politician and Prime Minister of Canada 1948-57. An intense Canadian nationalist, St-Laurent was universally respected and familiarly called "Uncle Louis".

Louis-S. St-Laurent National Historic Park★. – *Main St. Open daily mid May - Labour Day ; Wed - Sun Labour Day - mid Oct ; closed 12-1pm ; ☎ (819) 835-9222.*

The simple clapboard house where St-Laurent was born has been restored to represent various times of his life. The adjoining general store run by his father, almost the village social centre, has also been recreated. The warehouse attached to the latter today houses an excellent audio-visual show *(20 min)* on St-Laurent's life and importance.

Granby. – Pop 38 069. Set on the banks of the Yamaska River, this city is a small industrial centre in the middle of a rural area.

Zoo★. – *347 ave Bourget. Open daily May - Oct ; $5.50 ; snack bar, picnic sites ; ☎ (514) 372-9113.*

This is a pleasant zoo with a wide range of animals from all over the world.

Automobile Museum. – *288 ave Bourget opposite Zoo. Open daily May – mid Oct ; $3.00 ; ☎ (514) 372-4433.*

The museum displays a large number of pre–1931 automobiles in prime condition.

Valcourt. – Pop 2 601. In 1907, this community was the birthplace of **J. Armand Bombardier,** mechanic and inventor of some genius, who in 1935 developed a drive-wheel and track mechanism to power vehicles over snow. The first Bombardier machines held up to seven people and were used as industrial tractors, logging machines, for military purposes and by school boards. Later, Bombardier produced smaller models for recreational purposes culminating in his **Ski-doo** of 1958-9. Today, there are about 1 1/2 million snowmobiles in the world, more than half of which are made by Bombardier.

J. Armand Bombardier Museum★. – *Behind plant on rue J. A. Bombardier. Open afternoons 1pm - 4.30pm ; ☎ (514) 532-2258.*

This fascinating museum relates the history of this extraordinary man and his inventions. There are many examples of his snowmobiles. The original garage built for the young Bombardier by his father, where he worked as a mechanic inventing in his spare time, can also be visited.

Arthabaska. – Pop 6 827. This town has a pleasant site at the foot of Mount St-Michel in the Bois-Francs. For many years, it was the home of **Sir Wilfrid Laurier,** Prime Minister of Canada 1896-1911 *(see also Laurentides p. 157).*

Musée Laurier★. – *16 Laurier St W. Open daily mid Jan - mid Dec ; closed Mon, hols and 12-1.30pm ; $2.00 ; ☎ (819) 357-8655.*

This two-storey brick house in attractive surroundings was built by Laurier in 1876 before he entered politics. He maintained it until his death in 1919 although only as a summer residence after he became Prime Minister *(see Ottawa p. 121).*

Several rooms contain his original furniture and there are exhibits and a slide show *(15 min in French)* on his life especially as it affected Arthabaska.

Drummondville. – Pop 27 347. Set on the banks of the St. François River, this city is an industrial centre particularly associated with the garment industry.

Village Québécois d'Antan. – *Rue Montplaisir, 3 km - 2 miles from exit 181 Trans-Canada Hwy (Rte 20). Open daily June - Labour Day ; $5.00 ; refreshments ; ☎ (819) 478-1441.*

An interesting collection of 19th century buildings, including homes, school, tavern, forge, etc, has been moved to this pleasant spot beside the river.

Costumed guides perform chores and explain daily life of about a hundred years ago *(in French only).*

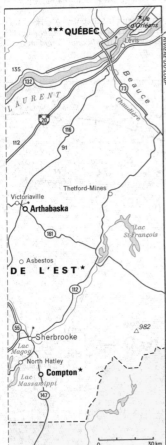

GASPÉ Peninsula ★★★ (Gaspésie)

Map p. 10 – 752 km - 467 miles by Route 132 - allow about 5 days

This large peninsula which protrudes into the Gulf of St. Lawrence between the river's estuary and Chaleur Bay (Baie des Chaleurs) is more or less separated from the rest of the province by the Matapedia River and Lake. The interior is a largely impenetrable wilderness of mountain and forest, the only settlement being around the copper mine at Murdochville. The **Chic-Choc Mountains,** a continuation of the Appalachians, have the highest peaks in Québec (**Mount Jacques Cartier** 1 268 m - 4 160 ft). In the north, these mountains seem in places to drop straight into the St. Lawrence. This wild, rocky and sea-battered coast is stunningly beautiful culminating in the scenic wonders of Forillon and Percé. The inhabitants live in tiny villages which cling precariously to the coast. They make their living from fishing – cod, herring, mackerel, lobster, salmon, smelt, shrimp, etc. The south shore, by contrast, is less abrupt and a little agriculture thrives amidst the forestry activities. The main activity on both shores, however, is tourism.

It is not only the spectacular scenery which attracts visitors but the charm of a simple lifestyle close to nature which still respects the traditions of another age. The region also offers excellent cuisine and some of the best salmon fishing available anywhere. Many local handicrafts are produced but the Gaspé is particularly noted for its model ships made during the long winter and sold along the highway.

■ THE NORTH COAST ★★

From Ste-Flavie to Forillon National Park – *351 km – 218 miles - Local map below*

From Ste-Flavie (Pop 921), Route 132 runs along the coast plateau to reach the resort area around the village of Grand-Métis.

Métis Park★★ (Parc de Métis). – *Open daily early June – Labour Day 8.30am – 8pm; parking $3.25 ; restaurant ; cafeteria ; handicraft boutique ; ☎ (418) 775-2221.*

These **gardens ★★**, which come as a complete surprise on this rocky coast, are an exceptional display of the horticulturist's art. They are unique on the continent for the variety of species which flourish so far north (winter temperatures can drop to – 40 °C ; – 40 °F) and in such poor soil. Paths wind along beside a stream where exotic and brilliantly coloured flowers bloom – lilies, rhododendrons, azaleas, Asiatic gentians, Tibetan blue poppies, etc. Because spring arrives so late in the region (June) and the summer is so short, many of these flower at the same time as each other whereas further south they bloom as much as two months apart.

The gardens were the creation of **Elsie Reford,** niece of George Stephen, President of the Canadian Pacific Railway Company and a prime mover in the building of the transcontinental line *(p. 16).* Stephen bought the estate for the excellent salmon fishing but in 1919 gave it to his niece. Mrs. Reford, who preferred horticulture to fishing, set about creating a garden – with these incredible results.

In the centre of the gardens stands the elegant house built by Stephen. A guided tour *(20 min in French)* enables visitors to see the Reford apartments and displays of regional life at the turn of the century. The house also contains a restaurant *(traditional Canadian food)* and a boutique run by local handicraftsmen.

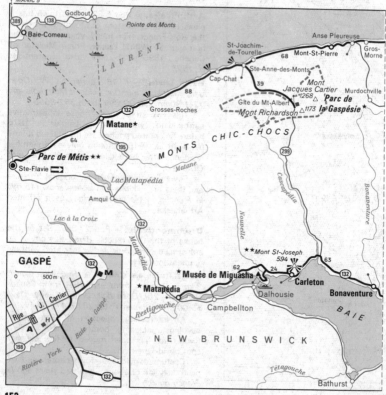

Matane★. – Pop 13 612. This small industrial centre lies on the Matane River which is reputed for its salmon. In the centre just behind the *Hôtel de ville*, a migration **channel**★ has been built around a dam. Between mid June and October every year, visitors can watch the salmon negotiating it on their way upstream to spawn.

After Matane the route becomes more rugged. At times the coastal strip disappears as the mountains approach the water's edge although agriculture is still practised in places. Particularly notable are the large rocks at Grosses-Roches and Cap-Chat.

Excursion to Park de la Gaspésie ★. – *39 km – 24 miles to Gîte du Mont-Albert by Rte 299.*

The road gradually climbs into hilly forested country and, after entering the park, follows the wide valley of the Ste-Anne River. The park encompasses the highest peaks of the Chic-Choc mountains including Mount Jacques Cartier, Mount Richardson and Mount Albert. This is a rugged region with deep valleys between the forested slopes with their bare peaks.

At the **Gîte du Mont-Albert** the air is almost alpine. There are a variety of hiking trails and a **nature centre** *(open afternoons daily late June - Aug)* with displays and films on the park. A rough road *(34 km – 21 miles)* leads to a trail up Mount Jacques Cartier.

Return to Ste-Anne-des-Monts.

The road winds up and down twisting and turning sometimes at water level, other times high above on the cliffs. The **coast**★★ is one rocky headland after another and there are constantly changing views of cove and cape – and of course of the ever-present sea. Waves smash on the rocks, seagulls fly overhead and one tiny fishing village succeeds another all clustered in sheltered coves and dominated by their large churches. In some of them, the racks used for drying cod now little used can be seen. Of particular note are the impressive shale cliffs surrounding the bay at **Mont-St-Pierre**. Just before the village of **Grande-Vallée**, there is a pulloff with a fine view of the village and bay. In the centre of the community, a wooden covered bridge can be seen from the main road. Built in 1923, it is still in use.

The road passes through **Rivière-au-Renard**, the most important fishing centre of the Gaspé. Then the road begins to follow the Forillon peninsula where the view becomes more open and some of the land is cultivated. From Cap-des-Rosiers, there is a **view**★ across the bay of Cap Bon Ami and Cap Gaspé.

■ **FORILLON NATIONAL PARK** ★★ – *Local map below*

Camping ; hiking, swimming, nature walks, fishing, boat trips ; admission to National Parks p. 21 ; ☎ *(418) 368-5505.*

Like a massive tilting block emerging from the sea, this park sticks out into the Gulf of St. Lawrence at the tip of the Gaspé peninsula. It has a rugged coastline of sheer limestone cliffs on its north side. Its southern face on the Bay de Gaspé is less tortured but nonetheless impressive. Many species of bird inhabit these cliffs and whales are often seen plying the waters off the coast.

Route 132 makes a tour of the park *(about 17 km – 10 1/2 miles)*. At Cap des Rosiers the park **interpretive centre** can be visited *(open daily)* where there are displays, films and an introductory slide show *(10 min)*. A secondary road leads to the **Cap Bon Ami** area, where a trail descends to the beach from which there are stunning **views**★★ of the limestone cliffs and **Cap Bon Ami.**

Crossing the peninsula on Route 132, there is a sudden **view**★★ at the height of land of the Bay de Gaspé and beyond to Percé – on a clear day the famous *rocher (see below)* can be seen.

On the south side of the peninsula, a secondary road leads to **Anse aux Sauvages**, where a trail can be followed to **Cap Gaspé,** the easternmost tip of the park. There are fine **views**★ of the Bay de Gaspé from the now deserted little villages along the route.

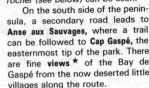

■ **GASPÉ**★ Pop 17 261

This small city has a fine **site**★ on a hillside which slopes down to the York River at the point where it joins the Bay de Gaspé. It is the administrative and commercial centre of the peninsula, and it has a deep-water port. Its fame, however, comes from the fact that it was the spot where Jacques Cartier *(p. 144)* first set foot in North America in July 1534, where he raised a wooden cross and took possession of the land in the name of the King of France.

Museum★ (M) (Musée régional). – *Open daily, except hols and Sat in winter; $1.50;* ☎ *(418) 368-5710.*

On a fine **site★** overlooking the bay and the Forillon peninsula stands this attractive wooden structure housing a museum devoted to the history and popular traditions of the Gaspé. In addition to displays on Jacques Cartier's voyages and the Anglo-French struggle, there are exhibits on the origins of the population of the region and on their various means of making a livelihood. There are also regular slide shows on folklore and cultural themes.

In front of the museum overlooking the bay is an interesting collection of bronze slabs which form a **monument to Jacques Cartier★** *(National Historic Site).* Carved in 1976 by two of the Bourgault family from St-Jean-Port-Joli *(p. 158),* they have bas reliefs on one side and descriptions of Cartier's voyages on the other. This harmonious ensemble blends well with its setting.

Cathedral★ (A). – This remarkable modern church is almost completely built of wood. Finished in 1968, it has a fine yet simple interior with huge wooden beams, a large stained glass window and other windows offering views of the Bay de Gaspé.

Stone Cross. – Reached by steps close to the *Hôtel de Ville* **(H)**, this granite cross erected in 1934 commemorates the wooden one placed there by Cartier 400 years earlier.

The **drive★★** to Percé *(75 km – 47 miles)* offers lovely views after Douglastown of Cap Gaspé especially from **Auberge Fort-Prével** *(hotel run by Québec government).* Then, Route 132 rounds a cape to Belle-Anse with **views★★** across the Bay of Malbaie of *Rocher Percé* and Bonaventure Island, also fish drying racks. Approaching Percé, the road climbs and drops, and winds precariously before its sudden descent into the village. This first **view★★** of Percé is breathtaking.

■ PERCÉ★★★

Pop 4 839 – Tourist Office ☎ (418) 782-2933

Once a tiny fishing village cut off from the rest of the world, Percé has become a resort renowned for the extraordinary beauty of its **site★★★**. It is the culmination of all the scenic wonders of the Gaspé peninsula, and at no other point is the effect of the geological forces on the landscape more marked. The reddish gold limestone and shale rock has been pushed, folded and squeezed into a wonderful variety of cliffs, bays and hills. Most famous of all is the great rock pierced with a hole which has given the community its name *(Percé).*

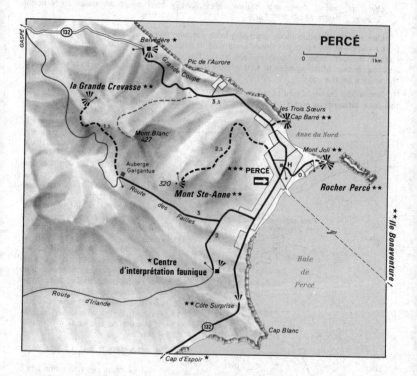

Percé also boasts some of the best restaurants in the region, cafes, summer theatre, a boardwalk stretching along the south beach, and a wharf where visitors can watch fishermen filleting their catch.

The Coast★★★. – Each cliff and cape offers a new view of this incredible landscape. They all rise sheerly from the sea but have gentler grassy slopes inland making it quite possible to climb them for the view *(the light is exceptionally good as the sun rises).*

The **Belvédère★** on Route 132 just before entering Percé has a fine view of the **Pic de l'Aurore**, which rises like a giant tooth from the sea, and of the **Grande Coupe**. A little further along the road, a path leads up **Cap Barré★★**, from the top of which the cliffs known as the **Trois Sœurs** (Three Sisters) can be seen to the west, and an end-on view of Rocher Percé with the north beach (l'anse du nord), Mont Joli, Bonaventure Island and the town spread out to the east.

From **Mont Joli**★★ itself *(access in town near hôtel de ville)*, the sculptured limestone of the famous rock can be admired *(steps to north beach and rocher – see below)*, with to the east the Three Sisters and Cap Barré, and inland the red cliffs of Mount Ste-Anne.

On the other side of the town, a viewpoint at **Côte Surprise** ★★ offers a fine view of the rock straight on with the town and island. From **Cap d'Espoir** ★ *(11 km - 7 miles map p. 153)*, Percé's site can be appreciated and Bonaventure Island seen although the Rock is hidden.

The Rock★★ (Rocher Percé). – Rising like a great ship at anchor just offshore, this great wall of limestone is 433 m - 1 420 ft long and 88 m - 288 ft high. Once it boasted two arches. All that remains of the first is the slab of rock which stands isolated at one end, called the Obelisk. The Rock is connected to Mont Joli by an isthmus of sand *(access from north beach)*. At low tide, it is possible to walk across to it *(check times of tides at tourist office)*.

Percé

Boat Trip to Bonaventure Island★★ **(Ile Bonaventure).** – *Departs from wharf on south beach daily June - mid Oct, 8.00am - 5-6pm, every 15 min in July and Aug ; $8.00 ; trip around island and return – 1 hr ; until 2pm, visitors can disembark on island and return by later boat ; snack bar on island ; guided walks ; binoculars advisable ;* ☎ *782-2974.*

This flat-topped island (4 sq km - 1 1/2 sq miles) with its high cliffs is formed of the same rock as Mount Ste-Anne *(see below)*. It is a bird sanctuary, home in summer to North America's largest gannet colony (about 50 000 birds). These large white seabirds with their black tipped wings nest in the crevices, cracks and ledges of the 90 m - 300 ft cliffs of the island's east side. They are joined by a variety of other birds including kittiwakes, murres, puffins, razorbills, guillemots, cormorants and gulls.

The boats circle the island with fine views of the cliffs and their inhabitants. A **trail** across the island from the wharf *(40 min)* affords visitors a unique opportunity to see these colonies close up from the top of the cliff.

Mount Ste-Anne★★. – *Steep but not difficult trail starts near church on Ave de l'Eglise ; 2 hrs Rtn.*

This flat-topped mountain which rises to 320 m – 1 050 ft has extraordinary red rock formations which fall away steeply on three sides. From just below its summit, there is a superb **view**★★★ of Percé and region. A statue of St. Anne stands at the summit.

The Great Crevass★★. – *Trail from Auberge de Gargantua, Route des Failles ; 1 1/4 hrs Rtn.*

This trail follows the top of the sheer cliff on the west side of Mount Ste-Anne. The great crevass, which is actually part of **Mount Blanc,** is a deep fissure rent in the red conglomerate rock and is an impressive sight *(unfenced ; not recommended for children or sufferers of vertigo)*. The trail also offers **views** over the valleys and forested slopes of the Chic-Choc Mountains to the west, and towards the Bay of Malbaie to the north.

The Crevass can also be seen from below, from Route des Failles.

Wildlife Centre★ (Centre d'Interprétation faunique). – *Open daily late June - Aug ; films ; nature walks ;* ☎ *(418) 782-2240.*

This attractive centre built entirely of wood has fine **views** ★★ of Percé and offers interesting displays on the wildlife of the region (birds, fish and inter-tidal life) as well as the development of Percé geologically and historically.

■ **THE SOUTH COAST**★ (Baie des Chaleurs) – *Local map pp. 152-3*

From Percé to Matapedia – *284 km - 176 miles including excursions*

Gaspé's south coast is a gentler, more tranquil land than the wild north coast which culminates in Percé. In the south, the coastal plain is often cultivated, the places are bigger and there is a wider range of activity with a thriving forestry industry. Yet, the mountains still rise to the north, and at the mouth of every creek lies a little fishing village complete with fish drying racks. There are lovely vistas of the low coastline and on clear days the coast of New Brunswick is visible across the waters of Chaleur Bay.

Bonaventure. – Pop 2 950. This small resort lies on an attractive bay. It was founded by Acadians fleeing the Deportation *(p. 188)*.

Carleton. – Pop 2 710. This attractive community on a bay nearly closed by a sand spit is dominated by the bulk of **Mount St. Joseph** (594 m - 1 949 ft) which rises to the north. A road leads to its summit *(6 km – 4 miles ; signed to Sanctuarie St. Joseph)*. From the shrine to St. Joseph, there is a fine **panorama** ★★ of Chaleur Bay from Bonaventure to the Miguasha peninsula and beyond, and of the coast of New Brunswick. A marked contrast is apparent between the fields of Carleton spread out below and the forested hills just behind the coastal plain.

Miguasha Museum★ (Musée de Miguasha) . – At Nouvelle turn left for 5 km - 3 miles, then turn right for 1 km - 1/2 mile. Open daily, June - Labour Day, ☎ (418) 794-2475.

This attractive museum overlooking Chaleur Bay is devoted to paleontology. It forms an interesting introduction to the study of fossils which are very numerous in the cliffs and rocks of this region. Not only are the fossils seen in display cases, but the laboratory where they are separated from the rock can be visited and the cliffs themselves viewed (1 hr on foot Rtn - in good weather only).

Return to Route 132.

The Miguasha peninsula marks the beginning of Chaleur Bay and the end of the estuary of the Restigouche River. The road follows this attractive valley with its farms beside the river and its forested slopes as far as the Matapédia River.

Matapédia★. – Pop 845. This little village has a pretty **site★** at the confluence of these two famous salmon rivers. The mountains rise green and sombre on all sides.

GATINEAU Park ★★ (Parc de la Gatineau)

Maps pp. 9 and 99 – Description p. 123

LAKE ST-JEAN ★ (Lac St-Jean)

Map p. 10 – Local map p. 182

This vast saucer-shaped lake (971 sq km - 375 sq miles) is an ancient glacial trough which was once an arm of the sea. It is fed by several big rivers (the Péribonka, Mistassini and Chamouchouane) as well as many smaller ones, but it is drained by only one - the mighty **Saguenay**, which leaves the lake via two channels known as the Grande and Petite Décharges. Lying in the middle of wild forested Shield country, the lake comes as a surprise as it is surrounded by a strip of fertile land where wheat is cultivated and dairy cattle reared.

Lake St-Jean was part of Cartier's mystical kingdom of the Saguenay (p. 182) but it is named for the first white man to view it, **Father Jean Duquen,** who reached it overland from Chicoutimi in 1647. No permanent settlement occurred until the mid 19th century, however, when sawmills and pulp mills were built and the land was first cultivated. All the neat farms and little white churches which line the lake date from this time.

The region is known for its **blueberries** which are harvested in August, and for its **ouananiche,** the famous land-locked salmon which survive in the lake. The region is also known for two sporting events held in the summer, an international **swimming marathon** across the lake from Péribonka to Roberval and a 426 km - 265 mile **bicycle race** around the lake.

Val-Jalbert★. – 8 km - 5 miles W of junction of Rtes 155 and 169. Open daily June - Labour Day ; parking $3.25 ; Provincial Park ; camping, snack bar ; ☎ (418) 275-3132.

This deserted village has a lovely site beside 72 m - 236 ft high falls on the Ouiatchouane River. This spot was selected in 1901 by **Damase Jalbert** to build a pulp mill. To house his employees, who at one time numbered 950, he built a series of wooden shingled houses, all alike and all equipped with electricity and running water. The village also boasted a hotel, store, post office, church and Ursuline convent. In 1927, however, the mill closed as it was unable to compete with the big companies exploiting the area, and the village was abandoned.

Today, visitors can wander around this ghost town and see the restored hotel and mill. A film shown regularly (20 min ; in French) explains the history of the community. Beside the mill, a path leads up to the top of the waterfall from which there is a rare **view★** of Lake St-Jean from above, elsewhere its banks are too flat.

St-Félicien Zoo★ (Jardin Zoologique). – 5 km - 3 miles from town on Rte 167. Open daily May - Sept ; $4.00 ; refreshments ; ☎ (418) 679-0543.

This zoo has a splendid setting on an island in one of the tributaries of the Chamouchouane River which joins Lake St-Jean at St-Félicien. It has a collection of animals in cages and a section of particular interest called the Sentiers de la Nature. In a huge enclosure, native Canadian animals roam at liberty and are viewed by visitors from a small train (1 1/4 hrs ; $3.50 ; commentary in French).

Péribonka. – Pop 675. This pretty village which lies at the mouth of the river of the same name is best known for being the setting of one of the most famous novels of French Canada, **Maria Chapdelaine.** The author, **Louis Hémon,** lived in the community for a few months in 1912 and was inspired by the life of the inhabitants and his own experiences as a farmhand to create his story.

A small **museum** (Musée Louis Hémon) beside the river recreates the farmhouse where Hémon lived and relates the story of the book (5 km - 3 miles E of village on Hwy 169 ; open daily mid May - Labour Day ; $2.50 ; commentary in French). English-speaking visitors will find it helpful to have read the book first (p. 148).

(after photo by Musée des Anciens Canadiens, St-Jean-Port-Joli)

Québec Wood Carving - Returning from Mass

LAURENTIANS ★★ (Laurentides)

Map p. 10 – Local map p. 150

The Laurentian Mountains in Québec form part of the age-old Precambrian Shield which covers most of the province *(p. 13)*. They are rounded, heavily-wooded hills rising to a maximum of 960 m - 3 150 ft (**Mount Tremblant**) which stretch across the province between the Ottawa and Saguenay Rivers north of the St. Lawrence. However, when any Québecker talks of the Laurentians, he is referring specifically to the region just north of Montréal between St-Jérôme and Mount Tremblant Park. Places like Ste-Agathe, Ste-Adèle, Val-David, Estérel, St-Donat, St-Jovite, Mont-Gabriel, Val-Morin, St-Sauveur, Morin-Heights and Mont-Tremblant itself are well-established resorts offering an attractive blend of sporting activities, fine cuisine and night life which has made the region famous.

A Moose

In winter, more than one hundred ski lifts and tows operate for the alpine skier and hundreds of kilometres of trails exist for the cross-country enthusiast. In summer, water sports prevail on the innumerable lakes which lie interspersed between the hills, but there are also facilities for golf, tennis and horseback riding. Summer is also the season for theatre and the **boîte à chansons,** literally song boxes, where Québec performers sing traditional and popular songs. In the Spring there are sugaring-off parties, and the Fall sees a brilliant display of colours gracing the hillsides making a drive through the region a glorious experience.

Highway to the Laurentians★★. – *80 km - 50 miles from St-Jérôme to St-Jovite by Autoroute 15 and Rte 117.*

This stretch of road is most attractive in all seasons. It weaves through the forest clad hills which are a deep green in summer, alive with colour in the Fall and covered with skiers in winter.

Ste-Adèle. – Pop 4 675. This community has a pleasant setting around Lake Rond and on the slopes of the mountain of the same name. It is a writers' and artists' colony as well as a resort.

Village de Séraphin★. – *4 km - 2 1/2 miles N on Rte 117. Open daily mid May - mid Oct ; $3.75 ; parking $1.50 ; refreshments ; ☎ (514) 229-4777. Explanations in French.*

Agreeably set in the woods near Ste-Adèle, this reconstructed 19th century village was inspired by Claude-Henri Grignon's 1933 work *Un Homme et son Péché* which was later a successful television series. Some of the buildings illustrate episodes in the life of **Séraphin Poudrier,** a miser in the book, but they also show the life of the first settlers in the region. These people came mainly due to the efforts of **Curé Labelle,** the parish priest of St-Jérôme who hated to see his compatriots departing for jobs in the United States. His attempts to encourage farming in this region met with failure but the communities he founded form the basis of the successful tourist industry of today.

Ste-Agathe-des-Monts★. – Pop 5 641. The principal community of the Laurentians, Ste-Agathe has a fine **site★** on the shores of Lake des Sables. **Boat trips★** *(daily mid May - Oct, frequent service ; 50 min ; $5.50 ; ☎ (819) 326-3656)* on this H-shaped lake spotted with islands make a pleasant excursion on fine summer days. Many of the large and beautiful homes of wealthy Montréalers can be seen along its shores.

Laurentides. – Pop 1 947. *26 km - 16 miles E of Autoroute 15 (Exit 39) by Rte 158.*

This small town due north of Montréal is famous as being the birthplace of **Sir Wilfrid Laurier,** Prime Minister of Canada 1896-1911. The first French Canadian to hold this office, Laurier devoted his whole life to the cause of Canadian unity. His years in power were a time of tremendous growth in Canada. His government promoted the mass immigration to and settlement of the West *(p. 75)* and he felt the country's future was unbounded. Indeed, it was he who said : "The 18th century belonged to Britain and the 19th to the United States, but the 20th century belongs to Canada".

Wilfrid Laurier House★. – *Guided tours daily May - Labour Day ; National Historic Park ; ☎ (514) 439-3702.*

This tiny house with its red brick veneer finish is furnished as it might have been during Laurier's boyhood. Beside it stands an **Interpretive Centre★** with interesting displays on Laurier's life, achievements and the Québec of his day. *(See also Arthabaska p. 151 and Ottawa p. 121).*

Use the **Map of Principal Sights** (pp. 4-11)

and the **Suggested Automobile Tours** (pp. 22-27)

to help you plan your vacation.

LOWER ST. LAWRENCE ★★ (Bas Saint-Laurent)

Map p. 10

The south shore of the St. Lawrence between the capital and the Gaspé peninsula *(p. 152)* is called simply *Bas Saint-Laurent* in French - an adequate description of the region dominated by this huge river, now an estuary with wide tidal mud flats, fishing weirs and flocks of sea birds. Unlike the rocky and mountainous Charlevoix coast on the north side *(p. 149)*, this is a land of soft rural landscapes where the remains of the seigneurial system are evident with long narrow farms and old manor houses. Going north, the hills of the Appalachian chain approach the river's edge and the land becomes more rocky and barren anticipating the Gaspé.

From Lévis to Ste-Flavie

329 km - 204 miles by Rte 132 – allow 1-2 days – local map pp. 182-83

Soon after leaving Lévis, there are fine views of Ile d'Orléans *(p. 180)* and the smaller islands in the river with the Laurentians rising to the north. This is a rural area except for the industrial centre of Montmagny.

L'Islet-sur-Mer. – Pop 774. This little community has spawned many seamen including the famous Captain **Joseph-Elzéar Bernier.** He made a total of twelve voyages to the Arctic 1904-25, establishing, among other things, Canada's sovereignty over the islands of the Arctic archipelago.

A **museum** (Musée Maritime Bernier) in an old convent commemorates Bernier's trips and displays many mementos of maritime life *(open daily ; $2.50)* ; ☎ *(418) 247-5001.* Behind the museum, two vessels can be boarded : the *Ernest Lapointe*, an ice-breaker constructed in 1940, and the *Bras d'Or*, a hydrofoil used by the Canadian Navy 1968-72.

St-Jean-Port-Joli★ . – Pop 3 420. In this village are gathered together the largest number of sculptors and other artisans of any place in Québec. Their specialty is woodcarving, an art which flourished in 18th and early 19th century Québec but which had nearly died out when it was revived in St-Jean by the three **Bourgault brothers** circa 1930.

In the **Musée des Anciens Canadiens★★** *(open daily ; $1.00 ; boutique ; cafeteria ;* ☎ *(418) 598-3392)* there are many fine examples of the work of the Bourgault brothers - mainly figures of ordinary people doing everyday tasks. The sculpture of other artists is also represented.

In the centre of the village stands a large **church** with a red roof and two bell towers. It was built in 1779 and has been little altered since. Its highly decorated interior is especially notable.

The **views** of the north shore are particularly fine along the next section of road. The Laurentians can be seen rising on both sides of the valley of the Gouffre river, site of Baie-St-Paul *(p. 149)*.

St-Roch-des-Aulnaies. – Pop 218. This village is one of the few in Québec which still has its seigneurial estate with mill and manor house intact. **La Seigneurie des Aulnaies** *(on Hwy 132 ; guided tours daily late June - Labour Day ; 1 hr ; $2.00 ;* ☎ *(418) 354-2800)* was built 1850-53. The adjacent grist mill *(moulin banal)* of similar date is in full working order and its machinery is demonstrated for visitors *(flour on sale)*.

La Pocatière★. – Pop 4 560. This cathedral town has a pleasant site on a terrace above the coastal plain. The **Musée François Pilote★** *(part of college Ste-Anne near the cathedral ; open daily except hols, and Sat in winter ; $2.00 ;* ☎ *(418) 856-3145)* has an important collection of agricultural, social and wildlife displays, each with its accompanying tape recording *(in English and French)* which adds greatly to the interest of the exhibits.

Kamouraska★. – Pop 442. This is one of the prettiest places on the river. A minor road leads to the water's edge where lines of stakes can sometimes be seen in the tidal flats. These weir traps divert fish and especially eels into enclosures where they can be netted. The **view★** across the river extends from Ile aux Coudres past La Malbaie towards St-Siméon.

Along this section of the drive, a number of large odd-shaped rocks can be seen on the shore and in the river sometimes forming tiny islets. The edge of the coastal plain is clearly marked by a cliff.

Rivière-du-Loup★. – Pop 13 459. Set on the terrace above the coastal plain, this city is a commercial and resort centre linked as it is by the ferry to St-Siméon and the Trans-Canada Highway to New Brunswick. The du Loup river drops over the cliff terrace in **falls★** about 30 m - 100 ft high *(access by Rte 185 and Frontenac St)*.

Offshore along the next section of road, several islands can be seen including **Ile aux Basques.** Today, it is a bird sanctuary but once it was a stopping place for Basque fishermen who came to the region even before Cartier in 1535 to catch whales in the mouth of the Saguenay *(p. 182)*. On the island there are remains of furnaces built by the Basques in order to extract oil from the whales.

Bic★★. – Pop 2 994. This village has an exceptionally beautiful **site★★** in hilly terrain overlooking a rocky bay and a series of tiny islands and islets offshore. The great number of these hills and islands has given rise to the legend that, when the world was created, one angel was responsible for giving out the topography. At the end of the day, he had a lot left over, so he dropped it all on Bic.

Rimouski★. – Pop 29 120. On descending the hill into this city, the metropolis of the region and an ocean port, there is a good **view★** of the bay, Ile St-Barnabé and the St. Lawrence which is so wide now that the opposite shore is only a blue haze.

In the Parc de la Rivière Rimouski *(5 km - 3 miles west by Blvd de la Rivière and Ave Tessier)*, there are **falls★** in rocky terrain. A wooden dam has been built across part of them forming a pool for swimming.

After Ste-Flavie, the road enters the Gaspé peninsula *(p. 152)*.

MAGDALEN Islands ★★ (Iles de la Madeleine)

Maps pp. 10 and 187 – Pop 14 130 – Tourist Office ☎ (418) 986-5462

Access. – *Car ferries run from Souris, P.E.I., daily except Tues in summer, less regularly rest of year (no service Feb and Mar) ; 5 hrs ; no advance reservations ; long line-ups in high season. Also, boats run from Montréal weekly April - mid Dec ; 2 days ; for details of both contact Coopérative de Transport Maritime* ☎ *(418) 986-2214 (Cap-aux-Meules)* ☎ *(514) 527-8361 (Montréal).*

There are flights daily from Charlottetown, P.E.I., by Eastern Provincial, and also from Gaspé (Québec and Montréal) by Québecair.

The islands offer camping, limited accommodation (make reservations in advance), bicycle and car rentals. They keep Atlantic Standard Time (map p. 20).

This isolated and windswept outpost of the province of Québec lies in the middle of the Gulf of St. Lawrence nearer to Cape Breton and Prince Edward Island than to Gaspé. Comprising about a dozen islands, the archipelago is little more than a 100 km - 60 mile - long string of rocky outcrops connected by sand spits enclosing lagoons.

In places, there are red sandstone cliffs sculpted into incredible shapes - arches, tunnels and caves, by the sea. Elsewhere, fine beaches stretch towards the horizon, and at the centre, the stubby treeless hills support little except grass.

Visitors to the islands have never failed to be enchanted by their isolation and windswept beauty ever since **Jacques Cartier** wrote of them in glowing terms after his visit in 1534. The inhabitants (Madelinots) are in the main descendants of refugees of one kind or another. The majority of the population trace their origins to Acadians who fled the Deportation *(p. 188)*, but there is also a sizeable group of Cape Breton Scots forced from their native land by enclosures for sheep farming *(p. 188)*. Today, these people live in little white houses, seemingly dropped higgledy-piggledy all over the place. They are fishermen taking lobsters, scallops, herring, cod, crab and mussels. Their catch comprises more than a quarter of Québec's total. There is also an annual seal hunt when the ice floes come south from Labrador in the spring *(see also p. 218)*. The only other livelihood on the islands, apart from a naissant tourist industry, comes from salt mining or working for Hydro Québec. The latter are conducting various wind experiments because the islands register an average wind speed of 31 km - 19 miles an hour, which is twice that of anywhere else in the province.

Cap-aux-Meules Island ★★ . – The community of the same name (Pop 1 507) is the main port and commercial centre of the archipelago. It is dominated by the Cape for which it is named.

In the centre of the island is its highest point – the **Butte du Vent.** From here, there are splendid **views ★★** of the entire archipelago *(from La Vernière church on Rte 199 turn right on Chemin de l'Eglise, then left on Chemin Arsène).*

On the other side of the island at **Etang du Nord,** the sea has carved some spectacular **rock formations ★★** (rochers) *(from Chemin des Caps turn left on Chemin du Phare).*

Havre-Aubert Island ★. – The community of the same name has an attractive site on a harbour almost closed by Cape Grindley. Behind it rise several hills including the Colline de la Demoiselle with a cross on its summit. It is also the location of a little **Maritime Museum ★** (Musée de la Mer) – *open daily ; $1.50.* There are interesting displays on different methods of catching fish, types of boats used, etc, as well as slide shows *(in French - ask for showing)* illustrating life on the islands.

Havre-aux-Maisons Island ★. – Some of the land on this island is cultivated and examples of the unique Madelinot **baraque** can be seen - a haystack with a roof to stop the hay blowing away.

At the **Dune du Sud** *(park in picnic area and descend to beach)* there are fine **rock formations ★** (rochers) including a detached arch usually covered with birds.

Isle de l'Est ★. – At Old Harry Point *(follow sign from village),* there are more excellent **rock formations ★** (rochers) carved into the cliffs by the sea.

MONTRÉAL ★★★

Map p. 10 – Metro Pop 2 828 349 – Tourist Office ☎ (514) 871-1595

The city of Montréal, built around an extinct volcano, sits majestically on its island in the St. Lawrence. There are many Montréals, some of them seemingly incongruous. It is the heartbeat of Québécois culture, the second largest French-speaking city in the world (after Paris) full of Roman Catholic churches and religious institutions, yet a third of its population is non-French and the visitor is struck by the amazing mélange of cultures. It is a city divided between the "English" and the "French", yet in its atmosphere there is great cultural vitality and a *joie de vivre* unknown elsewhere in North America. It is a thousand miles from the ocean yet it is a major port lying at the head of a vast inland waterway connecting the Great Lakes. It is a city of huge and expensive world projects – Expo '67, the 1976 Olympic Games – yet the old is preserved in its midst and there are parts where the clock seems to have stood still.

There was nothing incongruous however about the choice of the site of Montréal for a city. The confluence of the **St. Lawrence** and **Ottawa Rivers** is marked by a series of islands, by far the largest of which is Montréal *(map p. 150)*. The waters of these two rivers, the major water-courses of Eastern Canada, meet not in harmony but with the rush of many rapids. For early explorers the site of the future city was the head of navigation. It could only be passed by strenuous portaging and trekking. Yet beyond it lay the great waterways giving access to half a continent. It was a natural place for a city.

Mont Réal. – The first white man to visit Montréal island was **Jacques Cartier** during his voyage of 1535. He was received with great pomp at the Indian Village of Hochelaga (approximately where McGill University now stands) and taken to the top of the mountain to admire the view. "It's a Royal Mountain" he exclaimed *(un mont réal)* and the name stuck. The site was not again visited by white men until Samuel de Champlain arrived in 1608 *(p. 175)*.

A Sacred City. – Unlike Québec, Montréal did not start its existence as a commercial centre. It was founded as a mission to convert the Indians to Christianity. The early 17th century saw a revival of Roman Catholicism in France after the onslaught of the Protestant Reformation. Many ladies of the Court, soldiers and nobles wished to pass on their faith to those whose lives had so far been deprived of it. The name "Montréal" came to mean somewhere in need of Christ and a "Montréal Movement" began. Two men, **Jérôme Le Royer de la Dauversière** and **Jean-Jacques Olier,** founder of the Sulpician Order, separately had visions telling them to found a city. They met, raised the money and formed an association with this aim. Paul de Chomedey, **Sieur de Maisonneuve,** was chosen as the leader of the sacred mission. He set off across the Atlantic in 1641 with forty companions including a woman, **Jeanne Mance,** whose personal mission was to found a hospital in the new settlement which they named Ville Marie de Montréal.

(after photo by Délégation Générale du Québec)

Statue of de Maisonneuve, Place d'Armes

This group finally reached the island in May 1642 despite attempts in Québec to dissuade them from venturing so far away from the other settlers for fear of Indian attack. And indeed they did not find the Iroquois receptive to their ideas. In fact anyone who was foolish enough to wander away from the hastily constructed palisade risked being ambushed and killed. This situation plagued the history of the settlement for the rest of the century but nevertheless Montréal grew and thrived becoming less and less a mission and more and more a trading settlement and centre of exploration. *Coureurs des bois* went out into the wilderness beyond the city and brought back rich loads of furs. Explorers began travels which took them all over the Great Lakes, the Ohio lands, the Mississippi valley and to the foot of the Rockies *(p. 145)*. Farming under the seigneurial system thrived as the Iroquois threat subsided. By the time of the English Conquest in 1760 the city was firmly established.

The English Conquest. – Montréal had a population of 5 000 when the British arrived. It occupied roughly the area now called the "Old City" and it was surrounded by thick but indefensible stone walls. Its sole business was the fur trade. **Vaudreuil,** the French Governor, surrendered rather than have the city blasted to pieces by the vastly superior British forces. The majority of the French nobility and soldiery departed for France.

The English Regime saw the arrival of a large number of Scots, who might almost be called the "other" racial group in Montréal. They set about expanding the fur trade and diversifying Montréal's economy. This progress was halted briefly by the arrival of an American army in 1775.

The American Occupation (1775-76). – The American States rising in revolt against their British rulers decided to persuade the Canadians to join them. Two armies invaded Québec. One of them commanded by **Richard Montgomery** arrived at the gates of Montréal. The city surrendered for the second time without a fight, the British garrison having withdrawn to concentrate forces in Québec City. The Americans stayed over the winter waging a propaganda campaign to gain Canadian support. **Benjamin Franklin** arrived in the city with a printing press. But all these efforts were to no avail and so the Americans left in the spring after being defeated at Québec City *(p. 175)*.

The Revolutionary War affected Montréal very little after that. Much more important to the city was its aftermath – the arrival of thousands of Loyalists to bolster the English-speaking population.

The North West Company. – The late 18th and early 19th centuries saw a vast expansion of the fur trade which brought great prosperity to Montréal. Various companies sent men far out into the woods to seek furs and there was great competition. In 1783 a partnership was formed between the leading men of this enterprise called the North West Company, one of the great names in the history of Montréal. The leading men in this Company, and indeed the leading men of their time in Canada, were Simon McTavish, Joseph Frobisher, William McGillivray, Alexander Henry, Peter Pond explorer of the Athabasca country, **David Thompson** who mapped a vast area of western Canada, **Simon Fraser** explorer of British Columbia and especially of the river which bears his name, and last but not least **Alexander Mackenzie,** the first man to cross the continent by land (in 1793) and explorer of the river which bears his name. Instead of sending *coureurs des bois* out into the woods, the North West Company set up a series of trading posts all over the northwest to which the Indians brought their furs. Once a year these furs were taken to Fort William on Lake Superior and exchanged for trade goods brought from Montréal by canoe *(see Thunder Bay p. 128)*. The furs were exported to Europe from Montréal. This system led to the formation of the **Beaver Club** in Montréal which had as its only condition of membership the requirement of having wintered in the northwest.

The year 1821 saw the beginning of the end of Montréal's pre-eminence in the fur trade. The North West Company was merged with the more powerful Hudson's Bay Company *(p. 74)* for long its main rival. Since the latter operated out of ports on Hudson Bay, Montréal lost its position as export centre but it did not lose all interest in the fur trade. Even today it is important for making and selling fashion furs.

The Rebellion of 1837. – The year 1837 saw revolts in both Upper and Lower Canada over who controlled the reins of government. Upper Canada's revolt was a class and religious struggle for responsible government by the elected representatives of the people. This was also the case in Lower Canada except that the elected representatives were in the main French and the government was controlled by English officials. The rebels called themselves the **Patriotes** and they were led by **Louis-Joseph Papineau.** The revolt was speedily crushed yet many of its objectives were achieved later. The two Canadas were united and responsible government – control by elected representatives, was granted.

After the Rebellion Montréal was for a short time the capital of the united "Canada". However, in 1849 some members of the English community burnt down the Parliament building in outrage against the passing of an act to compensate victims of the rebellion. To them these victims were rebels whose lands had been trampled by British soldiers because they had rebelled. The burning of the Parliament did not stop the act, it only caused Montréal to lose its position as capital, an honour it never regained.

Montréal's Development to Today. – After Confederation in 1867 Montréal was the most important city in Canada. It dominated the new nation both economically and politically. It was also in the forefront of railway development and St. James Street was the Wall Street of Canada, all the major banks and trust companies having their offices there. In the early part of the century, Montréal was also the largest grain port in the world with this commodity arriving by train from the Prairies. The opening of the St. Lawrence Seaway *(p. 170)* in 1959 changed this, but as the port declined the city developed industrially – the most important industry by dollar value is now oil-refining.

Today Montréal is a very different city from that founded by de Maisonneuve . Its religious heritage is still evident in the number of churches and religious communities but the city is dominated by the "temples of finance". The huge cruciform skyscraper of the Royal Bank **(Place Ville Marie)**, the Stock Exchange Tower **(Place Victoria)** and the **Bank of Commerce Building** are today the city's landmarks. The centre of Montréal has moved to the St. Catherine's, Peel and Dorchester Streets area. Much of it has moved underground connected to the metro system with its attractive stations. This is well-adapted to the winter climate and it is said Montréalers can leave their apartments adjoining the metro stations, travel to work, shop, eat, and entertain themselves, all without going out-of-doors.

Huge world projects such as the 1967 World Fair – **Expo '67** – and the 1976 **Olympic Games** brought world recognition to Montréal and have established it as an international centre. Visitors appreciate not only the fine restaurants and shops but the atmosphere and vitality of the city. A hundred years ago **Pierre Chauveau,** the first premier of Québec, wrote : "English and French, we climb by a double flight of stairs towards the destinies reserved for us on this continent, without knowing each other, without meeting each other, and without even seeing each other except on the landing of politics. In social and literary terms we are far more foreign to each other than the English and French of Europe". This is still true today. But it is exactly this situation which makes Montréal unique, and therefore interesting as all the vitality and flavour of the city spring from this source.

The City where the Sun Rises in the South. – In general the St. Lawrence River flows in a west to east direction from Lake Ontario to the Atlantic. A custom grew up of referring to the two banks of the river as the north shore and the south shore. This custom was and is used in Montréal although at this point the river is flowing almost due north *(map p. 150)*. In general Montréal's streets run parallel to the river or at right angles to it. Thus those perpendicular are called north-south streets although they are actually east-west and of course the east-west streets are almost exactly north-south ! Mount Royal is always referred to as being north of the centre – it is actually west. If your hotel room has a river view you will be surprised to see the sun rise. Montréal is therefore the only city in the world where the sun rises in the south !

Cultural Activities. – Montréal is the centre for French Canadian theatre, radio, television and publishing. There are many theatre groups performing in the city and summer festivals held outside *(contact Tourist Office for information)*. Montréal also supports a symphony orchestra, an opera and ballet company. The main celebration of the year is during the week of June 24th – **St. John the Baptist Day** – the Québec national holiday.

Visiting Montréal. – The subway system known as the **Metro** is an excellent means of travelling around the city and avoiding the traffic. Maps are available at any metro station or from the Tourist Office. Information can be obtained by telephoning A-U-T-O-B-U-S.

■ DOWNTOWN ★★
(Centre-ville)

Bordered roughly by Atwater, St-Denis, St-Jacques and Sherbrooke Streets, Montréal's downtown is too large to visit all at one time. It is presented here by centres of interest so that visitors may either wander at leisure or select their sights and travel by metro.

Place Ville Marie and the Underground City★★. – At the heart of Montréal's very extensive underground network of shopping concourses and walkways is Place Ville Marie, a complex of four buildings dominated by the 45-storey, cruciform **Royal Bank Tower★★** (Banque Royale), one of the most attractive modern buildings in the city. Above ground the four structures of Place Ville Marie are connected by a concrete courtyard full of cafes and people in summer, but bleak and deserted in winter. Beneath it, there are elegant and popular stores as well as restaurants and cinemas. Not only has Place Ville Marie revolutionized life in downtown Montréal but it has become a forerunner of many such developments across the country.

From Place Ville Marie visitors can walk underground to the **Queen Elizabeth Hotel, Central Station** and thence **Place Bonaventure,** another vast shopping and office complex topped by the Hôtel Bonaventure. In one direction lie **Place du Canada,** the **Château Champlain Hotel** and **Windsor Station**; in the other, the **Hyatt Regency Hotel** (short stretch above-ground) and the massive 47-storey Stock Exchange tower, **Place Victoria★.** This tower of darkened glass with its triple "waists" (floors housing mechanical equipment) has four concrete corner supports rising the height of the building, 190 m - 624 ft.

Dominion Square★. – In summer the large open space which makes up Dominion Square could be considered the centre of Montréal. Tours of the city both by bus and by horse-drawn *calèche* (carriage) begin here. It was not always considered such a central spot. When the Roman Catholic Bishop of Montréal, **Ignace Bourget,** decided in 1855 to build his new cathedral in the square, there was great opposition from his parishioners who objected to travelling so far from their homes in Old Montréal *(p. 164)* to attend church !

Mary Queen of the World Cathedral★ (Cathédrale Marie Reine du Monde). – Bishop Bourget overcame the objections and today his cathedral stands in the square, its dome, once considered large, dwarfed by the surrounding highrise. It is modelled after St. Peter's in Rome, covering in total about one quarter of the area of the original. The front, just as its counterpart in Rome, looks like a palace with ornate decoration, Greek columns and a row of statues on the top. Inside, there is a fine reproduction of Bernini's *Baldacchino* – the columns supporting a cover over the altar.

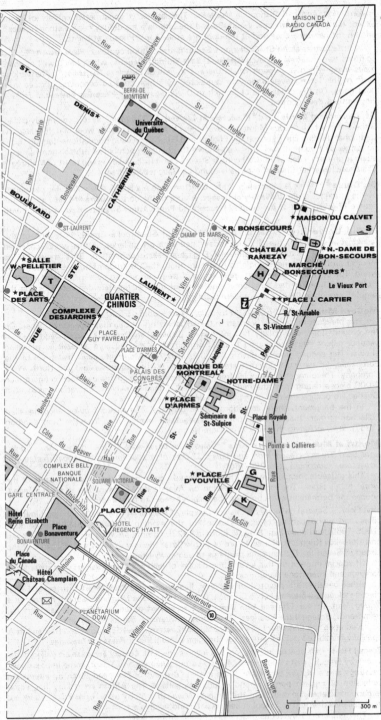

Also in Dominion Square stands the **Château Champlain** Hotel, a slim building with semicircular windows, the **Bank of Commerce**, a tall slim shiny glass box, and the **Sun Life Building,** the first skyscraper in Montréal built in stages 1918-33 and indeed rising in stages in true wedding cake tradition. The vaults in its basement were used to house British government securities during the Second World War.

In the centre of the square, there are statues of Canadian Prime Ministers Sir John A. Macdonald *(p. 108)* and Sir Wilfrid Laurier *(p. 157)*, Robert Burns and Queen Victoria.

St. Catherine's Street ★ (Rue Ste-Catherine). – This is the main shopping street of Montréal. The **Crescent Street** area is Montréal's Yorkville *(p. 137)*. Further along the Department Store area is reached : Ogilvy's, Simpson's, Eaton's and The Bay where the crowd is thick and the traffic noisy. On one side of Eaton's, there is a shopping area called **Les Terrasses** and on the other a small oasis of green surrounds the **Anglican Cathedral.**

Christ Church Cathedral ★. – This ivy-covered limestone church with its slender spire is a fine example of Gothic Revival architecture. It was built 1857-59 at the instigation of Francis

MONTRÉAL★★★

Fulford, first Anglican Bishop of Montréal. The **interior** is constructed entirely of stone except the high roof which is wood. Behind the altar is a beautifully carved stone **reredos**★ and on the nearby arches and at the door are stone carved heads of saints.

A little further along St. Catherine's Street is the cultural complex, **Place des Arts**★. This contains two theatres and a concert hall, **Salle Wilfrid Pelletier**★, which has a wall of enormous glass windows through which there is a view of **Complexe Desjardins**★. The various parts of this latter development are connected by a high covered concourse glassed in at both ends. On the other side of Complexe Desjardins stands **Place Guy Favreau**, a Federal Government development.

St. Lawrence Boulevard★ **(Boulevard St-Laurent).** – "The Main" as it is commonly called is the street which divides Montréal – everything is numbered east or west of it. It is also the traditional dividing line between the English and French-speaking populations, though this is no longer as true as it was. It is well-known for the large number of ethnic shops situated along it on both sides of St. Catherine's Street. Two blocks away is the heart of Montréal's **Chinatown** (Quartier Chinois) especially along La Gauchetière Street.

St. Denis★. – This is Montréal's "Latin Quarter" with numerous sidewalk cafés patronized by the students of the **University of Québec.** A little to the north is **Carré St-Louis**, a pleasant square of lovely turn-of-the-century houses and **Prince Arthur Street** *(closed to traffic)* with its restaurants.

McGill University. – Set on the north side of Sherbrooke Street, once one of the fashionable streets of the city and today lined with art galleries, is this world-renowned university – the bastion of Montréal's English-speaking population. Best known for its medical and engineering schools, it has more than 15 000 students from all parts of the world. The campus is a pleasant green space of trees surrounded by a mélange of buildings – older structures of dark grey limestone some of them elaborately decorated jostling the simpler, straighter lines of the modern buildings.

McCord Museum★★. – *Open Wed - Sun, 11am - 5pm ; $1.00 ;* ☎ *392-4778.*

This pleasant museum is devoted to the social history of Canada, especially Québec. On the ground floor, one gallery has interesting displays on Canada's Indians and Inuit. A second gallery houses changing exhibits organized by the museum as well as travelling shows. The second floor is devoted to the history of Montréal since the arrival of the Europeans. Of particular interest are the displays on the fur trade and the North West Company. There are also examples from the museum's large costume collection (more than 7 000 pieces dating from the mid 18th century). Changing exhibits on various aspects of Québec life occupy the rest of the second and the third floors.

In the basement, there are photographic displays. The McCord owns an unequalled collection of more than 700 000 prints and negatives, many dating from Pre-Confederation (1867) days, including the work of William Notman.

Montréal Museum of Fine Arts★★ **(Musée des beaux-arts).** – *Open daily 11am - 5pm ; until 9pm Thurs ; closed Mon and hols ; $2.00 ; plan available at entrance ; restaurant, bookstore, auditorium ;* ☎ *285-1600.*

This museum founded in 1860 has a collection covering all the arts of all parts of the world at all times. The modern extension on Avenue du Musée, which is open-planned, houses the permanent collection and the displays seem to flow into one another.

First Floor. – Several galleries on this level display **Canadian art** from the paintings, furniture, silver and wood carving of early Québec to the modern works of Paul-Emile Borduas (1905-1960) and Jean-Paul Riopelle (born in 1923). Of note are the paintings of Paul Kane and Cornelius Krieghoff, the sculpture of Suzor-Coté, the few examples of the work of the Group of Seven *(p. 139)* and the paintings of James Wilson Morrice.

Of special interest on this level is the display of **Inuit and Amerindian art** with its argillite carvings and soapstone sculptures.

Other galleries are devoted to **Medieval, Renaissance and Baroque art** with several fine pieces including works by Lucas Cranach, El Greco and Hans Memlinc's superb *Portrait of a Young Man.* In the **17th and 18th Centuries European art** galleries, there are paintings by Rembrandt, Brueghel the Younger, Gainsborough, Ramsay, Batoni and others.

In addition the first floor has displays of Near Eastern, Greek, Etruscan and Roman art. A specially humidified gallery is used for changing exhibitions of **Prints and Drawings.**

Second Floor. – Of special interest on this level is the **19th Century European art** gallery with works by French artists Bouguereau, Fantin-Latour, Daumier and Tissot, some Impressionist paintings and sculpture by Rodin. There are fine displays of European silver, an interesting collection of English porcelain and a furniture gallery. The **African art** gallery has some remarkable pieces, among them the intricate *Mwaash a Mboy* mask from Zaïre. There are also galleries devoted to Precolumbian, Asiatic and Islamic art.

The temporary exhibitions galleries are found on this level.

Third Floor. – The two small galleries on this level display works by Picasso, Feininger, Salvador Dali and Hans Hofman as well as sculpture by Henry Moore and Jean Arp. An Alexander Calder mobile hangs in the stairwell.

■ THE OLD CITY★★ (Le Vieux Montréal) Plan p. 163

Wandering around this area bounded by the port, St-Jacques, Berri and McGill Streets which is so full of life and history, it is hard to realize that in 1960 it was a deserted collection of derelict houses in danger of being demolished. It was of course the original city where de Maisonneuve landed and built his fort. For nearly a hundred years it was surrounded by a high stone wall. But the early 20th century saw the population move away from it. People built their houses further and further north and west, retail business also moved in these directions leaving the Old City an area of warehouses, wholesale businesses and activity to do with the developing port. City Hall, the Law Courts and the "temples of finance" along **St. James Street** (rue St-Jacques) remained but otherwise the area declined.

The 1960s saw the beginning of a movement to change this. The **Viger Commission** which controls all development in the area was set up. The Provincial Government declared the region south of Notre Dame Street an "historic area" where nothing could be pulled down or built without the approval of the Commission. Slowly the area came back to life, restaurants and shops opened, houses were restored. Today the process is far from complete but what has been done has made the area a major tourist attraction and a pleasant place to wander around.

Place Jacques Cartier★★. – In summer this lovely square is the heart of Québecois life and culture. There are outdoor cafes, street musicians, restaurants and artisan shops. Visitors can admire the works of art on sale along narrow **rue St-Amable,** buy flowers from the vendors in the centre of Place Jacques Cartier or join with the crowd to listen to the latest chansonnier on **rue St-Vincent** or **rue St-Paul.** *Tours of the Old City by horse-drawn calèche (carriage) can be taken from here.*

At one end of the square stands a column with a statue on the top. This rather surprisingly is **Admiral Nelson,** the British commander who defeated the French fleet at the Battle of Trafalgar. When the news of this victory reached Montréal, the population was so delighted that a fund was started and this monument was the result. Completed in 1809 it predates the famous column in Trafalgar Square, London. On the other side of Notre-Dame Street from the column stands Montréal's **City Hall (H)**, a fine ornate building with four storeys, a tower and a mansard roof. Note the second floor balcony from which General de Gaulle made his *Vive le Québec libre* speech in 1967.

At the other end of Place Jacques Cartier, a park, **Le Vieux Port**, stretches to the St. Lawrence *(open during summer months only)*. It is part of a large federal government project to reuse space in the port of Montréal and give people a "window on the river" *(☎ 283-5256 for more information)*.

Jet Boat Trips on the Lachine Rapids★★ (S). – *From wharf in port of Montréal near bottom of Berri St ; May - mid Oct ; 1 1/2 hrs ; $25.00 ; ☎ 284-9607. Protective clothing provided.*

This is a thrilling trip by shallow-draft jet boat up the St. Lawrence to the Lachine Rapids *(p. 172)*. This still formidable piece of water rises in great waves as the river drops about 6 m - 20 ft. The boats mount and descend the rapids several times enabling all participants to appreciate the power of the river... and to get soaking wet despite the protective clothing ! The trip to and from the rapids offers fine **views★★** of the city.

Château Ramezay★. – *Open daily 10 am-4.30 pm ; closed Mon and hols ; $1.00 ; ☎ 861-7182.*

This low-lying fieldstone house with a tower at one end and two cannons at the front was built in 1705 by **Claude de Ramezay,** the Governor of Montréal. It has been much altered since by later occupants - the tower for example was added in the 19th century - but the walls which are more than 1 m - 3 ft thick and the deep stone vaults which de Ramezay built can still be admired. In 1755 it became the headquarters of the **Compagnie des Indes,** a French company which held a monopoly on the export of beaver pelts until the Conquest. They used it as a combined office, warehouse and residence until it was sold to the British Government in 1763 to serve as the official residence of the British Governors. When the Americans occupied Montréal during the winter of 1775-76 the Château was used as Montgomery's headquarters and **Benjamin Franklin** stayed in it on his mission to persuade the Canadians to join the Revolution. Today, it houses a museum.

The displays cover the history of Montréal and the Château's part in this history. One room is a reconstruction of the **Grande Salle★** of the Compagnie des Indes in Nantes, France (the location of the headquarters of that company). The very fine carved panelling which once graced the above was transported to Montréal and re-erected in the Château. Other rooms are furnished and decorated to evoke the de Ramezays' and the work of a Governor of Montréal in the French Regime. In the **basement** the stone vaults, now whitewashed, can be seen. Bread is sometimes baked in the huge oven and there are displays on the life of the Indians who once inhabited the Montréal area.

On the corner of Berri Street stands the **Sir George Etienne Cartier House (D)** with its mansard roof. It was once the home and legal office of this Québec politician who was also one of the Fathers of Confederation *(p. 209)*. It is being restored by Parks Canada.

Rue Bonsecours★. – This is one of the most attractive streets in the Old City. It descends from Notre-Dame to St-Paul Street and is dominated by the lovely church of Notre-Dame de Bon-Secours which stands at the bottom. On the right just after the corner, note the grey house with two sets of dormer windows in the pitched roof (no 440). This is the **Papineau House (E)** built in 1752 of fieldstone covered with a façade of wood carved and painted to look like limestone. It was home to six generations of Papineaus including Louis-Joseph Papineau, the leader of the 1837 Rebellion in Lower Canada *(p. 161)*.

Maison du Calvet★. – Built about 1725 this lovely three-storey stone house with its distinctive high chimneys is considered one of the best examples of urban architecture remaining from the French Regime. It is named not for its builder but for its most famous or infamous occupant. **Pierre du Calvet** was a French Huguenot who settled in Montréal during the last years of the French Regime. After the Conquest he quickly offered his services to the British which were accepted because he was a Protestant and French-speaking, and he became a Justice of the Peace. When the Americans arrived in 1775 he was just as quick to offer his services to them. But this time he chose the wrong side. The Americans left the next year without paying him for the supplies he had acquired for them and the returning British threw him into jail. After his release a few years later he tried to get compensation for his services from the Americans - without success - and at the same time he appealed his imprisonment to the British. While pursuing both these "injustices" he was drowned when his ship sank en route for London from New York.

Notre-Dame de Bon-Secours★. – *Open daily except Mon ; ☎ 845-9991.*

This pretty stone church with its central spire and two side pinnacles is among the most photographed in the city. The original church on this site was built by **Marguerite Bourgeois,** a devout lay teacher who was recruited by de Maisonneuve to establish a school in Ville Marie. She arrived in 1653 and immediately set about raising the money to build the church. She was assigned the duty of chaperoning and training **les filles du roi,** the young women who were sent out from France at the King's expense to marry the lonely bachelor settlers and increase the population *(see also p. 171).* In 1671 she and some other similarly-minded women were officially recognized as an order of teaching nuns - **La Congrégation de Notre Dame.** It was the first religious order established in Canada.

The original wooden church which Marguerite Bourgeois built was replaced in 1678 by a stone one which was burnt down in 1754. The present structure dates to 1772 except for the tower at the back with the large statue of the Virgin standing with arms outstretched towards the river. This was added in the 19th century. The statue became a landmark for sailors coming up river and the church became known as the "sailors' church". The interior has a definite nautical look with ship-shaped votive lamps.

The **tower** at the back can be mounted *(open daily except Mon and hols ; 75¢)* to the level of the statue of the Virgin. From

(after photo by Canadian Government Office of Tourism)

Notre-Dame de Bon-Secours

this point there is a good **view**★ of the harbour and river. Once the church stood on the water's edge – all the land between the church and the river has been reclaimed. The **clock tower** on the pier in front of the church is a memorial to sailors who lost their lives during the two World Wars.

In the basement of the chapel is a small **museum**★ *(same admission as for tower)* devoted to the life of Saint Marguerite Bourgeois. She was canonized in 1982. Her life is portrayed by means of dioramas using dolls. A spoken commentary describes each scene.

Next to the church on St-Paul Street stands the **Marché Bonsecours**★, a striking two-storey grey stone structure with its central dome. Built between 1845 and 1852 as Montréal's City Hall and central market, it today houses municipal offices.

Place d'Armes★.

In 1644, this square was the site of a battle between the French and the Iroquois when the Sieur de Maisonneuve personally killed the Indian chief. The monument in the centre commemorates this victory *(see illustration p. 160).* It was sculpted in 1895 by the Québec artist Philippe Hébert.

In the southeast corner of the square, hidden behind a wall with a façade dominated by a clock stands the old fieldstone **Seminary of St-Sulpice.** The Sulpician order was founded in Paris in 1641 by the Abbé Jean-Jacques Olier to train aspirants to the priesthood. It was involved in the creation of Ville Marie and took over all the obligations and rights of the Compagnie de Ville Marie in 1663. The present building was commenced in 1685 and first occupied in 1712. The Sulpicians still occupy the seminary today and are responsible for the neighbouring church.

Notre-Dame★.

Open daily ; guided tours May - Oct ; ☎ 842-2925.

This twin-towered church was completed in 1829 to replace an earlier structure. The exterior was the work of two architects : **James O'Donnell** an Irish-American and **John Ostell** who was responsible for the twin towers.

On entering Notre-Dame visitors will be struck by its size and the richness of its decoration. The overall interior design was the work of the architect, **Victor Bourgeau.** The carvings on the main altar were executed by the French sculptor, Bouriché, those of the pulpit were carved by Philippe Hébert (note especially Ezechiel and Jeremiah at the bottom) and the baptistry was the work of Ozias Leduc.

In the Sacré-Cœur Chapel behind the altar, note the magnificent bronze **reredos**★ by Charles Daudelin (1982).

Bank of Montréal★

(Banque de Montréal). – This Classical revival building with its portico of six columns and its squat dome was built in 1847. It houses the main branch of the oldest Canadian bank founded in 1817. To the left of the main entrance is a small **museum** *(open banking hours ;* ☎ 877-6892) displaying banknotes, coins, piggybanks and the history of the bank in pictures.

The street on which the Bank of Montréal stands is **St. James Street** (rue St-Jacques) which was once the Wall Street of Canada. Although Bay Street in Toronto is today considered to be Canada's financial centre, St. James Street still retains some of the grandeur from its days of financial primacy. Many highly decorated Victorian buildings housing banks and insurance companies can be seen along it.

Place Royale.

The obelisk in the centre of this small square commemorates the arrival of the first inhabitants of Ville Marie. It is difficult to envisage this spot as they saw it. A small river, the St-Pierre, ran along **Pointe à Callières** and entered the St. Lawrence in front of Place Royale. The river is still there but underground. The edge of the St. Lawrence has been pushed back to build the port installations. The statue at the end of Pointe à Callières stands on what was once a point of land between the two rivers. It was on this point that de Maisonneuve actually disembarked and built a fort, the first structure of Ville Marie. The statue is of **John Young** under whose guidance the port of Montréal began the expansion which led to its importance today.

Place d'Youville★. – The red brick building at the centre of this square was once a fire station *(la vieille caserne)*. Today it houses an interesting **Interpretation Centre**★★ (F) *(open daily except Mon, 10am - 4pm; visit 1 hr; $2.00; ☎ 845-4236)* which traces the history of Montréal through the ages by means of slide shows, films and taped commentaries.

On the east side of Place d'Youville stands a long low structure of grey stone with a gable at either end. Through the archway there is a central courtyard. The buildings around this yard, known as the **Youville Stables**★ (G) (les écuries d'Youville), were constructed between 1825 and 1860. They have been beautifully restored and today house offices and a restaurant. The courtyard itself is a pleasant spot in summer with its trees and cafe tables. Although these structures mainly date from the 19th century, the layout is a left-over from the early days of the settlement when the inhabitants needed to protect themselves from Indian attacks. Later this arrangement of buildings was continued to protect gardens from the extremes of the climate and to enclose other buildings such as stables, thus the name.

Nearby, between St-Pierre and Normand Streets, stands the restored **Grey Nuns Convent** (K) erected in 1692 by François Charon de la Barre and extended by Marie d'Youville, the foundress of the Order of Grey Nuns (les sœurs grises) in 1753. The **Musée Marc Aurèle Fortin** *(118 rue St-Pierre; open Tues-Sun; $1.00)* has changing exhibitions devoted to Québec artists in addition to the works of Fortin (1888-1970).

■ MOUNT ROYAL★★ (Le Mont-Royal) *Plan p. 168*

Known familiarly to Montréalers as "The Mountain", Mount Royal is situated roughly in the centre of the island. It rises rather suddenly from the otherwise flat landscape and is the best known and indeed the namesake of a series of eight peaks called the Monteregian Hills (Collines Montérégiennes) (derived from the latin *mons regius* - Mount Royal) which lie between the St. Lawrence and the Appalachians *(map pp. 150-51)*. These hills – Mount St. Bruno, Mount St. Hilaire, Rougemont, Yamaska Mountain, Shefford Mountain, Brome Mountain, Mount St. Gregoire and Mount Royal itself – are the stubs of extinct volcanoes formed about three million years ago. They rise abruptly from the otherwise flat plain and thus seem more prominent than their actual heights (rnaximum 535 m - 1 755 ft) would suggest.

Mount Royal Park★★ **(Parc du Mont Royal).** – *20 min on foot from Peel and St. Catherine Sts. By car approach from Côte des Neiges or Voie Camillien Houde, parking areas ($) on Remembrance Rd; cafeterias at Beaver Lake (Lac des Castors) and the Chalet (A).*

Mount Royal is cut in two by Côte des Neiges Road. To the north is this pleasant park with its tree-lined walks which circle and climb the mountain giving fine views of the city on all sides. This mountain park is a feature unique to Montréal because it lies in the centre of the urban area. Despite its natural look the park was actually the result of careful planning. It was laid out in 1874 by **Frederick Law Olmstead,** the American landscape architect responsible for many city parks in the United States including Central Park in New York. His design for Mount Royal is a work of art – the more so because its very naturalness seems to suggest that it has no design.

The park has become a popular spot in all seasons. Summer visitors walk, jog, sit, picnic, sail model boats on Beaver Lake (Lac des Castors) or enjoy the views of the city. Winter activities include skating on Beaver Lake, downhill and cross-country skiing and snow-shoeing. Horses pull carriages *(calèches)* full of tourists in summer and sledges of revellers in winter.

Viewpoints. – The terrace in front of the **Chalet (A)** *(short walk from parking area)* offers a splendid **view**★★ of the city by day and night. The downtown area below the terrace seems squashed between the mountain and the St. Lawrence. This was not always the case. Once McGill University *(to the left of the lookout)* was the country estate of James McGill to which he retreated from his town house beside the river! The St. Lawrence is particularly attractive from this viewpoint in the winter when large chunks of ice can be made out in the blue waters. Beyond the river some of the other Monteregian Hills can be distinguished and on clear days the Adirondack Mountains of New York State can be seen to the south.

From the Chalet follow the path around the summit of the Mountain. It passes a huge metal **Cross (B)** which at night is lit up by hundreds of bulbs. This was erected in 1924 in memory of the cross placed there in 1643 by de Maisonneuve. There are views of eastern Montréal through the trees, the Olympic Stadium and several oil refineries are clearly distinguishable. Continuing along the path the view changes to the north and west especially near to the television transmission tower.

Voie Camillien Houde★. – One of the most attractive drives in Montréal is down this road from the car parks to Park Avenue. The road winds down steeply past imposing cliffs. There is a **viewpoint**★ of eastern Montréal *(parking, path to the Cross).*

University of Montréal (L'Université de Montréal). – *Access from Blvd. Edouard-Montpetit.*

This imposing structure with its high tower and symmetrical wings houses the largest French university outside France. Set on the western flank of Mount Royal, it is well known for its medical and dental faculties and for its polytechnical school.

Westmount Lookout★ **(Belvédère de Westmount).** – On the southern side of Côte des Neiges Road is this small park offering a fine **view**★ from its terrace. In the trees immediately below is Westmount the heart of English-speaking Montréal, with its tree-lined streets and gracious stone houses of great size. A group of black glass and metal towers of classic Mies van der Rohe design can be seen to the left and indeed he was the architect. This is **Westmount Square**★ *(access from Atwater metro)* which contains elegant living, shopping and office areas.

St. Joseph's Oratory★★ **(Oratoire St-Joseph).** – *Entrance from Queen Mary Rd. Open daily all year; refreshments; ☎ 733-8211.*

On the western flank of Mount Royal stands this well-known shrine to St. Joseph (husband of Mary, mother of Christ). Its dome is a Montréal landmark rising 260 m - 856 ft above sea level (higher than Place Ville Marie and the Cross on the main summit of the mountain). The shrine was created by a lay brother from St-Grégoire, Québec, called Alfred Bessette, who joined the Congregation of the Holy Cross in 1870 and took the name under

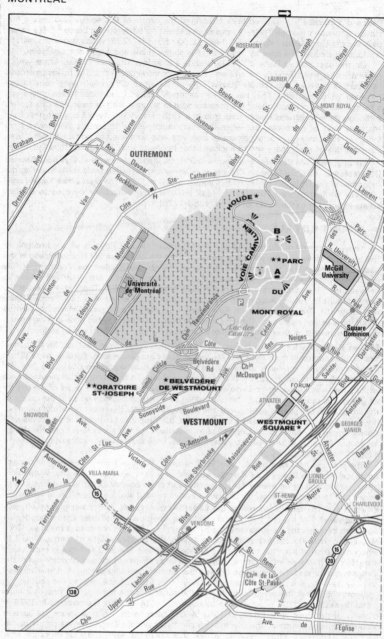

which he is better known, **Brother André**. In 1904 he built a small wooden chapel on the west slope of Mount Royal to honour St. Joseph. He treated the sick and preached that complete devotion to St. Joseph would relieve suffering. Many left the Oratory cured, their abandoned crutches, canes and wheelchairs bearing witness to their recovery. When he died in 1937 at the age of 91, Brother André's fame was so widespread that nearly a million people filed past his coffin. Today, an estimated two million pilgrims visit the Oratory every year.

The original chapel erected by Brother André still stands but the site is dominated by the huge basilica topped by the dome. The base of this is built in terraces. The lowest part, the crypt chapel, was constructed in 1924 but the basilica church and dome were not completed until 1967 although the plans were approved by Brother André.

The Basilica Interior★. – *Either climb up the series of steps outside to the main terrace or enter crypt chapel and ascend by escalator.*

The Basilica is entered through carved bronze doors designed by Robert Prévost. The interior is impressive, almost austere. Concrete columns support the nave and dome designed by **Dom Paul Bellot**. There are large and fine carved oak statues of the apostles by Henri Charlier, who also designed the stone altar and wooden crucifix. Regular recitals are given on the huge organ.

From the terrace a view to the north and west is obtained and the University of Montréal can be seen to the right.

The Original Chapel. – *Follow signs from basilica.* This tiny chapel and Brother André's room above it can be visited. A statue of Brother André by Emile Brunet stands beside the chapel. In the grounds there are some fine carvings representing the Stations of the Cross.

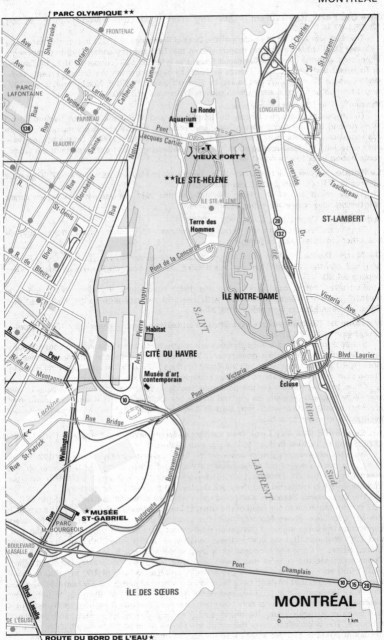

■ **ST. HELEN'S ISLAND AND AREA★★** (Ile-Ste-Hélène)

Access : by metro from Berri de Montigny ; by bus no 167 (McGill) or 169 (Papineau) ; by car over Jacques Cartier Bridge, or Pont de la Concorde (summer only) ; parking $4.00 during Man and His World.

St. Helen's Island lies in the St. Lawrence directly east of the main island of Montréal. It was named by Samuel de Champlain in honour of his wife **Hélène Boulé**. It was on the island that the **Chevalier de Lévis** burnt the regimental flags of the Compagnie Franche de la Marine *(p. 170)* before surrendering to the British in 1760. Following the War of 1812, the island was fortified and British troops remained there until 1870. The City of Montréal purchased it at the beginning of this century and turned it into a park.

In 1967, the island was artificially extended and connected by bridge to its neighbour Ile-Notre-Dame which had been built for the St. Lawrence Seaway *(p. 170)* and which was also extended. This formed the site for the great international exhibition, **Expo '67**, which was held in the year of the centennial of Canada's Confederation. Ile-Notre-Dame was also the site of the **International Floralies** held in 1980.

Man and His World (Terre des Hommes). – *Open late June - Aug daily ; restaurants, cafeterias ;* ☎ *872-6222.*

The pavilions which were built to house the displays of Expo '67 were turned into an annual summer show with displays from all over the world. Visitors can wander among them, sit at the cafes, and enjoy the **views★** of the river and the city from the island. There are concerts, rock shows and other activities.

MONTRÉAL ★★★

The Old Fort★ (Le Vieux Fort). – *Open daily 10am - 5pm ; closed Mon in winter ; $1.50 ;* ☎ 861-6738.

This fort was built on the orders of the **Duke of Wellington** in 1822. In summer *(late June - Labour Day)* students perform manœuvres in the 18th century uniforms of two regiments connected with the Island. **La Campagnie Franche de la Marine** was founded in 1622 by Cardinal Richelieu and sent to New France in 1683 to defend it from the British. **Fraser's Highlanders** was a Scottish regiment raised by Simon Fraser to fight in North America in 1757, and it formed part of the army which captured Montréal in 1760.

Museum★. – *In Old Fort ; same hours.*

This museum traces the history of New France and of Canada until the Second World War. Among the many examples of weapons, uniforms and other military mementos, there are some scale models. Note particularly the **Model of Montréal in 1760★**. On the second floor note especially the **Firearms Collection★** which includes weapons from all parts of the world, some dating back four hundred years.

La Ronde. – *Open daily late June - Aug ; weekends in May and early June ; $2.50 general admission, $10.00 unlimited access to all rides.*

At the north end of St. Helen's Island lies this vast amusement park which offers hair-raising rides, cafes and other entertainment.

Aquarium. – *Open daily ; $2.00 ;* ☎ 872-4656.

The Alcan Pavilion contains a series of aquariums with a variety of fish, marine animals and other creatures such as penguins.

Ile-Notre-Dame. – *Open daily in summer and for winter sports ; closed during Spring and Fall months. During Man and His World, balade from Ile-Ste-Hélène metro, 50¢ ; parking $4.00.*

Converted into a **floral park★** after the 1980 International Floralies, this island is a pleasant place to wander in summer with views of the city and the St. Lawrence. The Canadian Grand Prix is also held on the island.

Museum of Contemporary Art (Musée d'art contemporain). – *Open daily 10am - 6pm ; closed Mon ;* ☎ 873-2878.

Set back off the road stands this austere concrete structure housing the contemporary art collection of the Québec government. The permanent collection stresses Québec art since 1940 and includes work by Paul-Emile Borduas, Alfred Pellan and Jean-Paul Riopelle. These paintings are however not always on show as there are many visiting shows.

Close to the museum on the peninsula stands a structure of modular blocks placed seemingly higgledy-piggledy on top and across one another. This is **Habitat,** the creation of architect Moshe Safdie which was built in 1967 for Expo. Each block is a self-contained living unit *(not open to public).*

St. Lawrence Seaway Lock (Voie maritime du Saint-Laurent). – Access from Hwy 132 at eastern end of Victoria Bridge ; follow signs for "écluse".

From the observatory *(upper tower on the lock ; open daily May - Oct ;* ☎ 672-4110), there is a good view of the huge vessels (lakers and ocean-going ships) passing up and down through the St. Lambert Lock. The working of this lock in co-ordination with the Victoria Bridge is explained and there are displays on the rest of the Seaway.

The **St. Lawrence Seaway** is a shipping route which provides navigation at a depth of 8 m - 27 ft from Montréal to the head of the Great Lakes *(see Thunder Bay p. 127).* The rapids in the St. Lawrence above Montréal and the various falls and rapids on the other rivers connecting the lakes impeded navigation until canals were built to bypass them in the 18th and 19th centuries. But the draft in these canals was small so the 20th century saw a joint United States - Canadian proposal for a deep waterway which would take ocean boats. Construction started in 1954 and it was completed in 1959. The Seaway begins at Montréal, 1 650 km - 1 000 miles from the Atlantic, and rises a total of 180 m - 600 ft above sea level between that city and Lake Superior, a distance of another 2 160 km - 1 342 miles *(see also Welland Canal p. 114, and Sault Ste Marie p. 124).* Because of the winter freeze-up, the entire seaway is only open between April and mid December each year, but it has become a major route for world trade, especially iron ore, grains and petroleum products. The ships which carry this cargo are for the most part specially built to hold the maximum possible and yet still fit into the locks. They are called **lakers** and are long and narrow – as long as 222.5 m - 730 ft with a maximum width of 23.16 m - 76 ft *(see Thunder Bay p. 127).* These lakers are each capable of carrying over one million bushels or 25 000 metric tonnes - 27 600 tons of grain.

■ OLYMPIC PARK AREA★★ (Parc Olympique)

The fine collection of sports facilities constructed for the 1976 Olympic Games are located in the east end of Montréal in the area which was once the **City of Maisonneuve.** This city was developed at the turn of the century by wealthy French Canadian businessmen to rival Montréal. Fine houses such as the Château Dufresne *(p. 171)* were built along wide tree-lined boulevards. The municipal buildings were grandiose and parks abounded. Unfortunately this development was too costly and in 1918 the practically bankrupt city was annexed by Montréal.

The Olympic Park★★. – *Sherbrooke St at Pie IX ; metro - Pie IX or Viau ; parking ($) ; cafeteria ; souvenir shop ;* ☎ 252-4737.

This vast complex was designed by the French architect **Roger Taillibert.** Controversial from the first, very expensive and still unfinished, these buildings offer a remarkably fine and attractive set of sports facilities. Visitors should wander around the site to admire the concrete supports of the stadium. The sheer amount of concrete used is impressive and their size is somewhat overwhelming.

The **guided tours** *(daily, 1 hr $4.00)* are the only means of entering the buildings (except for baseball and football games in the stadium ; and public swimming in the Olympic pool). The tour begins with the swimming pools (piscine) and then moves into the **Stadium** (stade) itself. This huge oval structure with its sideways V-shaped concrete ribs is Roger Taillibert's masterpiece. It is built almost entirely of precast reinforced concrete and the thirty eight ribs which are self-supporting - there are no interior columns - in turn support the roof over the rows of seats. The sports area itself is open to the elements as is required for the Olympic Games but in the future it may be covered by a retractable roof. The stadium seats 60 000 people and the field can be easily changed to accommodate baseball, football, athletics (the Olympic track is underneath the artificial grass surface which covers the floor) and even pop concerts and political meetings.

The tour continues into the **Velodrome,** the site of the Olympic cycle events. This attractive structure has a vast arched roof with a span of 190 m - 560 ft made of concrete with large acrylic glass panels which let in the daylight. It contains a cycle track of Cameroon redwood but is used for many other events. The central part can be frozen to form a skating rink and it has also been used for exhibitions and meetings.

Across Sherbrooke Street near Viau stands the **Olympic Village** *(accessible by passage under Sherbrooke - not open to public).* This striking pair of half-pyramids, used to house the athletes during the Olympic Games, has been converted into apartments.

Château Dufresne★★ (Musée des Arts Décoratifs - Museum of Decorative Arts). - *Sherbrooke St at Pie IX. Open Thurs - Sun 12am - 5pm ; $1.00 ; free parking ; refreshments ; ☎ 259-2575.*

This elegant neo-classical building, restored by the Macdonald-Stewart foundation, was constructed 1915-19 by **Marius Dufresne** for himself and his brother Oscar. It is in fact two residences. Part of the development of the City of Maisonneuve *(see above),* it shows the wealth and way of life of the early 20th century business aristocracy. The richly decorated rooms with their wood panelling, plaster sculpturing and fine furniture reflect many styles. In the basement there is a small collection of Québec art, and the museum mounts changing exhibitions f the decorative arts.

Botanical Gardens★★ (Jardin botanique). – *4101 Sherbrooke St. E. Open daily ; parking $3.00 weekends ; cafeteria ; guided tours by mini-train 55¢, 20 min ; ☎ 252-1171.*

Started by Brother Marie-Victorin in 1931, the founder of the Botanical Institute of the University of Montréal, these gardens are the largest of their type in North America. Covering 73 ha - 180 acres, they contain about 26 000 species of which 3 000 are trees. These species are displayed in thirty specialized sections which provide a comprehensive picture of plants used by man, particularly what will grow in southern Québec, as well as showing plants native to all five continents. Among the specialized sections are gardens devoted to annuals and perennials, a rose garden, a recreated monastery garden, an enclosure of poisonous plants, Alpine gardens with the species particular to several great mountain ranges, an aquatic garden with pond and stream, and an incredible Bonsai garden with 100-year old miniature trees.

Pleasant as the gardens are for wandering around, no visit is complete without entering the **conservatories★★** (serres) *(open daily 9am - 6pm, later in summer months ; $2.00).* A wide range of tropical, semi-tropical and plants native to arid regions are on display. Of particular note are the orchids (1 200 varieties), begonias (200 species) and cacti. One conservatory is reserved for changing displays on varying themes.

■ **RIVER AND LAKESHORE DRIVE★** (Route du bord de l'eau)

33 km - 21 miles from Dominion Square to Pointe Claire – about 1hr not including visit – Plans pp. 169 and 172

This drive beside the St. Lawrence River and Lake St. Louis enables visitors to appreciate the size and force of this great waterway and thus the importance of Montréal's site. For much of the route, parks border the river with picnic spots and viewpoints. The road can be followed all the way to Ste-Anne-de-Bellevue at the western tip of the island or it can be followed just in part depending on the time available.

From Dominion Square take Peel St to its end at Wellington St, turn right, take the tunnel and after 3 km - 2 miles turn left at Parc Marguerite Bourgeois.

Musée St-Gabriel★. - *2146 Favard. Guided tours afternoons daily mid April - mid Dec ; closed Mon ; 1 1/2 hr ; reservations recommended ; ☎ 935-8136.*

This attractive three-storey stone house with its steeply pitched roof was built in 1698 on foundations dating back to 1668. It belongs to the nuns of the Congrégation of Notre-Dame who restored the house and opened it to the public in 1966. The land on which it stands was bought by Marguerite Bourgeois, the foundress of the Order *(p. 165)* in 1671. At that time it stood beside the St. Lawrence and faced Nun's Island (Ile-des-Sœurs) which also belonged to the Congregation. A convent and a farm were built and from time to time the house was temporary home to some of the *filles du roi (p. 166).*

The tour allows the visitor a glimpse into the life of the 17th and 18th centuries. The solid construction of the house is evident in the massive stone walls and huge timber beams of the basement, and the ash and oak timbers of the roof which have been held together by wooden pegs since 1698. A replica of the room of one of the *filles du roi* can be seen.

Return to Wellington St. and after 1 km - 1/2 mile turn left onto Lasalle Blvd.

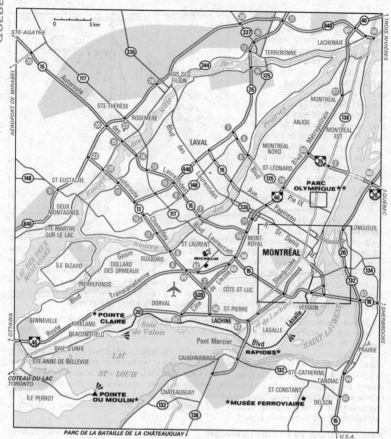

The road runs beside the St. Lawrence entering the town of Lasalle *(9 km - 5 1/2 miles)* where there are good **views**★ of the rapids, in particular from the end of the causeway across the old power house opposite 8th Avenue.

Lachine Rapids and Canal★. – *For boat trips see p. 165.* This turbulent water upstream from Montréal is still impressive despite the lessening in the water level since the building of the St. Lawrence Seaway. These rapids frustrated Cartier's hopes of mounting the river in 1535 – and those of many after him. They were called the *Sault St-Louis* by Champlain in 1611 when one of his companions named Louis was drowned there. They were later renamed Lachine after the place that grew up near their beginning, part of the seigneury of **Robert Cavelier de LaSalle.** LaSalle was a great explorer, one of his hopes being to find the elusive Northwest passage to China *(p. 230).* His seigneury and thus the rapids were given the name **La Chine** (the French for China) partly in derision by his colleagues.

It was possible to run the rapids coming down the river and many brave souls did but usually they sent their baggage overland first. Going upstream however was a different matter, and provisions were hauled the 13 km - 8 miles from Montréal by land. The idea of building a canal to avoid this navigational hazard was first suggested in 1670, but it was abandoned as too massive an undertaking until 1824 when the first channel was completed. This remained an important transportation route, starting as it did in Montréal harbour, until the opening of the Seaway in 1959. Since then it has been little used for commercial purposes but it is being converted into a recreational corridor by Parks Canada. An **Interpretation Centre** *(7th Ave and Boul. St-Joseph in Lachine ; open daily mid May - mid Sept)* explains some of its history.

The road passes under the Honoré-Mercier road bridge and a railway bridge and enters Lachine *(18 km - 11 1/2 miles).*

The City of Lachine. – Granted to LaSalle as a seigneury in 1667 it was from here that he began his explorations. Settlement soon followed but was set back by the **Lachine Massacre** of 1689. The Iroquois attacked the village during a dark night killing about two hundred people and taking away about another hundred as prisoners never to be seen again. More than two-thirds of the houses were burnt to the ground. This event was the most brutal massacre suffered by the French.

Lachine, however, recovered and became the major embarkation point for fur traders and explorers going west. After the Conquest it continued to be a fur trading centre and embarkation point for immigrants to Upper Canada. The building of the canal gave Lachine additional importance until the Seaway superseded it, but Lachine remains an important industrial centre.

The road crosses the Lachine Canal and becomes Blvd. St. Joseph.

The road follows almost continuously the shores of **Lake St. Louis,** an enlargement of the St. Lawrence for the next 13 km - 8 miles. Then it rounds **Baie de Valois** and enters the city of Pointe Claire.

Pointe Claire★. – This pleasant city on the lakeshore is full of tree-lined streets and large houses. It is the beginning of the area known as the "West Island" where wealthy Mont-réalers, largely English-speaking, have their homes. There are several yacht clubs and in summer the lake is dotted with sails. The "point" of Pointe Claire is reached 32 km - 20 miles from downtown. *(Turn left off Lakeshore Road onto Ste-Anne and park beside the attractive church of St-Joachim).* An old stone windmill stands in the grounds of the convent of the sisters of the Congrégation of Notre Dame, the only surviving part of a series of forts built in the early 18th century near the Lachine rapids by the Sulpicians. The Lachine Massacre *(p. 172)* led to the building of such fortifications as a sort of outer line of defence for Montréal. This windmill served not only to grind flour but as a refuge in time of attack. From this point there is a fine **view★** back towards Montréal. The west flank of Mount Royal is evident with the dome of the Oratory and the tower of the University of Montréal standing out clearly.

The road continues through **Beaconsfield, Baie d'Urfe** and **Ste-Anne-de-Bellevue,** all pleasant residential areas with tree-lined streets and attractive houses. For the most part the road is a little inland and the lake is glimpsed only occasionally.

EXCURSIONS

Canadian Railway Museum★ (Musée Ferroviaire). – *Plan p. 172. 120 rue St-Pierre, St. Constant 19 km - 12 miles by Mercier Bridge, Rtes 132 and 209. Open daily May - Oct ; $3.00 ;* ☎ 632-2410.

This museum has one of the largest collections of railway equipment on the continent. In addition to numerous locomotives (steam, electric and diesel), there are railway cars, electric trams and a mass of other equipment including a hand-operated turntable. Many of these pieces are exhibited outside but the gems of the collection are housed in two large sheds. Visitors can climb into the cab of **CPR 5935,** one of the largest steam engines ever built, and handle the controls. Also on view are CPR 2850 the **Royal Hudson** which took King George VI and Queen Elizabeth across Canada in 1939, and BR 60010 which hauled the famous *Flying Scotsman* on the London - Edinburgh run (one of its sister locomotives holds the all-time speed record for steam trains – 204 km - 126 1/2 mph).

The railway cars on display include Sir William Van Horne's private one, the *Saskatchewan,* in which he travelled while supervising the building of the Canadian Pacific Railway *(p. 16),* and a school car which served children in the Chapleau - White River area of Ontario earlier this century (the teacher lived in it).

The second shed houses a collection of trams including two open *Golden Chariots* which were once used by visitors to tour Mount Royal *(p. 167),* and the first electric streetcar used in Montréal, the *Rocket.*

Regular tramway rides are offered free to visitors.

Pointe du Moulin★. – *Plan p. 172. 40 km - 25 miles from downtown by Route 20 ; turn left at 2nd set of traffic lights on Ile-Perrot. Provincial Historical Site. Open daily mid May - Labour Day ; refreshments ; picnic sites ;* ☎ 453-5936.

In this pleasant park at the tip of Ile-Perrot, with its **views★** of Montréal across Lake St. Louis, stands a stone windmill constructed in the early 18th century. Today, restored by the Québec government, the windmill is in full working order *(operated summer weekends if wind is favourable).* Its mechanism is explained by guides and also in the Interpretation Centre *(film 15 min in French).*

Battle of the Châteauguay National Historic Park (Parc de la Châteauguay). – *Map p. 150. 53 km - 33 miles by Mercier Bridge, Rte 138 and Rural Route 4, at Allan's Corner between Howick and Ormstown. Open daily May - Labour Day, weekends Sept-mid Oct ;* ☎ 829-2003.

This interpretive centre beside the Châteauguay River commemorates the battle of the same name fought on this spot in 1813. An American invasion force of about 3 000 men was stopped by **Charles-Michel de Salaberry** at the head of 350 Canadian Voltigeurs. Apart from describing the battle itself, displays explain the historical background and the daily life of a soldier. An animated film *(30 min)* is shown on request. From the top floor of the building, there is a **view** over the battlefield. A maquette explains the scene at the time of the battle, today quiet and rural.

Coteau du Lac National Historic Park. – *Map p. 150. 58 km - 36 miles W by Rtes 20 and 338. Open daily mid May - Labour Day, weekdays only until mid Oct ;* ☎ 763-5631.

In this park, the remains of the earliest canal with locks in North America can be seen. It was built 1779-80 to bypass the treacherous rapids on this section of the river and was a forerunner of the Beauharnois Canal, part of the St. Lawrence Seaway *(p. 170)* used by shipping today.

The fort itself first served as a commercial centre where tariffs for the use of the canal were collected and goods stored. Threats of American invasion during the War of 1812 caused it to be fortified. Today it stands in ruins but an unusual **octagonal block house** built in 1812 has been reconstructed. Inside, there are interesting displays on the history of the fort and on its commercial importance. The **Information Centre** has a maquette of the fort as it once was.

The rapids on the St. Lawrence can be seen from the fort but their ferocity has been much reduced by the lowering of the river level due to dam construction upstream.

All symbols on the city plans are explained
in the key p. 28.

For maximum information from city plans
consult the key p. 28.

NORTH SHORE ST. LAWRENCE ★ (Côte Nord)

Map p. 10 – *Local maps pp. 152 and 183*

When natives of the province of Québec talk of the *Côte Nord,* they are not referring to some distant region on Ungava Bay but to the left bank of the lower St. Lawrence. More precisely, they mean the section between the Saguenay and the end of Highway 138 - at present just east of Sept-Iles *(for details on other sections of the left bank of the St. Lawrence see Charlevoix p. 149 and Québec City p. 180).*

Until this century, this was a region of small fishing villages strung out along the coast with no land connection and backed by a mountainous and forested wilderness. The 1920s and 30s, however, saw the beginning of the exploitation of the forest resources and the building of **pulp mills.** This was later followed by the discovery of the rich **iron ore** deposits of Labrador and Northern Québec *(see also Newfoundland p. 218).* Railways were built south from the mines to the river where ports sprang up almost overnight. Then in the 1960s, the wild rivers of the region were harnessed for **hydro-electricity.** Highway 138 was built and heavy industry began to move to a region rich in electric power.

(courtesy Hydro-Québec)

Daniel Johnson Dam

Today, despite all these developments, much of the **Côte Nord** is still a wilderness and a drive between Tadoussac and Sept-Iles is an incredible mixture of lonely forest and mountain, river vistas and then suddenly a highly developed city in a bay.

Sept-Iles (Pop 29 262) is the region's chief centre. It has an impressive **site**★ on an almost circular bay which has made a fine deep water port. Open all year, it is always busy shipping out the iron ore from Labrador City and Wabush and trans-shipping grain to ocean-going vessels from the lakers of the Seaway *(p. 170).*

Port-Cartier (Pop 8 191) also serves the mines and **Baie-Comeau** (Pop 12 866) on its attractive **bay**★ is an industrial centre with a newsprint mill and aluminum smelter in addition to grain elevators.

■ THE MANIC-OUTARDES COMPLEX

The **Manicouagan** and **Outardes Rivers** rise deep in the mountains of the *Côte Nord* and rush in almost parallel courses south to the St. Lawrence. On their way they traverse rapids and falls, or at least they did. Since 1959, they have both been extensively harnessed for hydro-electricity. Today, the seven power plants which have been built in their valleys generate over 5 500 000 kw.

This electricity is transmitted to Montréal and Québec City by power lines of very high voltage - 735 000 volts.

Several of these power plants can be visited but no trip is complete without seeing the huge dam built on the site of the fifth set of rapids on the Manicouagan River, known as Manic 5.

Excursion to Manic 5★★. – *Round trip of 432 km - 268 miles from Baie-Comeau on partially unpaved road ; possible in one day including visit. Daily mid June - Labour Day ; for information contact Hydro-Québec office at junction of Rtes 138 and 389 ; ☎ (418) 296-7902 ; gas and snack bar at Manic 5.*

This is a long drive through mountainous terrain typical of the Canadian Shield. Just before Manic 2 *(19 km - 12 miles)* there is a fine **view**★ from above of the Manicouagan River in its deep valley.

Daniel Johnson Dam★★. – *Guided tours mid June - Labour Day ; 1 1/2 hrs ; 4 times a day ; include film in French (20 min), visit to generating station and bus trip over dam.*

This massive multiple arch dam, the biggest of its type in the world, is a most impressive sight as it is approached from afar. Completed in 1968, it blocks the wide valley of the Manicouagan creating a doughnut-shaped reservoir covering 1 950 sq km - 750 sq miles and regulating the flow to the other power plants downstream. It has a crest length of 1 314 m - 4 310 ft and the central arch rises a total of 214 m - 703 ft and could contain Montréal's Place Ville Marie with room to spare.

On the tour, visitors are taken by bus right up to the massive arches and across the top of the dam, from whence there are good views of the reservoir and of the surrounding country.

The dam is named for the man who was Premier of Québec in 1968 – and who died at the site on the morning of the official opening.

WHEN IN EUROPE

use the **Michelin Red Guides (hotels and restaurants)** for :

Benelux	France
Deutschland	Great Britain and Ireland
España Portugal	Italia

QUÉBEC City ★★★

Map p. 10 – Metro Pop 576 075 – Tourist Office ☎ (418) 643-2280

Citadel, seaport, provincial capital - Canada's oldest city, built on the slopes of a lofty rock rising from the St. Lawrence River, has charmed visitors for centuries. **Charles Dickens** raved about it in 1842, and in 1912 **Rupert Brooke** asked "Is there any city in the world that stands so nobly as Québec ?". A walled city with fort, gates and cannon, narrow cobbled streets, ancient graystone houses, venerable churches, sweeping views of the St. Lawrence... all these delight tourists. But Québec is also a French city with a distinct European flavour enhanced by fine restaurants, outdoor cafes and a lively nightlife.

Birthplace of New France. – The promontory on which the city stands was named *Cap aux Diamants* (Diamond Cape) by **Jacques Cartier** in 1535 for the wealth he hoped to find in this new land. He spent a winter at the Indian village nearby *(p. 179)* and then gave up his search. It was not until 1608 that anyone else became interested in the site. In that year, **Samuel de Champlain** arrived and built a fort below the cliff face. Over the next 150 years, this settlement grew in size and importance becoming the centre for all activities in French North America - an empire which stretched from the Gulf of Mexico through the Great Lakes to the Rockies *(map p. 145)*. Throughout this period, however, it was constantly threatened by the English colonies established on the coast to the south (in addition to the Iroquois *(p. 144)* and the naval power of Great Britain. In 1629, it was captured by **David Kirke** and only re-established in 1632. In 1690, it was again besieged by **Admiral Phipps**, but unsuccessfully. The 18th century saw England and France almost continually at war *(p. 146)* and every year the residents of Québec expected to see an enemy fleet below their walls.

The Conquest. – This fleet arrived in 1759 fresh from the capture of Louisbourg, France's fortress on the Atlantic *(p. 205)*. The British army under the command of 31-year-old **General James Wolfe** attacked and bombarded the city from Lévis for nearly two months. Finally, on the night of September 12th, Wolfe's troops stole silently up the river and landed at **Anse au Foulon** (Wolfe's Cove), the only break in the sheer cliff face. They scaled the heights and were in position the next morning on the **Plains of Abraham** before the city. The French, caught unprepared, marched out of the city under the command of the veteran soldier the **Marquis de Montcalm**, who had many victories in North America to his credit. In twenty minutes it was all over – the French were defeated, Québec fell, Wolfe lay dead on the field of battle and Montcalm, mortally wounded, died next day.

Despite a French victory at nearby Ste-Foy in the next year, the British held onto Québec and the battle on the Plains of Abraham proved to be the end of New France. The official secession came in 1763 by the **Treaty of Paris** – and the city founded by Champlain assumed a new role as the capital of a new British colony.

The British Regime. – Québec had not, however, seen the end of fighting. Twelve years later an American army arrived before its walls. The Thirteen colonies to the south, in revolt against their British rulers, dispatched troops in an attempt to persuade the French Canadians to join them. The latter, however, refused and, although Montréal was captured by Montgomery *(p. 160)*, both he and **Benedict Arnold** were repulsed before Québec.

This battle in the winter of 1775 marked the end of warfare for Québec. Instead the city developed apace as the seat of British government. This was also the era of the legendary French Canadian log drivers. Trees cut in the forests of the province and in Ontario were brought to Québec where throughout the 19th century a wooden shipbuilding industry flourished. Indeed, between 1827-67, a total of 3 000 ships were constructed in the city's shipyards. In 1864, Québec was the site of the negotiations which led to Canadian Confederation *(p. 209)*, and when that came about in 1867, the city became the capital of the Canadian province of the same name.

Québec Today. – In addition to its old city full of the charm of a bygone age, Québec today is also a bustling metropolis, the seat of government for the province, a major port, industrial centre (leather and fur goods, clothing, food products, pulp and paper, tobacco, etc), and home to two universities – Laval and a college of the University of Québec.

One major celebration in the city is during the week surrounding **June 24th** – St-Jean-Baptiste (John the Baptist) day, Québec's national holiday.

The Château Frontenac and Lower Town

"Carnaval". – However, the main event in the city's year is its famous winter carnival in February when the population doubles for about ten days. There is much merrymaking in the streets, a great parade, an ice palace, a street of ice sculptures *(rue Ste-Thérèse)* **(A),** and canoe races across the partially frozen St. Lawrence – a mixture of canoeing and pushing craft over ice floes *(see also Ile aux Coudres p. 149).* Everything is overseen by an enormous snowman – called **Bonhomme Carnaval.** Visitors to Québec during this period are advised to make reservations well in advance.

The best way of arriving in Québec is by the ferry from Lévis *(plan p. 179).* Alternatively, the drive along Champlain Boulevard from the two bridges which span the St. Lawrence is interesting.

■ THE OLD CITY★★★

Set both on top of the cliff and below it, the oldest part of Québec is best visited on foot as streets are narrow, crowded and sometimes closed to traffic. Cars can be left in one of the garages which exist expressly for this purpose. The Old City is also the most pleasant area in which to stay. There are numerous small *pensions* and *maisons de chambres* with charming if modest accommodation.

Place d'Armes and Vicinity★★★

Walk of about 1 hr – allow 1/2 day with visits

This pleasant square is the heart and soul of old Québec. Crowds throng here in all seasons and *calèches,* the attractive horse-drawn carriages, stand ready to take visitors on leisurely tours. The square is dominated by the **Château Frontenac** hotel, a massive structure of turrets and towers built in 1893 on the site of the former governor's residence. Below, at the edge of the square stands a statue of Samuel de Champlain, the city's founder.

Behind the statue is the **Dufferin Terrace★★★** (Terrasse Dufferin), a wide wooden board-walk stretching 671 m - 2 200 ft along beyond the Château Frontenac, and suspended high above the river. From it there are fine **views★★** of the St. Lawrence, the opposite shore and *Basse Ville,* the section of the city at the foot of the cliff. The terrace is also the site of a toboggan slide in winter and many of the St-Jean-Baptiste day celebrations in summer.

At the far end of the Dufferin Terrace, a flight of steps ascends to the **Governors' Walk★★** (Promenade des Gouverneurs ; *open May - Oct, 20 min one way ; excellent means of arriving in the Old City),* a spectacular route clinging to the cliff face which goes around the outer walls of the Citadel *(p. 178)* to the National Battlefields Park.

Next to the Château Frontenac behind the Dufferin Terrace is a little square called the **Governors' Garden** (Jardin des Gouverneurs). At its centre is a monument which commemorates both Wolfe and Montcalm - probably the only one in the world where both victor and vanquished are jointly remembered. Its inscription reads in translation : "Valour gave them a common death, history a common fame, posterity a common monument".

Return to Place d'Armes.

Musée du Fort★ (MI). – *Open daily all year except Dec ; $2.75 ; performances every 1/2 hr in French or English ;* ☎ *692-2175.*

On a large-scale model of the city indicating its unique relief, a *son et lumière* show is presented explaining the city's history and particularly the various sieges and battles it has experienced. This show forms a good introduction to Québec City.

Rue du Trésor★. – This delightful little street is the haunt in summer and during *Carnaval* of artists selling their wares and sketching portraits for visitors. On its corner with Place d'Armes stands a **wax museum (M2)** (musée de cire) which has a series of scenes of Québec's history *(open daily ; $2.00).*

Follow rue du Trésor to the end.

Basilica of Notre-Dame de Québec (B). – The grey stone Roman Catholic cathedral has a massive portal opposite Québec's **City Hall (H)** and two quite different towers. This classic facade was designed by Thomas Baillairgé in 1844.

In the square stands a statue of **Elzéar Alexandre Taschereau** (1820-98), the first Canadian bishop to be made a cardinal of the Roman Catholic Church.

Seminary★ (Séminaire). – *Entrance to left of Basilica. Guided tours daily mid May - mid Aug ; 1 hr ; 50¢ ;* ☎ *692-3981.*

This is Canada's oldest institute of higher learning. It was founded in 1663 by **François Xavier de Laval** to train priests for the infant colony. Monsignor de Laval, the first bishop of Québec, ruled the religious life of New France 1674-1688 encouraging missionary effort and opposing the sale of liquor to the Indians.

The junior section of the seminary remains in these buildings. The senior section, which became Laval University in 1852, moved to Ste-Foy in 1970 *(plan p. 179).*

Only the seminary **chapel** with Bishop Laval's tomb and the fine interior courtyard can be seen without taking the tour. The latter is notable for its sundial on the wall of a wing dating from 1678.

Highlights of the tour are : a little **chapel★** with fine wood carving executed in 1785 for **Jean Olivier Briand,** bishop of Québec 1766-84, the reception hall and elegant *parloir* used for official occasions, the great staircase in the priests' residence dating from 1880, and, in the oldest part, the refectory and flagstone kitchen with its stone vaults.

At the end of the tour, visitors leave by the gate on rue de l'Université.

Seminary Museum★ (M3). – *9 rue de l'Université. Open daily except Tues ; $2.00 ;* ☎ *692-2843.*

The Seminary owns a fine collection of works relating to the arts and sciences. It is particularly well known for its European paintings and gold and silver plate, but there are also galleries devoted to Québec art, Oriental art and scientific instruments. In addition, temporary exhibitions are given on varying themes including a changing selection from the Seminary's collection of prints and drawings.

Follow rues Couillard, Collins and Charlevoix.

THE OLD CITY

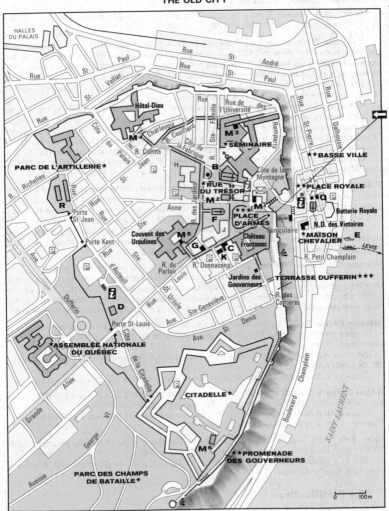

Hôtel-Dieu. – This large hospital, which was founded by an order of Augustinian nuns in 1637, has existed on this site since 1644. Its **museum (M4)** *(entrance 32 rue Charlevoix, ring bell ; guided tours daily ; 1 hr ; reservations ☎ 692-2492)* has many mementos of its early days as well as some fine pieces of furniture and religious paintings. The stone vaults where the nuns took refuge during the siege of 1759 can also be visited.
Follow rues Collins, Côte de la Fabrique and Desjardins.

Holy Trinity Anglican Cathedral (F). – Standing amongst trees with its back to Place d'Armes is this church constructed in 1804, the first Anglican cathedral consecrated outside Britain. It is a copy of the church of St. Martin's in the Fields in Trafalgar Square, London.
Follow rues Desjardins and Donnacona.

Ursuline Convent (Couvent des Ursulines). – This convent was founded in 1639 to provide a Christian education for Indian girls. It was the life's work of **Marie de l'Incarnation,** its first mother superior and the first missionary nun in Canada, and of **Mme. de la Peltrie,** a rich benefactress of the Ursuline order who wished to devote her entire fortune to establish Christianity in the New World. Together they opened a school for Indian and French girls and Mother Marie compiled dictionaries of the Algonkian and Iroquoian languages. The girls' school still exists today.

On rue du Parloir, there is an entrance to the **chapel** *(open daily May - Oct)* where the tomb of Marie de l'Incarnation can be seen, and nearby there is a **museum★ (M5)** *(12 Rue Donnacona, open daily except Mon, hols and 12 - 1.30pm ; $1.00 ☎ 694-0694)* with displays recalling the early life of the Ursulines and the work of their foundress. The skull of the French general, Louis Joseph Marquis de Montcalm, is also exhibited.

Follow rue du Parloir to rue St-Louis.

Rue St-Louis. – Some of the oldest houses in Québec can be seen along this street. At the corner of rue Desjardins stands the **Maison Jacquet (G)** with its pretty red roofs. Built in 1677, it has remained substantially unchanged. Today, it houses a restaurant, *Aux Anciens Canadiens.* Across the street at no 25 is the **Maison Kent (K)** built 1648-50 and home to the Duke of Kent, father of Queen Victoria, when he was Governor of Canada 1791-94 *(see also Halifax p. 201).* It now houses the French Consulate *(not open to public).* Next to it at no 17 the **Maison Maillou (C)** with its steeply sloping roof, built 1736 - 53, houses the Québec Chamber of Commerce.

177

Lower Town★★ (Basse ville)

Access from Dufferin Terrace by funiculaire, 60¢, or by steps beside "kiosque". Time : 2 hours including visits - plan p. 177

This piece of land at the foot of the cliff was the original site of Québec. Champlain built his *habitation* or fort there in 1608 and, although all the religious and administrative institutions later moved up the cliff, it remained the commercial centre of the city until the 19th century. It was almost completely destroyed during Wolfe's bombardment of 1759, rebuilt but later deserted as commercial activities moved further east towards the present location of the port in the mouth of the St. Charles River.

Today, the Québec government is in the process of rebuilding and restoring the area to its 18th century appearance, and it has become a popular spot for tourists and residents alike. Restaurants, cafes and boutiques have located in the newly restored buildings, many of the streets are closed to traffic, and there are outdoor activities in the summer. Along rue Petit Champlain, a number of artisans have established workshops and craft stores.

Guided tours of the area start from the Maison Soumandre (i) at 29 rue Notre-Dame, daily May - Sept, about 1 hr ; ☎ 643-6631.

Place Royale★★. – This pleasant square has been almost completely restored to its 18th century appearance and it is assuming once more its role as the centre of Lower Town. Tall stone houses with sloping roofs and high chimneys line it and, in the centre, there is a bust of Louis XIV, a copy of the original erected in 1686 which gave the square its name.

The little church of **Notre-Dame des Victoires** at one end is so named for the various sieges the city successfully resisted – only a shell remained after the bombardment of 1759. It has been restored to its appearance in 1688 when it was built.

Maison Chevalier★ (Musée de l'Habitation). – *Open daily except Mon in winter.* This attractive graystone house with its red roofs and high chimneys was built around three sides of a little garden in 1752 for the wealthy merchant Jean-Baptiste Chevalier. Restored in 1959, it houses a fine collection of French Canadian furniture including a long wooden dining table with pewter utensils. In the stone vaults, a series of changing exhibitions can be seen.

Maison Fornel★ (Q). – *Entrance Place Royale. Open daily mid June - Labour Day.*

A slide show *(12 min in French or English)* presents the history of Place Royale and its restoration.

Entrance rue St-Pierre. Open daily mid June - Labour Day ; less frequently rest of year ; ☎ 643-6631 first.

Displays in the vaulted cellars describe the restoration work and the city's history.

Royal Battery (Batterie Royale). – Originally built in 1691, this was the city's first defence structure. Once it stood at the water's edge and was subject to flooding.

Close to it, a ferry crosses the river to Lévis *(pedestrians $1.10, cars $2.20 with driver).* This trip offers a splendid **view★★** of Québec and its site.

Boat Trip★ (E). – *M/V Jolliet. Daily May - mid Sept ; trips of varying lengths ; from $6.00 ; from Quai Chouinard in Basse Ville ; ☎ 692-1159.*

This is a pleasant trip with fine **views★★** of the city, port, Ile d'Orléans and Montmorency Falls from a distance.

The Fortifications★ - *plan p. 177*

Québec is the only walled city in North America and part of its attraction today is these fortifications. In the main they date from the 19th century. Although some were built prior to 1759, the French relied on the strength of the city's natural site as its main defence. Thus the existing walls, gates, batteries and the Citadel were built by the British through fear of renewed American attack after the siege of 1775 *(p. 175)*. They were never needed.

A **Visitor and Interpretaion Centre (D)** in an old powder magazine *(100 rue St-Louis ; open daily in summer ; National Historic Park ; ☎ 694-4206)* offers an introduction to these fortifications and tours *(mid May - Labour Day ; 1 hr).*

The Citadel★ (La Citadelle). – *Entrance at end of Côte de la Citadelle, parking. Guided tours daily mid June - Labour Day, Mon - Thurs rest of year ; closed Dec - Feb ; 50 min ; $2.25 ; ☎ 694-3563.*

This mighty fortress constructed 1820-32 on the orders of the **Duke of Wellington** is still today very much a military institution. The **Royal 22ᵉ Régiment,** the only completely French-speaking regiment in the Canadian army, has its headquarters here. The citadel is built in the shape of a four pointed star with bastions and huge earthworks. It covers more than 16 ha - 40 acres. Inside, a large parade ground is surrounded by buildings bearing the names of the various campaigns of the 22ᵉ Régiment - Vimy, the Somme, Korea, etc. One house is the summer residence of Canada's Governor-General *(see also Ottawa p. 122)*. A powder magazine dating from the French regime (1750) houses a small **museum (M6)** of military history.

In summer, visitors can watch the Royal 22ᵉ Régiment, dressed in red tunics and bearskins, perform **Changing of the Guard** *(10am daily)* and **Retreat** ceremonies *(7pm Tues, Thurs, Sat and Sun).*

From the citadel, there is a pleasant **walk** along the top of the ramparts to Artillery Park *(see below)* passing the St-Louis, Kent and St-Jean gates *(portes).*

Artillery Park★ (Parc de l'Artillerie). – *Entrance corner rues St-Jean and d'Auteuil. National Historic Park. Open daily ; guided tours 1 1/2 hrs ; ☎ 694-4205.*

This complex of buildings following the walls from rue St-Jean to Côte du Palais is in process of being renovated by the federal government. The majority of the buildings were constructed for military purposes but some were later used for other purposes.

The **Interpretation Centre (R)** describes the evolution of the site over three centuries. It also houses a fascinating **model★★** of the city of Québec made 1806-08 by Jean-Baptiste Duberger and Colonel John By *(of Rideau Canal fame p. 116)*. Although restored several times, this model is a reasonably accurate representation of what Québec City looked like at the beginning of the 19th century.

Among the restored structures is the **Dauphine Redoubt** , a fine stone edifice dating from the French regime (1712-48) which is notable for its exterior supporting buttresses. An exhibit incorporating costumes, paintings, reproductions and other artifacts depicts scenes in the lives of the soldiers who lived in the building at various times. The neighbouring **Officers' Quarters** houses an interpretation centre for children.

■ OUTSIDE THE WALLS

Legislative Building★ (Assemblée Nationale). – *Plan p. 177. Guided tours daily June - Sept, weekdays only rest of year except during Parliamentary sessions ; about 1/2 hr ; restaurant ;* ☎ *643-7239.*

This elegant Renaissance style structure built 1877-86 houses the Parliament of the province of Québec. It stands among other more modern buildings containing government offices. The interior is very richly decorated with a combination of British, French and French Canadian emblems.

National Battlefields Park★ (Parc des Champs de Bataille). – *Access by Governors' Walk - p. 176, or by car - strict one-way system, restricted parking. National Historic Park.*

This park on the Plains of Abraham offers fine **views★★** of the river and city. There are pleasant walks and drives, and mementos of the famous battle of 1759. Today, a road (Côte Gilmour) mounts the cliff at **Anse au Foulon** (Wolfe's cove) and it is hard to reconstruct the British landing because of land reclamation for port facilities at its foot. There are also two Martello Towers built in 1812 in the park *(see Halifax p. 203).*

Québec Museum★ (M7) (Musée du Québec). – *In National Battlefields Park, entrance at rear of building, parking. Open daily ;* ☎ *643-2150.*

This museum has a very fine collection of Québec art both old and new including paintings, sculpture, needlecraft and other decorative arts. This collection is presented in a series of changing exhibitions. The museum also displays the works of young Québec artists and has visiting shows.

Cartier-Brébeuf National Historic Park★. – *75 rue de l'Espinay, 3 km - 2 miles from Porte St-Jean (plan p. 177) by Côte d'Abraham, rue de la Couronne, Pont Drouin and 1ᵉʳ Avenue. Open daily except certain hols ;* ☎ *694-4038.*

This spot at the confluence of Lairet and St. Charles Rivers was the site of two famous events in Québec's history. **Jacques Cartier** spent the winter of 1535-6 here, and in 1626 some Jesuit missionaries, including **Jean de Brébeuf,** built their first residence in this place. Brébeuf was later martyred by the Iroquois in what is now Ontario *(see Midland p. 104).*

An interesting **interpretive centre** explains the background to Cartier's voyages and describes the terrible winter he and his men spent – they would all have died of scurvy but for the help of Indians from the nearby village of Stadacona. The highlight of the visit is, however, the reconstruction of the biggest of his three ships, **La Grande Hermine★.** This tiny two masted sailing vessel which is less than 24 m - 80 ft long *(see illustration p. 144)* was not only home to sixty men for a winter but carried them across the stormy Atlantic *(guided tours regularly, about 30 min).*

Zoo★ (Jardin zoologique). – *11 km - 7 miles N by Autoroute 73, exit rue de la Faune. Open daily ; $2.75 ; cafeteria ; picnic spots ;* ☎ *622-0312.*

This pleasant zoo has a wide variety of animals with emphasis on Canadian species.

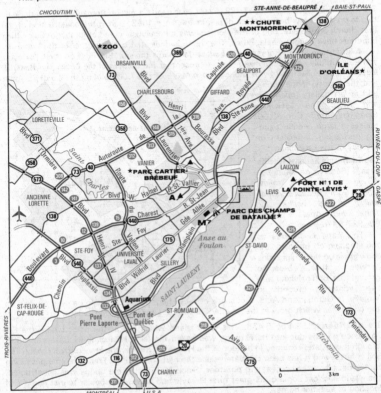

QUÉBEC City★★★

Aquarium. – *11 km - 7 miles by Rte 175 and Chemin St-Louis. Open daily ; $2.00 ; cafeteria ; picnic sites ; explanations in French ;* 🕿 *659-5264.*

This aquarium has an interesting collection of Québec fish both fresh and salt water varieties, and an outdoor seal pool.

EXCURSIONS

The Beaupré Coast★ (Côte de Beaupré). – The region between Québec city and Cap Tourmente is known as the Beaupré coast because it appeared to Cartier as a lush, green meadow *(beau pré)*. Highway 360 passes through a string of little communities whose origins go back to the beginning of New France.

(after photo by Musée du Québec)

The Montmorency River in Winter by Cornelius Krieghoff

Montmorency Falls★★ (Chute Montmorency). – Just before its mouth in the St. Lawrence, the Montmorency River drops over 83.5 m - 274 ft high falls. This is a spectacular sight but especially in the winter when spray from the falls builds up an ice cone which in some years surpasses 20 m - 70 ft in height.

The falls can be viewed either at their crest or at their foot. From the **upper viewpoint★★** *(in Montmorency Park, access from Route 360 immediately after crossing river)*, the full height of the falls can be appreciated. Nearby stands a **redoubt** used by General Wolfe during the siege of 1759.

The **lower viewpoint★★** *(access from Route 138)* enables visitors to approach the base of the falls.

Ste-Anne-de-Beaupré★ . – Pop 3 292. Every year nearly a million Roman Catholics flock to this town which has been a place of pilgrimage since 1658. During the construction of the first church on the site, one of the workers was miraculously cured of lumbago. Since then hundreds have sought similar cures. The shrine is dedicated to the mother of the Virgin.

A large twin-spired Romanesque **basilica** dominates the site. Behind it on the hillside are some beautifully carved life-size figures representing the **Stations of the Cross.** The **Historial Museum** has a collection of wax models *(open May - Oct ; $1.00)* relating the life of St. Anne and the history of the shrine, and an art gallery *(open July and Aug).* The **Cyclorama** *(open daily April - Oct, $3.00)* houses a large circular painting portraying Jerusalem on the day of the Crucifixion.

Cap Tourmente National Wildlife Area★ (Réserve de Faune). – *48 km - 30 miles, follow signs from Beaupré. Open daily, guided walks and films mid April - Oct ;* 🕿 *827-3776.*

This cape is famous as the stopping-off place for the **snow geese** on their migrations between their breeding grounds on Baffin Island and their wintering grounds in Virginia. In October and April, thousands of these huge white birds can be seen feeding on the bullrushes which grow in the mudflats of the St. Lawrence at this point.

Ile d'Orléans★. – Pop 6 436. This large island which lies at the point where the St. Lawrence widens out into its estuary, was called the Isle of Bacchus by Cartier in 1535 though it was later renamed in honour of the House of Orleans, the French royal family. The soil is fertile and it has been cultivated since the early days of the French regime producing fruit especially strawberries, and potatoes. Since 1935 when the bridge was constructed, the island has lost some of its quiet rural lifestyle and become a popular tourist haunt and location of summer homes.

Route 368 makes a circular tour of the island *(71 km - 44 miles)* passing some old houses and the pretty churches of the French regime. It also offers some fine **views** of the St. Lawrence and its two shores.

Highlights of the tour include the little community of **St-Jean** on the south side with its pretty **site**★ on a rocky beach. The **Manoir Mauvide-Genest** built in 1734 can be visited *(open daily mid June - mid Oct ; restaurant).* **St-François,** at the northeast tip of the island, offers fine **views**★ of Cap Tourmente *(see above),* and the prettiest church on the island built in 1734 and renowned for its finely carved interior. Between St-François and Ste-Famille there are **views**★ of Mount Ste-Anne and the twin spires of Ste-Anne-de-Beaupré. One of the old stone farmhouses along this route has been converted into a restaurant, **L'Atre**★. It dates back to 1680 and visitors are brought from the main road by horse and buggy *(open daily late May - Labour Day ; weekends in Sept and Oct ; reservations* ☎ *829-2474).* **Ste-Famille** boasts an elaborate parish church with three bell towers which was consecrated in 1749. This makes an interesting contrast with the simple structure in **St-Pierre** which was built in 1717.

Fort No. 1 at Point Lévis★. – *Chemin du Gouvernement, Lauzon. Open daily May - Labour Day ;* ☎ *694-2470.*

This fort, the highest spot on the south shore opposite Québec, was built 1865-71 to protect the city from a possible American attack. It is a massive earthwork, roughly pentagonal in shape, and a good example of mid 19th century European fortification techniques. From the walls, there are fine **views**★ over the river to Montmorency Falls and Ile d'Orléans.

Opening hours of museums and other sights change frequently. We advise you to telephone in advance to avoid disappointment.

RICHELIEU Valley ★ Vallée du Richelieu

Map p. 10 – *Local map p. 150*

This important tributary of the St. Lawrence runs about 130 km - 80 miles across Québec from its source in Lake Champlain to join the main river at **Sorel** (Pop 20 347), a port and industrial centre. In its short length, it traverses a rich agricultural region and one much frequented by Montréalers for leisure activities.

The Richelieu, named for the great French Cardinal, has served as an invasion route on several occasions. Indeed, it was originally called the *Rivière des Iroquois* by Champlain because these "scourges of New France" *(p. 144)* mounted their attacks from it. A series of forts were built along it – at Sorel, Chambly *(see below),* **St-Jean** which is still the location of a military college, and Ile-aux-Noix *(see below).* But these did not impede successful invasions by the British in 1759-60 and Americans in 1775. The valley was also the location of some of the events of the Revolt of 1837 *(p. 161).* A monument to the **Patriotes** stands in St-Denis.

Today, the Richelieu still serves as a transportation artery between Montréal and New York for both leisure and commercial craft. Canals between St-Jean and Chambly *(see below)* and connecting Lake Champlain with the Hudson River in New York State have made this possible.

Chambly★. – Pop 12 190. This little town has a pleasant **site** ★ at the point where the river widens to form the **Chambly Basin,** just below rapids. The basin which is a haven for yachtsmen is dominated by the looming form of **Mount St-Hilaire,** one of the Monteregian Hills *(p. 167)* which rises 438 m - 1 437 ft to the north.

The rapids can be admired from **Park des Rapides**★ on rue Richelieu which is lined with fine houses mainly Georgian in style. The canal built in the 19th century to avoid the rapids can also be seen.

Chambly was the home of Charles de Salaberry, the victor of the battle of the Châteauguay in 1813 *(p. 173).*

Fort Chambly★. – *Open daily mid May - Labour Day ; closed Mon and hols rest of year ; National Historic Park ; picnic tables ;* ☎ *(514) 658-1585.*

Set in a pleasant park beside the river, this small stone fort was constructed 1709-11 to replace an earlier wooden one built by Jacques de Chambly in 1665 as part of a concerted attack on the Iroquois. The Iroquois threat was overcome but, despite its 9.75 m - 32 ft walls, the fort fell to the British in 1760 and to the Americans in 1775.

Inside, the buildings have been restored to their 18th century appearance. They contain interesting displays on the history of the fort and the area.

Fort Lennox★. – *Access by ferry from Interpretive Centre in St-Paul de l'Ile-aux-Noix on west bank of river ; 5 min ; $1.25. Open daily mid May - Labour Day, weekends until mid Oct ; National Historic Park ; picnic sites ;* ☎ *(514) 291-5700.*

This fort has a most attractive **site**★ on an island in the river. The island was fortified during the French Regime and it served as a shipbuilding centre during the War of 1812, but the present star-shaped structure surrounded by a moat was built between 1819 and 1838 by German mercenaries and has never seen military action.

Inside, there is an impressive collection of **stone buildings**★ housing guard house, barracks, officers' quarters, etc. Some have been restored to illustrate military life of the mid 19th century. The Officers' Quarters has interesting displays on the history of the fort.

Safari Park★★ **(Parc Safari).** – *7 km - 4 1/2 miles W of Rte 15, exit 6, by Rte 202 W, near Hemmingford. Open daily May - Sept ; $6.50 ($20 a car load) ; refreshments ;* ☎ *(514) 247-2727.*

This park lies in the middle of an apple growing and cider making region west of the Richelieu River. Visitors drive their own cars *(9 km - 5 1/2 miles ; about 1 hr)* through large enclosures where the animals – elephants, lions, tigers, rhinoceros, giraffes, baboons, bears, wolves, etc. roam at liberty. Tape recordings *(free)* explain the characteristics and habits of the various animals.

SAGUENAY River ★★

Map p. 10 – Local map pp. 182-83

The Saguenay River, major tributary of the St. Lawrence, drains Lake St-Jean *(p. 156)* and thus a large section of northwestern Québec. In its short length (160 km - 100 miles), it assumes two characters at complete variance to each other. Between Alma and Chicoutimi, the once roaring torrent, which dropped more than 90 m - 300 ft in 56 km - 35 miles, has been harnessed and has spawned one of the most industrialized areas of the province. Then suddenly and dramatically in its lower section, the Saguenay widens, deepens and flows majestically between mountainous shores almost untouched by man.

A Spectacular Fjord. – About 1 500 m - 1 mile wide, an average 240 m - 800 ft deep and lined with precipitous cliffs which rise over 460 m - 1 500 ft in places, the lower section of the Saguenay is a fjord in every respect except that it never reaches the sea. This gigantic slash in the Canadian Shield came about during the last Ice Age. Always a river bed, the valley was deepened and enlarged by the glaciers, and then, when the latter withdrew, it was invaded by the sea as far as Chicoutimi. In fact, this invasion still occurs as tidewater reaches Chicoutimi every day. The rush of the incoming water is sometimes quite violent and the difference in level between high and low tides can be as much as 6 m - 20 ft.

The deep waters of the Saguenay fjord are, in summer, the breeding grounds of the **beluga whale.** This mammal, which has no dorsal fin, can be as much as 5.5 m - 18 ft in length when it is full grown and it is white in colour. In addition, the shallow waters at the point where the Saguenay joins the St. Lawrence are rich in all kinds of aquatic life including capelin and shrimp. These attract not only belugas but minke, finback, humpback, pilot, sei and blue whales, the latter being the biggest of all (as long as 30 m - 100 ft). These can be observed in the St. Lawrence from the shore at Tadoussac and boat excursions are organized during the period of their visit *(generally August, for information contact Hotel Tadoussac* ☎ *(418) 235-4421).*

An Industrial Valley. – In 1534, Jacques Cartier visited the mouth of the Saguenay and returned to France with tales of a mystical kingdom where all manner of riches, gold and silver existed. No one ever found any gold but riches of other kinds awaited exploitation. At first it was the animals trapped for their furs. Then, in the 19th century, the tall trees of the region were cut to be used as masts on British naval vessels. This led to the building of pulp and paper mills, still an important aspect of the region's economy.

It was not, however, these resources which gave the Saguenay its industrial importance. It was instead the 20th century demand for **aluminum.** The production of this metal which is obtained from bauxite requires vast amounts of electricity, and so smelters are generally

ST. LAWRENCE VALLEY - QUÉBEC CITY TO RIMOUSKI

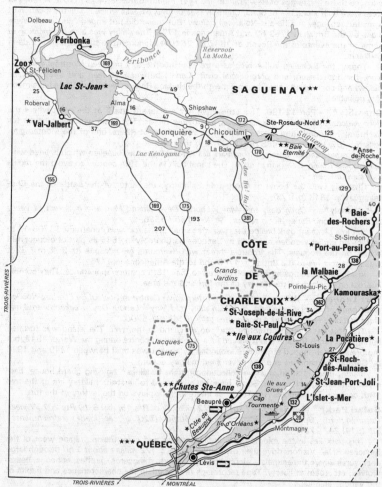

built where electric power is cheaply and easily available. The upper Saguenay with its wild water was a natural site for hydro-electric plants and the first of these was built in 1926. During the Second World War when the demand for aluminum increased apace, the huge dam and generating plant were built at **Shipshaw** and an enormous smelter which is still one of the biggest in the world was constructed at **Arvida** (now part of Jonquière).

■ VISIT

Cruises on the Fjord★★. – *From Chicoutimi daily June - Sept, whole day and shorter excursions ; ☎ (418) 543-7630. From Tadoussac in summer depending on demand, contact Hotel Tadoussac, ☎ (418) 235-4421.*

The only way to really appreciate this incredible fjord is to take a boat trip. The roads on both north and south shores run far from the river with only the occasional side road to a tiny hamlet from which a view can be obtained *(see below)*. For those without a day to spare, the shorter cruise from Tadoussac gives an adequate impression of this formidable waterway but it is only on the longer trips that the bay at the mouth of the Eternité River, the highlight of the fjord, is reached. Two giant capes, **Cap Trinité** and **Cap Eternité**, rise a sheer 457 m - 1 500 ft and 510 m - 1 673 ft respectively. Another 240 m - 800 ft is out of sight below the black water. Part way up Cap Trinité stands a **statue of the Virgin.**

Viewpoints of the Fjord★★. – The pretty village of **Ste-Rose-du-Nord★★** on the north shore is set in a bay of the Saguenay. Apart from its site, the community offers an interesting **Nature Museum** in an artisan's shop *(open daily, $1.50)*. This is a collection of driftwood and other natural phenomena which has been collected and polished. Further east, the little community of **Anse-de-Roche★** lies on the edge of the fjord *(19 km - 12 miles from Tadoussac by Hwys 138, 172 and a rough road from Sacré-Cœur)*.

On the south shore, the famous twin capes at the mouth of the Eternité River can be reached by road from the community of **Rivière Eternité** *(8 km - 5 miles, open daily mid June - Labour Day ; weekends until mid Oct ; cars $3.25)*. From this splendid **bay★★**, visitors can climb up to the statue of the Virgin for another fine **view★★** *(4 hrs Rtn on foot)*.

To the west, Route 170 follows Baie des Ha ! Ha ! for several miles with good **views★** through the city of **La Baie** of the port. The best lookouts of the fjord however are on the descents to the community on Route 170 from Chicoutimi and Route 381 from Baie-St-Paul.

Tadoussac★. – Pop 900. This little community with its lovely **site** in hilly terrain at the mouth of the Saguenay, is today a resort centre although its origins go back to the very beginning of New France. Visited by Jacques Cartier in 1535, the location soon became a meeting place for the fur trade. In 1600, **Pierre Chauvin** built the first trading post in Canada and in 1615 a mission was established to convert the Indians to Christianity. Tadoussac, an Indian name for the sand dunes beside the St. Lawrence, was an important trading centre throughout the French Regime and indeed until the mid 19th century when settlers moved into the region.

The village is dominated by the **Hotel Tadoussac** with its long façade and red roofs. In front of it, gardens lead down to the **Anse de l'Eau** on the St. Lawrence from which cruise boats depart for the fjord and on whale-sighting excursions *(see above)*. A **boardwalk** beside the river connects the reconstruction of **Pierre Chauvin's trading post,** now an artisan's shop, and a tiny **wooden chapel** built in 1747 by the Jesuits.

A fine **view** of the site is obtained on descending Route 138 towards the wharf and there are pleasant walks along the beach from the Anse de l'Eau to the area called the **Desert** *(3 km - 2 miles)* where in summer ski enthusiasts climb a set of wooden steps and ski down a 112 m - 367 ft sand dune overlooking the river.

TROIS RIVIÈRES ★

Map p. 10 – Metro Pop 111 453 – Tourist Office 168 rue Bonaventure
☎ (819) 375-9628 - *Local map p. 148*

Situated on the north bank of the St. Lawrence about midway between Montréal and Québec, Trois Rivières was so named because at this point the once wild and turbulent **St. Maurice River** joins the main stream via three channels separated by islands. This "delta" remains but the river has been tamed by hydro-electric developments on its rapids and falls, and it has been harnessed as a transportation route for the logs cut in the forests of the north. These two resources have created in Trois Rivières a great industry - the manufacture of newsprint. In fact, the vast pulp and paper mills have given Trois Rivières the epithet "newsprint capital of the world".

The city has not always been so industrial. It was founded in 1634 by the **Sieur de Laviolette** who built a fort, on the orders of Champlain, to regulate the fur trade in the St. Maurice valley and protect the local Indians from attack by the Iroquois. The community flourished and was indeed the home of many of the great explorers of New France - Radisson and Groseilliers *(p. 145)*, Nicolet and the La Vérendryes. It was also the site of the first industry of the colony – iron smelting *(see below)*. It was only in this century that the great forest wealth north of the city was exploited and the region developed its present industrial potential. Trois Rivières also has a fine harbour on the St. Lawrence and it is the location of one of the colleges of the University of Québec.

Boat Trip★. – *Departs quay at foot of rue des Forges. Daily May - mid Sept ; 2 1/2 hrs ; $5.50 ; refreshments ;* ☎ *375-3000.*

This cruise on the St. Lawrence enables visitors to see Trois Rivières' giant pulp and paper mills and its port where grain is transferred from the lakers used on the St. Lawrence Seaway *(p. 170)* to ocean-going vessels. The shrine at Cap-de-la-Madeleine *(see below)* and the high arched **Laviolette bridge** which crosses the river at this point are also viewed. An interesting commentary *(in French)* provides a good introduction to the city and area.

Rue des Ursulines. – *In centre of city near junction rues Notre-Dame and Laviolette.*

This quiet little street is almost all that remains of Trois Rivières before this century. In 1908, a disastrous fire wiped out most of the city leaving only this corner intact. The street is dominated by the large dome of the **Ursuline Convent** with its bell tower and sundial on one wall. Some of it was built in 1700 but it has been much modified since. Next to it stand several fine 17th and 18th century houses and, on the other side of the street, the tiny **Anglican Church of St. James** also built in 1700 by the Recollet fathers.

From the **Turcotte Terrace** (terrasse Turcotte) – *access beside church*, there is a **view** of the river and a monument to Pierre Gaultier de la Vérendrye *(p. 145)* and other famous residents of Trois Rivières.

EXCURSIONS

St. Maurice Ironworks★ (Les forges du St-Maurice). – *13 km - 8 miles N by Blvd des Forges. National Historic Park. Open daily mid May - Labour Day, guided tours ;* ☎ *378-1663.*

Established in 1730, these ironworks, the first in Canada, produced a wide variety of goods including cauldrons, kettles and wood burning stoves. They remained in operation until 1883 when the iron ore and wood of the region were exhausted. Today, only ruins remain but some of these are being restored. An **interpretive centre** has interesting displays on the ironworks and on how iron was made. A pleasant path leads down to the river where the **Devil's Fountain** can be seen. Natural gas escaping from the earth is contained in a fireplace and can be lit.

Cap-de-la-Madeleine★. – Pop 32 626. *Map p. 148.* This sister city of Trois Rivières on the opposite side of the St. Maurice is a well known place of pilgrimage. This has come about because of two miraculous happenings. The first occurred during an extension of the parish church in 1878-9. The stone for the new structure was assembled across the St. Lawrence from the city to await the annual freezing-over of the river. However, the winter passed without the ice collecting and it seemed the church would not be built that year. The priest, Father Desilets, prayed to the Virgin and, against all odds, an ice bridge formed across the river at the end of March, and it remained for a week – the time required to bring the stone across. This happening brought many visitors to the new church and it was before three of these that the second miracle occurred in 1888 - a statue of the Virgin in the church opened her eyes. Since 1888, millions of people have made the pilgrimage to Cap-de-la-Madeleine.

The Sanctuary★. – *Corner rues Notre-Dame and du Sanctuaire.* Set in attractive grounds beside the river stand the original stone chapel built in 1714 and the extension constructed in 1879. The jewel of the site is, however, the huge and imposing octagonal **basilica★** erected between 1955 and 1964 to receive the hordes of pilgrims. This impressive building boasts fine **stained glass windows★** designed by a Dutch Oblate father, Jan Tillemans, in Gothic style.

Mauricie★. – *Map p. 150.* Apart from its important hydro and forest resources, the valley of the St. Maurice river and the surrounding country form a beautiful region of wooded hills, lakes and rivers. This can be appreciated by following Highway 155 between Grand-Mère and La Tuque *(121 km - 75 miles)*. The **road★** hugs the river, which is frequently full of logs, for this entire stretch making it among the more attractive drives in the province.

North of Grand-Mère on the other side of the river, the **Mauricie National Park** (Parc national de la Mauricie) a glorious wilderness of water and trees can be visited *(access from St-Mathieu or St-Jean-des-Piles ; Visitor Reception Centre open daily mid May - Labour Day, weekends until mid Oct ; camping, canoeing, winter sports ;* ☎ *536-2638).*

MARITIME PROVINCES

Canada's three smallest provinces – **New Brunswick, Nova Scotia** and **Prince Edward Island,** lie huddled together on the eastern side of the continent. They are battered by the often violent waves of the Atlantic on one side and washed by the gentler waters of the Gulf of St. Lawrence on the other. Their coastline is long and deeply indented with the result that no part of them is more than 160 km - 100 miles from the sea and most of them is less than 48 km - 30 miles. The effects of the sea are thus noticeable everywhere, contributing in great measure to the economic, political and cultural development of the three provinces – and indeed giving them their name.

DESCRIPTION

Parts of the region, notably northern New Brunswick and Cape Breton Island, are quite hilly lying as they do near the end of the **Appalachian Chain** of mountains. There are however stretches of lowland, in particular the whole of Prince Edward Island. Some areas are fertile – the Saint John River valley, the Annapolis valley and Prince Edward Island, but much of the region is densely forested inland, and barren and rocky by the sea. The coast itself is ruggedly beautiful with granite capes, inlets, cliffs and stretches of sandy beach. The **Bay of Fundy** is remarkable for its tides which have a range of as much as 12 m - 40 ft, and rush in with great rapidity causing the phenomenon known as the tidal bore *(p. 206)*. The highest recorded tide in the world occurred at **Burncoat Head** *(map p. 187)* on the Nova Scotia shore. A difference of 16.6 m – 54 ft was measured between high and low tides !

Climate. – The sea is of course the determining factor in the climate of this region. The cold **Labrador Current** moves south down the Atlantic coast and enters the Gulf of St. Lawrence by the Strait of Belle Isle. However, the region also lies on the eastern side of an immense land mass and it thus receives air currents from the interior, as air masses generally move from west to east at this latitude.

Winters are very stormy along the Atlantic coast but milder than inland. Halifax records a mean daily maximum of 0 °C - 32 °F in January, Saint John records – 2 °C - 28 °F, Charlottetown – 3 °C - 26 °F and Fredericton – 4 °C - 24 °F whereas extreme minimum temperatures of – 34 °C - – 30 °F are experienced in northwestern New Brunswick.

Summers are not as hot as they are in Ontario and Québec at the same latitude but they are far less humid. The coast is cooler than inland with Halifax and Charlottetown registering mean daily maximums of 23 °C - 74 °F in July and Saint John registering 21 °C - 70 °F, whereas extreme maximum temperatures in excess of 38 °C - 100 °F have been recorded in northwestern New Brunswick. Along the coasts, the Labrador current cools the air passing over it and often produces fogs – prevalent all summer but less frequent in later months (August and September) than in earlier ones (June and July).

Precipitation is greatest along the Atlantic coast of Nova Scotia (Halifax 1 372 mm - 54 ins annually) and least in northwestern New Brunswick (1 016 mm - 40 ins). Saint John records 1 194 mm - 47 ins and Charlottetown 1 092 mm - 43 ins fairly evenly distributed throughout the year. Snow falls in all regions but is heaviest in northwestern New Brunswick (254-305 cm - 100-120 ins) and lightest on the Atlantic coast (Halifax 163 cm - 64 ins).

Population. – More than a million and a half people live in the Maritime Provinces, with Nova Scotia and New Brunswick having fairly comparable populations (Nova Scotia 847 440, New Brunswick 696 400) and Prince Edward Island having considerably less (122 505). In all three provinces the majority of the inhabitants claim origins in the British Isles (England, Scotland and Ireland) but there is also a noticeable French-speaking minority largely Acadians – 4 % in Nova Scotia, 5 % in Prince Edward Island and 34 % in New Brunswick, where they are concentrated mainly in the north and east. Nearly 30 % of Nova Scotia's population are of Scottish origin and they live mainly in Cape Breton Island and along the shores of Northumberland Strait, another 4 % have German origins and they live along the south coast west of Halifax.

MARITIME PROVINCES

RIMOUSKI · GASPÉ

QUÉBEC

RIVIÈRE-DU-LOUP / MONTRÉAL

Cabano

Edmundston

Saint

John

Grand Falls★★

River

105

Florenceville

Hartland★

Valley

119 Woodstock

Mactaquac Prov. Park

★★ King's Landing

Woolastook Wildlife Park

FREDERICTON★

Houlton

U. S. A.

M A I N E

BOSTON

Bangor

Bar Harbor

PORTLAND

Matapédia

Campbellton

Carleton · Bonaventure

Chaleur Bay

★★ Village historique Acadien

Caraquet

Shippagan ★

Mount Carleton Provincial Park

820 △

Nepisiguit River

Bathurst

124

NEW BRUNSWICK

Newcastle · Chatham

Little Sw. Miramichi River

Kouchibouguac National Park

135

Southwest Miramichi River

Salmon River

Shediac

Moncton

55

St-Joseph

77 ★★ Hopewell Cape

★ Sussex

Alma

★★ Fundy National Park

Grand Lake

197

163

St. John River

Canaan River

109

St. Croix River

Saint John ★★

114

★★ Passamaquoddy Bay

Fundy Islands ★★

Bay

of

Fundy

Chignecto Bay

★ Prescott House

Middleton

Lawrencetown

Bridgetown

★★ Annapolis Valley ★★

★★ Annapolis Royal

Digby

168

NOVA

10

Kejimkujik National Park

106

8

Yarmouth

Shelburne

187

Barrington

★ Liverpool

Mersey

103

HISTORICAL BACKGROUND

Before the arrival of white settlers, the Maritime Provinces were inhabited by Indians of the Eastern Woodlands culture *(map p. 15)* – **Micmacs** who lived by hunting and fishing, and **Malecites** who cultivated the land in southern New Brunswick like their Iroquoian brothers in Ontario *(p. 98)*. There is a school of thought that believes the Norse settled in Nova Scotia about 1000 AD *(see Newfoundland p. 224)* but no irrefutable evidence has been found of this. It is certain, however, that the coast was visited by many of the early explorers and fishermen *(see also Newfoundland p. 219)* and there were several attempts at settlement. None met with any success until the Sieur de Monts and Samuel de Champlain established **Port Royal** in 1605 *(p. 191)*.

"New Scotland". – Port Royal fell to a force from Virginia in 1613 and, although the French re-established it later, in the interim it was British. In 1621, James I granted the entire region to **Sir William Alexander** on the condition he establish a "New Scotland" there (both men were Scots). Alexander did this, calling the region *Nova Scotia*, the Latin for New Scotland used on the original charter. The settlements he founded did not, however, last very long as in 1632, Charles I – who obviously did not share his father's desire to establish a New Scotland, returned the region to the French by the Treaty of St-Germain-en-Laye. Nevertheless, this was the origin of the future Nova Scotia and the coat of arms granted in 1621 is still the province's emblem today.

"Acadie". – The rather vague area covering much of the Maritime Provinces and Maine was called *Acadie* (Acadia) by the French. Although one or two of the original Port Royal settlers may have remained throughout the British occupation, the Acadians as we know

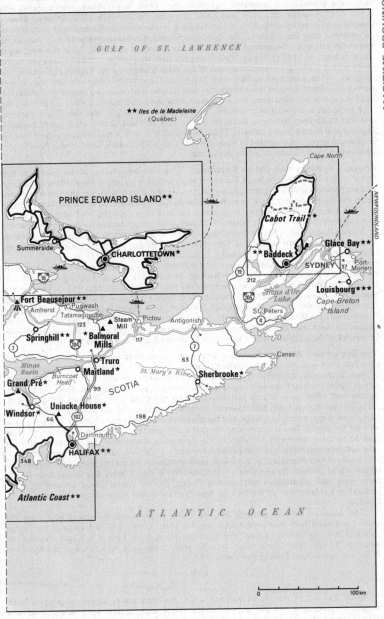

GULF OF ST. LAWRENCE

★★ Iles de la Madeleine
(Québec)

PRINCE EDWARD ISLAND ★★

Cape North

Summerside

Cabot Trail ★

Baddeck ★★

Glace Bay ★★

CHARLOTTETOWN ★

SYDNEY

Port-Morien

19

212

NEWFOUNDLAND

Fort Beausejour ★★

Amherst   Pugwash

Tatamagouche

105

Bras d'Or Lake

Louisbourg ★★★

Cape Breton Island

St. Péters

123   Steam Mill

Pictou

Antigonish

Springhill ★★

104

2

Balmoral Mills

117

4

Canso

Truro

7

Maitland ★

63

St. Mary's River

Sherbrooke ★

Minas Basin

SCOTIA

Grand Pré ★

Burncoat Head

99

Windsor ★

Uniacke House ★

66

102

198

Dartmouth

348

HALIFAX ★★

Atlantic Coast ★★

ATLANTIC   OCEAN

0   100 km

them today are mainly descendants of French colonists who came to La Have and Port Royal 1632-51 from the west of France. As their numbers grew, settlements spread along the Annapolis valley to the Minas Basin and Chignecto Isthmus (p. 198). But these settlements were constantly attacked by expeditions from New England during the Anglo-French wars of the 17th century and even changed hands several times. The end of French rule came in 1713 when, by the Treaty of Utrecht, the French ceded all of mainland Nova Scotia to the British, and Port Royal renamed Annapolis Royal became the capital (p. 190).

Nova Scotia Again. – The terms of the Treaty of Utrecht gave the Acadians a choice – leave British territory for Cape Breton Island (still French) within a year or stay and become British subjects by taking an oath of allegiance. The Acadians did not want to take the oath because it obliged them to bear arms if necessary, perhaps against fellow Frenchmen, but neither did they want to leave their rich farmlands for barren Cape Breton. They maintained they were neutral and said they would take an oath if they were exempted from military service. At first the British governor in Annapolis Royal agreed, mainly because he needed provisions for his soldiers which the Acadians readily supplied – there were no British settlers at that time who could fill this need. Had times been peaceful this arrangement might have become permanent but there was renewed Anglo-French fighting in Europe, and British rule in Nova Scotia was threatened by the building of Louisbourg (p. 205). Also there was undeniable sympathy for the French cause among the Acadians, even aid, though it seems likely that most of them were truly neutral. Then in 1747, a French force from Québec made a surprise attack at night on the village of Grand Pré where five hundred New England soldiers were billeted. Nearly a hundred of these were killed as they slept, and treachery among the Acadian inhabitants was suspected.

The Deportation of the Acadians. – This attack and the fear of others hardened the British line towards the Acadians, especially after 1749, when Halifax was founded with 2 500 English settlers (p. 201) who could provision the army. In 1755, **Governor Charles Lawrence** delivered his ultimatum to the Acadians – take an unqualified oath of allegiance or be removed from Nova Scotia. The Acadians refused. Lawrence moved fast, in August he issued his infamous **Deportation Order** – with no reference to Britain. Over the next eight years, a total of 14 600 Acadians were forcibly deported to the American colonies to the south where it was considered they would not pose a threat as the English population was so great. What was more terrible than the actual Deportation Order was the way it was carried out. Some families were separated and no one was given any choice of destination. In addition, the Acadians were not welcomed in the American colonies. Only in Louisiana did they establish some kind of community and as **Cajuns** survive to this day. Some escaped and fled to Québec but most found their way back to Nova Scotia when peace between England and France finally came in 1763, only to find their rich farmlands occupied by new English colonists. They settled in other parts of the region, mainly what is now New Brunswick where their descendants live to this day.

Scots, Loyalists and Other Settlers. – After the Deportation of the Acadians, the British offered free land in Nova Scotia to anyone willing to settle there. Many New Englanders moved north and other groups came from the British Isles and the German states along the Rhine. Among these were two hundred Scots who landed at Pictou, Nova Scotia, in 1773 from the ship *Hector*. They were the first of a vast wave of Highlanders who crossed the Atlantic seeking a better life, having been dispossessed by the big landowners in Scotland who found raising sheep more profitable than renting land to tenant farmers. These highlanders settled mainly in Cape Breton (p. 196) but also in the Pictou and Antigonish area, and on Prince Edward Island.

In 1775 when revolution broke out in the American colonies, it seemed for a time likely that Nova Scotia would join the other thirteen. In the event, this did not happen and thus it became one of the main receiving points for the flood of Loyalists who fled the new United States after the war (p. 99). In all, about 30 000 people settled in Nova Scotia mainly along the Atlantic Coast and in the valley of the Saint John River, but also in Prince Edward Island. The arrival of so many people, some of them very influential, transformed Nova Scotia. To meet their needs, a separate administration was set up in 1784, and called New Brunswick (Prince Edward Island had been separated from Nova Scotia in 1769).

The Era of the Wooden Ships. – One great industry established by Pre-Loyalists and Loyalists alike was the building of wooden ships. The forests of the region, especially those of New Brunswick, offered rich resources of timber already exploited for use as masts in British Naval vessels. From this beginning, the industry grew especially at Saint John which by the mid 19th century was numbered among the world's great shipbuilding centres. Shipyards sprang up along the coasts of all three provinces and skilled craftsmen perfected the clipper ships, schooners, brigs and barques that made the region famous and were used all over the world. Two brothers who opened a shipyard in Chatham, New Brunswick, were later to become famous as founders of the **Cunard line.** Along Nova Scotia's south coast it was not only the schooners that became legend, but also the sailors who manned them – universally called **Bluenoses,** an American term of derision for people who could survive the region's cold climate. By the time of Confederation in 1867, Nova Scotia and New Brunswick were well established and wealthy (Prince Edward Island joined Canada in 1873, p. 209). In the latter half of the century New Brunswick was the most prosperous region in Canada.

This situation did not however last. By 1900, steam power had taken over from sail power and steel hulls had superseded wooden ones. Only a few shipyards in the region changed their operations to meet this development and this lack of foresight doomed the industry. By the First World War, wooden ships were built no more and the Maritime Provinces' great age of prominence was over.

RESOURCES

Since the end of the era of wooden ships, the Maritime Provinces have never been prosperous compared with the rest of Canada. The Atlantic coast is not well-endowed with natural resources, except for its magnificent scenery which has made tourism a major factor in the economy of all three provinces.

Fishing. – This is another resource that the three provinces share. Today, the most valuable catch is **lobster.** Since these can only be taken in tightly controlled seasons, numerous saltwater pounds have been constructed where the creatures can be kept all year and sold fresh to meet world demand. Most of these pounds are in New Brunswick notably on Deer Island (p. 207). Many other crustaceans are caught including Prince Edward Island's famous Malpeque **oysters,** Nova Scotia's Digby **scallops,** shrimps, clams, crab, etc. In addition, New Brunswick is known for its sardines and its Atlantic salmon, and giant **bluefin tuna** are caught off all three provinces. Nova Scotia is the only province with an off-shore fleet which fishes the Banks (p. 221).

Agriculture. – Although agriculture plays a part in the economy of all three provinces, it is Prince Edward Island's backbone. The Island supports a great range of farming but it is most famous for its **potatoes.** Indeed potatoes are to Prince Edward Island what wheat is to Saskatchewan. With New Brunswick, the Island produces 80 % of Canada's domestic seed potatoes and 90 % of the country's exports. The Saint John River valley of New Brunswick and the Annnapolis valley of Nova Scotia are the region's other great agricultural areas. The land which is not cultivated in the latter two provinces supports a considerable **forestry** industry, especially in New Brunswick.

Mining, Hydro-Electric Power and Manufacturing. – New Brunswick is the only one of the three provinces in which mining contributes significantly to the economy. There are zinc, lead and copper deposits near Bathurst, antimony near Fredericton and potash near Sussex. In Nova Scotia, **coal,** gypsum and salt are mined. Once the coal industry was a mainstay of the economy (pp. 200 and 215) but it slumped badly after the Second World War. A recent revival due to high oil prices is gradually changing this however.

New Brunswick is also the only province with significant electric power resources. The Saint John River has been harnessed in several places, notably at Mactaquac *(p. 213)*. There are plans on foot in both New Brunswick and Nova Scotia to harness the mighty Bay of Fundy tides *(p. 185)*. Generating stations built across tidal inlets could produce power as the water level rises and drops. A pilot project opened at Annapolis Royal in 1983 *(p. 191)*.

There is relatively little manufacturing industry in this region due to its distance from markets in central Canada, although Nova Scotia and New Brunswick have good road and rail links and their ports, being ice-free, are open all year. What industry there is relies largely on local products – fish packing, food processing, pulp and paper making, etc. However, steel is refined at Sydney, Nova Scotia, oil at Saint John, New Brunswick, and Nova Scotia supports an auto assembly and auto parts manufacturing industry (three Michelin tire factories).

SPORTS AND OUTDOOR ACTIVITIES

All three provinces have excellent national and provincial parks offering camping facilities and many other activities. Prince Edward Island is famous for its fine beaches washed by the surprisingly warm waters of the Gulf of St. Lawrence *(p. 208)*. **Kouchibouguac National Park** in New Brunswick also has miles of sand dunes. Both New Brunswick and Nova Scotia are well endowed with hiking trails, notably in Cape Breton Highlands National Park *(p. 196)*, Fundy National Park *(p. 200)* and Mount Carleton Provincial Park in northern New Brunswick. The size of Prince Edward Island makes it suitable to visit by bicycle or on horseback.

Water Sports. – With so much coastline between them, the three provinces offer unequalled opportunities for boating and sailing. Those who find Atlantic waters a little rough may prefer Bras d'Or Lake in Cape Breton or the beautiful Saint John River *(p. 213)* where Mactaquac Provincial Park among other places offers good facilities. Canoeing is not as popular an activity in this part of Canada as in other regions, nevertheless **Kejimkujik National Park** in Nova Scotia has several canoe routes.

Fishing. – Deep sea fishing is an activity popular with visitors to all three provinces. Boats can be chartered and a wide variety of fish caught including the giant bluefin tuna, a worthy opponent of any sportsman. Inland, the region is especially noted for its Atlantic **salmon** – the Miramichi and Restigouche valleys of northern New Brunswick and the Margaree valley of Nova Scotia *(p. 196)* being the most famous areas. Information on seasons, limits, restricted areas and outfitters can be obtained from the provincial tourist offices *(p. 190)*. This is also true of hunting which is popular in the remoter areas of northern New Brunswick.

Other Activities. – Farm vacations are possible in all three provinces but Prince Edward Island is particularly known for them *(for details contact the tourist office)*. The Island also offers some excellent golf courses. In winter, cross-country skiing and snowmobiling are popular throughout the region. Skating on frozen lakes is possible in Prince Edward Island and northern New Brunswick offers some alpine ski centres.

PRINCIPAL FESTIVALS

May – June	**Annapolis Valley N.S.**	Blossom Festival
June - Labour Day ...	**Charlottetown P.E.I.**	Summer Festival *(p. 210)*
June – July	**Campbellton N.B.**	Salmon Festival
July	**Saint John N.B.**	Loyalist Days *(p. 211)*
July	**Shippagan N.B.**	Provincial Fisheries Festival
July	**Antigonish N.S.**	Highland Games
July	**Pugwash N.S.**	Gathering of the Clans
July	**Shediac N.B.**	Lobster Festival
July 24th	**Halifax N.S.**	Natal Day
July - August	**Edmundston N.B.**	*Foire Brayonne* (Brayonne Fair)
August	**Halifax N.S.**	Nova Scotia Festival of the Arts
August	**Caraquet N.B.**	Acadian Festival *(p. 216)*
August	**St. Ann's N.S.**	Gaelic Mod *(p. 198)*
September	**Lunenburg N.S.**	Nova Scotia Fisheries Exhibition and Fishermen's Reunion *(p. 194)*
September......................	**Halifax N.S.**	Joseph Howe Festival

PRACTICAL INFORMATION

Access. – Prince Edward Island can be reached all year round by air and by two car ferries which cross the Northumberland Strait.

From New Brunswick : *Cape Tormentine to Borden, daily ; non-stop service in peak periods, less frequent off season ; about 45 min ; no reservations ; for details contact : CN Marine, P.O. Box 250, North Sydney, N.S. B2A 3M3 ☎ (800) 565-9470 from N.B., N.S. and PEI. Busy in peak periods, try to cross before 10am or after 6pm.*

From Nova Scotia : *Caribou to Wood Islands, daily May - Dec 20th, minimum of 6 round trip sailings, 20 in peak season ; 1 1/4 hrs ; no reservations ; for details contact : Northumberland Ferries Ltd., P.O. Box 634, Charlottetown, P.E.I. C1A 7L3 ☎ (902) 894-3473. There can be long line-ups at peak periods.*

From Souris, Prince Edward Island, a ferry crosses to the Magdalen Islands (Iles de la Madeleine) regularly in summer *(p. 159)*.

Nova Scotia, which is practically an island, is accessible by three car ferry services in addition to the road connection.

From Maine : *Portland to Yarmouth, daily May - Oct ; 11 hrs ; for reservations and details contact Prince of Fundy Cruises, Portland, Maine 04101,* ☎ *(207) 775-5616 or (902) 742-5164.*

From Maine : *Bar Harbor to Yarmouth, daily in July and Aug ; less frequently rest of year ; about 6 hrs ; for details and reservations contact : CN Marine (see above).*

From New Brunswick : *Saint John to Digby, daily year round ; about 3 hrs ; for reservations and details contact : CN Marine (see above).*

From North Sydney, two car ferries cross to Newfoundland *(p. 220).*

Road Conditions. – Roads in all three Maritime Provinces are kept in very good condition. Speed limits, unless otherwise indicated, are 90 kmh (55 mph) in New Brunswick and Prince Edward Island, 100 kmh (62 mph) in Nova Scotia.

Accommodation and Road Maps. – The governments of all three provinces produce annually revised lists of approved accommodation in their regions, including campsites. These are available free of charge, with regularly updated road maps, from most tourist bureaus or from :

Tourism New Brunswick, *P.O. Box 12345, Fredericton, N.B., E3B 5C3 ;* ☎ *(506) 453-2377 (1-800-561-0123 toll free in Canada).*

P.E.I. Tourist Information Centre, *P.O. Box 940, Charlottetown, P.E.I., C1A 7M5 ;* ☎ *(902) 892-2457.*

Nova Scotia Department of Tourism, *P.O. Box 130, Halifax, N.S., B3J 2M7 ;* ☎ *(902) 424-4247.*

Time Zone. – All three Maritime Provinces are on **Atlantic Standard Time** (one hour in advance of the eastern United States, Québec and Ontario). Clocks are advanced one hour in summer *(map p. 20).*

Taxes. – A sales tax of 10 % is charged on all purchases except food and clothing in all three provinces. A tax of 10 % is added to hotel bills and restaurant meals over $3.00 in New Brunswick and Nova Scotia.

Liquor Laws. – Liquor, beer and wine can only be publicly consumed on licensed premises and can only be purchased from government stores.

The legal drinking age is 19 in New Brunswick and Nova Scotia, 18 in Prince Edward Island.

BOOKS TO READ

The Fascinating World of New Brunswick by Stuart Trueman *(McClelland and Stewart)*

Halifax - Warden of the North by Thomas Raddall *(McClelland and Stewart)*

The Town that Died by Michael Bird *(McGraw Hill Ryerson)* (Halifax Explosion)

The Acadians of the Maritimes by Jean Daigle (translation) *(Université de Moncton)*

The Governor's Lady by Thomas Raddall *(McClelland and Stewart)* FICTION

Anne of Green Gables by Lucy Maud Montgomery *(McGraw Hill Ryerson)* FICTION

His Majesty's Yankees by Thomas Raddall *(McClelland and Stewart)* FICTION

*When in Europe use **Michelin maps** (1 :1 000 000 – 1 inch = 14 miles)*

Great Britain – Ireland 986	*Spain - Portugal 990*
Germany – Austria - Benelux 987	*Yugoslavia 991*
Italy – Switzerland 988	*Greece 980 (1 :700 000)*
France 989	

ANNAPOLIS ROYAL ★★ Nova Scotia

Map p. 186 – Pop 631

Annapolis Royal has a pleasant **site**★ near the point where the great basin of the Annapolis narrows into the river of the same name. This marshland area was reclaimed by building a dam across the river with flood gates to control the water level. Twice a day the tides of the Bay of Fundy *(p. 185)* rush in reversing the flow of the river. A causeway over the top of the dam offers views of this phenomenon and of the experimental tidal power project *(p. 191).*

The first settlement in this area was the French colony at **Port Royal** of 1605. This was destroyed by a force from Jamestown, Virginia, in 1613 after most of the colonists had returned to France. However, by 1635 a French nobleman, **Charles de Menou d'Aulnay,** had built a new Port Royal on the site of the present town. Over the next century other settlements grew up in the area and further east forming the region called Acadia *(p. 186).* As these communities grew they came more and more into conflict with the New England colonies to the south. Port Royal suffered many raids which led to the construction of a fort – the predecessor of the present Fort Anne. There was never sufficient money to properly maintain the fort however, and it fell to a New England expedition under Colonel Francis Nicholson in 1710.

Renamed Annapolis Royal after **Queen Anne,** it was the capital of Nova Scotia when the mainland part of the present province was ceded to the British by the Treaty of Utrecht in 1713. It was constantly threatened and frequently withstood French attack surrounded as it was by Acadian settlements sympathetic to the soldiers from Québec or Louisbourg. In 1749, the capital was switched to Halifax and Annapolis Royal lost its importance though troops were stationed there until 1854.

Today, the old centre (**Lower Saint George St**) is being renovated. Houses, shops, a theatre and an inn have been restored and there is a pleasant boardwalk beside the Annapolis Basin.

■ **SIGHTS** *time : 1/2 day*

Fort Anne★. – *Open daily mid May - mid Oct, weekdays rest of year ; National Historic Park ; guided tours and self guiding tour ; ☎ 532-2397.*

Approaching Annapolis Royal from the west, Fort Anne is visible with the high chimneys of the Officers' Quarters protruding over its earthworks. Today it is peaceful though once it was the most fought over place in Canada suffering fourteen sieges during the Anglo-French wars, numerous changes of possession and garrison, and a few pirate raids thrown in for good measure. The existing earthworks were built by the French 1702-8 with some later alterations by the British. In one of the bastions stands a stone powder magazine of the French period. From the earthworks there is a fine **view★** of the Annapolis Basin.

Officers' Quarters★. – This distinctive building with its high chimneys and dormer windows stands in the centre of the fort. It is a reconstruction of the original built in 1797 on the orders of Prince Edward *(p. 201)*. Inside, a **museum★** contains displays on the military history of the fort including details of the various sieges and changes of control.

Over the fort flies the flag of the Grand Union. It is a combination of the English cross of St. George and the Scottish cross of St. Andrew. The Union Jack as we know it today did not come about until the union with Ireland in 1800 when the cross of St. Patrick was added.

Historic Gardens★. – *On Upper Saint George St (Rte 8) just S of Fort Anne. Open daily mid May - mid Oct ; $2.00 ; ☎ 532-5104.*

Paths wind in and out of a series of theme gardens laid out on a 4 ha - 10 acre site overlooking Allain's River, a tributary of the Annapolis. The Acadian Garden has a typical cottage and a replica of the dike system *(p. 192)*. The Governor's Garden is formal in style typical of the early 18th century when Annapolis Royal was the seat of the English Governor. The Victorian Garden has more natural landscapes, a trend which became fashionable in the 19th century. The Rose Garden traces the development of this ever popular species.

Annapolis Tidal Power Project★. – *On the Causeway (Rte 1). Information Centre open daily mid May - mid Oct ; ☎ 532-5104.*

This experimental project is North America's first tidal power generating station. Low-head, straight-flow turbine generators are being tested to see how the enormous energy of the Bay of Fundy tides can be harnessed. If successful, they will be used for future much more major harnessing of tidal power. The information centre enables visitors to look at the project and have it explained to them.

EXCURSIONS

North Hills Museum★. – *In Granville Ferry on road to Port Royal. Open daily mid May - mid Oct ; ☎ 532-2168 ; Nova Scotia Museum.*

This small wood-framed 18th century house has retained its pioneer look despite a series of modifications. It provides a fitting setting for the largely 18th century antique collection of a retired Toronto banker which includes English furniture, ceramics, silver and Georgian glass. It was bequeathed to the province on the banker's death in 1974.

Port Royal Habitation★★. – *10 km - 6 miles from Annapolis Royal Causeway. Open daily mid May - mid Oct ; National Historic Park ; self guiding tour ; ☎ 532-2898.*

This is an exact replica of the buildings constructed in 1605 by the **Sieur de Monts,** a French nobleman, who had been granted permission by Henry IV of France to colonize the New World between the 40th and 46th lines of latitude and to develop the fur trade. He chose **Samuel de Champlain** as his captain and navigator and the expedition departed in 1604. Their first winter in Canada was spent on an island in the mouth of the St. Croix River *(map p. 207)* which proved to be a poor choice cut off as it was from the mainland and fresh food by the storms and ice of the Bay of Fundy. The next year they moved to the Annapolis Basin and Champlain constructed his Habitation.

Champlain's Habitation

The Order of Good Cheer. – For the next winter Champlain organized this order, which could be called the first social club in Canada, because boredom as much as sickness had made the first winter so unbearable. There were fifteen charter members and they took it in turns to be the Grand Master and to organize gourmet feasts. This was very successful as was the first play performed in Canada **The Theatre of Neptune** written by Marc Lescarbot in 1606. All in all the small colony flourished. Crops were grown, trade with the Indians was organized and there seemed every chance that Port Royal would become a permanent settlement when suddenly in 1607 de Monts' trading monopoly was revoked and the whole expedition returned to France.

The Habitation was left in the care of the Micmac Indians until 1610 when one of the original settlers, the **Baron de Poutrincourt,** returned having been granted the land. But again the colony was short lived. In 1613 an English expedition from Virginia destroyed the Habitation while all the men were in the fields. The Habitation was not again revived until the Canadian Government reconstructed it in 1938-39 using the writings of Champlain, Lescarbot and the Jesuits.

ANNAPOLIS ROYAL★★

Visit. – The Habitation has a very distinctive form unlike anything else found in Canada. From the exterior, it is a collection of fortified black buildings all joined together with steeply pitched roofs built around a central courtyard. This style was often employed for farms in 16th century France. The walls are actually of **colombage** construction - upright posts placed several feet apart with the spaces between them filled in horizontally with logs caulked with clay. On the exterior this construction is covered with lapped boarding so it can only be appreciated from inside. No nails or spikes join the timbers, they are mortised and tenoned and then pinned together. Each building has a fieldstone chimney.

The Habitation is entered through a narrow gateway above which hang the arms of France and Navarre, of which Henry IV was king. A well with a shingled roof stands in the middle of the courtyard and around it there are residences for the governor, priest, artisans, etc. All the furnishings are meticulous reproductions of early 17th century styles. The kitchen, forge, community room where the Order of Good Cheer met, and chapel can be visited as can the storerooms, wine cellar and a trading room where the Indians brought their furs. A **slide show** depicting life at Port Royal can be seen in the latter *(ask for showing)*.

On leaving the Habitation, note the view of the river and the circular fences in the water. These are weirs for catching fish and they are frequently seen in tidal areas.

ANNAPOLIS Valley ★★ Nova Scotia
Maps pp. 10 and 186-187

The Annapolis River flows about 112 km - 70 miles southwest to the sea widening out into a tidal lake called the **Annapolis Basin** and emptying into the Bay of Fundy through a narrow opening known as **Digby Gut**. However, the area commonly referred to as the Annapolis Valley comprises several other rivers and extends from Digby to Windsor on the **Minas Basin**. This was the region where some of the earliest French colonists settled and from which they were deported by the British in 1755 *(p. 188)*. The valley is sheltered on both sides from heavy wind and fog by the North and South Mountains, a situation which has long made it famous for its **apple orchards.** Today, many other fruits and crops are grown in the fertile soil and dairy cattle are kept on the meadow land bordering the river.

From Digby to Windsor
168 km - 104 miles by Route 1 – allow 1 day

Digby. – Pop 2 558. From this small town, home of the famous scallop *(p. 188)*, ferries cross to New Brunswick.

Route 1 follows the shore of the Annapolis Basin with pleasant **views★** especially at the estuary of the Bear River.

Annapolis Royal★★. – *Description p. 190.*
Remains of the old French dike system can be seen along the route. Route 1 crosses the river and continues through country which becomes more and more rural. Apple orchards line the hills and there are meadows beside the river.

At **Bridgetown★**, elm shaded streets contain fine houses many built by Loyalists. **Lawrencetown** and **Middleton** are similarly attractive and gracious. This drive is particularly pleasant in apple blossom time *(late May or early June).*

Prescott House★. – *5 km - 3 miles N of Rte 1 at Greenwich in Starr's Point. Open daily mid May - mid Oct ; Nova Scotia Museum ; ☎ (902) 542-3984.*
This attractive brick house set in fine grounds was built by **Charles Prescott**, a successful merchant and legislator, but much more famous as a horticulturalist. On this estate, Prescott tried out new kinds of wheat, planted nut trees, grapes, pears, and introduced many varieties of cherries and apples, particularly the latter. He gave away cuttings to many valley farmers and is at least partially responsible for the growth of the great apple industry in this area.

Prescott built this house in the early 19th century. The interior is attractively furnished with some original pieces. There is a pleasant sun room at the back. The garden is also worth visiting.

Grand Pré National Historic Park★. – *Just N of Rte 1, 4 km - 2 1/2 miles E of Wolfville. Open daily mid May - mid Oct ; weekdays only rest of year ; ☎ (902) 542-3631.*
Before the Deportation *(p. 188)*, Grand Pré was the most important Acadian settlement in Nova Scotia with about two hundred farms spread out along the edge of the Minas Basin. The inhabitants had moved to this region from Port Royal *(p. 190)* and quickly realized the richness of the soil covered by the sea at high tide. A system **of dikes** was constructed to keep the sea out while the marsh water was allowed to escape through flood gates. In this way, the land was brought under cultivation and soon supported crops, livestock and orchards. After the Acadians were deported, the farmlands were given to settlers from New England who moved north, and later to Loyalists.

Today, this park stands as a permanent memorial to the Acadians. Set on land reputedly the site of the first church of Grand Pré is a little **chapel** surrounded by poplar and willow trees. It was built 1922-30 of local stone in a style recalling the French origins of the settlers. Inside, there are interesting **displays** detailing Acadian settlement, the problems after the British takeover, and the final Deportation. A copy of the original order signed by Governor Lawrence can be seen.

Home of Evangeline. – Grand Pré was chosen by the American poet **Henry Wadsworth Longfellow** as the setting for his poem *Evangeline – A Tale of Acadie*, written in 1847. In this work, he describes the separation of a young couple during the Deportation, and the subsequent search of the woman, Evangeline, for her lover, Gabriel, which took her all over the eastern United States only to find him in the end – dying. This poem has become part of the popular culture of the Acadians typifying as it does the tragedy of the Deportation.

A bronze statue of Evangeline by Philippe Hébert stands in the grounds.

Windsor★. – Pop 3 646. Famous as the home of Thomas Haliburton, the town of Windsor is set at the confluence of the Avon and St. Croix Rivers. It was once the site of the Acadian settlement of Piziquid which was taken over by New Englanders after the Deportation and renamed Windsor. A causeway over the Avon today closes the river above the town to the tides of the Bay of Fundy *(p. 185)*. Windsor is a shipping point for lumber and gypsum mined nearby.

Clifton - Haliburton Memorial Museum★. – *On Clifton Ave - follow signs from causeway. Open daily mid May - mid Oct ; Nova Scotia Museum ;* ☎ *(902) 798-2915.*

At the end of a long and impressive drive stands this house in a lovely park full of fine trees. It was built in 1833 by **Thomas Chandler Haliburton,** famous as the creator of **Sam Slick.** Judge, legislator, and last but not least author and humourist, Haliburton was one of the foremost Nova Scotians of his day. He first started publishing stories in 1836 under the title *The Clockmaker ; or, The Sayings and Doings of Samuel Slick of Slickville.* Slick, a Yankee clock pedlar, travelled all over Nova Scotia making fun of its unenterprising inhabitants. This volume and later ones gave Haliburton an international reputation for wit. Many of the epigrams he coined are still in use today : "six of one and half a dozen of the other", "an ounce of prevention is worth a pound of cure", "facts are stranger than fiction", "the early bird gets the worm", "as quick as a wink", "jack of all trades and master of none", etc.

The interior of the house reflects the man with a spacious entry hall, elegant dining room and sitting room. The walls are decorated with numerous Sam Slick cartoons.

Fort Edward. – *Off King St near the causeway. Open daily June - Labour Day ; National Historic Park ;* ☎ *(902) 542-3631.*

From these grassy fortifications, there are good **views★** of the tidal river, the causeway and lake above it. Constructed in 1750, the fort established British authority in this Acadian area and safeguarded the communications route between the Bay of Fundy and Halifax. It was used as a major gathering place for the Acadians during the Deportation *(p. 188)* and was garrisoned until the early 19th century.

The black wooden **blockhouse** is the only remaining building of the fort and it is in fact the oldest original such structure in Canada. It is made of squared timbers with two storeys, the upper overhanging the lower. The walls are pierced by square portholes out of which cannon could be fired, and loopholes for musket fire. Inside, there are displays on the blockhouse system of defence and on Fort Edward.

ATLANTIC Coast ★★ Nova Scotia

Maps pp. 10 and 186-187

The Atlantic coastline of Nova Scotia is famous for its rugged scenery, indented granite coves, sandy beaches, pretty fishing villages tinged by the spray of the ocean, and for its wealthy and attractive tree-lined towns with their elegant houses. The latter were built from the proceeds of a flourishing shipbuilding industry *(p. 188)* as well as, in some cases, from the vast profits made from privateering on the high seas.

The entire coast from Canso to Yarmouth can be followed by road. Some of the roads are small and narrow but by following them, the true charm of this peaceful region will be captured.

The best time of year for this trip is between mid July and October since fogs, which can descend on this wild Atlantic coast at any time, are least common in these months.

From Halifax to Liverpool

300 km - 186 miles – allow 2 days – Local map p. 194

Leave Halifax (p. 201) on Rte 3, then turn left on Rte 333.

Very soon the landscape becomes wild almost desolate. There are huge boulders on all sides left behind by retreating glaciers and stunted vegetation giving the area a lunar look as the coast is approached.

Peggy's Cove★★. – Pop 54. This tiny village, immortalized by artists and photographers across Canada, is the most attractive of all the settlements on the coast and it is surprisingly uncommercialized despite the number of visitors. There is a delightful little harbour with boats and fishermen's shacks built on stilts in the water. The lighthouse stands alone on one of the huge granite slabs against which the Atlantic pounds during storms – a complete contrast to the tranquillity of the harbour.

Before leaving, note the carvings of Peggy's Cove residents sculpted in the granite rock by W. De Garthe.

After Peggy's Cove, the coast is pretty with small villages, views of **St. Margaret's Bay,** and sandy beaches at the head of the bay.

Rte 333 joins Rte 3 at Upper Tantallon, follow 3 until Rte 329 turns off after Hubbards, make the tour of the peninsula, rejoin 3 just before Chester.

Chester★. – Pop 1 131. This charming town perched on the cliffs as they rise out of Mahone Bay has attractive frame houses of New England style and beautiful trees. It was founded by New Englanders in 1759 and is still popular among Americans as a place to have a summer home. It is also a favourite retirement place for wealthy Canadians.

Take Rte 12, 7 km - 4 miles after Chester for 24 km - 15 miles.

Ross Farm★. – *24 km - 15 miles N by Rte 12. Open daily mid May - mid Oct ; $1.50 ; Nova Scotia Museum ;* ☎ *(902) 389-2210.*

Hacked out of the wilderness in 1816 by William Ross, this farm belonged to five generations of his family before the Nova Scotia Museum acquired it. It is run as a living and extremely realistic museum of 19th century farm life. Activities vary with the season. A variety of crops and animals can be seen including oxen and farm horses which give wagon rides. There are also displays of farm implements and machinery.

Return to Rte 3.

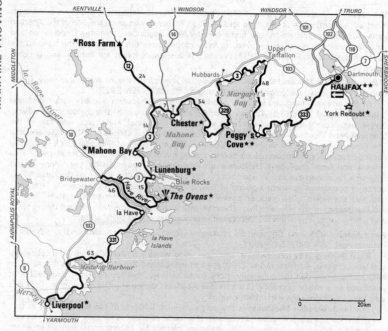

Mahone Bay★. – Pop 1 228. Approaching this pretty town at the head of the bay, there is a fine **view★** of its churches reflected in the water.

Founded in 1754 by Captain Ephraim Cook, Mahone Bay has experienced a checkered history of pirate raids and wealth garnered by privateering. Between 1756 and 1815, hundreds of small ships sailed from Nova Scotia ports to harass the vessels of the French, Spanish, Dutch and Americans from New England to the Caribbean. These acts of piracy were carried out with Royal blessing. A privateer owner had to obtain a license, he could only attack enemy ships, and he had to take all prizes to Halifax where the Court of Vice Admiralty decided if they were legal. Despite these restrictions, profits were enormous and these coastal communities prospered.

Today, Mahone Bay is more respectable with a shipbuilding industry, elegant frame houses and churches set along tree-lined streets.

After Mahone Bay, the road is very pretty with considerable agricultural activity in evidence, rare so close to this rocky coast.

Lunenburg★. – Pop 3 014. Situated on a hilly peninsula with "front" and "back" harbours, Lunenburg is named for the town in Germany from whence its first settlers came in 1753 (Lüneburg). It has always been known for its fishing fleet and, like Mahone Bay, was once a pirates' haven, although it suffered for this when it was sacked by American privateers in 1782.

Lunenburg is also famous for its shipbuilding industry both past and present. Many of the schooners which fished the "banks" *(p. 221)* were constructed here, including the **Bluenose** which was the undefeated champion of the North American fishing fleet and winner of four international schooner races 1921-46. The **Bluenose II**, a replica of the original *(see Halifax p. 203)*, was also constructed here in 1963.

Every September, the popular **Nova Scotia Fisheries Exhibition and Fishermen's Reunion** is celebrated. There are dory, yacht and schooner races, fish filleting and scallop shucking contests, parades, displays, etc.

Fisheries Museum★. – *On "front" harbour. Open daily mid May - mid Oct ; $2.00 ; Nova Scotia Museum ;* ☎ *(902) 634-4794.*

This is the official fisheries museum of Nova Scotia. It comprises an exhibit building which houses an aquarium of the salt water fish caught off the coast and three vessels moored in the harbour which can be boarded.

The **Theresa E. Connor,** a schooner built in 1938, fished the Grand Banks for twenty five years. She has been completely refurbished to illustrate the era of "dory" fishing. These small boats were usually manned by two men and they would set the long trawl lines and haul in the fish, using the schooner as a supply and delivery centre. On board the schooner the fish were salted which is the origin of the name "saltbanker" commonly used of these vessels. On the *Theresa E. Connor,* the dories are all set to go fishing, and in the holds there are displays on the saltbankers and on the *Bluenose.*

Moored beside the *Theresa E. Connor* is the **Cape North,** a wooden trawler built in 1945. These ships took over from the schooners, hauling the trawl nets themselves instead of using dories.

The third vessel is the **Reo II** built in 1930 specially for the illicit trade of "rum-running". During the prohibition era in North America, such vessels picked up cargoes of rum from the French islands of St. Pierre and Miquelon *(p. 222)* and sold them for vast profits to coastal communities in the United States.

Follow Rte 3 and turn left on Rte 332 for 15 km - 9 miles.

This is a pretty **drive★** with views of Lunenburg harbour.

Ovens Natural Park★. – *Open daily mid May - mid Sept, 8am - 9pm; $1.00;* ☎ *(902) 766-4621.*

These caves, cut into the cliffs by the action of the sea, have a lovely site with **views**★ across Lunenburg Bay to Blue Rocks. A path along the cliff top leads to several sets of stairs by which visitors can descend to see the caves which resemble ovens hence their name. The rock is of a slanting formation, the reason why the sea was able to wear it away, but also an indication of the presence of gold. Gold was found here in 1861 but not enough to support for long the town that sprang up almost overnight to exploit it.

Continue on Rte 332, and then left on Rte 3.

The road follows the wide and tranquil estuary of the La Have River. Boats of all types will be seen along this pretty stretch of water which is lined with white frame houses and trees. At **Bridgewater** (Pop 6 669), a small industrial town (Michelin tire factory), the river is crossed.

Turn left on Rte 331.

The road passes the town of **La Have** itself (Pop 195), one of the earliest settled places in the province. Isaac de Razilly, the Lieutenant Governor of Acadie *(p. 186),* built a fort here in 1632. The road continues along the coast with many pretty views of sea and fishing villages especially around **Medway Harbour.**

Liverpool★. – Pop 3 304. Founded in 1760 by New Englanders, Liverpool, like its great English namesake, is on the Mersey River. It is a pretty place with many grand houses several storeys high with fine gardens. The wealth was accumulated partly by privateering, partly by fishing, and partly by ship repairing.

Simeon Perkins House★. – *On Main St. Open daily mid May - mid Oct; Nova Scotia Museum;* ☎ *(902) 354-4058.*

This low lying house of New England style with odd shaped corners and winding hidden stairs was built in 1767 by Colonel Simeon Perkins who emigrated to Nova Scotia from Cape Cod. A merchant and ship owner, Colonel Perkins also assumed certain military, judicial and legislative roles. His diary, a copy of which is on display in the house, records in detail the life of a colonial town 1766-1812. The house is set in fine gardens among enormous trees and surrounded by other elegant homes.

BALMORAL MILLS ★ Nova Scotia

Map p. 187 - 9.5 km - 6 miles SE of Tatamagouche by Rte 311 and a left turn in The Falls

Set in a pleasant valley beside a stream stands a fully operational **gristmill** built in 1830 *(open daily mid May - mid Oct; Nova Scotia Museum; picnic grounds;* ☎ *(902) 657-3016).* Although not in commercial use since 1954, it has been completely restored. It is in operation for a few hours each day and during this time the interior is a hive of activity. The various milling processes are explained to visitors by guides. The original mill stones weighing 1 1/2 tons grind oats, wheat, barley and buckwheat into flour and meal *(on sale),* and the grain is moved from storey to storey by means of a series of buckets mounted on leather belts. The water wheel can be seen in operation below the mill.

EXCURSION

Sutherland Steam Mill. – *10 km - 6 miles NE by Rte 311, minor road and Rte 326, in Denmark. Open daily mid May - mid Oct;* ☎ *657-3365; Nova Scotia Museum.*

When Alexander Sutherland built this sawmill in 1894, steam was replacing water power as the most efficient means of cutting up wood. He made sleighs, carriages and sleds, while his brother and partner produced doors, windows and other trim for local houses. All the machinery is in working order and the mill "steams up" once a month *(Sat,* ☎ *for dates).*

CABOT TRAIL ★★ Nova Scotia

Maps pp. 11 and 187 – round trip of 301 km - 187 miles from Baddeck – allow 2 days – Local map p. 197

This route named for **John Cabot** who is said to have landed at the island's northern tip in 1497 is one of the most beautiful drives in eastern North America. It makes a circular tour of the northern part of Cape Breton Island passing at first through tranquil farmland, then hugging the coast and winding up and down with fine views of the ocean, craggy mountains, rocky inlets, magnificent headlands and dense forests. Many parts are reminiscent of the Highlands of Scotland and indeed that is where many of the inhabitants originally came from. *Much evidence of their culture can be seen especially on the east coast.*

The Trail can be driven in either direction but many visitors prefer to do it clockwise for the security of hugging the sides of the mountains while driving up and down some of the steep and curvy stretches. Attractive in all seasons, it is especially fine in September and October when the hills are bright with Fall colours.

Baddeck★★. – Pop 972. The village of Baddeck is a popular resort centre with a lovely **site**★ on the north shore of **Bras d'Or Lake.** This vast inland sea almost cuts Cape Breton Island in two. It is fed by the Atlantic via two channels, the **Great Bras d'Or** and the **Little Bras d'Or,** on either side of Boularderie Island. Far away to the south, a narrow strip of land separates the lake from the sea again. The St. Peters Canal crosses this strip.

Summer Home of Alexander Graham Bell. – Bras d'Or Lake's resemblance to a Scottish loch has attracted many settlers of Scottish origin to its shores. Among these was Alexander Graham Bell (1847-1922), humanitarian, inventor and researcher of great genius not only in communications science, for which he is best known, but also in medical and aeronautical sciences. It was his work as a teacher of the deaf which led to his invention of the telephone which he conceived in Brantford, Ontario *(p. 103),* in 1874 and tested in Boston the next year. This discovery made him famous and gave him the money to carry on his other research. In 1885 he first visited Baddeck and built a summer home called **Beinn Bhreagh,** the

CABOT TRAIL★★

Gaelic words for beautiful mountain. There he did much of his work in the aeronautical field. He built kites and other heavier-than-air craft, using combinations of the tetrahedron shape - an almost perfect engineering form because it is light but strong. In 1907 with other pioneer aviators he founded the **Aerial Experiment Association** and sponsored the first manned flight made in Canada when the **Silver Dart** flew across Baddeck Bay in 1909. Before his death he was also able to see one of his hydrofoil craft, the **HD-4**, reach the incredible speed (for 1919) of 114 km - 70.86 mph on Bras d'Or Lake.

Alexander Graham Bell National Historic Park★★. – *On Hwy 205 in Baddeck. Open daily ;* ☎ *(902) 295-2069.*

The unique shape of this fascinating museum is due to the extensive use of Bell's favourite tetrahedra in its structure. Inside, there are many displays illustrating the variety and scope of the genius of this remarkable man. For example, there are models of the telephone, the vacuum jacket - a forerunner of the iron lung, the surgical probe - a device used before the advent of X-ray, and various ways of making drinking water from fog, breath and salt water - work carried out by Bell to prevent sailors from dying of thirst when stranded at sea. There are also models of Bell's kites and a tiny one of the *Silver Dart (a full-scale replica can be seen in the National Aviation Museum in Ottawa p. 121).* A highlight of these displays is the superb **photograph collection** on Bell's life and work. Another wing of the museum is devoted to Bell's hydrofoil - the *HD-4.* Both the dismembered original and a replica are exhibited.

From the terrace of the museum there is a fine **view**★ across Baddeck Bay to the headland on which Bell built his summer home. *Beinn Bhreagh* can be seen among the trees *(not open to public).*

■ FROM BADDECK TO CHETICAMP★

88 km - 55 miles

After leaving the Trans-Canada Highway, the Cabot Trail follows part of the valley of the Middle River, passes the O'Law Lakes and joins the Margaree River in a lush green **valley**★ of meadows and fine salmon pools. This valley is reputed to offer some of Canada's finest salmon fishing.

North East Margaree. – Pop 325. This small community has two museums of interest.

Museum of Cape Breton Heritage★. – *Open daily mid June - mid Oct ; 50¢ ; gift shop.* This interesting little museum displays the handicrafts of the various peoples of Cape Breton : Micmac Indians, Acadian French and Highland Scots, but particularly the latter. There is a fine collection of tartans, a display of weaving and spinning equipment and an exquisite collection of embroidery.

Margaree Salmon Museum. – *Open daily mid June - mid Oct ; 50¢.* This pleasant little museum operated by the Margaree Anglers' Association has displays on the life cycle of the Atlantic salmon from the egg to the full-grown adult's return trip up the river to reproduce. Unlike its Pacific cousin *(p. 38),* the Atlantic salmon can make several such trips. There are also displays of fishing tackle including illegal spears used by poachers.

The Cabot Trail crosses the estuary of the Margaree River at Margaree Harbour and heads north with some views of the Gulf of St. Lawrence.

Chéticamp. – Pop 1 022. This fishing community is the centre of the Acadian area where the tricolour flag is frequently seen *(p. 216).* It sprawls along the coast opposite Chéticamp Island for some distance with a protected harbour and a fine stone church dedicated to St. Peter. However, Chéticamp's main claim to fame is the very fine hand hooked rugs made by its womenfolk.

Acadian Museum. – *Open daily May - mid Oct ; snack bar.* Run by a cooperative of Acadian women, this museum and gift shop have a fine collection of hooked mats, rugs and other items. Sometimes there are demonstrations of this art which is much more difficult than it looks. There are also occasional demonstrations of spinning, carding and weaving.

■ CAPE BRETON HIGHLANDS NATIONAL PARK★★

From Chéticamp to Cape Smoky *124 km - 77 miles*

For admission to National Parks see p. 21 ; camping ; hiking ; swimming ; Information Office in Ingonish Beach ; ☎ *(902) 285-2270.*

"Where the mountains meet the sea" is the apt description given to this park, where hills rise directly from the water to form a tableland more than 370 m - 1 200 ft high above which rounded summits rise again to a peak of 532 m - 1 747 ft. The waters surrounding the Park are among the most hazardous in North America with the Atlantic pounding on the bare rock. Yet there are many fine beaches. Inland the park is heavily forested and boggy, the realm of deer, moose, lynx and beaver with overhead the occasional bald eagle. There are a series of trails to the interior *(details from Park office)* but the Park's main attraction is its beautiful coast.

From the Chéticamp River, the Cabot Trail winds up a narrow valley to emerge on the coast which it follows for some time with several fine **viewpoints**★★ *(parking and picnic tables)* of the road weaving along the coast. Heading inland, it slowly climbs French Mountain, the highest point on the highway. It descends to Mackenzie Mountain after crossing several deep stream-lined valleys and thence, by a series of switchbacks, it reaches Pleasant Bay (Pop 293) with outstanding **views**★★ on the descent.

The Lone Shieling. – *About 6.5 km - 4 miles from Pleasant Bay, short walk.* This tiny structure of stone with its rounded corners and thatched roof is a replica of a Scottish crofter's cottage common in the Highlands and Islands of Scotland. It was built to form a visible link between the adopted home of the many Highland Scots who settled Cape Breton and their ancestral land.

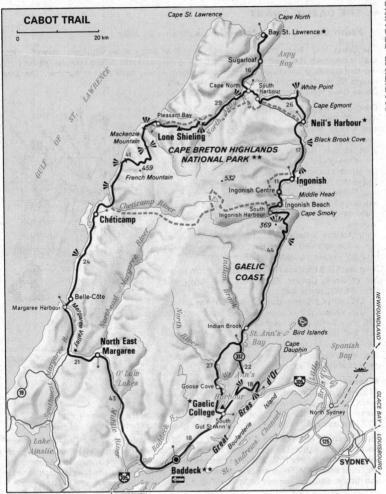

CABOT TRAIL

0   20 km

The Cabot Trail climbs over North Mountain and then descends steeply in the gorge of Mac-Gregor Brook with fine **views★** entering the valley of the North Aspy River which is followed to the village of **Cape North** (Pop 152).

Excursion to Bay St. Lawrence★★. – *16 km - 10 miles.* This is a pretty trip around Aspy Bay with views of its long sand bar, and then inland across grassy hills with spots of pink rock to St. Lawrence Bay at the north end of Cape Breton Island. Before leaving Aspy Bay, the road stops at **Sugarloaf.** This is the supposed first North American landfall of the explorer John Cabot in 1497 *(see also p. 221).* Whether visited by Cabot or not, it is a pretty spot with a fine beach backed by Sugar Loaf Hill.

The highlight of the trip, however, is **Bay St. Lawrence★** (Pop 218), a tiny fishing settlement built around a small lake with a narrow exit to the sea. Approaching the village, stop at the large white clapboard church for the **view★★.** The church has a fine wood interior with a ceiling like the hull of a ship.

Return to Cabot Trail. After South Harbour, take coast road.

This is a pretty route with fine **views★** of Aspy Bay, its sand bar and the pink cliffs of Cape North. After White Point, the road turns south to **Neil's Harbour★** (Pop 283), a charming little fishing village with an artificial harbour beside a sandy bay.

Rejoin Cabot Trail.

This is a splendid drive along the coast especially after **Black Brook Cove.** Pink rocks stretch into the sea with green forest inland. There are many little bays and coves. Ahead Cape Smoky and Middle Head can be made out, sometimes rising from a mist which reminds visitors of the Scottish Highlands.

The Ingonishs. – Pop 1 262. The relative solitude of the Trail is left behind. The various Ingonishs - Ingonish Centre, Ingonish Beach, Ingonish Harbour, etc, form a resort centre popular for fishing, boating, swimming (fine sandy beaches), golf, tennis and skiing in winter. Many cruise ships stop over in Ingonish Harbour. The bay itself is cut into two parts - north and south - by Middle Head, the location of **Keltic Lodge,** one of Canada's best known resort hotels. It has a fine setting on this narrow peninsula with **Cape Smoky** towering out of the sea (369 m - 1 210 ft) to the south. Sometimes this headland is partially obscured by cloud which is the origin of its name "smoky".

View from Cape Smoky★★. – On a clear day, there is a splendid view from the top of the **chairlift** *(on Cabot Trail after South Ingonish Harbour; daily July - Labour Day; $3.00; single trip 13 min).* The south and north bays of Ingonish Harbour can be seen as well as Middle Head, Keltic Lodge, Ingonish Island and the various settlements around the bay.

■ **THE GAELIC COAST**

From Cape Smoky to Baddeck *89 km - 55 miles*

The Cabot Trail climbs over Cape Smoky and then drops again with good **views**★. After that, it descends the coast a little inland passing several Gaelic fishing villages. Offshore are the **Bird Islands,** a sanctuary where vast numbers of sea birds nest in summer. The Trail rounds St. Ann's Harbour with some fine views after Goose Cove but especially at South Gut St. Ann's.

Gaelic College★. – *Summer school in July and Aug ;* ☎ *295-2877.* Founded in 1939 by the Reverend A.W.R. MacKenzie, this college offers immersion courses in an ancient culture. Young people from all over North America vie to go there and "have the gaelic". It is the only school on the continent which teaches the Gaelic language and the arts and crafts of the Highlander - bagpipe music, clan law, Gaelic singing, Highland dancing and the hand weaving of family and clan tartans. Visitors may see students performing Highland flings and sword dances.

In August, a **Gaelic Mod** is held for a week when prizes are awarded to the best performers in each field *(for details, contact the College).*

Giant MacAskill Highland Pioneers Museum. – *On campus of Gaelic College. Open daily mid May - mid Oct ; $1.00 ; snack bar.*

This small museum displays some of the effects of Angus MacAskill of Cape Breton who grew to be 236 cm - 7 ft 9 ins in height and weighed 193 kg - 425 lbs. He died in 1863 at the age of 38 after touring in the United States with his extreme opposite, the midget Tom Thumb, who danced on the palm of MacAskill's open hand.

(after photo by Canadian Government Office of Tourism)

Bagpipers

Alternative Route★. – *22 km - 14 miles by Rte 312 and Trans-Canada Hwy.* This road crosses St. Ann's Bay via a narrow spit of land which divides the bay from St. Ann's Harbour. At the end of the spit, there is a ferry across the 270 m - 300 yd outlet *(24 hr service ; cars 50¢ ; hoot to summon ferry).*

Excursion to Great Bras d'Or★. – *18 km - 11 miles NE along Trans-Canada Hwy from South Gut St. Ann's.* The road climbs up Kelly's Mountain with a fine **view**★ of the harbour, spit of land and ferry from above. It crosses the Cape Dauphin peninsula and descends to the Great Bras d'Or. There are fine **views**★ of this stretch of water, the bridge which spans it and, in the distance, the city of **Sydney** (Pop 29 444) with the chimneys of its steel mill.

Return to Cabot Trail.

The Trail returns to the starting point at Baddeck along Baddeck Bay. On entering the community on Route 205, there are good views of its site.

FORT BEAUSEJOUR ★★ New Brunswick _____

Maps pp. 10 and 187
Just off Trans-Canada Hwy at Aulac near Nova Scotia border.
Open daily mid May - mid Oct ; National Historic Park ; self-guided tour - ask for brochure ; ☎ *(506) 536-0720*

Today, the exceptional thing about Fort Beausejour is its impressive panoramic **view**★★ over the surrounding country *(since this area experiences frequent fog and rain, this view may not be available).* It overlooks the Cumberland Basin, an arm of Chignecto Bay, as well as the Missiguash River valley and the Tantramar Marshes. The latter were reclaimed from the sea by an extensive system of dikes built by the pioneer Acadian settlers.

Fort Beausejour stands on the **Chignecto Isthmus,** the narrow strip of land which today joins the provinces of New Brunswick and Nova Scotia but which once marked the division between French and British lands. The Acadians first settled in this area which they called **Beaubassin** in 1672. After the Treaty of Utrecht ceded mainland Nova Scotia to Britain in 1713, they found themselves in the middle of border conflict. The British built Fort Lawrence on their side of the isthmus, the French Fort Beausejour on theirs. In 1755 a force led by Colonel Robert Monckton captured the latter and renamed it Fort Cumberland, a name it retained until it became a National Park in 1926. Immediately after its capture, the Acadians of the area were deported *(p. 186).* The fort was considerably strengthened by the British and it withstood an attack in 1776 by New England settlers sympathetic to the American Revolution ; it has seen no further military action.

Visit. – Just outside the earthworks of the fort, there is a Visitor Centre, housed in a stone building with a steeply pitched roof, which has interesting displays on the history of the fort, on the Acadians, on the Chignecto Isthmus and on the later history of the region. The earthworks themselves are in good repair but no buildings remain inside.

In the peak summer season,
you may have difficulty finding hotel accommodation.
We advise you to make reservations in advance.

FREDERICTON ★ New Brunswick

Maps pp. 10 and 186 – Pop 43 723 – Tourist Office ☎ (506) 455-9426

Set on a bend of the wide and placid **Saint John River** opposite the point where the Nashwaak River joins it, Fredericton, the provincial capital of New Brunswick, is a quiet city of elm lined streets and elegant houses. The French governor of Acadie, Joseph Robineau de Villebon, constructed a fort at the mouth of the Nashwaak in 1692. It was soon abandoned but a settlement of Acadians called St. Anne's Point grew up and survived until the Seven Years' War (p. 146).

However, Fredericton's real start in life came, like Saint John's, with the arrival of the **Loyalists** in 1783. The settlement they founded complete with college - now the University of New Brunswick, was chosen as the capital of New Brunswick with the creation of that province in 1784. Governor Thomas Carleton considered it a more central site and less open to sea attack than Saint John, the more obvious choice. He called the new capital Fredericton after the second son of George III, and it soon became an elegant and gracious place to live. Social life revolved around the governor and the military garrison. Garden parties, gala dinners and visits from Royalty were the order of the day.

In many ways, little has changed this century. The vast majority of the population work either for the Provincial Government or are involved with the university. Fredericton is also New Brunswick's cultural centre, a factor which is at least partly due to the munificence of one man.

Lord Beaverbrook. – Born William Maxwell Aitken in Maple, Ontario, in 1879 and raised in Newcastle, New Brunswick, Lord Beaverbrook was a successful businessman in Canada before he left for England in 1910. He entered politics and was elevated to the peerage in 1917 taking his title from a small place in New Brunswick. He formed Beaverbrook Newspapers and built up a vast empire on Fleet Street. During the Second World War he held several key cabinet posts and was very influential in the government of **Winston Churchill.** He died in 1964. Although most of his life was spent away from New Brunswick, he never forgot it. In addition to many gifts to the town of Newcastle, he built and endowed the Beaverbrook Art Gallery in Fredericton, helped finance the **Playhouse Theatre,** home of New Brunswick's premier dramatic company, and donated the money for several of the buildings of the **University of New Brunswick.**

■ SIGHTS time : 3 hours

One of Fredericton's most attractive features is the strip of parkland known as **The Green**★ which stretches along the southern bank of the Saint John River.

Beaverbrook Art Gallery★★. – Open daily except hols ; $1.00 ; ☎ 455-6551.

This unique art gallery was the vision of one man. Lord Beaverbrook designed and built the simple one storey structure overlooking the Saint John River, filled it with a collection of paintings he had personally selected, then gave it to the people of New Brunswick. Opened in 1959, it has become the major art centre of Atlantic Canada and well known internationally for its collection.

On entering the gallery, the view of the Saint John River through the enormous window in the entrance is immediately striking. Beside it hangs the huge surrealistic canvas of **Santiago el Grande** by Salvador Dali, one of the gallery's masterpieces. This remarkable work depicts St. James on a horse being carried upward into heaven.

One wing of the gallery is devoted to a particularly fine selection of **British Art,** the most comprehensive in Canada and especially strong in its portraits. There are some fine examples of the great British painters of the 18th century (Gainsborough, Reynolds, Romney, etc) and also more recent works, notably Graham Sutherland's portrait of Lord Beaverbrook. A second wing is devoted to **Canadian works** which are regularly rotated. Among them are some fine paintings by Cornelius Krieghoff.

The gallery has recently opened a new East Wing comprising the Hosmer-Pillow-Vaughan Gallery and the Sir Max Aitken Gallery. The former displays continental European paintings, tapestries and furniture from 15-19th centuries ; the latter British portraits and landscapes from 17-19th centuries, both in period settings. The gallery also features an important collection of 18th and 19th century English porcelain.

Legislative Building★. – Guided tours daily mid June - mid Sept ; weekdays rest of year ; 1/2 hr ; ☎ 453-2527.

Opposite the Art Gallery stands this attractive building with its small silver dome constructed in 1880.

The tour enables visitors to see the Assembly Chamber with its tiered balcony and portraits of **George III** and **Queen Charlotte** by Joshua Reynolds, and also the Parliamentary Library which is reached by a striking wooden spiral staircase.

FREDERICTON★

Christ Church Cathedral★. – This elegant stone church with its slender spire stands surrounded by trees and the attractive frame houses built by the Loyalists when they first settled in Fredericton. Built 1845-53, it is a fine example of decorated Gothic architecture, modelled on the parish church of St. Mary in Snettisham, Norfolk. The gracious interior is dominated by the pointed wooden ceiling known as a **hammer beam roof.** At the entrance to the south transept, there is a cenotaph with a **marble effigy** of the Rt. Rev. John Medley, the first bishop of Fredericton. This is similar to effigies found in Europe and extremely rare in North America.

Military Compound★. – The central location of this compound, which once stretched from Queen Street to the river between Regent and York Streets, shows the importance of the infantry garrison in the early life of Fredericton. (This is still true today as Canadian Armed Forces Base Gagetown, the country's major military training area, lies just to the southeast.) Today, only a few of the original buildings remain but there are plans to restore the entire compound.

The old parade ground is now a pleasant park (**Officers' Square**), and the site in summer of a **Changing of the Guard** ceremony performed by students in the Reserve dressed in the turn-of-the-century uniforms of the Royal Canadian Regiment *(Mon - Fri ; mid July - August ; 10am).* On one side of the Square there is a three storey stone building with white arches at ground floor level. Built in 1839 and added to in 1851, this was once the **Officers' Quarters.**

A few blocks to the west the old **Guard House (A)** built in 1827 can be seen. It stands close to the **Soldiers' Barracks (B)**, a stone building with red painted wooden terraces. Both have been restored and suitably furnished *(guided tours daily mid May - Labour Day ; 15 min each).*

York - Sunbury Historical Society Museum (M). – *In old Officers' Quarters. Open Mon - Sat mid May - Labour Day, Sun in July and Aug ; Mon, Wed and Fri afternoons rest of year ; $1.00 ;* ☎ *455-6041.*

This museum has military exhibits recalling the elegant and gay life of Fredericton as a British Garrison town and a reconstruction of a First World War trench in memory of the many New Brunswickers who lost their lives at this time ; also domestic exhibits which include fine examples of Loyalist furniture.

EXCURSION

King's Landing Historical Settlement★★. – 37 km - 23 miles. Description p. 213.

FUNDY National Park ★★ New Brunswick
Maps pp. 10 and 186 – 77 km – 48 miles from Moncton by Rte 114. Open daily ; admission to National Parks p. 21 ; camping ; hiking ; information centre near eastern entrance ; ☎ (506) 887-2000

Note : the Bay of Fundy is notorious for its fogs, thus the views described below may be obscured.

This park extends about 13 km - 8 miles along the rugged coastline of the Bay of Fundy. Cliffs rise steeply from the sea to form an area of rolling parkland cut by rivers and streams in deep valleys. The Bay of Fundy tides *(p. 185)* rise and fall about 9 m - 29 ft in the park (sometimes more). Thus the bays and coves at the mouths of the rivers have vast tidal flats to explore at low tide with a wide array of marine life - limpets, barnacles, sea anemones and sand hoppers.

Eastern Park Entrance. – From the park gate, there is a fine **view★** of the tranquil Upper Salmon River, the hills to the north, the small fishing village of Alma, Owl's Head and the Bay of Fundy. If possible, try to visit this place at both high and low tides to appreciate the difference.

Herring Cove. – *11 km - 7 miles from entrance.* At the end of the road, there is a good **view★** of Herring Cove from above and a display on the tides of the Bay of Fundy. A path leads down to the cove which has tidal pools full of life at low tide.

Point Wolfe★★. – *10 km - 6 miles from entrance.* The road crosses the Wolfe River by a wooden covered bridge. Below the bridge is a waterfall, dam and small gorge by which the river enters Wolfe Cove. Once a sawmill existed at this spot and the dam was built to collect the logs floated downstream from the forests of the north. A small community grew up around the mill and there were wharves in the cove at which schooners loaded the sawn wood. Today, only the bridge and dam remain.

At the end of the road, a path leads to the cove with good **views★★** on the descent. At low tide, the sand and rock pools are alive with small creatures.

GLACE BAY ★★ Nova Scotia
Maps pp. 11 and 187 – Pop 21 466

This sprawling Cape Breton town has been in the centre of a coal mining area since the days of the French regime when soldiers from Louisbourg found coal in the cliffs at **Port Morien.** They named the bay *glace* after the ice they found in it. The whole region is underlain with bituminous coal seams which dip seaward under the Atlantic. By the late 19th century a large number of coal mines were operating and, when iron ore deposits were found nearby in Newfoundland, a steel industry grew up in the **Sydney** area using the coal as coke in the refining process. The early 20th century saw immigrants pouring into the area. Some, unable to speak English, pinned a note on their coats with two words on it - "Glace Bay" knowing only that Glace Bay meant jobs.

By the early 1950s, however, the demand for coal had dropped. Oil and gas replaced it as fuel. The mines began to shut and economic depression hit Cape Breton. The Federal government stepped in and set up the **Cape Breton Development Corporation.** Today, with the renewed interest in coal as a fuel, several mines are in operation again producing coking coal for refining steel and thermal coal for making electricity.

Cape Breton Miners' Museum★★. – At Quarry Point, follow signs from town. Open daily mid June - Labour Day ; $1.00 ; mine tour 30 Min ; $2.00 ; protective clothing provided ; restaurant ; ☎ 849-4522.

This museum has displays on the formation of coal, on early coal mining methods and equipment, and on modern day methods. There are also films (20-30 min) on the industry in Cape Breton.

The **mine tours** are conducted by retired miners who have spent up to fifty years working the mines. They explain everything about mining past and present with many tales from their own experiences. Visitors walk down a sloping tunnel under the Atlantic in part of the old Ocean Deeps Colliery (note : mine ceilings are low) to see the coal face and mining machinery (coal samples can be collected as souvenirs).

Beside the museum building, there is a reconstructed **miners' village.** At one time, the mining company supplied all the houses and ran the store where transactions were carried out by means of credit secured against the wages a miner earned. Thus, it sometimes happened that, after a week of toil, a miner drew no pay and found instead that he owed the store for food, clothes and the other necessities of life. In addition to the store, a miner's house of 1850-1900 has been recreated, and there is a restaurant serving good home cooking.

Use the Map of Principal Sights (pp 4-11) and the Suggested Automobile Tours (pp 22-27) to help you plan your vacation.

HALIFAX ★★ Nova Scotia

Maps pp. 10 and 187 – Metro Pop 277 727 – Tourist Office ☎ (902) 421-8736

The city of Halifax, capital of Nova Scotia, is situated on a deep inlet of the Atlantic Ocean which gives it one of the finest harbours in the world. The outer part of the inlet is 6.5 km - 4 miles long and it is lined with docks and piers where it narrows. The inner harbour - called the **Bedford Basin,** is 5 km - 3 miles long by 2.5 km - 1 1/2 miles wide, very deep and protected by the boot-shaped peninsula on which the city stands. Despite recent highrise construction, this peninsula is still dominated by a hill on top of which lies a star-shaped **citadel.** These two factors - natural harbour and fortress - were the reasons for Halifax's foundation.

Early History. – Halifax was founded in July 1749 when **Edward Cornwallis** and a large group of settlers arrived and constructed a fortified settlement. The idea of a fortress on the inlet called *chebucto* (big harbour) by the Indians was not new. Indeed the French had considered it themselves before settling for Cape Breton Island after the loss of mainland Nova Scotia in 1713 (p. 187). In fact it was due to the existence of Louisbourg (p. 205) that Halifax came into being. The New Englanders successfully captured the French fortress in 1744 only to see it returned to France at the end of the war. Their justified anger prodded the British government into building another fortress as a counterweight to Louisbourg.

From the start, therefore, Halifax was a military stronghold full of soldiers in the citadel and the other fortifications, and sailors off the numerous Royal Naval vessels always in the harbour. The military presence shaped the town from the balls and gatherings of the nobility - officers in both services - to the plethora of whorehouses along the wharves and beneath the Citadel. Indeed, even the law was martial and it was nearly a hundred years before Halifax achieved city status allowing its citizens some control of their own affairs.

The Royal Princes. – Halifax played home to two of the scapegrace sons of **George III** when they were forbidden to remain in England by their father. The future **William IV** spent his 21st birthday in wild revels off the port and passed many nights in the arms of Frances Wentworth, the future governor's wife.

His brother **Edward,** Duke of Kent, the future father of Queen Victoria, spent six years in Halifax as Commander in Chief. During this time he spent a fortune on defences for the city and established Halifax as part of the famous quadrilateral of British defences – the homeland, Gibraltar, Bermuda, Halifax. He was a rigid disciplinarian, his men being flogged or hanged for minor misdemeanours. He also established the first telegraph system in North America by which he could relay orders to his men from Annapolis Royal on the other side of the peninsula (p. 191) or from his lovenest on the Bedford Basin where his mistress the beautiful Julie St. Laurent lived.

The Halifax Explosion. – Halifax's history has not always been so colourful but its periods of prosperity have coincided with times of war whereas peace has often brought economic depression. The Napoleonic Wars, American Civil War, First and Second World Wars saw great military activity in Halifax, great wealth - and tragedy. During both World Wars the Bedford Basin was used as a convoy gathering point so that ships could cross the Atlantic in the safety of numbers to better protect themselves from German submarine attack. In December of 1917 the **Mont Blanc,** a French munitions ship, arriving to join one of these convoys had a fatal collision with a Belgian Relief ship, the **Imo,** in the Narrows. The *Mont Blanc* was carrying a lethal combination of picric acid, guncotton, T.N.T. and benzol. The explosion which followed the collision was the greatest man-made one the world had seen until the atom bomb was dropped on Hiroshima in 1945. The entire north end of Halifax was wiped out, rail yards and docks were destroyed, 1 400 people were killed outright, an estimated 600 died later, another 9 000 were injured and 199 were blinded. Windows were shattered as far as Truro 100 km - 60 miles away and the sound was heard 160 km - 100 miles away. All that was ever found of the *Mont Blanc* was a cannon in Albro Lake behind Dartmouth and an anchor shaft which landed in the woods across the North West Arm more than 3 km - 2 miles away (the crew however survived as they abandoned ship in time). There are people in Halifax today who, injured for life as children, are still receiving compensation.

HALIFAX★★

Halifax Today. – In addition to being the administrative centre of Nova Scotia, Halifax is the commercial and financial capital of the Atlantic Provinces, and an important centre for scientific research with six degree-granting universities and colleges in the immediate area. The military presence is still strong even though soldiers no longer man the Citadel and the other defences. Halifax is the Atlantic base of the **Canadian Navy** with a large naval dockyard and research establishment, the latter located in **Dartmouth.** This twin city of Halifax lies on the other side of the inlet connected to it by two bridges.

The port of Halifax handles more than 14.5 million metric tonnes - 16 million tons of cargo annually, and is especially busy in the winter when the St. Lawrence Seaway *(p. 170)* is closed to shipping. Apart from a large container terminal and autoport, there are shipyards for the building and repairing of vessels.

Special dates in Halifax are : July 24th, Natal Day, when the anniversary of the founding of the city is celebrated, mid August for the Nova Scotia Festival of the Arts, and late September for the Joseph Howe Festival.

■ **SIGHTS** *time : 1 day – plan p. 203*

The Citadel★★. – Behind the commercial centre of Halifax rises Citadel Hill - much as Mount Royal rises above Montréal *(p. 167)*. Once a tree-covered bluff, the hill has been levelled off to build the series of fortifications that have graced it since the 18th century. The Citadel is easily approached on foot from downtown or driven around on Citadel Road. There are excellent **views★★** of the city, harbour, the Dartmouth shore, little George's Island and the Angus McDonald suspension bridge. Note in particular the attractive **Clock Tower★** which has become the symbol of Halifax. The original was ordered by Prince Edward with four faces and bells to ring out the hours. Restored in 1962, it remains a memento to the punctiliousness of that rigid disciplinarian.

The Clock Tower

Interior of Citadel. – *Open daily 9am - 5pm ; until 8pm in summer ; guided tours 45 min ; snack bar ; National Historic Park ;* ☎ *426-5080.*

Three citadels occupied this site before the present star-shaped masonry structure was begun in 1828 on the orders of the Duke of Wellington. The fortress is entered by a bridge over a dry moat. In the centre is a large parade ground where soldiers in 19th century uniforms can sometimes be seen performing guard duties. Visitors can climb on the ramparts and look at the guns which were the Citadel's main defence. They can also walk beneath the moat by tunnel, noting the thickness of the walls, to the ravelins built in the outer perimeter. These structures added greatly to the strength of the fortress as they were shell-proof. Also built into this outer wall is a musketry gallery from which invaders could be shot at if they succeeded in entering the moat.

Tides of History★★. – This excellent audio-visual display *(50 min)* graphically illustrates the history of Halifax and its defences which have ebbed and flowed with the "tides of history". It forms a good introduction to the city.

Army Museum. – Housed in the casemates, this museum has some interesting models of the Halifax area in addition to a collection of weapons, uniforms and decorations.

Other Displays. – There is a display on gunpowder in the old powder magazine, and exhibits on communications and the construction of the Citadel. A reproduced defence casemate and garrison cell can also be visited.

Historic Properties and the Harbour★★. – The area on both sides of Lower Water Street between Duke Street and the Cogswell interchange is commonly known as Historic Properties. There are several 19th century stone warehouses and wooden structures which have been completely renovated and now house interesting shops and studios, restaurants and pubs with outdoor seats overlooking the harbour. The streets have been closed to traffic making a pleasant pedestrian area and the space between two of the warehouses has been enclosed to form an attractive mall.

Various companies offer harbour tours, sometimes in a sailing vessel.

Harbour Cruise★★ (A). – *Departs from Privateers' Wharf. Daily June - mid Oct ; 2 hrs ; $9.25 ; snack bar ;* ☎ *423-7783.*

The best tour of the port and the environs of Halifax is however given by the *Haligonian III.* An interesting commentary explains the numerous things seen, such as the Halifax shipyards where 7 000 vessels were repaired during the Second World War ; the vast naval dockyards with destroyers, preservers, submarines and other vessels ; the National Harbours Board terminals with a huge grain elevator *(busier in winter when the St. Lawrence Seaway p. 170 is closed to shipping) ;* and the container terminal where giant gantry cranes load the strange-shaped ships specially constructed to carry containers.

The cruise rounds Point Pleasant and enters the **North West Arm★** *(plan p. 204),* a lovely stretch of water bordered by expensive homes and yacht clubs, making a complete contrast to the harbour.

Maritime Museum of the Atlantic★★. – *Open daily except hols in winter ;* ☎ *429-8210.*

Located on the waterfront with a view of Halifax harbour, this interesting museum has a variety of small craft, ship models, photographs and displays on maritime history. Note in particular the restored **ship's chandlery** housed in an old warehouse where a range of mariner's equipment is exhibited. Sections are also devoted to the days of sail and the age of steam.

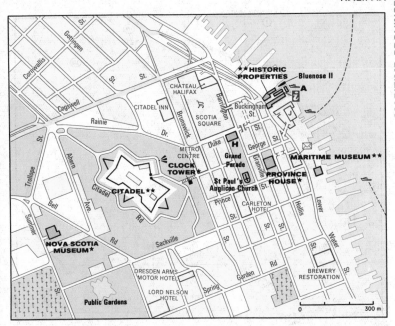

Outside, the **CSS Acadia**, a steamship built in 1913 for the Canadian Hydrographic Service, is moored at the museum's wharf. She can be boarded *(summer months only)*. Sometimes the **Bluenose II** is also moored here. This replica of the schooner which captured the International Fishermen's trophy in 1921 and held onto it throughout her twenty year career *(see also p. 192)* was constructed in 1963 as a goodwill ambassador for Nova Scotia. In summer, when she is not employed in this role visiting foreign ports, she gives cruises in Halifax harbour *(July and Aug, three times daily except Mon ; 2 hrs ; $10.00 ; ☎ 422-2678)*.

Province House★. – *Main entrance on Hollis St. Guided tours daily except Sun, and Sat and hols in winter ; 20 min ; ☎ 424-5982.*

Completed in 1819 this Georgian structure built of sandstone houses the Legislative Assembly of Nova Scotia. This institution has existed since 1758 – though not in this building. The tour includes a visit to the **Red Chamber** where the Council used to meet. Note the twin portraits of *Caroline of Anspach,* wife of George II, and her father-in-law *George I.* His portrait was sent from England in 1820 in error for one of his son !

The **Assembly Chamber** and **Legislative Library** are also visited on the tour. The latter, with its twin curving staircases, was at one time the Supreme Court of Nova Scotia. It was in this room in 1835 that the journalist **Joseph Howe** defended himself against the charge of criminal libel. His acquittal is counted as the beginning of a free press in Nova Scotia. He later entered politics, led a fight against Confederation *(p. 209)* but eventually joined the Dominion Government in Ottawa. There is a statue of him in the Library and another outside the building in the grounds.

Finally, the tour visits the Office of the Chief Clerk where two sculptures of falcons can be seen without heads. This execution was performed in the height of anti American feeling in the 1840s because the birds looked too much like the American eagle.

Grand Parade. – This pleasant square, bordered by **City Hall (H)** at one end and by **St. Paul's Anglican Church** at the other, has been the centre of Halifax since its founding. The militia mustered here, the town crier proclaimed the news and sedan chairs could be hired. The small timber-framed church was built in 1750 and is the oldest Protestant church in Canada.

Nova Scotia Museum★. – *Entrance on Summer St. Open daily except Mon and hols in winter ; ☎ 429-4610.*

This museum gives a comprehensive picture of the province by covering geological, historical, social and natural (flora and fauna) aspects. On entering, a beautifully restored stagecoach used on the Yarmouth to Tusket run in the late 19th century can be seen. Note also the Micmac Indian displays, the furniture and glass of the early settlers, the natural history dioramas, and the room devoted to marine life especially the whales and sharks.

The museum also maintains numerous historical houses in various parts of the province. These are indicated in the text of the appropriate places.

Point Pleasant Park★. – *Plan p. 204. Closed to cars ; parking on Point Pleasant Drive at Tower Rd and near container terminal ; snack bar.*

This lovely park situated at the southernmost point of the Halifax peninsula has fine **views★★** of Halifax harbour and the North West Arm. It is also a good place from which to observe the **Bluenose II** cruising with sails extended. There are many paths and trails as well as facilities for barbecueing, picnicking and swimming along its shores. It was for many years dominated by the military who filled it with batteries and forts. The remains of some of these can be seen.

Prince of Wales Martello Tower (B). – *Open daily mid June - Labour Day ; National Historic Park ; ☎ 426-5080.*

This circular stone tower was erected in 1796 by Prince Edward. It was the first in North America and indeed the prototype of what came to be called a **Martello Tower.** This design was adapted by Prince Edward from a tower on Mortella Point in Corsica which had proved almost impregnable. The idea was to combine barracks, storehouse and gun platform in a

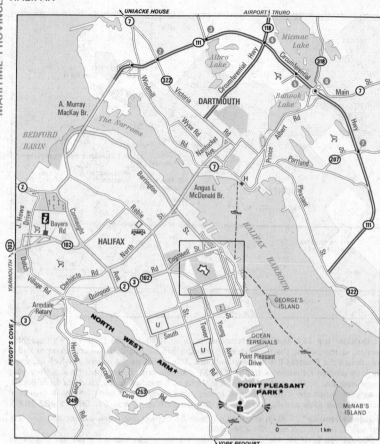

self-defensible unit with immensely thick walls and no access except a removable stairway to the upper floor. Later, many of these towers were built in Canada and indeed along the coast of England to counter invasion by the troops of Napoleon. The viability of such towers as defensive fortifications ended in the 1870s when rifled artillery and steam and ironclad ships were developed.

The Prince of Wales Tower, named by Edward for his brother the future **George IV,** was built to overlook and guard Halifax Harbour – a fact it is difficult to appreciate today due to the high trees which have grown up around it. Inside, the powder magazines and the gun emplacements on the roof can be seen.

Public Gardens. – *Plan p. 203. Open daily May - Oct, dawn - dusk.*

This 7 ha - 17 acre park was opened to the public in 1867. It is a fine example of a Victorian garden complete with ornate bandstand, weeping trees, ponds, fountain, statues and formal plantings.

EXCURSIONS

Peggy's Cove★★. – *43 km - 27 miles. Description p. 193.*

Uniacke House★. – *40 km – 25 miles NW by Rtes 7 and 1, in Mount Uniacke. Open daily mid May - mid Oct ; Nova Scotia Museum ; ☎ 429-4610.*

Set in pleasant gardens near a lake stands this fine example of plantation style colonial architecture with its wide portico rising the two storeys of the house. It was constructed 1813-15 by Richard Uniacke, Attorney General of Nova Scotia 1797-1830. The interior looks today as it did in 1815 with the original furnishings of the Uniacke family.

York Redoubt★. – *Map p. 194. 11 km – 7 miles by Rte 253. Open daily mid June - Labour Day ; grounds open all year ; picnic area ; National Historic Site ; ☎ 426-5080.*

The first defences on Sandwich Point were constructed in 1793 but they were extensively strengthened by Prince Edward. He built a tower which was an integral part of his signal telegraph system. Extensive renovations were made later to the redoubt, named by Edward for his brother the Duke of York. Indeed, it continued in military use as late as the Second World War when it was the centre for coordinating the defence of harbour and city against German attack.

The **command post,** which is a maze of tunnels beneath a tower, can be visited. The tower contains displays on Halifax's fortifications, and from it on fine days there are good **views★** of the harbour.

Along the walls of the Redoubt are huge 250 mm – 10 inch rifled muzzle-loading cannon, and in the adjoining buildings there is a collection of military equipment including a furnace to heat up cannon balls and the tool used to carry the hot balls to the guns (balls were only heated for smooth-bore cannon).

HOPEWELL CAPE ★★ New Brunswick

Map p.186 – Pop 144 – 35 km - 22 miles S of Moncton by Rte 114

Near this little village overlooking Shepody Bay, part of the larger Chignecto Bay, is a collection of phenomena of great interest known as **The Rocks★★** *(signed from Rte 114,*

parking, cafeteria, stairs to beach). These red sandstone rock formations on the beach stand as much as 15 m - 50 ft high. They have been cut off from the cliffs and sculpted into weird shapes by the action of the Bay of Fundy tides *(p. 185)* aided by wind and frost. At high tide, they are tiny tree covered islands ; at low tide, they become giant "flowerpots" with narrow bases widening at the top to support, in some cases, balsam fir and dwarf black spruce. At low tide, visitors can walk around them and look at the crevices in the cliffs which in time will become new flowerpots.

Flowerpot Rocks

However, be sure to mount the stairs at the time posted at their head – the tide rises about 9.8 m - 32 ft at this point ! *(Morning light is best for photography.)*

LOUISBOURG ★★★ Nova Scotia

Maps pp. 11 and 187 – 37 km - 23 miles S of Sydney by Rte 22.
National Historic Park ; open daily June - Sept ; $2.00 ; no cars allowed beyond Reception Centre, bus to fortress ; guided tours 2 hrs ; restaurant ; coffee shop ;
☏ *(902) 733-2280*

Note : although the weather is generally good, visitors should be prepared for cool temperatures, rain and fog. Good walking shoes are also recommended.

Louisbourg was once the great fortress of New France guarding the entrance to the St. Lawrence, the approach to Québec. Not only did it have the largest garrison in North America but it was an important commercial centre with a harbour full of fishing boats. Captured and destroyed it lay in ruins for nearly two centuries.

Today, it is rising again from the largest reconstruction project ever undertaken by the Canadian Government. One quarter of the fortress will be rebuilt following the original plans. Meticulous care is taken to make sure everything is as authentic as possible. The furnishings are either original or copies made in some cases by the same companies in France that produced the originals.

The Not-so-Impregnable Fortress.

– The French had long planned a fortress in what is now Nova Scotia. They even considered the site of Halifax *(p. 201)* but in 1713 they lost mainland Nova Scotia to the British. Thus an eastern peninsula on Isle Royale (now Cape Breton) was chosen and the construction of a fortified town was commenced in 1719. The plan, prepared in the style of the great French military engineer, **Vauban,** called for a star-shaped fort and a large harbour. These took so long to build and were so expensive (equivalent of about $200 million – the reconstruction to date has cost $25 million) that **Louis XV** said he expected to see Louisbourg rising above the Atlantic ! Part of the reason for the expense was the site. The boggy marshland caused the mortar to crumble and buildings collapsed (a problem also encountered during the reconstruction). Another reason was the corruption rife among French officials who

The Porte Dauphine

lined their pockets at the expense of the King. Among them was the **Intendant Bigot** who was blamed later for the fall of New France *(p. 175)*. Yet another reason was the living conditions and lack of discipline among the common soldiers which led them to mutiny in 1744.

In 1745 before it was really finished the "impregnable" fortress was attacked by 4 000 New Englanders. Less than two months later it surrendered. However, three years afterwards the British returned it to King Louis without consulting the colonists who had lost many lives in its capture and whom it threatened daily. The furore this caused in New England led to the founding of Halifax as a counter-fortress *(p. 201)*. And such is the unpredictability of governments that only ten years later Louisbourg was under siege again this time by British regulars. An impetuous 31-year old Brigadier named **James Wolfe** managed to land and the fate of the "impregnable" fortress was sealed – it surrendered for a second time. Wolfe went on the next year to capture Québec *(p. 175)*. Louisbourg was destroyed to make sure it never threatened British interests again.

LOUISBOURG ★★★

■ **VISIT** *time : 1/2 day*

In the **Reception Centre** there are audio visual presentations on the history of Louisbourg and on the reconstruction plans. Then visitors are taken to the fortress by bus. At the **Porte Dauphine,** soldiers ask questions before allowing anyone to enter to make sure they are not spies ! Inside, the town looks very French. The houses are built of wood or roughcast masonry with roofs of bark, board, shingle or slate. Some are open to the public *(the number increases every year)* including a **bakery,** where visitors can buy the type of bread King Louis' troops queued up for in 1744, and the **Hotel de la Marine,** where an 18th century meal can be eaten off earthenware and pewter. Near the latter stands a high wooden gate, **Porte Frédéric,** the entrance through which important visitors were once ushered from the harbour. Roaming the streets and inside the houses the "inhabitants" will be seen. In all about 100 people work as animators in Louisbourg.

King's Bastion (Bastion du Roi)★★. – In this building, the quarters of the military men stationed in Louisbourg have been recreated. The **Governor's Apartment★★** consists of ten elegant rooms as tastefully and comfortably furnished as anywhere in the 18th century world. The **Officers' Quarters** are not as elegant but are quite acceptable. The **Soldiers' Barracks,** however, have a raw spartan air and are not conducive to a long stay even though the damp lice-infested straw once used has not been recreated ! The soldiers who inhabited them will however be seen, the mutinous, slovenly look is deliberate.

MAITLAND ★ Nova Scotia

Maps pp. 10 and 187 – Pop 230

Once an important shipbuilding centre, Maitland on Cobequid Bay of the Minas Basin is best known for having been the site of the construction of the **William D. Lawrence,** the largest wooden ship ever built in Canada. Today, this industry exists no more but the remains of the wealth it created for some can be seen in the fine houses in the village.

W. D. Lawrence House★. – *On Rte 215. Open daily mid May - mid Oct ; Nova Scotia Museum ;* ☎ *(902) 261-2628.*

This is a splendid example of the great shipbuilders' and sea captains' houses in Nova Scotia. It stands two and a half storeys high surrounded by elm trees with a portico reminiscent of a ship's bridge with a double curved staircase. It was built by William Dawson Lawrence about 1870 to overlook his shipyard on the Shubenacadie River at the point where it joins Cobequid Bay. There is a good **view★** of the tidal flats from a lookout area across the road from the Lawrence house. In this shipyard, Lawrence constructed his *William D. Lawrence* gambling that he could double a ship's size without doubling her operating costs. Thus his ship was 80 m - 262 ft long with three masts the highest more than 60 m - 200 ft, and she weighed 2 459 tons. To complete her, Lawrence had to mortgage his house but his investment paid off handsomely. Launched in 1874 she sailed all over the world with many varied cargoes, a wonder to all who saw her.

The house contains most of its original furnishings including shipbuilding artifacts, pictures of 19th century ships and a 2 m - 7 ft model of the *William D. Lawrence.*

Opening hours of museums and other sights change frequently.
We advise you to telephone in advance to avoid disappointment.

MONCTON New Brunswick

Maps pp. 10 and 186 – Pop 54 743 – Tourist Office : City Hall, Main Street, ☎ (506) 853-3333

Set on a bend of the Petitcodiac River, Moncton is famous for its tidal bore which rushes up the river from the Bay of Fundy, and for its university, the only French college in Atlantic Canada. It was named after **Robert Monckton,** the commander of the British force that captured Fort Beausejour in 1755 *(p. 198).* The first settlers were German and Dutch families from Pennsylvania but they were joined later by many Acadians when the latter were allowed to return to British territory after the Deportation *(p. 188).* Today, one third of the population is French-speaking and it is generally considered the capital of *Acadie.*

Moncton has always been connected with transport. In the 19th century, it was a shipbuilding town, today it is a railway city. The headquarters of Canadian National Railways' Atlantic region are located here including rail repair shops and freight yards.

The Tidal Bore★. – The rise and fall of ocean tides is caused by the gravitational pull of the moon and to a lesser extent the sun on the earth's watery surface. Along ocean shores high tides occur every 12 hours and 25 minutes. In the open ocean, the ebb and flow of the tide is barely noticeable but in certain V-shaped bays or inlets the tide enters the broad end and literally piles up as it moves up the bay. This occurs in the Bay of Fundy which is 77 km - 48 miles wide at its mouth narrowing and becoming shallower along its 233 km - 145 mile length *(see also p. 185).* The tide is thus squeezed as it goes up the bay becoming a wave which varies from a ripple to several feet in height as it enters the rivers emptying into the bay. This wave is known as a "bore" which simply means any tidal wave of unusual height. At Moncton the bore varies from a few inches to nearly two feet. The highest bores occur when earth, moon and sun are in line.

Boreview Park. – *Off Main St by the river. Details of times of Bore available from Tourist Office ; arrive 15 min before bore to view river at its lowest level, and if possible return 2 hrs later to see it at high tide ; parking 25¢ per hour.*

This is the best place to view the tidal bore and the change in level of the Petitcodiac River. At low tide, the river is just a small stream in the centre of a vast bed of red mud. At high tide, it is 1.6 km - 1 mile wide with no mud visible. The tide changes the level by 7 m - 23 ft !

EXCURSION

Survival of the Acadians National Historic Site★. – *30 km - 19 miles SE by Rte 6 in St-Joseph. Open daily mid May - mid Oct 10am - 6pm ; ☎ (506) 758-9783.*

Maps, displays and audio-visual presentations trace the Acadians' long and hard struggle to maintain their distinctive culture, and illustrate their strength today.

This National Historic Site is located appropriately in **Collège St-Joseph**, the first Acadian institute of higher learning. Founded by the Reverend Camille Lefebvre in 1864, it trained Acadian leaders for nearly one hundred years before its amalgamation with the Université de Moncton. It was also the site of the first National Convention of Acadians in 1881. The Memramcook Valley including the community of St-Joseph is among the very few regions in which Acadians maintained continuous settlement despite the Deportation (p. 188).

PASSAMAQUODDY Bay and the FUNDY Islands ★★ New Brunswick

Maps pp. 10 and 186 - *Local map below*

Passamaquoddy Bay is an inlet of the Bay of Fundy between Maine and New Brunswick. It includes the estuary of the **St. Croix River** and has many islands and harbours along an irregular shoreline. A popular resort area, it is also famous for its lobsters and for its edible seaweed known as **dulse** a great New Brunswick delicacy. According to Indian legend, the islands were created by the god **Glooscap** who one day saw wolves about to attack a deer and a moose. He turned them all into islands. In 1604, the bay was selected by **Samuel de Champlain** as the site of his first settlement. With his followers, he spent the winter on St Croix Island (today in Maine) in the estuary of the river of the same name. They found it so bleak, however, that they moved across the Bay of Fundy to Nova Scotia in the next year *(p. 191)*. Finally, in 1783 the **Loyalists** arrived and settled St. Stephen, St. Andrews, St. George, Deer and Campobello Islands. They gave the bay its distinctive character of quiet rural charm and gracious living which has existed ever since.

St. Andrews★. – Pop 1 760. This charming little town at the end of a peninsula sticking out into Passamaquoddy Bay has a quaint main street – **Water Street,** lined with interesting boutiques, and quiet tree-lined avenues with elegant houses, many more than one hundred years old. Some indeed were floated lock, stock and barrel across the St. Croix estuary in 1842 when the Webster-Ashburton Treaty declared that river to be the Canadian – US border and some Loyalists discovered they were on the "wrong" side of it. St. Andrews became a prosperous mercantile and fishing town but today it is also a resort centre for summer visitors who like the quiet calm, the boating and fishing in pleasant surroundings. It supports the **Algonquin Hotel,** perhaps New Brunswick's foremost resort hotel. It has always been popular as a summer retreat. Among the famous Canadians who have owned homes here is **Sir William Van Horne,** President of the Canadian Pacific Railway Company *(p. 16)*.

Huntsman Marine Laboratory Museum and Aquarium★. – *At Brandy Cove. Open daily June - mid Sept ; $2.00 ; ☎ (506) 529-3979.*

This is an interesting little aquarium with tanks of fish and displays on the 200 mile fishing limit, sea bird migration routes, and salmon spawning in the Atlantic Provinces. The stars of the place are, however, three harbour seals which perform all kinds of antics for visitors. Films are shown regularly in the theatre.

St. Andrews Blockhouse. – *On Joe's Point Rd. Guided tours daily June - mid Sept ; 20 min ; National Historic Park.*

This square wooden structure with an overhanging second storey was constructed during the War of 1812. It stands on a small hill overlooking the harbour. Inside, there are displays on the settlement of the town and on the building of the blockhouse, which is unusual in that it was erected by the citizens at their own expense.

■ THE FUNDY ISLANDS★★

Visits to Deer, Campobello and Grand Manan Islands can be beautiful, however fogs and cold weather sometimes come off the Bay of Fundy even in summer.

Deer Island★. – Pop 868. *Government car ferry from Letete every 1/2 hr 8am - 5pm, later and earlier in mid summer ; 20 min ; ferry from Eastport, Maine, every hr mid May - mid Sept, 15 min, car and driver $6.00, passengers $1.00 ; ferry from Campobello Island - see below ; line ups for ferries at weekends and peak times.*

The most pleasant way to reach this island which nearly closes Passamaquoddy Bay is the ferry **trip**★ from Letete to Lord's Cove. It weaves in and out of other smaller islands

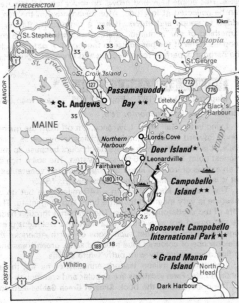

covered with birds. Deer Island itself is a quiet place inhabited by fishermen. **Northern Harbour** on its western side has an enormous lobster pound, the world's largest. By means of nets and fences, part of this narrow inlet has been made into a corral swept by the tide where lobsters are kept year round. There are smaller pounds at Leonardville and a sardine canning plant at Fairhaven. Just off the coast at the southern end of the island, there is a large whirlpool when the Fundy tides are running strong. It is called the **Old Sow** for the noise it makes. It is visible from Deer Island Point or from the ferry to Campobello Island.

Campobello Island★★. – Pop 1 424. *Car ferry from Deer Island late June - Labour Day, 25 min, car and driver $8.00, passengers $2.00 ; ☎ (506) 747-2168 ; or access by bridge from Lubec, Maine, non Americans need suitable visa or identification to enter USA. See also Michelin Green Guide to New England.*

The rather primitive ferry **trip★** from Deer Island passes the Old Sow whirlpool, the town of Eastport, Maine, and hundreds of birds, making it a pleasant way of reaching Franklin D. Roosevelt's "beloved island".

First settled in the 1770s, Campobello was named for the governor of Nova Scotia, **William Campbell,** and for its beauty. By the end of the 19th century it had become a summer retreat for wealthy Americans. This is still the case today and many fine "cottages" can be seen. Visitors are attracted by the island's sandy beaches, its picturesque coves and inlets where herring seiners and fish draggers tie up, its headlands and lighthouses, and by, last but not least, the International Park devoted to the memory of **Franklin D. Roosevelt.**

The future President of the United States first came to Campobello Island in 1883 - when he was one year old. After that he spent every summer on the island with his parents and later with his wife Eleanor. He taught his five children to enjoy and appreciate nature and he took them boating, boating and swimming much as he had done as a child. Then in 1921 tragedy struck. F.D.R. contracted polio after a swim in the chill Bay of Fundy waters. He left the island on a stretcher and did not return for twelve years – by that time he was President of the United States. In 1964, an International Park was set up jointly by the Canadian and American governments. It stands as a memorial to a great and brave man.

Roosevelt - Campobello International Park★★. – *Open daily late May - early Oct ; ☎ (506) 752-2922.*

The southern part of Campobello Island is preserved as natural parkland in memory of the pleasure F.D.R. derived from nature there. Several fine **drives★★** have been laid out through landscapes of forests, bogs, lakes, cliffs, beaches and the sea. Note in particular the view of Passamaquoddy Bay from Friar's Head *(turn right at sign marked Picnic Area just S of Visitors' Centre)* and that of Herring Cove from Con Robinson's Point *(follow Glensevern Rd E).*

The **Visitors' Centre** offers films on the life of Roosevelt which make a good introduction to the visit.

The red-shingled, green-roofed **cottage★** (34 rooms) which belonged to F.D.R. is built in Dutch colonial style. It is simply, almost rustically, furnished with just a few reminders of the fame of its owner : four water-colours on rice paper given to Mrs Roosevelt by Mme Chiang Kai-shek, and of his tragedy : the stretcher improvised by friends to carry him to the boat after he had contracted polio. The rooms on the west side especially the living room have pleasant views over Friar's Bay.

East Quoddy Head Lighthouse★. – *12 km – 7 1/2 miles from Visitors' Centre ; follow road N to Wilson's Beach, then gravel road to the Point.*

This lighthouse has a picturesque site overlooking Head Harbour Island.

Grand Manan Island★. – Pop 686. *Car ferry from Black's Harbour 3-5 times daily in summer, less frequently in winter ; 2 hrs ; cars $9.00, passengers $3.00 ; no reservations, line up in peak summer season ; snack bar ; ☎ (506) 662-3606 or 642-7317.*

The biggest of the islands, Grand Manan is noted for its rugged scenery including 120 m - 400 ft cliffs and picturesque harbours, for its large and varied bird population - in all about 230 species have been sighted including puffins, bold eagles and Arctic terns, and for its **dulse.** This edible seaweed grows on rocks under the water mainly in the Bay of Fundy and can be collected at low tide. After being dried in the sun, it can be eaten raw, toasted or added to soups and stews. It has a tangy salty flavour rich in iron and iodine, and it is something of an "acquired" taste. **Dark Harbour** on the rocky western coast of the island supplies some of the best dulse in the world. A natural rock breakwater across the mouth of the harbour is perfect for collecting and drying the purple seaweed.

PRINCE EDWARD ISLAND ★★

Maps pp. 10 and 187 – Pop 122 505 – *Local map below*

Access. – *See Introduction p. 189.*

Lying in the Gulf of St. Lawrence, cut off from the mainland by the **Northumberland Strait,** Prince Edward Island, Canada's smallest province, is a charming, attractive and peaceful place. It is very different from its neighbours because so much of its low, rolling countryside (highest point 142 m - 465 ft) is cultivated. The soil is rich and brick red in colour - the result of an excess of iron. All kinds of crops, fruit and vegetables are cultivated and livestock kept but it is especially famous for its **potatoes** *(p. 188).*

The island is about 225 km - 140 miles long but its width varies greatly because the coastline is very indented by large bays and long inlets. These have red sandy beaches and cliffs of red sandstone in places. The rivers run through beds of red soil and those roads that are not paved are also red. It is a neat and well-kept province almost entirely lacking the huge hoardings and other such signs of North American life. Instead, its landscapes are a kaleidoscope of colours : blue sea, red sand, green trees and crops, red soil and above them on fine days a blue sky with puffy white clouds.

About half a million visitors annually come for the peace and quiet, and the slow unhurried life. **Farm vacations** are popular and community **lobster suppers** are another speciality. The popularity of the book **Anne of Green Gables** also encourages people to visit Anne's island.

Ile-St-Jean. – Although Jacques Cartier claimed the Island for France in 1534 and named it Ile-St-Jean, there was no serious attempt to colonize it until the 18th century when a settlement called **Port La Joie** was founded near the present site of Charlottetown. Some of the Acadians fleeing the Deportation *(p. 188)* settled on the island and then it was captured by a British expedition under **Lord Rollo** in 1758. The population was deported except for a small settlement in the Malpeque area which was left untouched. These few Acadians who remained are the basis of the Island's French-speaking population of today.

The British Regime. – After the British take-over, St. John's Island as it became known was annexed to Nova Scotia. The land was divided into lots and given away to wealthy Englishmen on the condition that they organized settlement. Most of them did not do this, nor did they ever visit the island preferring to live in England. They did, however, petition the government to have the island declared a separate colony. After the American Revolution the population was bolstered by the arrival of many **Loyalists** and the name was changed to Prince Edward Island in 1799 in honour of the father of Queen Victoria *(p. 201).*

Confederation. – Prince Edward Island's population increased slowly but steadily in the 19th century with the addition of such people as the Selkirk settlers *(p. 211).* Agriculture, shipbuilding and fishing were the main occupations. In 1864, Charlottetown was the location of the historic meeting of the **Fathers of Confederation.** Representatives of Nova Scotia, New Brunswick and the Island, meeting to discuss maritime union, were joined by a delegation from Canada (then only Ontario and Québec). A union of all the British colonies in North America was discussed which led to Confederation in 1867. At first the Island refused to join this union but impending bankruptcy because of railway construction and heavy pressure from Britain eventually persuaded Islanders to change their minds, and the Island entered Confederation in 1873.

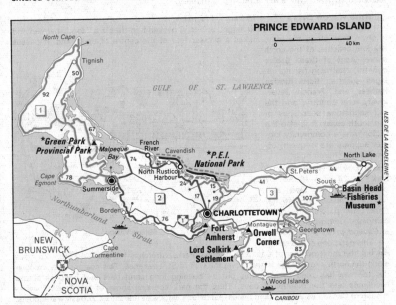

■ **CHARLOTTETOWN★** Pop 15 282 – Visit 2 hrs

Tourist Office : Royalty Mall, University Ave, ☎ (902) 892-2457

Situated on a sheltered arm of Northumberland Strait, Charlottetown is the Island's capital and commercial centre. It lies in the middle of a rich agricultural area, the produce of which is funnelled through its port. It is named for the elegant wife of George III and it is a city of large and spacious clapboard houses and big trees. An especially attractive area is **Victoria Park** with its **views★** of the harbour. The remains of **Fort Edward** built about 1800 can be seen, also **Government House,** the imposing white colonial style residence of the province's Lieutenant Governor.

Confederation Centre★★. – Queen St between Grafton and Richmond Sts. Open daily ; guided tours mid June - mid Sept, 30 min ; restaurant ; ☎ 892-2464.

This collection of grey concrete block structures was built to celebrate the 100th anniversary of the historic meeting of 1864. All the provinces in Canada contributed 15¢ per resident to meet the cost of construction and they make annual payments for its support. The main entrance is by **Memorial Hall** which has an interesting system of glass window structures on its roof to provide lighting. The Centre contains theatres, an art gallery, library, display areas, restaurant and the provincial archives. The **Art Gallery★** *(open daily except Mon in winter ; $1.00 in summer)* has a large collection of Canadian works. The exhibitions change frequently.

Province House★. – Richmond St beside above. Open daily except weekends and hols in winter ; ☎ 892-6278.

Note : when Legislature is sitting, certain rooms are not open to the public.

This three storey sandstone structure built 1843-47 houses the Provincial Legislature. The Legislative Chamber can be visited and also the famous room where representatives of Canada, Nova Scotia, New Brunswick and Prince Edward Island met to discuss union *(see above)*. **Confederation Chamber** is set out as it was in 1864. There are also displays and a slide show on that meeting.

PRINCE EDWARD ISLAND★★

■ SCENIC DRIVES★★ *Map p. 209*

The charm of Prince Edward Island lies in its lovely countryside and sea views. The best way of appreciating these is to follow the scenic drives worked out by the provincial government. They are easy to follow as they are clearly marked with separate symbols. Full details and maps can be obtained from any tourist office on the Island ; allow about one day for each drive.

① **Lady Slipper Drive**★. – *287 km - 178 miles. Information Centre on Rte 1A E of Summerside (open daily early June - mid Oct).*

Named for the pretty pink orchid which is the province's official flower, this drive follows the narrow indented western end of the Island in a figure of eight. It is usually less frequented than the other two but no less beautiful. There are many attractive villages and lovely views especially at the extreme western end. Along the way, the homes of the Island's Acadian population can be seen, and the drive touches **Malpeque Bay** famous for its oysters and fine sandy beaches. **Summerside** (Pop 7 828) is the chief community and the centre of a rich agricultural area.

Green Park Provincial Park★. – *Off Rte 12 near Port Hill. Usually open late June - Labour Day but not daily - telephone first ; $1.50 ; ☎ 892-9127.*

This park is devoted to shipbuilding, a major Island industry in the 19th century *(p. 188)*. Green Park was the home of James Yeo Jr. who owned one of the important shipyards. The distinctive house he built in the 1860s, with its high gables and cupola on the roof, can be visited. It was once the centre of business, political and social life of the area.

Nearby stands an **Interpretive Centre** with interesting displays and explanations on the importance of shipbuilding and the various stages of ship construction. Outside, there is a recreated shipyard with a full sized ship in frame.

② **Blue Heron Drive**★★. – *191 km - 119 miles.*

This drive, named for the long legged and long necked bird that is a keen fisherman and is often seen along the way, makes a circular tour of the centre of the Island. It passes

the fine beaches of the north shore, **Anne of Green Gables** country, charming fishing villages such as **North Rustico Harbour** and French River, lovely rural country, and the red sandstone seascapes of the south coast. It is also the region where community lobster suppers are frequent, often held in church halls.

Fishing Village

Prince Edward Island National Park★. – *24 km - 15 miles N of Charlottetown. Open daily ; for admission to National Parks see p. 21 ; beaches, camping ; information office in Cavendish ☎ 672-2211.*

This park, one of the smallest but the most popular of Canada's National Parks, stretches for about 40 km - 25 miles along the north shore of the Island facing the Gulf of St. Lawrence. This coast is very irregular but the sea has tried to even this out by building long sand bars and beaches across headlands and the mouths of bays. Thus the park contains some of the finest beaches in eastern Canada as well as sand dunes, sandstone cliffs, salt marshes and fresh water pools.

The best way to visit the park is to drive along the **Gulf Shore Road** to see the beaches and cliffs, especially Orby Head, take a walk in the dunes, and stop at the Park **Visitor Centre** in Cavendish for the slide presentations and exhibits *(open daily mid June - Labour Day).*

Green Gables. – *Near Cavendish in the Park. Open daily mid May - mid Oct ; ☎ 963-2675.*

This little green and white house was the one-time home of **Lucy Maud Montgomery.** After the death of her parents, Miss Montgomery lived here with her grandparents and in 1908 published **Anne of Green Gables,** one of the most popular children's books ever written. It tells the story of a young orphan girl adopted by a strict but kindly brother and sister who lived in a farm called Green Gables on the outskirts of Avonlea, Prince Edward Island. Once described by **Mark Twain** as "the sweetest creation of child life ever written", this story has so caught the imagination of its readers that thousands visit Green Gables every summer from as far away as Japan. The house is organized to reflect the story.

Every summer, a musical on the life of Anne is performed as part of the **Charlottetown Festival.** It is always the festival's most popular event. Miss Montgomery wrote many sequels to the story, the backgrounds for which can be seen all over the Island.

Fort Amherst National Historic Park. – *32 km - 20 miles S of Charlottetown on Rte 19 at Rocky Point. Open daily June - mid Oct ; ☎ 675-2220.*

Only the earthworks of this British fort built in 1758 stand today. They are on the site of Port La Joie, the French settlement of 1720. There are displays and a slide show in the Visitor Centre.

③ **Kings Byway**★. – *367 km - 228 miles. Information Centre on Rte 4 at Pooles Corner N of Montague (open daily early June - mid Oct).*

This drive at the eastern end of the Island is named for the county in which most of it lies. The northern section is less cultivated than other areas of the Island and it has some interesting fishing villages. Note especially **North Lake,** famous for its tuna fishing and as a centre for the collection of **Irish Moss.** This is a type of seaweed gathered on the shore, dried and used in soups or for industrial purposes. Lobster traps are also a common sight. A ferry to the Magdalen Islands (Iles de la Madeleine) leaves Souris regularly in summer *(p. 159).* In the south, Kings county is much more rural with lovely sea views over Northumberland Strait.

Basin Head Fisheries Museum★. – *Usually open mid June - mid Sept but not daily - telephone first ; $1.50 ;* ☎ *357-2966.*

Devoted to the life and work of the inshore fisherman, this fascinating museum has a fine site overlooking the Gulf of St. Lawrence and surrounded by rolling sand dunes. All the day-to-day equipment of an inshore fisherman is on display – boat, nets, hooks and other gear, whilst other artifacts and photographs recreate his life. On the shore, some recreated fishing shacks and an old cannery can be visited. There is also a box factory where various sizes of salt fish box are made.

Lord Selkirk Pioneer Settlement. – *Off Rte 1 at Eldon near Lord Selkirk Provincial Park. Open daily mid June - mid Sept ; $2.50 ; craft shop ;* ☎ *659-2425.*

In 1803, three ships set sail from Scotland carrying crofters (tenant farmers) who had lost their land in the big movement to enclose land to rear sheep *(p. 188)*. This expedition was financed by Thomas Douglas, **Lord Selkirk,** with the express purpose of helping some of his less fortunate fellow Scots. The settlers he brought to Prince Edward Island surmounted great difficulties and went on to create a flourishing settlement. *(See also the Red River Settlement, p. 93).*

This recreation is a tribute to these Highlanders. An example of the first type of shelter built by the new arrivals, no more than a crude wigwam, is on display. These were replaced by simple cabins with walls of undressed logs and roofs of bark covered with a thatch of grass and twigs. Finally, when the settlers were better established, they built two-storey houses of squared logs with dove-tailed corners and shingled roofs. The example of the latter in the settlement is an original home, the others are reconstructed.

Orwell Corner Rural Life Museum. – *Usually open late June - Labour Day but not daily - telephone first ; $1.50 ;* ☎ *651-2013.*

This site, recreating a late 19th century rural crossroads, preserves the flavour and spirit of the times. A farmhouse which also served as post office and general store can be visited along with animal barns, a church, school, community hall, forge and shingle mill.

SAINT JOHN ★★ New Brunswick

Maps pp. 10 and 186 - Metro Pop 114 048 - Tourist Office ☎ (506) 658-2990

Saint John always spelt out in full and without an apostrophe 's' (residents will quickly point out that **St. John's** is in Newfoundland) is the province's largest city, industrial centre and major port. Fondly called "fog city" by other New Brunswickers because of the dense sea mists which sometimes roll in off the Bay of Fundy, Saint John has a barren, rocky and hilly site at the point where the Saint John River joins the Bay. This site has created a city where few of the roads are straight and many are dead ends. Yet on a clear day in summer, when the wind blows the aroma of the big pulp and paper mill on the river away from the city, Saint John is an attractive and interesting place.

Part of Acadie. – In 1604 Samuel de Champlain and the Sieur de Monts *(p. 191)* landed briefly at the mouth of the river. Some years later another Frenchman, **Charles de la Tour,** founded a trading post there. In 1645 this was destroyed by his compatriot from Port Royal, de Menou d'Aulnay *(p. 190),* an act which issued in a period of trading rivalry among the French in Acadia in addition to the Anglo-French struggle. In 1763, the area was ceded to England by the Treaty of Paris and an English trading post was established. However, Saint John counts the year 1783 as its true beginning.

The Arrival of the Loyalists. – On May 18th 1783, a fleet of square-rigged ships sailed into the river mouth and more than 3 000 Loyalists landed. Overnight the tiny trading post became a boom town. (By the end of the year, 4 200 people had landed but many went north to settle the river valley and Fredericton). Those who came were mainly wealthy people who had lost everything or nearly everything during the American Revolution *(p. 99)* and had few if any of the pioneer skills necessary to carve new homes for themselves out of the wilderness. Somehow they survived and indeed went on to create a prosperous city of shipyards and trade along with a lively social life.

During the 19th century, Saint John was known as the **"Liverpool of America"** thriving as it did on shipbuilding and trade. Unfortunately a great fire in 1877 destroyed more than half of the city. Then as the era of wooden ships came to an end *(p. 188)* Saint John declined as did so many places in the Atlantic Provinces. Its port remained active but it was not until the 1960s that some general economic revival occurred. Then huge investments were made in pulp and paper, sugar and oil refining. A container shipping service was set up and a deep water terminal was built for tankers. There is still shipbuilding in Saint John but today the economy of the city is much more diversified.

Loyalist Days. – Once a year in July the city looks back to its foundation which it celebrates in style. Everyone dresses up in 18th century costume and the landing of the Loyalists is re-enacted. A large parade, street dances and sidewalk breakfasts complete the festival.

■ SIGHTS *time : 1 day - plan p. 212*

Reversing Falls Rapids★★. – The Saint John River runs through Maine and New Brunswick to empty into the Bay of Fundy at Saint John. At this point on the Bay the tides are 8.5 m - 28 ft high *(p. 185)*. At low tide the Bay is more than 4 m - 14 ft below the level of the river and the river water thus rushes out into it. As the tide rises the rush of the river water is gradually brought to a halt and the river becomes as calm as a mill pond (slack tide) before gradually being reversed in direction. At high tide when the water of the Bay is more than 4 m - 14 ft above the level of the river, the water flows swiftly upstream. The force of the ocean tide is felt as far away as Fredericton *(129 km - 80 miles upstream)*.

This reverse of the river current is highlighted just before the river enters the Bay of Fundy because it narrows and curves around a bend in a deep gorge. This narrow bend creates rapids and whirlpools in the water whenever the current is great in either direction. This is the phenomenon known as the Reversing Falls Rapids.

SAINT JOHN★★

To fully appreciate the Reversing Falls Rapids, visitors should try to see the river several times : at low tide when it is rushing downstream, at slack tide as it begins to reverse and at high tide when it is swiftly flowing upstream. For times of tides contact Tourist Office.

Lookout at Reversing Falls Bridge★ (A). – *Parking at west end of bridge ; restaurant.*

At slack tide, boats can be seen ascending and descending the river, as it is the only time they can negotiate the rapids.

Lookout at Falls View Park ★ (B). – *Parking at end of Falls View Ave.* The views of the rapids are good from here but not as dramatic as from the bridge lookout.

Viewpoints of Saint John★★. – On a fine clear day Saint John's splendid site can be appreciated from two very different points.

Fort Howe Lookout★★. – *From Main St take Metcalfe St and then a sharp right turn onto Magazine St.*

This wooden blockhouse *(not open)* stands on a rocky cliff above the surrounding hills and from it there is an excellent panoramic **view★★** of the docks, harbour, river and city.

Carleton Martello Tower★. – *Open daily mid May - mid Oct ; National Historic Park ;* ☎ *672-5792.*

This Martello Tower *(p. 203)* was built in 1813 to help defend Saint John from possible American attack. It was used intermittently in the 19th century and during both World Wars. In the Second World War a two storey steel and concrete structure was built on the top to house the anti-aircraft and fire control headquarters for the Saint John area. Inside the tower, costumed guides explain the life of an 18th century soldier and there are displays on various episodes in the history of the area.

The tower stands above its surroundings providing a panoramic **view★★** of Saint John harbour, the docks, rail yards, a breakwater which leads to Partridge Island, the Bay of Fundy, the river and of course the city.

New Brunswick Museum★★. – *Open daily May - Sept, 10am - 5pm ; Oct - April 2pm - 5pm ; $2.00 ;* ☎ *693-1196.*

For well over a hundred years, this museum has devoted itself to all aspects of the human, natural and artistic life of the province and it has accumulated an interesting collection.

Ship models, watercolours and other displays bring alive the golden age of ship-building in New Brunswick (19th century). Saint John's importance at this time as a commercial emporium as well as a shipbuilding centre is stressed with exhibits showing the range of imports and exports which entered and left the port.

A bicentennial display on the history of the province is being installed *(scheduled opening 1984).* The development of New Brunswick is also shown by means of Indian birchbark, quill and bead work, period furniture, costumes, etc. The museum owns a splendid collection of watercolours, sketches and photographs of Saint John, New Brunswick and Canada in general. These are exhibited in changing displays on varying themes.

In the natural science galleries, the native fauna - birds, insects, fish and mammals, are illustrated and the geological structure of the province explained.

Two **art galleries** have changing exhibitions, often devoted to the works of local artists.

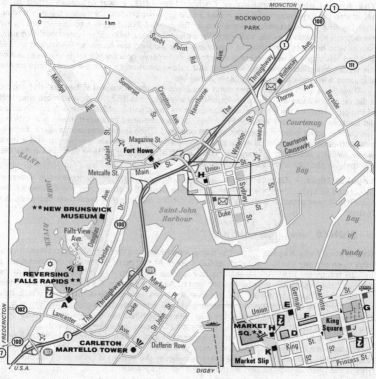

Downtown★★. – Saint John's downtown has been revitalized in recent years making it a pleasant area for visitors to explore on foot (various "trails" can be followed, contact Tourist Office for details).

Market Square Area★★. – The Market Square complex which opened in 1983 comprises an attractive shopping centre with central atrium and several levels, hotel, convention centre and residences. A row of late 19th century warehouses were incorporated into it and they front onto a pleasant plaza around the **Market Slip** where the Loyalists landed in 1783. Today, a tugboat, the *Ocean Hawk II*, is moored at the Slip and in summer there are outdoor cafes and concerts in the plaza.

On the south side of the plaza stands **Barbour's General Store (K)** (open daily, closed mid April - mid May), a red and cream clapboard structure with gingerbread decoration dating from 1867. It is well stocked with merchandise of that era.

A pedestrian bridge over Dock Street links Market Square with Saint John's **City Hall (H)** which has an observation gallery on its top floor (open weekdays), and thence to **Brunswick Square (D)**, a complex of shops, offices and hotel.

Loyalist House (E). – Guided tours daily June - Sept, 1/2 hr ; $2.00 ; ☎ 652-3590.

This house built in 1817 by David Merritt, a Loyalist who fled from New York State in 1783, was one of the few buildings to escape the great fire of 1877 and thus it is one of the oldest structures in the city. On two sides the exterior is clapboard, on the other two it is shingled. Clapboard was expensive and thus it was put only on the north and east sides as it offered better protection against the weather. This rather plain exterior belies the elegant and spacious Georgian interior. Note especially the arches between the rooms and the fine curved staircase. On leaving, note the solid rock foundations on the Germain Street side. All of Saint John is built on this rock.

King Square Area. – Generally considered the centre of Saint John, King Square has trees and flowerbeds arranged in the form of the Union flag (p. 191), and a two-storey bandstand. In one corner is the old **City Market (F)** where all kinds of New Brunswick produce can be bought including dulse (p. 208). On the other side of the square, the **Loyalist Burial Ground (G)** can be seen.

To find the description of a point of interest which you already know by name, consult the index p. 237.

SAINT JOHN RIVER Valley ★★ New Brunswick

Maps pp. 10 and 186

This wide and scenic river rises in northern Maine and flows 673 km - 418 miles to the Bay of Fundy through varied and beautiful country. In the north it traverses hilly almost mountainous forest but as it heads south its valley becomes increasingly rolling and rural supporting some of the richest farmland in New Brunswick especially important for the potato crop. South of Fredericton the river is a maze of channels, lakes and bays before finally reaching the sea at Saint John where it is forced back in its tracks twice a day by the powerful Fundy tides (p. 185).

The river was named by **Samuel de Champlain** who landed at its mouth on the feast day of St. John in 1604. Few people settled along it, however, until the year 1783 brought 4 000 Loyalists to Saint John (p. 211). Then settlements sprang up throughout the valley and the 19th century saw great activity with numerous steamboats moving between them. This era ended in the 1940s when traffic took to the roads, but the valley remains New Brunswick's principal transportation route as the Trans-Canada Highway now follows it for much of its length in the province. Today, the river itself carries little except pleasure boaters and sailing enthusiasts who find its wide expanses and deep waters a veritable paradise especially in the lower sections.

From Fredericton to Edmundston

285 km - 177 miles – allow about one day

Leave Fredericton (p. 199) on the Trans-Canada Hwy (Rte 2).

After traversing the provincial capital, the Trans-Canada Highway follows the river upstream to the Mactaquac Dam, New Brunswick's biggest power project. The dam has created a reservoir or headpond about 105 km - 65 miles long affecting the valley as far as Woodstock. On the north bank of the headpond lies **Mactaquac Provincial Park,** a haven for sports enthusiasts. The Trans-Canada follows the south side of the headpond with fine **views**★ as the country becomes increasingly rural.

Woolastook Wildlife Park. – 29 km - 18 miles. Open daily mid May - Sept ; $3.25 ; snack bar ; ☎ (506) 363-2352.

This is a pleasant park devoted to animals native to New Brunswick and the other Maritime Provinces. There is a good **view**★ of the Saint John River from the parking lot.

King's Landing Historical Settlement★★. – 37 km - 23 miles. Open daily June - mid Oct ; $4.00 ; restaurant, snack bar ; emporium ; ☎ (506) 363-3081.

This restored village has a very beautiful **site**★★ on the sloping banks of the Saint John beside a little creek which joins the main river by a small cove. The land on which it stands was given to veterans of the King's American Dragoons after the Revolutionary War and it is typical of the many Loyalist settlements which sprang up along the river making their living by lumbering, farming, and some shipbuilding. The houses and other buildings were for the main part moved to this site when the Mactaquac dam project

SAINT JOHN RIVER Valley★★

flooded their original sites. Each has retained the character of one of its original owners and thus the village provides an authentic glimpse of life in the Saint John valley between 1790 and 1870. Indeed, walking along the village road is like taking a step back in time to the calm and rural peace of the 19th century. There are about one hundred village "inhabitants" who explain everything as they carry out the chores of the routine life of another age.

Apart from the beautifully restored farms with their fields of crops, the village has a church, school, forge, well-stocked village store and a **theatre** with live entertainment *(ask for details at entrance).*

(after photo by Tourism New Brunswick)

Water-Powered Sawmill

Beside the mill stream, there is a water-powered **sawmill** which operates regularly, its large water wheel activating a saw blade which cuts through logs by moving along a wooden carriage. The **King's Head Inn**, a typical 19th century road stop, serves appropriate refreshments. The commodious Morehouse residence stands near the elegant Ingraham house with its delightful garden overlooking the river.

At the wharf - the "landing" of the name, a reconstructed half size replica of a 19th century **wood boat**★ is moored. Its name comes from what it carried rather than from what it was made from. It is typical of the boats which once carted lumber from the sawmills or possibly hay from the farms to market.

Between King's Landing and Woodstock, there are excellent **views**★★ from the Trans-Canada of the wide and tranquil Saint John traversing lovely rolling country of farms and forests.

After Woodstock, leave Trans-Canada Hwy and take Rte 103 to Hartland.

Hartland★. – Pop 846. Settled by Loyalists, this town is in the centre of a prosperous agricultural district especially important for its potatoes. Hartland is, however, much better known for its **covered bridge**★ across the Saint John - the longest in the world. Built in 1897 and rebuilt in 1920, this 391 m - 1 282 ft bridge crosses the river in seven spans and carried the Trans-Canada until 1960. Today, it links Routes 103 and 105. There is a good **view**★ of it descending the hill on Route 103.

The first bridges built in New Brunswick as in many other provinces were of wood, and they were covered to protect the large timbers from weathering. These "covers" lengthened the life of a bridge to seventy to eighty years from perhaps only fifteen to twenty. There are many such bridges in New Brunswick but none as extensive as that of Hartland. It resembles a barnlike tunnel from the exterior, the fine woodwork construction can only be appreciated from the interior *(travellers can drive through).*

Take Rte 105 on the east bank to Florenceville, then the Trans-Canada to Grand Falls.

The area north of Florenceville is very agricultural both in and outside the valley and there are fine **views**★ from the Trans-Canada of the river and farms. The Saint John gradually approaches the Maine border going north and enters more mountainous country.

Leave Trans-Canada and enter Grand Falls.

Grand Falls★★. – Pop 6 203. Built on a plateau above the river, Grand Falls is the centre of the potato belt. The river changes suddenly and dramatically here. Instead of being a wide and tranquil stream with gently sloping banks, it plunges over falls and, for about 1.5 km - 1 mile, it flows through a deep and narrow gorge. Unfortunately, the falls are not very impressive these days as much of the water is diverted through a power plant, but there are two good viewpoints of the gorge.

Falls Park★. – *Accessible from Reception Centre on Madawaska Rd. Open daily June - mid Sept.* This park offers a good view of the gorge and the falls below the power plant.

La Rochelle in Centennial Park★. – *Accessible from Reception Centre on Madawaska Rd. Open daily June - mid Sept ; $1.00.* Steps descend into the gorge which has walls as high as 70 m - 230 ft in places. There are some deep holes in the rock called wells at the bottom, but it is the **gorge**★★ itself which is impressive.

Return to Trans-Canada Highway.

After Grand Falls, the Saint John returns to being a wide and placid stream. It forms the international boundary, thus the towns and villages seen across it are in Maine.

Edmundston. – Pop 12 044. Situated at the junction of the Saint John and Madawaska Rivers, this industrial city contrasts sharply with the rural nature of the rest of the valley. It is dominated by the twin spired **Cathedral of the Immaculate Conception.** Once called *Petit-Sault* (little falls) to distinguish the rapids at the mouth of the Madawaska from Grand Falls further south, Edmundston was renamed in honour of Sir Edmund Head, governor of New Brunswick in 1856. Its population is mainly French-speaking, although they boast Acadian, Québecois, Indian, American, English and Irish origins.

The Republic of Madawaska. – The land south of Lake Témiscouata in Québec and New Brunswick and the area north of the Aroostook River in Maine were once collectively called Madawaska. These lands were long in dispute between the provinces of Canada (then only Ontario and Québec) and New Brunswick, and between both of them and the United States. When the boundaries were finally settled, New Brunswick was left with this strange thumb-shaped peninsula *(map p. 186)* and the city of Edmundston. The result of these years of dispute was to make Madawaskans rather independent-minded though not in a political sense. Thus they created a legend for themselves – the Republic of Madawaska. Known as Brayons because they used to crush flax with a tool called a "brake", Madawaskans have their own flag with an eagle and six stars (representing their six different origins) and their own president, the Mayor of Edmundston. *More details can be obtained from Edmundston Tourism Services at City Hall, 7 Canada Rd, during office hours.*

The **Madawaska Museum** *(195 Hebert Blvd ; open daily except Mon and hols in winter ; $1.00)* presents the history of this region.

SHERBROOKE ★ Nova Scotia
Maps pp. 11 and 187 – Pop 390

Sherbrooke occupies a pretty site on the St. Mary's River once the location of a French fort. After its capture by the English in 1669, settlement ceased to exist until people were attracted by the rich timberlands and arrived to exploit them in 1800. Sawmills sprang up and wooden ships were built during the earlier part of that century. Then in 1861 gold was found and the town flourished for about twenty years. The gold did not last but Sherbrooke survived as a lumber town and recently as a centre for sports fishing and tourism.

Sherbrooke Village★. – *Open daily mid May - mid Oct ; $1.50 ; Nova Scotia Museum ; restaurant ;* ☎ *(902) 522-2400.*

This is not the normal reconstructed pioneer village with buildings removed from various locations and set down in artificial surroundings. What is visited is actually part of the town. Certain streets have been closed to traffic and most of the houses are no longer inhabited, but it is still difficult to know where "village" ends and town begins. The buildings open to visitors were constructed 1860-70. They have been renovated to reflect this period.

The church, schoolhouse, post office, forge and several homes can be visited. Of particular interest is the **boatbuilding shop** where wooden boats are constructed. Above the Cumminger Brothers general store, there is an **ambrotype photography studio.** This process was used in photography until about 1900. Visitors can dress up in 19th century costume and have their photograph taken. The tea room serves 1880 fare, the telephone exchange still works and the Court House is still in use.

Removed from the rest of the village *(0.4 km - 1/4 mile)* is the **McDonald Brothers' Mill★**, an operational water powered sawmill capable of full production. Nearby, there is a reconstructed **lumber camp** of the 1880s.

SHIPPAGAN ★ New Brunswick
Maps pp. 10 and 186 - Pop 2 471

This town on the Acadian peninsula *(see also Village Historique Acadien p. 216)* has an important commercial fishing industry and peat moss processing plants. A bridge leads to Lamèque Island with its peat moss bogs from whence a ferry *(toll free)* crosses to Miscou Island which has fine beaches on the Gulf of St. Lawrence.

Marine Centre★ (Centre Marin). – *Open May - Sept 10am - 6pm ; $2.00 ;* ☎ *(506) 336-4771.*

This pleasant museum is devoted to all aspects of the marine life of the Gulf of St. Lawrence. An audio-visual presentation *(20 min)* explains the history of the fishing industry - the discovery of the Banks *(p. 217)* and their subsequent exploitation, etc. All the fish native to these waters can be seen in a series of aquariums and an outdoor seal pool. Other exhibits feature the types of ship used for fishing and how they are built. Finally, visitors can enter the cabin of a modern trawler (reconstructed) to see the mass of electronic devices now employed in the fishing industry.

SPRINGHILL ★★ Nova Scotia
Maps pp. 10 and 187 - Pop 4 896

Commemorated in song and legend, the "town of Springhill, Nova Scotia" is famous as a coal mining centre which has suffered more disasters than any other place of its size in the country. In 1891 there was a terrific blast in one of the mines which tore out a vast area and which was followed by a flame which swept through all the mine workings : 125 men died. In 1916 a subterranean fire swept through the galleries. No one died this time but much damage was done. In 1956 an explosion and fire caused 39 deaths. The next year a fire wiped out most of the business district of the town proving that disasters did not only occur in the mines. Finally in 1958, an underground upheaval or "bump" caused the deaths of 76 men, entombing twelve men for six days and seven more for eight days.

This final disaster proved the death knell of an industry already doomed by the change to oil and gas as heating fuels, and all the mines closed.

Miners' Museum★★. – *On Black River Rd – follow signs along Rte 2 (Parrsboro direction). Open daily May - Oct ; mine tour $2.00 ; 45 min ; protective clothing provided ;* ☎ *(902) 597-3449.*

This museum commemorates the terrible disasters and the bravery of the rescuers. There are newspaper clippings and displays on these and also on mining equipment. The highlight of the visit is however the **mine tour** given by retired miners with many years of experience. Equipped in hard hat, rubber coat and boots, visitors descend about 270 m - 900 ft into the old Syndicate Mine via a tunnel of regular height, not by the tunnels used by the miners, along which they had to crawl ! Both old and new methods of mining are demonstrated, and those desiring souvenirs can hack them out with a pick axe.

TRURO Nova Scotia

Map p. 187 – Pop 12 552 – Tourist Office ☎ (902) 893-2922 (summer only)

Set on the Salmon River near its mouth, Truro experiences the high tides of the Bay of Fundy and also the tidal bore *(pp. 185 and 206)*. It was the site of a thriving Acadian community called Cobequid before the Deportation *(p. 188)* and was later settled by people from Northern Ireland and New Hampshire. Today, it is a manufacturing centre and home to the Nova Scotia Agricultural College.

Tidal Bore★. – *Viewpoint : leave Hwy 102 at exit 14 and take Tidal Bore Rd (left on Robie and then left on Tidal Bore Rd if coming from Halifax). Parking area beside Palliser restaurant ; clock gives time of next bore or ☎ Tourist Office ; arrive 15 min before bore and stay if possible for about 1 hr to see high tide.*

Twice a day the tide rushes up the Salmon River from the Bay of Fundy causing the phenomenon known as the tidal bore *(p. 206)*. This wave may vary from just a ripple to several feet in height. However, what is more interesting than the actual bore is the tremendous inrush of water and the extremely rapid rise in water level immediately following it. In fact, high tide is reached just over an hour after the arrival of the bore.

VILLAGE HISTORIQUE ACADIEN ★ New Brunswick

Maps pp. 10 and 186 – 11 km - 7 miles W of Caraquet by Rte 11. Open daily June - Sept ; $4.00 ; refreshments ; souvenirs ; ☎ (506) 727-3468

This is a reconstructed village depicting the life of the Acadian people 1780-1880, a time of great hardship re-establishing after the Deportation *(p. 188)*. This site was selected for the village because Acadians had originally reclaimed it from a marsh, although it is no longer inhabited. Also it resembles the type of area where Acadians took refuge after the Deportation.

This part of New Brunswick and indeed most of the Gulf of St. Lawrence shore in the province is still inhabited by Acadians living traditional lives of farmers and fishermen. **Caraquet** (Pop 4 315) nearby has an annual Acadian Festival each August which is opened by a **Blessing of the Fleet,** symbolic of Christ's blessing of the fishermen of Galilee. As many as sixty fishing boats arrive each year from all over the province decked out with bunting to be blessed by the Bishop of Bathurst.

Visit. – The village is entered through the Reception Centre (Centre d'Accueil) where a **slide show** *(15 min)* provides a good introduction to the village. The entire history of the Acadians is explained : who they were, their situation in the Anglo-French wars, why they were deported, where they settled later, and what they do today.

The village itself is spread out along a road about a mile long *(transport by horse and oxen drawn carts)*. The houses were moved to their respective sites from various parts of the province and they have been furnished to represent life

(After photo by Canadian Government Office of Tourism)

Demonstration of spinning

1780-1880. Only the little wooden church is a copy of an original building. The village is "inhabited" by Acadians wearing traditional costumes.

Over the village flies the **flag of Acadie** – the French red, white and blue tricolour with a star at the top left hand corner symbolizing the Virgin Mary. This flag is often seen in the Acadian regions of the Maritime Provinces.

NEWFOUNDLAND

This wild and rocky island off Canada's shores, constantly buffeted by the Atlantic, harbours the most individualistic part of North America. Where else are there settlements with names such as : Stinking Cove, Useless Bay, Dildo Pond, Jerry's Nose, Cuckold Cove, Witless Bay, Happy Adventure, Heart's Content, Heart's Desire and Little Heart's Ease ? These settlements cling precariously to Newfoundland's coasts and have for centuries been cut off from each other – and from the rest of the world. It was only in 1949 that Newfoundland joined Confederation, and visitors from other Canadian provinces can expect to be asked : "Are you from Canada then ?". This isolation has always thrown Newfoundlanders on their own resources and a deeply rooted and highly original culture has emerged. Jokes about **Newfies,** as the inhabitants are generally known, are legion all over Canada in both French and English but, unlike other racial groups, Newfoundlanders respond in kind with their own special brand of humour.

Labrador. – To use the term "province of Newfoundland" of the island in the gulf of the St. Lawrence alone, is incorrect. The province also comprises a considerable stretch of the coast of the Canadian mainland. Known as Labrador, this is a rugged land of high mountains (Cirque Mountain in the **Torngats** of the north reaches 1 676 m - 5 500 ft), deep coastal settlements nestling under high cliffs, and inland a barren largely treeless terrain. Unlike the island, it forms part of the Canadian Shield *(p. 13).* It is largely uninhabited except along the coast and around the mines in its rich iron ore belt.

The Island. – Called "The Rock" for its craggy profile, the island part of the province has a 9 660 km - 6 000 mile coastline which is ruggedly beautiful, deeply indented and studded with bays, coves, "tickles" and islands. In the north and west, the coast is grandiose with towering cliffs and deep fjords *(see Gros Morne and Terra Nova National Parks pp. 222 and 228).* The hills of the western part of the island are a continuation of the Appalachian Chain – the **Long Range Mountains.** From these heights the land slopes east and northeast. Parts of the interior are heavily forested whereas elsewhere there are expanses of rocky barrens and boggy peatlands, the legacy of the glaciers. There are also a multitude of fine lakes and attractive rivers.

THE FISHERY

Newfoundland's number one resource, which first brought it to prominence in the 15th century and is still its mainstay, is the vast and rich fishery off its coasts. The submerged continental shelf, which extends as much as 500 km - 300 miles from the coast and is known as the **Grand Banks of Newfoundland** *(see also p. 221),* provides the most extensive fish breeding grounds in the world. Cod is the great catch and indeed in Newfoundland "fish" is cod, all other varieties are referred to by their name (herring, caplin, salmon, etc).

Inshore Fishery. – Along the coasts of Newfoundland, fishermen operate from small boats, their method varying with the season. Early summer is the time of the **caplin run.** These small fish swim ashore to spawn bringing with them their main predator, the cod. Large square traps of nets are used to catch the cod at this time and a fisherman may gain most of his livelihood during the few weeks of the caplin run. At other times of the year, cod are caught by **longlining** - paying out a trawl line from a boat to which are attached smaller lines with baited hooks, or **jigging.** Cod do not always respond to bait but they will snap at shiny lead "jiggers" bobbing in the water. Cod-jigging is one of Newfoundland's great traditions but it is a relatively slow and inefficient way of catching fish.

More recently, **gill-netting** has been used by inshore fishermen. The net is weighted to keep it on the bottom and it is held vertical by floats. Another recent development has been the use of larger boats called **longliners** which can stay at sea several days and pursue schools of fish catching them either by longlining or gill-netting. Also, cod are no longer the only fish caught. Squid and caplin are taken (once only used as bait) as well as salmon and lobsters.

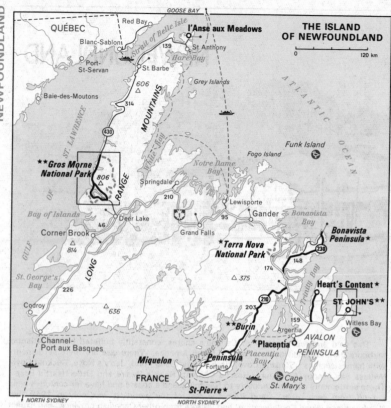

The province of Newfoundland also contains Labrador, map pp. 10–11.

Offshore Fishery. – Large schooners have left Newfoundland ports for hundreds of years to fish the Banks. They were usually away for several months at a time. The actual fishing was done from **dories,** small flat-bottomed open craft carried on the deck of the schooner and only launched when schools of fish were located. The catch was either salted on the deck of the schooner and stored in the hold (the **"wet" fishery**) or taken ashore and dried on wooden racks known as **flakes** (the **"dry" fishery**).

Since 1945, however, the trend has been towards using draggers, trawlers and long-liners on the Banks instead of schooners and dories because fish can be caught en masse instead of singly. Also, filleting plants ashore have taken the place of the flakes and refrigeration is used instead of salting.

Sealing. – The catching of seals for their skins and meat is as old as settlement in Newfoundland and for many families it is an important part of their livelihood. In the spring, the adult seals and their white-coated whelps leave their breeding grounds in the Arctic and float south on the ice floes carried by the Labrador current. At this time scores of small ships set sail full of sealers determined to have their share of the valuable skins of these babies. In recent years, these hunts have become controversial, not so much for the number of seals killed as for the means of killing them. Sealers carry long poles, to enable them to vault from ice floe to ice floe, which double as clubs to kill the baby seals.

Other Resources. – Although it is still a major primary resource, fishing has been surpassed in production value in recent years by **mining** and **forestry.** Iron ore has been exploited in Newfoundland since the turn of the century. The workings on Bell Island in Conception Bay *(map p. 228)* are now closed but they were so important during the Second World War that they were twice attacked by German submarines. Today, however, it is the mines of the so-named **Labrador Trough** in western Labrador that produce the province's iron ore. Indeed, Labrador City is the site of the largest open-pit iron ore mining, concentrate, and pelletizing operation in the world. The province also exploits lead, zinc, copper, gold, silver, asbestos and gypsum in small quantities.

In recent years, it has been established that there are considerable reserves of **natural gas** and **oil** off the coast of the island and off Labrador. Marine technology is being developed to enable exploitation of these reserves hindered at present by such problems as drifting icebergs, etc.

The forests of Newfoundland support a considerable **pulp and paper** manufacturing industry. The completion of the Trans-Canada Highway across the island (1962) greatly aided this as previously only transportation by water existed. The big centres of the industry are **Corner Brook** and **Grand Falls.** Agriculture, on the other hand, in this land ravaged by the glaciers does not play an important role in the economy. The farms which do exist in the **Avalon Peninsula** and **Codroy Valley** supply local markets only.

The hydro-electric potential of Labrador is enormous. At present there is a huge generating station at **Churchill Falls** (the power all goes to Québec) and there are plans for another development on the lower Churchill, from which electricity will be carried to the island by means of cables underneath the Strait of Belle Isle.

218

Population. – Newfoundland's population of 567 685 people is the most homogeneous of any province in Canada. More than 98 % of the inhabitants have English as their mother tongue. About the same percentage was born in the province – a proportion unequalled elsewhere in Canada. The non-Anglophones include French-speaking Acadians in the St. George's – Port au Port region, Québecois in western Labrador and Inuit in the north.

The Outports. – About one fifth of the total population lives in the general area of the provincial capital, St. John's (*p. 225*), the rest live mainly in the fishing villages along the coasts known as outports. Traditionally, an outport was any community outside St. John's, but today, with the rise of industrial centres such as Corner Brook, the term is applied to the tiny settlements of the coast epitomized by their dories and trap skiffs along the shore, their weather-beaten fishing stages perched on poles above the water and their colourful and varied two-storey "box" houses (*illustration p. 217*).

Newfoundland English. – All visitors to Newfoundland are charmed by the wonderful accents of its inhabitants, by their humour and by the wealth of unusual words and idioms. There is a quite remarkable variety of dialects. Some have definite Irish overtones, others are more reminiscent of the English West Country (Dorset, Devon, Cornwall, etc). A few examples of Newfoundland expressions follow :

    to have a noggin to scrape   (a very hard task)
    he's in a hobble about it   (not worrying about it)
    you are moidering my brains   (you are disturbing me)
    to be all mops and brooms   (to have untidy hair)
    Long may your big jib draw   (good luck for the future)
    Go to law with the devil and hold court in hell   (the odds are against you)
    Pigs may fly but they are very unlikely birds   (a vain hope)
    A fisherman is one rogue, a merchant is many.

Climate. – The sea exerts a dominating influence on the climate of the island of Newfoundland moderating both summer and winter temperatures. Winters are cold in the interior, milder on the coasts. (St. John's mean maximum in January is –1°C - 30° F, Gander –3°C - 26° F). Summers are cool along the coasts, hotter in the interior (St. John's mean maxium in July is 21°C - 70° F, Gander 22°C - 72° F). There is abundant precipitation everywhere especially along the coasts and it is evenly distributed throughout the year (St. John's 1 346 mm - 53 ins, Gander 1 016 mm - 40 ins annually). The Great Northern peninsula is the driest region. There can be fogs all year along the coasts caused by the cold waters of the Labrador current meeting warmer air currents off the continent. The least foggy period is late summer.

Labrador experiences a much more severe climate than the island with more extreme temperatures but less precipitation. Goose Bay registers mean maxima of –14°C - 7° F in January, 21°C - 70° F in July with 737 mm - 29 ins of precipitation annually.

HISTORICAL BACKGROUND

The Native Peoples. – Archaeological research has proved that people have inhabited the island of Newfoundland for many thousands of years. The earliest known inhabitants used a red powdered ochre on their bodies and have become famous as the **Red Paint people.** The term "red indian" is thought to have originated in tales of these Indians brought back to Europe by Cabot.

At the time of white contact, the island was inhabited by the **Beothuck Indians,** part of the Eastern Woodlands culture (*p. 98*). Hostility between these Indians and the first white settlers arose quickly, partially due to the Beothuck belief that all goods were held in common, an idea not shared by early fishermen when they found their gear missing. In the 17th and 18th centuries, this hostility grew into an appalling sport or rivalry between settlers to see who could kill the most Beothucks. By 1800, when the government finally took action against these hunters, it was too late. The last known surviving Beothuck died in St. John's in 1829.

The native Inuit and Montagnais Indians of Labrador did not share the Beothucks' fate and they still survive in their small communities today.

The "Discovery" of Newfoundland. – Although he has long received the credit for it, it has now been conclusively proved that **John Cabot** in 1497 was not the first white man to set foot in Newfoundland. Norsemen settled on the coast nearly 500 years before his epic voyage (*see L'Anse aux Meadows p. 224*) and there is also reason to believe that the **Irish** touched the island shores in the 6th century. Indeed, Cabot was not even the first man of his own time to view the island. It is possible that the **Basques** fished in the North Atlantic in the 14th century and certainly **English mariners** from Bristol crossed the "western sea" to the "Isle of Brasil" before Columbus (1492).

Cabot's importance is not so much his landing on the island (even this is disputed, *see Cabot Trail p. 197*) as the fact that he publicized the existence of the rich fishery off its shores. The news of his voyages spread quickly in a Europe already excited by Columbus' discoveries. In 1500, the Portuguese equipped an expedition under **Gaspar Corte Real** to search for a route to Asia through the "islands" which apparently stood in the way. After exploring the coast of Labrador, he returned home – unsuccessful.

Fishing Station. – It was not long before the waters off Newfoundland were swarming with small fishing vessels. The Basques, English, French, Portuguese and Spanish all came after the cod for which there was a ready and increasing market in Europe, and which, when dried on racks on the shore, were light, easily transportable and almost indestructible. It was a seasonal activity and the fishermen returned to their homelands for the winter. In fact, settlement on the island was actively discouraged by the English West Country merchants who owned the fishing fleets, because they feared competition from a resident population.

There was great rivalry in Europe over Newfoundland, which led to the proclamation of the sovereignty of Elizabeth I at St. John's in 1583 (*p. 225*). As the century wore on, only the French made really determined efforts to wrest control of the island from the English.

The First Settlements. – Despite the harsh anti-settlement laws, many small communities of English fishermen were established in the coves of the Avalon Peninsula before the close of the 16th century. Then in the 17th century, several charters were granted by the English Crown for the establishment of colonies on the island, notably those of **John Guy** at Cupids in 1610 and **Lord Baltimore** at Ferryland in 1622. Nevertheless, the island was not as a whole treated as a colony. By a charter granted by Charles I in 1634, which remained in force for nearly 150 years, authority for enforcing law and order in any particular harbour was the responsibility of the master of the first British ship to enter it in any one season, regardless of whether there were resident inhabitants or not. These **Fishing Admirals,** as they were called, frequently abused and oppressed the local fishermen.

In the end, it was fear of French expansion which changed the attitude of the British government to permanent settlement. The French established a colony at **Placentia** in 1662 *(p. 225)* and proceeded to mount attacks on British harbours especially St. John's. Proper defence was only possible with a strong permanent community. Although France recognized British sovereignty over the whole island in 1713 (Treaty of Utrecht), fighting and raids went on throughout the 18th century. At the end, France only retained the small islands of **St. Pierre and Miquelon** *(p. 222)* and the exclusive right to dry fish on a large stretch of the coast (given up in 1904). But settlers had proved their worth and finally in 1824, Newfoundland was recognised as a British colony for the first time in British law.

Confederation Rejected and Accepted. – When the other British colonies in North America decided to form a Confederation in 1867 *(p. 209)*, Newfoundland chose not to join although its representatives attended the final Québec Conference *(p. 175)*. The early 20th century saw the Dominion struggling economically only to be bankrupted during the Depression. Responsible government was suspended and administration was carried out by a Commission of six men appointed by Westminster. The Second World War saw a boom and full employment, so afterwards the British government arranged a vote to decide the colony's future. After two referendums, Newfoundlanders decided to join Confederation by a vote of 52 % for and 48 % against. On March 31st, 1949, Newfoundland became Canada's 10th province.

SPORTS AND OUTDOOR ACTIVITIES

The Newfoundland government has established an excellent system of provincial parks on the island for camping and other activities *(details from Department of Tourism - see below)*. The two National Parks also offer facilities for boating and hiking *(pp. 222 and 228)*, and there are opportunities for sailing and canoeing in the province's lakes and rivers. But Newfoundland is probably best known for its **fishing.** Trout and salmon fishing are unequalled elsewhere in eastern North America. This is true of Labrador as well as the island. One famous place to watch the salmon leap *(August)* is the **Squires Memorial Park** near Deer Lake *(map p. 218)*. All details of season, limits, outfitters for both fishing and hunting can be obtained from the Department of Tourism.

In winter, cross-country skiing and skating on frozen ponds are popular.

Bird Watching. – This is one activity of special interest in Newfoundland. Of the 520 species found in any part of Canada, 300 have been recorded on the island. Many of these are migratory seabirds but there are also a significant number that remain all year especially birds of prey. Bald eagles are frequently sighted along the south coast, and even the occasional golden eagle. There are three famous seabird colonies – **Cape St. Mary's, Witless Bay** and **Funk Island** *(map p. 218)* where gannets, murres, kittiwake gulls, razor-billed auks, puffins, guillemots and dovekies can be seen.

PRACTICAL INFORMATION

Access. – Canadian National - Marine Division (CN Marine) operates a ferry service between North Sydney N.S. and Port aux Basques *(daily, about 6 hrs ; reservations required ; details from CN Marine, Box 250, North Sydney, N.S. B2A 3M3)*. In summer, CN Marine also operates a service between North Sydney and Argentia *(mid June - mid Sept, 3 times a week, about 18 hrs, overnight)*. Many summer visitors arrive by one ferry and leave by the other.

Also popular with tourists are the **coastal services** *(maps pp. 11 and 218)* run by CN Marine along both north and south coasts and between the coastal settlements of Labrador *(May or June - Nov or Dec, varying frequencies and times ; for details contact CN Marine, Coastal Reservation Bureau, P.O. Box 520, Port aux Basques, Newfoundland AOM 1CO)*. Labrador can also be reached by the St. Barbe - Blanc Sablon ferry *(daily May - Dec, 1 1/2 hrs ; for details contact Puddister Trading Company, P.O. Box 38, St. John's, Newfoundland A1C 5H5)*.

St. Pierre (France) can be reached by the coastal service or the Fortune Ferry *(p. 222)*.

Road Conditions. – The major highway is the Trans-Canada *(910 km - 565 miles Port aux Basques to St. John's)* which is paved and kept in reasonable condition. Other paved highways pose no special problems but there are also many miles of unpaved roads which can be very rough. However, it is only when the visitor leaves the main roads that the true Newfoundland can be appreciated. Speed limits, unless otherwise indicated, are :

90 kmh (56 mph)   Trans-Canada Highway   80 kmh (50 mph)   other roads

Accommodation and Road Map. – The provincial government produces an annually updated Accommodation Guide which includes campsites and approved **hospitality homes** - private homes which take paying guests, the only accommodation in some of the outports. This, a regularly updated road map, and much other useful information are available free from :

Tourism Branch, Department of Development,
P.O. Box 2016, St. John's, Newfoundland, A1C 5R8 ☎ 709-737-2830

Time Zone. – Newfoundland has its own time zone - 1/2 hour in advance of the Canadian Maritime Provinces (Atlantic Standard) or 1 1/2 hrs in advance of US East Coast (Eastern Standard). Summer time operates between May and October as elsewhere. *See map p. 20.*

Taxes. – A sales tax of 12 % is added to all purchases except food and a few other selected items, also to restaurant meals and hotel bills.

Liquor Laws. – Liquor and wine are available only from government stores except in some of the remote communities where local stores are licensed. Beer is available at the above and from local stores with the appropriate license. The legal drinking age is 19.

BOOKS TO READ

Newfoundland by Harold Horwood   *(Macmillan)*
Saint Pierre and Miquelon by William Rannie   *(W. F. Rannie)*
A Whale for the Killing by Farley Mowat   *(McClelland and Stewart)*
Outport People by Claire Mowat   *(McClelland and Stewart)*

BONAVISTA Peninsula ★

Maps pp. 11 and 218 - *119 km - 74 miles to Cape Bonavista from Trans-Canada Highway by Rte 230 – allow 1/2 day for round trip*

This interesting drive through some attractive fishing communities leads to the cape which was supposedly the first North American landfall of the explorer, **John Cabot.** Immediately after leaving the Trans-Canada, there are fine **views**★ of two arms of Trinity Bay – the Northwest Arm and Smith Sound.

Trinity★. – Pop 375. *74 km - 46 miles, turn off Rte 230 for 5 km - 3 miles.*

This little settlement has a picturesque **setting**★ on a hilly peninsula sticking out into Trinity Bay. Much of the land is cultivated and the colourful Newfoundland "box" houses have fine **views** of the sea, rocks, fields and the little protected harbour. Trinity is one of the oldest settlements in Newfoundland being sufficiently established in 1615 to be the site of the first Admiralty Court in Canada's history. Sir Richard Whitbourne was sent out from Britain to settle disputes between the resident fishermen and those who crossed the Atlantic just for the season.

The **Hiscock House** *(open daily July and Aug ; Provincial Historic Site)* has been restored to represent a typical local merchant's household in rural Newfoundland during the early 20th century.

Route 230 continues inland to **Port Union** and **Catalina,** two fishing communities set opposite each other on a pleasant bay.

Bonavista★. – Pop 4 460. *114 km - 71 miles.*

This is another and larger fishing community with attractive houses set around an outer harbour protected by a breakwater, and a sheltered inner harbour for small boats. European fishing fleets used this harbour throughout the 16th century but it had become a British settlement by about 1600 and remained so despite several attempts by the French to capture it in the 18th century. Beside the harbour there are also fishing shacks and drying racks now scarcely used as most of the fish caught (cod and salmon mainly) go directly into the big packing plants to be filleted and frozen.

Cape Bonavista★★. – *About 5 km - 3 miles from the village.*

An attractive **drive**★ through fields with views of the sea leads to the cape, supposedly named *Bonavista* (beautiful view) by Cabot in 1497. Although he sailed under British colours, Cabot was Genoese by birth which may explain the Italian name he gave it. The cape itself is superb with pounding waves, a clear blue sea and interesting rock formations. There is a statue of Cabot to commemorate his first North American landfall although recent research has thrown doubt on the authenticity of this claim.

The **lighthouse** on the cape built 1841-43 *(open daily July and Aug ; Provincial Historic Site)* has been restored to portray the 1870 period with guides in costume.

BURIN Peninsula ★★

Maps pp. 11 and 218

This rocky, mountainous and barren peninsula sticks down like a boot into the Atlantic from the southern coast of Newfoundland between Placentia and Fortune Bays. Just off the end of it are the island remnants of France's once great empire in North America – **St. Pierre and Miquelon**. The peninsula is on the doorstep of a vast off-shore fishery and its inhabitants are almost entirely bound up with this industry either as fishermen, workers in the fish plants or in the large shipyard at Marystown.

The Banks of Newfoundland. – In Newfoundland, "banks" are not money-lending institutions but vast areas of shallow water in the Atlantic to the south and east of the province which are extensions of the continental shelf. These shallow waters are fish breeding grounds which have attracted fishermen for 500 years – and are still doing so today. The biggest and richest of these banks is the Grand Bank where the Labrador Current meets the Gulf Stream. The cold current sinks below the warmer one stirring up the plankton on the sea bed as it does so. The plankton rises to the surface and attracts great schools of fish – and fishermen. Cod is the traditional catch though herring is also found. Newfoundlanders have always talked about "fishing the banks" and the boats used for this were called "bankers" in ages past.

■ ROUTE 210★

203 km - 126 miles from Trans-Canada Highway to Fortune – allow 3 hours

After a wild and deserted drive from the Trans-Canada, the traveller arrives in **Marystown** which has a pretty **site**★ on Little Bay. Its huge shipyard is the biggest in the province making trawlers used off all the shores of Newfoundland. After Marystown, Route 210 crosses the peninsula and descends to Fortune Bay. There are views across this bay of the southern coast of Newfoundland. Just before entering Grand Bank there is a fine **view**★ of the south coast and Brunette Island, with, to the west, the coast of the French island of Miquelon just visible.

BURIN Peninsula★★

Grand Bank★. – Pop 3 901. *199 km - 123 miles*. This is an important fishing centre with a fine **site★**. Once the home of the famous "bankers", it has some attractive houses from this era with widow's walks - small open galleries on the roof from which women could watch for the return, or not, of their men.

Southern Newfoundland Seamen's Museum★. – *Open daily ;* ☎ *(709) 832-1484.*

This museum is built of triangular-shaped blocks to represent a ship's sails. Inside, there are interesting displays on the history of the Banks fishery and the life of the men who fished it. Of particular interest are the photographs of ships and fishing. There are models of the types of ships used including a schooner loaded with equipment and dories (an actual dory is on display too). A relief model of Newfoundland and area shows the Banks and the depth of the Atlantic.

Route 210 continues to **Fortune,** another fishing community with an artificial harbour. A 48 km - 30 mile boat trip away lie the bleak and rocky French islands : little **St. Pierre** with its harbour around which nearly the whole population lives, and the larger **Miquelon** connected by a long sand bar to what was once a third island, **Langlade.**

■ ST. PIERRE AND MIQUELON★ (France)

To land on the islands, Canadian and American citizens require some form of identification, citizens of other countries need a valid passport. Daily passenger ferries from Fortune in the summer months ; 2 hrs ; $40 return ; reservations and details from Lloyd G. Lake Ltd in Fortune ; ☎ *(709) 832-1955. Also coastal services (p. 220).*

Regular flights from St. John's ; 1 hr ; Atlantic Airways ☎ *(709) 576-4100. Or regular flights from Sydney, N.S. and Halifax ; contact Air St. Pierre in Sydney* ☎ *(902) 562-3140.*

Warning : the sea crossing can be rough, flights can be delayed by fog.

For details of hotels, "pensions", etc, contact the St. Pierre Tourism Dept, P.O. Box 4274, St. Pierre and Miquelon, France ; ☎ *41-22-22.*

A Tiny Corner of the Old World. – Few people realize that part of metropolitan France lies off the coast of North America and indeed considering its hostile environment it is surprising that St. Pierre exists at all. From early in the 16th century the archipelago was used as a base for Basque and Breton fishermen working the Banks. It became an official French territory in the next century and saw several changes of ownership as France and England fought for hegemony on the North American continent in the 18th century. Although France was the loser in this battle, she did retain these islands as a *pied à terre* for her fishing fleets working the Banks.

Thus the cod fishery is the *raison d'être* of life on St. Pierre. The islands are too barren and too buffeted by the Atlantic to support much in the way of agriculture. They experienced a brief prosperity as an illicit "rum-running" centre during prohibition in the United States (1920-33) but this was short-lived and today only tourism adds to income from the fishery. Until 1976 the islands were an overseas French territory. Today, however, they are a full *département* or part of France itself sending a *député* to the French Parliament and a member to the Senate.

Visit. – From the sea, **St. Pierre★** (Pop 5 600) is a rocky and rugged island with little vegetation except stunted trees and low plants. Arriving in the harbour, the difference between St. Pierre and the rest of North America is however striking. An undoubtedly European atmosphere pervades it. Tall stone houses line the waterfront, the streets are narrow and full of hooting European cars. The people are friendly, the food good and there are some bargains in the tiny shops.

The same Customs regulations apply to visitors returning from St. Pierre as from any other country.

Excursions around the island and to **Miquelon** (Pop 600) and Langlade can be arranged by the St. Pierre Department of Tourism. A ferry crosses to Miquelon *(daily in summer)* where jeeps can be rented to drive along the sandspit known as the dune of Langlade. The remains of about 600 ships wrecked on this dangerous coast can be seen.

GROS MORNE National Park ★★

Maps pp. 11 and 218 – 84 km - 52 miles NE of Corner Brook. Camping ; hiking, cross-country skiing. Visitor Reception Centre near Rocky Harbour ; ☎ *(709) 458-2066 - Local map below*

This park on the western coast of Newfoundland includes some of the most spectacular scenery in eastern Canada. The flat topped **Long Range Mountains** are cut by several deep fjords and deep fjord-like lakes flanked by near vertical cliffs. They rise to a desolate boulder-strewn tableland where the snow remains in crevices even in August. Between them and the coast there is in places a narrow but poorly-drained plateau sometimes high above the sea with an infinite variety of cliffs, sandy shores, rocks, tidal pools and little fishing communities.

Bonne Bay★★. – *Circular drive of 83 km - 52 miles. Take Rte 431 at Wiltondale.*

This is a fascinating and beautiful tour of a deep fjord and its several arms surrounded by the chunky peaks of the Long Range Mountains. Route 431 proceeds through hilly lake country to reach Glenburnie. From here, the drive along the **South Arm★★** is magnificent. Fishing boats and small houses are set against the dark blue waters of the Arm with the flat topped mountains rising all around. Dominating the drive to the north is the vast bulk of **Gros Morne Mountain** (alt 806 m - 2 644 ft), the highest point in the park. At Woody Point, a little ferry *(regular schedule, 20 min trip ; $4.00)* crosses the mouth of the Arm to Norris Point, a pleasant **trip★**.

There are fine views of the main part of Bonne Bay as the road climbs out of Norris Point and heads for **Rocky Harbour★** which has a lovely site at the mouth of the Bay surrounded by cliffs with a lighthouse on a little point.

Take Rte 430 E.

The road descends to **Deer Arm** which it follows until it joins East Arm. The drive beside the **East Arm**★ is fine with views of sheer cliffs and rounded hills. The road climbs out of the glacial trough filled by Bonne Bay to join Route 431 again at Wiltondale.

Route 430 to North Park Exit★★. – *54 km - 34 miles.*

After Bonne Bay there is a narrow coastal plain between the sea and the Long Range Mountains on which the road has been built. This is a fine drive up the coast past Baker's Brook with **views**★ south of the mountains around Bonne Bay. Several small communities of fishermen still exist in the Park and tiny fenced gardens can be seen along the road. These are often far away from any houses as the people cultivate any fertile spot and fence it to keep animals out. Sometimes

the road is at sea level, sometimes high above a rocky coast, and all the while, just inland, the Long Range Mountains march along looking like a gigantic step up from the coast because of their flat tops.

Western Brook Pond★★. – *29 km - 18 miles from Rocky Harbour. Walk of 4 km - 2 1/2 miles, allow about 45 min each way ; boat trip of 2-3 hrs, contact Visitor Reception Centre (see above).*

Western Brook runs through a spectacular gorge in the Long Range Mountains (which in typical Newfoundland understatement is called a "pond") before it crosses the narrow coastal plain and reaches the sea. This gorge resembles a fjord because of its towering 600 m - 2 000 ft cliffs and its depth (approaching 200 m - 600 ft) but it is not a true fjord because it does not extend to the sea. Bonne Bay, St. Paul's Inlet, Parson's Pond (just north of the Park), and the large Bay of Islands *(map p. 218)* are on the contrary true fjords. All of these whether fjord or "pond" are the result of gouging out by glaciers in the last Ice Age.

(by permission of Parks Canada)

Western Brook Pond

There are fine **views**★ of the deep gorge cut into the mountains from the road and a trail leads across the boggy coastal plain *(boardwalks over marshy areas)* to the edge of the pond. The only way to view the interior, however, is to take a boat trip. The sheer cliffs and the depth of the water are impressive and cannot be appreciated without entering.

After Western Brook Pond, the road continues along the coast as before. There are views of mountains with odd patches of snow caught in crevices and of the shore covered with rocks, boulders and driftwood. The road traverses St. Paul's, a small fishing settlement, clustered at the mouth of a deep fjord with a backdrop of mountains.

After leaving the Park, Route 430 continues up the coast for another 300 km - 200 miles to L'Anse aux Meadows *(p. 224)* with similar sea views but less dramatic mountain ones as the Long Range peaks are further inland and smaller.

HEART'S CONTENT ★

Maps pp. 11 and 218 – *58 km - 36 miles N of Trans-Canada Highway by Rte 80* – Pop 625

The **drive**★ to this little town on Trinity Bay is very pretty, through charming fishing villages such as Dildo, Green's Harbour, Whiteway, Cavendish and Heart's Delight. Fishing nets are laid out to dry along the highway and there are strange rocks protruding from the bay especially at Whiteway.

Heart's Content, founded about 1650 with a pretty **site**★, is famous out of all proportion to its size and appearance. In 1866 the first successful **trans-Atlantic telegraph cable** was landed here. This was the result of many years of work by the New York, Newfoundland and London Telegraph Company led by Cyrus Field. The first attempt to lay a cable was made in 1858 but, after inaugural messages between Queen Victoria and US President James Buchanan, the cable failed. A second attempt was made in 1865 which also failed. Finally, Field used the liner *Great Eastern* to lay the cable between Valencia in Ireland and Heart's Content where it joined a cable to New York. This time it was successful and Heart's Content went on for nearly a hundred years to be the major relay station in North America. At first cables cost $5 a word and the station handled 3 000 messages a day. In 1965 with increasing automation, the Heart's Content station closed.

Cable Station★. – *Open daily July and Aug; Provincial Historic Site;* ☎ *(709) 737-2460.*

The Newfoundland government has converted the now obsolete relay station into an interesting and well-organized museum. Displays tell the story of communications from earliest times to today with special emphasis on how long it took for messages to cross the Atlantic before telegraph was used. There is a special section on the laying of the trans-Atlantic cables, the part played by the *Great Eastern* and the importance of Heart's Content. A replica of the first cable office of 1866 has been made with the original equipment. This can be compared with the very complex equipment of the station which closed in 1965.

L'ANSE AUX MEADOWS

Maps pp. 11 and 218 – *453 km - 281 miles N of Trans-Canada Highway by Rtes 430 and 436. National Historic Park. Site open daily; Interpretive Centre open daily mid June - mid Oct; closed weekends and hols in winter; guided tours 20 min. Accommodation available in St. Anthony (48 km - 30 miles); camping nearby on Pistolet Bay;* ☎ *(709) 623-2608*

On a grassy ledge facing Epaves Bay at the northernmost tip of Newfoundland's Great Northern Peninsula are the remains of what is the oldest European settlement in North America authenticated to date. A Norse community existed here about 1000 AD. This site is so important that it has been included on the UNESCO World Heritage List of cultural and natural properties of universal value.

The Location of Vinland. – About 800 AD Norwegians, Danes and Swedes left their native lands due to overpopulation and began establishing themselves elsewhere. The Danes and Swedes stayed in Europe, the Norwegians went further afield. In 900 AD they settled in Iceland and from there explored Greenland, Baffinland and beyond in search of falcons and polar bears. One ship returning to Iceland was blown off course and sighted land (maybe Labrador and Newfoundland). The account of this sighting inspired **Leif Erickson** to go exploring. About 1000 AD he landed at a fertile spot he named Vinland for the wild grapes he found there and constructed a settlement for the winter.

This story is preserved in two Norse tales - the *Saga of the Greenlanders* and the *Saga of Erik the Red.* These sagas were passed on by word of mouth for hundreds of years before being written down. The location of Vinland therefore is unknown though many scholars have tried to find it. Generally it was thought Vinland must be on the southeastern coast of the United States because of the grapes, even though no ship could ever have sailed so far in the time suggested in the sagas. Then in 1960 **Helge Ingstad,** a Norwegian explorer and writer, began a systematic search of the coast from New England north. He found a group of overgrown mounds near L'Anse aux Meadows and excavated them 1961-68. The foundations of eight sod houses of the type the Norse built in Iceland were uncovered, several artifacts undeniably Norse in origin were found, evidence of iron working, an art unknown to the North American Indian, was unearthed and finally samples of bone, turf and charcoal were dated at around 1000 AD using the carbon 14 method.

Thus, L'Anse aux Meadows is certainly a Norse settlement. It is impossible to prove if it is the elusive Vinland, as with no stretch of the imagination can one envisage grapes growing anywhere in Newfoundland. But it does show that the Norse settled, albeit briefly, on the North American continent about 1000 AD, the first Europeans to do so.

Visit. – The site has been completely excavated and returned to its natural state. Nonetheless, the layout of the houses, a smithy and what may possibly be the first North American sauna can be seen. Nearby, three **sod houses** (a long house, a workshed and an animal shed) have been reconstructed. In the **Interpretive Centre,** there are displays on the Norse way of life, what the settlement might have looked like, and replicas of the artifacts found.

To find the description of a point of interest which you already know by name, consult the **index** p. 237.

PLACENTIA ★

Maps pp. 11 and 218 – Pop 2 204 – 42 km - 26 miles from Trans-Canada Highway by Rte 100 – About 8 km - 5 miles from Argentia ferry

Set on the east side of the bay of the same name, Placentia has a very beautiful **site**★★ on a small peninsula at sea level facing the bay and flanked by hills. A small channel, **The Gut,** separates the bay from two deep inlets almost fjords which stretch miles inland. European fishermen especially the Basques came to Placentia as early as 1500 because the harbour was good, fresh water was plentiful and the beach was excellent for drying cod. No settlement occurred however until the French established a small colony in 1662 in order to protect their interests in the Newfoundland fishery. They called it **Plaisance** and built fortifications both at sea level and in the surrounding hills. From Plaisance they launched attacks on St. John's, the English capital, successfully capturing it during the wars at the turn of the 18th century. The **Treaty of Utrecht** of 1713, however, not only confirmed the above as a British settlement but handed over Plaisance as well. The French fortifications were rebuilt by the British and they successfully withstood French attack in 1762.

The **Treaty of Paris,** 1763, confirmed Newfoundland as British territory and afterwards Placentia (the original Basque name) settled down to a prosperous life of fishing and ship-building. The latter industry died with the end of the era of wooden ships but fishing is still important. The years immediately preceding the Second World War saw major changes in Placentia because of the building of a large American base at Argentia nearby. **Argentia** was the centre of anti-submarine patrol during the war and also the site, albeit offshore, of the famous 1941 meeting between Churchill and Roosevelt that produced the **Atlantic Charter.**

Castle Hill★. – *Between Rte 100 and Placentia. Open daily ; picnic sites ;* ☎ *(709) 227-2401.*

This park is made up of both French and English fortifications and is chiefly renowned for its commanding position overlooking Placentia. There is an interesting Interpretive Centre with displays on the history of the area, then visitors walk up to the remains of Fort Royal, built by the French at the turn of the 18th century, rebuilt and renamed Castle Hill by the British. From the fort, there is a splendid **view**★★ across the Gut of Placentia, the bay and fjords (the tide rip in the Gut is quite impressive and can be observed from here). A path *(10 min)* leads past dry stone walls to **Le Gaillardin,** a redoubt built by the French in 1692, with views as fine as from the fort.

ST. JOHN'S ★★

Maps pp. 11 and 218 – Pop 154 820 – Tourist Office ☎ (709) 737-2830

The capital of Newfoundland lies on the **Avalon Peninsula** facing the Atlantic Ocean in the extreme east of the province. It has a spectacular **site**★★ on a fine natural harbour which is entered by a passage called **The Narrows** about 207 m - 680 ft wide and flanked by 150 m - 500 ft cliffs on the north side which rise to form **Signal Hill.** Once past the Narrows the harbour widens out to nearly 800 m - 1/2 mile for about 1.6 km - 1 mile. It is surrounded by steep rocky slopes on which the city is built. Close to the port the narrow streets are a clutter of brightly-coloured wooden houses. Along **Water Street,** the sailors of many nations can be seen while their fishing vessels are being repaired or outfitted in the harbour.

The Harbour at St. John's

Early Years. – Tradition holds that **John Cabot** entered the harbour on Saint John's day in 1497. Whether this is true is impossible to prove now. What is certain is that by the turn of the century fishing ships from several European countries were using the harbour as a base for the fishery. By 1583 the fishery was so important to England that Queen Elizabeth I sent **Sir Humphrey Gilbert** to Newfoundland to claim it officially as an English colony. Gilbert made this declaration before a crowd of English merchants, and he allocated to them their fishing "rooms" (places to dry their cod) for the season. Thus began the era of the notorious "fishing admirals" *(p. 220).* Harsh laws were passed to prevent settlement but nevertheless a few hardy souls persevered.

The Anglo-French Wars. – By the 18th century, the attitude of the British government towards settlement had changed *(p. 220).* A French force from Placentia *(see above)* destroyed St. John's in 1696 and the British realized that if they were to hold on to the colony they must have settlers to defend it. St. John's fell twice more to the French in the 18th century, the final battle being in 1762 at the end of the Seven Years' War though it was recaptured soon afterwards. These attacks persuaded the British government to fortify Signal Hill and the harbour entrance but St. John's was never again threatened.

ST. JOHN'S★★

The 19th Century and Confederation. – The 19th century saw the rapid expansion of St. John's as a commercial centre, but it was also a time of tragedy as devastating fires wiped out vast areas of it. Nevertheless, it was a wealthy city in the early 20th century and during the Second World War when it served as a centre for North American convoys. After the war, the decision of the dominion of Newfoundland to enter Confederation *(p. 220)* brought about a decline in the importance of St. John's situated as it was "with its back to the Gulf" - Canada. In recent years, however, there has been a resurgence in the capital particularly with the discovery of offshore oil reserves. Today, the harbour serves mainly as a supply and repair depot for international fishing fleets.

Regatta Day. – *Quidi Vidi Lake* is the site each year of the St. John's Regatta, the oldest sporting event in North America. It is held on the first Wednesday in August – or the first fine day thereafter. This is probably the only civic holiday decided at 7 am on the morning of the holiday. If the day is fine the cry goes up "The races are on !" and the population crowds to the lakeshore to watch the boat races.

Some Newfoundland Specialities. – The province of Newfoundland has a very particular cuisine *(see also p. 20)* and St. John's is the place to taste some of its traditional dishes. One of the most famous is **fried cod tongues.** This can only be prepared with fish caught the same day otherwise the tongues become tough and glutinous. After washing one pound of cod tongues and drying them with paper towels, they should be sprinkled with fresh lemon juice (one tablespoon) and then rolled in 3/4 cup of flour to which 1/2 teaspoon of salt and some freshly ground pepper has been added.

About 1/4 pound of lean salt pork, diced and with the rind removed, should then be fried in a heavy skillet until the pieces are brown and have rendered all their fat. The cod tongues should then be dropped into this fat and fried gently for about ten minutes on each side or until lightly browned. Then they should be drained, the excess fat being removed with a paper towel, and served immediately. This recipe should serve four to six people and it is generally presented with boiled turnips and potatoes.

■ SIGHTS *time : 1 day*

Signal Hill★★. – *Open daily ; parking at Visitor Centre or Cabot Tower ; details of walks available from Visitor Centre, National Historic Park ;* ☎ *772-5367.*

The cliffs rise steeply at the mouth of the harbour to form Signal Hill, a natural lookout commanding the approaches to St. John's harbour topped by the squat stone structure of the **Cabot Tower,** St. John's best known landmark. From the hill the **views★★** of the city and surrounding area are splendid by day and night.

Signal Hill was not strongly fortified until after the Seven Years' War despite its obvious strategic value. The present defences (in ruins) date mainly from the War of 1812. The hill has, however, traditionally been used as a signal station to warn of the approach of enemy ships or in later years to tell merchants or their agents of the arrival of one of their fleet. In 1901 **Guglielmo Marconi** chose it for an experiment to show that signals could be transmitted long distances by electromagnetic waves. He made communications history when he received the letter "S" in Morse code from Poldhu in Cornwall, England, a distance of 2 700 km - 1 700 miles.

Visitor Centre★. – *Open daily.* There are interesting displays on the history of Newfoundland particularly emphasizing the development of St. John's.

Queen's Battery★★. – From this fortification which dominates the Narrows, there is a magnificent **view★★** of the harbour. Immediately below is Chain Rock – a white pillar in the Narrows from which a chain was stretched across the harbour entrance to keep out enemy vessels in the 18th century. On the other side of the Narrows stand the remains of Fort Amherst now housing a lighthouse.

Cabot Tower★★. – *Open daily.* This tower was built 1897-98 to commemorate the quadcentenary of John Cabot's visit to Newfoundland. It also commemorates the diamond jubilee of Queen Victoria's accession. Inside, there are displays on Signal Hill itself and on the history of communications with a special section on Marconi.

From the top of the tower, there is a panoramic **view★★** of the city and the coastline as far as Cape Spear, the most easterly point in North America *(map p. 12).* There are also fine walks with views over and around Signal Hill.

In mid July and August, students in the 19th century uniforms of the Royal Newfoundland Regiment perform a **Military Tattoo★★** near the Queen's Battery *(Tues, Thurs, Sat, Sun at 3pm and 7pm ; 1/2 hr).*

Old City and Harbour★★. – An interesting few hours can be spent exploring the narrow streets with their brightly painted houses which descend to Water and Duckworth Streets, and watching shipping activities along the **Harbour Drive.** Visitors can walk right up to the vessels moored in this section of the harbour, a rare occurrence in large ports today. Ships from Portugal, Spain, Poland, Russia, Japan and the Faeroe Islands can frequently be seen. There are also fine **views★** of the harbour and Signal Hill.

Newfoundland Museum★ (M1). – *Duckworth St. Open daily ; gift shop ;* ☎ *737-2460.*

This pleasant museum provides a good introduction to the province. There are interesting displays on the various native peoples of Newfoundland and Labrador going back over 7 000 years *(second floor),* and the life of the European settlers from the 18th to the 20th centuries *(third floor).* There are also temporary and travelling exhibitions.

Newfoundland Museum at the Murray Premises (M2). – *Harbour Drive. Open daily ;* ☎ *737-2834.*

Located in the **Murray Premises,** a collection of mercantile buildings dating from 1847 and recently restored to house shops, restaurant, offices, etc, this branch of the Newfoundland Museum *(opened 1983)* is devoted to the province's maritime history. Displays trace the development of sea trades from the 16th century Basque whalers to the early 20th century fish merchants.

In the future, exhibits on the province's military and natural history will be organized here. There are also facilities for temporary and travelling displays.

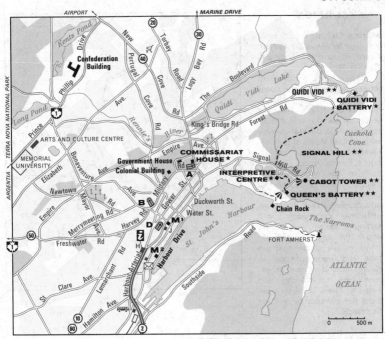

Commissariat House★. – *King's Bridge Rd. Open daily July and Aug ;* ☎ *737-2460.*
 This clapboard house with its tall chimneys and the little Anglican **Church of St. Thomas (A)** which stands beside it make an attractive ensemble. Dating from 1821 and 1836 respectively, they are among the very few buildings to escape the devastating fires of the 19th century. For many years the house was used by the Commissariat, the department responsible for supplying the military post of St. John's with provisions, fuel and storage and which also acted as the local government pay office. After 1871, it became the rectory for the church. It has been beautifully restored to reflect the 1830 period. The ground floor houses the commissariat offices and the kitchen, the second floor has entertaining rooms and bedrooms.
 A coach house has been reconstructed next to it to contain an interpretive centre showing how the house was restored.
 Not far away along Military Road stand two other interesting structures – **Government House,** a Georgian-style stone building constructed in 1830 and set in pleasant grounds, and the **Colonial Building,** a limestone structure with a classical portico built 1847-50 which once housed the provincial assembly and now houses the provincial archives.

Roman Catholic Basilica of St. John the Baptist (B). – *Corner Harvey Rd, Military Rd and Bonaventure Ave.* Situated on the highest point of the ridge above the city, this twin-towered church is a landmark from Signal Hill and in turn provides a fine **view★** of the latter and the Narrows. Opened for worship in 1850, the basilica has a decorated interior with a fine carving before the altar – Hogan's *Dead Christ.* In one of the transepts there is a statue of Our Lady of Fatima given to the basilica by Portuguese sailors who had survived ship-wreck on the Banks.

Anglican Cathedral of John the Baptist (D). – *Church Hill corner of Gower St.* This imposing stone structure was originally designed by Sir Gilbert Scott in 1843. Destroyed twice by fire it was only reconstructed this century and the tower and spire have yet to be added. It is a good example of Gothic architecture with a fine stone interior and tall windows.

Quidi Vidi★★. – This charming little community of fishing shacks, boats and nets is actually part of the city of St. John's. It is set on a tiny **inlet★★** flanked by steep cliffs just to the north of Signal Hill with an entrance so narrow as to barely admit the small fishing boats that use it. It is also connected by a narrow channel to the larger Quidi Vidi Lake, site of the St. John's Regatta *(p. 226).* Fresh fish and seafood are frequently on sale.

Quidi Vidi Battery★. – *Open daily July and Aug ; Provincial Historic Site ; accessible on foot or by road from Quidi Vidi,* ☎ *737-2460.*
 This battery, built by the French during their occupation of St. John's in 1762, stands above the community with a colonial-style wooden house at its midst. At the beginning of the 19th century the British tried to move the fishermen away from this inlet and block the channel as it provided a means of attacking St. John's from the rear. The fishermen, however, refused to move so the plan had to be given up and the battery strengthened. The house has been restored to the 1812 period.

Confederation Building. – *Information Office on ground floor ;* ☎ *737-3630.*
 The Newfoundland Parliament and some of the offices of the provincial government are housed in this brick building constructed in 1960. It stands high above the rest of the city providing a good **view** of the harbour and Signal Hill. The **Legislative Assembly** can be visited *(10th floor ; guided tours Mon - Fri ; 20 min).* It is interesting to note that the Government benches are on the left of the Speaker's chair. Accepted practice elsewhere is for the government to sit on the right. When the Newfoundland Assembly met in the Colonial Building *(see above),* there was only one fireplace - on the left of the Speaker, and govern-ments exercised their prerogative and sat by the fire. The tradition remains.

ST. JOHN'S★★

EXCURSION

Marine Drive★. – 29 km - 18 miles by Hwys 30 and 20. Leave St. John's on Logy Bay Rd (Rte 30).

This is an attractive and interesting drive up the coast to some little fishing villages north of St. John's. The road winds up and down in this almost treeless coastal country with endless views of the sea, headlands, cliffs, boats, fishing shacks and nets both in use and drying. It passes Outer Cove, Middle Cove, Torbay and Flat Rock and reaches **Pouch Cove★** an attractive community with fishing "flakes" on stilts above the sea. These traditional places to dry fish are less and less common in Newfoundland as most fishermen turn to filleting and freezing. There is also a view from the community of **Cape St. Francis.**

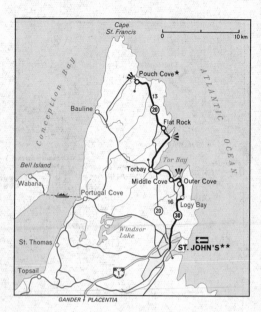

TERRA NOVA National Park ★

Maps pp. 11 and 218 - On Trans-Canada Highway ; camping, hiking, boating, cross-country skiing ; Information Office on Newman Sound ; ☎ (709) 533-2801

This 396 sq km - 153 sq mile area on the shores of **Bonavista Bay** is made up of rolling country and indented coastline much scarred by glaciers in ages past. Deep fjords or "sounds" reach inland and in early summer these coastal waters are dotted with icebergs which float down with the Labrador Current. The Trans-Canada Highway bisects the Park with some good views of these sounds but in the main visitors must leave the highway to appreciate this country.

Bluehill Pond Lookout★★. – 7 km - 4 1/2 miles from N Park entrance take branch road about 1.5 km - 1 mile to fire tower.

From the fire tower there is a fine panoramic **view★★** of the whole Park - deep inlets, cliffs, rocks, lakes, forest, bog and hills. Newman Sound, the Southwest Arm and Alexander Bay can be clearly seen.

Newman Sound★. – 12 km - 7 1/2 miles from N Park entrance take road to Park Information Office and Newman Sound, about 1.5 km - 1 mile.

There is a short walking trail along the shore of the Sound which is a deep inlet with low cliffs rising straight out of it.

Ochre Lookout Tower★. – 23 km - 14 1/2 miles from N Park entrance take road to tower, about 3 km - 2 miles.

From this lookout tower there is another panoramic **view★** of the Park with Clode and Newman Sounds standing out clearly. In the base of the tower, there is a display on how glaciers have shaped Newfoundland.

NORTHWEST TERRITORIES

No one who has visited the Northwest Territories in summer when day never ends – or barely, when the sun shines in a clear blue sky and when the land is alive with plant and animal life, can ever accept the common misconception of the North that it is a frozen wilderness. This vast region is more than a third of Canada's total area but it contains less than 1 % of the country's population. It encompasses all the land north of the 60th parallel between Hudson Bay and the Yukon including the islands in Hudson and James Bays and all the islands of the Arctic Archipelago between the mainland and the North Pole. Once the Territories were much greater encompassing most of Manitoba, Saskatchewan and Alberta as well as the northern regions of Ontario and Québec. Gradually these provinces have extended their land mass north leaving the Territories with their current borders *(map p. 16)*.

DESCRIPTION

Places referred to in the following text can be found on the accompanying Map of Canada.

The Northwest Territories are bordered by mountains on two sides. In the west rise the **Mackenzie, Selwyn** and **Richardson Ranges** which are part of the rugged western backbone of North America. In the east lie the shaggy glacier-strewn peaks of **Baffin, Bylot, Devon** and **Ellesmere Islands.** Next to the western mountains is a tongue of lowlands which is an extension of the plains of central Canada. Down this tongue runs the great **Mackenzie River.** East of this lowland lies the scarred face of the Canadian Shield pitted with lakes. The glaciers which retreated from this region 10 000 years ago scoured and gouged the ancient rocks leaving behind the intricate pattern of lakes and deep coastal fjords which exists today. They also left the land littered with glacial debris - huge boulders, piles of moraine, eskers (ridges of sand and gravel) and drumlins (elliptical-shaped hills inclining in the direction in which the glacier retreated).

Permafrost. – Another feature left behind by the glaciers is the layer of permanently frozen ground which underlies all regions where the annual mean temperature is below – 4°C - 20°F. This layer, known as permafrost, underlies a large area of Canada. It generally starts about 0.3 m - 1 ft or more below the surface and can be very shallow or as much as 370 m - 1 200 ft deep as at Resolute on Cornwallis Island.

Vegetation. – The tree-line crosses the Northwest Territories in a rough diagonal from the Mackenzie Delta to Hudson Bay at the Manitoba border. South and west of this line, the **boreal forest** of spruce, poplar, tamarack and jack pine common to all regions of Canada exists. To the north and east is the **tundra,** sometimes called the **barren lands** because of its bleak look in winter and because no trees grow. In summer, however, it is a colourful land of dwarf shrubs, a myriad tiny flowers of all hues, and **lichen** - a flat rootless growth part fungus, part algae, which flourishes where no other plant could possibly grow. These thrive in the surface ground above the permafrost because the latter prevents the moisture from draining away. Sometimes this surface ground is very boggy and swampy because it can not be drained and is known as **muskeg.**

Climate. – The annual precipitation over much of the Northwest Territories is so low (Yellowknife 254 mm-10 ins, Inuvik 276 mm-11 ins, Baker Lake 208 mm-8 ins, Frobisher Bay 409 mm-16 ins) that a great part of the region would be desert if the permafrost did not cradle what moisture there is on the surface. Generally, the winters are long, cold and dark and the summers surprisingly warm and sunny with long hours of daylight. During the summer months, the southern part of the Territories has 20 hours of daylight ; in the north, it never gets dark. The mean daily maximum temperatures for July are 21°C - 70°F in Yellowknife, 19°C - 66°F in Inuvik, 15°C - 59°F in Baker Lake and 12°C - 53°F in Frobisher Bay. The highest recorded temperature in July was 36°C - 97°F in Fort Simpson, the lowest was – 3°C - 26°F in Holman, Victoria Island.

The Aurora Borealis. – This amazing phenomenon also known as the **Northern Lights** can often be viewed in the Territories in the fall and winter. The sky seems to dissolve into folded curtains of elusive dancing lights sometimes of many colours, sometimes in black and white alone. Research into the cause of these displays is carried out at

Churchill, Manitoba *(p. 81)*, but it seems that they occur when electrically-charged particles emitted by the sun collide with atoms and molecules in the outer earth's atmosphere causing the latter to emit radiation which is sometimes in the form of visible light.

Population. – The inhabitants of the Northwest Territories number about 45 740. Of these nearly 16 000 are **Inuit** or eskimos (the name *eskimo* which means eaters of raw meat was given to the Inuit by the Indians of the south. *Inuit* is what these people call themselves ; it means the people). Another 10 500 are **Dene** or Athapaskan-speaking Indians. The rest are Metis *(p. 75)* or non-native.

HISTORICAL BACKGROUND

The first inhabitants of North America came from Asia across the land bridge which is now the Bering Strait *(p. 15)*. They settled south of the ice cap which covered the continent and as it retreated some of them moved north. Today, these people form two distinct groups.

The Inuit. – The life of the people of the Arctic Coast revolved largely around the hunting of sea mammals especially the seal and the whale. These animals provided them with food, blubber for heat and light, skins for clothing, shelter and boats, and bone or ivory for the blades of their harpoons or other tools. The smaller sea mammals were hunted from **kayaks** (one-man canoes), whales were hunted from **umiaks** which held up to twelve men. In winter animals were sought at openings in the ice. The occasional excursion south was made by **dog-sled** to hunt caribou, the skins of which were used for warm winter clothing or bedding.

The Inuit were nomadic, several families living and moving together. In winter they constructed **igloos**, dome-shaped snow houses made of blocks of snow and entered by a tunnel. The interior was lined with skins for insulation purposes. In summer they lived in tents of skins. Any time not spent seeking food and making clothes, especially their famous **parkas**, was devoted to carving in bone and soapstone for which they are today famous.

The lifestyle of the Inuit has changed drastically since the arrival of the white man. Igloos, dog-sleds and a nomadic way of life are today practically non-existent. On the other hand, many still live by hunting, supplemented by income from their arts and crafts, and they retain more of their traditional lifestyle than North America's other native peoples.

The Dene. – The Athapaskan-speaking peoples of the sub-Arctic lived a difficult life in a meagre environment. They hunted the caribou and fished, moving around all the time following the food supplies. Home was a conical-shaped lodge similar to the teepees of the Plains Indians *(p. 74)*. They travelled by canoe in summer and toboggan in winter. Today, some of these people still live a fairly traditional life of hunting and fishing but many live on the fringe of the white man's world.

The Northwest Passage. – The first white men to visit this vast region came looking for a trade route to the Orient around the north of the continent. The British sailor **Martin Frobisher** made the first attempt in 1576. His voyages were followed in short order by those of **John Davis**, **Henry Hudson** and **William Baffin**, all of whom have left their names on the map to mark their progress. Their reports of ice-filled seas somewhat dampened enthusiasm for the Passage and, except for exploration at the western end, no more attempts were made until the early 19th century.

The Fur Traders. – Meanwhile, other white men were penetrating the interior of the Northwest Territories after the trade in the skins of the many fur bearing animals. **Samuel Hearne** of the Hudson's Bay Company explored much of the region especially during his famous 1770-72 trip from Churchill to the Great Slave Lake and then down the Coppermine River to the Arctic Ocean. Not long afterwards in 1789 **Alexander Mackenzie** of the rival North West Company travelled down the river which bears his name. He, however, named it the "river of disappointment" as it led to the Arctic not to the Pacific as he had hoped. After the two fur companies were united in 1821 many trading posts were set up in the Territories, some of which remain to this day.

The Naval Explorers. – Mackenzie's voyage sparked new interest in a northwest passage and the first half of the 19th century saw the British Navy equipping expeditions to try to locate a navigable route. **John Franklin** made two overland trips to explore the western end. In 1845, he sailed a third time to try to find the connecting channel from the east. Years passed with no word from him, so eventually a series of expeditions, thirty eight in all, were sent to discover his fate. It was finally established that he and his entire crew had perished after years of being stuck in the ice. One effect of this tragedy was the exploration of a great part of the Northwest Territories by his would-be rescuers. The route of a passable Northwest Passage was also finally established although no one actually succeeded in navigating it until the Norwegian, **Roald Amundsen**, achieved it in 1903-6. Since then, many ships have followed the passage, among them the schooner *St. Roch (p. 59)*.

Later Explorers. – The Geological Survey of Canada mounted expeditions in the late 19th and early 20th centuries to explore and map the Territories under such men as Joseph Burr Tyrrell, Sir William Logan *(after whom Mt. Logan is named p. 72)*, George Mercer Dawson *(of Dawson City fame, p. 70)* and Vilhjalmar Stefansson. By this time there were already white missionaries in the region of both Anglican and Roman Catholic faiths. Soon afterwards, a new breed of explorer arrived - the prospector. Several major mineral finds *(see Yellowknife p. 235)* encouraged more white men to come to the Territories, a movement which is still continuing today.

RESOURCES

Since the 1930s the basis of the Northwest Territories' economy has been mining. Fur trapping, fishing, tourism and the sale of native arts and crafts also contribute but to a much lesser extent. Deposits of pitchblende and silver were discovered on the shores of the Great Bear Lake in 1930. This aroused interest in the mineral possibilities of other regions and led to the great gold discoveries at Yellowknife *(p. 235)*. Today, gold is still mined at Yellowknife. In 1964, the vast zinc and lead deposits at Pine Point on the Great Slave

Lake were found, and since then a mine of these same minerals has begun production at Nanisivik near Arctic Bay in the north of Baffin Island and on Little Cornwallis Island. Tungsten and copper are mined near the Yukon border in the Selwyn Mountains. There is a natural gas extraction and processing plant near Fort Liard, and producing oil wells and a refinery at Norman Wells on the Mackenzie.

The 1968 discovery of major oil and gas fields in northern Alaska spurred the search for these resources in northern Canada. Two potentially rich areas have been identified - the Mackenzie Delta - Beaufort Sea region and the high Arctic Islands. The question of pipelines and/or tanker routes through Arctic seas must be resolved before these resources can be tapped. Other minerals await exploitation for similar reasons.

Goods are transported to and from the Territories by either the Mackenzie Highway or the Great Slave Lake railway. Huge strings of barges float up and down the Mackenzie River all summer and the Delta is also accessible via the Dempster Highway. Winter roads criss-cross the frozen land between November and April giving heavy transport access to places which can only be reached by air for the rest of the year.

Handicrafts. – The distinctive arts and crafts produced by the native peoples of the Northwest Territories have long been popular among collectors and connoisseurs. This is due partly to their expressive nature and partly to the fact that they reflect a lifestyle different from that further south. The **soapstone sculptures** of the Inuit are the most famous. This grey or green-coloured stone can easily be worked with chisels and files before it is polished with emery paper to give it its distinctive finish.

Delicate carvings are also fashioned in ivory (from the walrus) and bone, and wall hangings and prints are produced. Cape Dorset on Baffin Island is especially famous for the latter *(see illustration p. 233)*. Certain items of clothing especially suited to this climate have become popular further south, in particular Inuit parkas and Indian mukluks beautifully decorated with beadwork.

SPORTS AND OUTDOOR ACTIVITIES

The Northwest Territories are a wonderland for outdoor enthusiasts and for those who want to get away from it all. Charter planes can take hikers, fishermen or **canoeists** (with their canoes) to remote lakes or regions where they are guaranteed never to see another soul. The northern summer with its twenty or more hours of daylight makes this a unique experience. Outfitters in the Territories *(list available from TravelArctic p. 232)* can organize and equip trips of all types in summer and winter. Canoes can be rented from one post of the Hudson's Bay Company and dropped off at another *(advance reservations required ; contact Hudson's Bay Company, U-Paddle Canoe Service, 77 Main St, Winnipeg, Man R3C 2RI ; ☎ (204) 943-0881)*. The Territories offer one of the world's great canoe trips down the **South Nahanni River** *(p. 235)* but a great variety of other routes of varying degrees of difficulty are available *(details from TravelArctic)*. There are also opportunities for hiking although this activity is less popular than canoeing in this land of rivers and lakes, with the exception of **Auyuittuq National Park** *(p. 233)*. All wilderness travellers (boaters, canoeists, hikers, etc) are asked to register with the Royal Canadian Mounted Police detachment nearest their point of departure for their own safety, and to notify the police when their trip is completed.

The Northwest Territories are liberally sprinkled with lodges on remote lakes and coasts where the **fishing** is superb (Arctic char, Arctic grayling, great northern pike among others) and the country is a wonder to the naturalist. All non-resident hunters of big game (wolf, moose, caribou, Dall sheep, grizzly, black and polar bears) must be accompanied by a licensed outfitter. *Details of seasons, bag limits and outfitters can be obtained from TravelArctic.*

Special Excursions. – A very special northern experience can be obtained by a visit to the **Naturalist Lodge** on Bathurst Inlet *(map p. 6)* on the Arctic Coast. The inlet is an outstanding habitat for wildlife and many excursions can be made to appreciate this (mid June - Aug). *For information write to : Box 820, Yellowknife NWT, X1A 2N6 ; ☎ (403) 873-2595.*

(after photo by National Museums of Canada)

Polar Bears

Another place well known as a wildlife habitat is **Wood Buffalo National Park** *(map p. 6)* which has the largest free-roaming and self-regulating herd of bison left in existence and is the last natural breeding habitat for the rare whooping crane. In addition, the Peace-Athabasca Delta is an outstanding area for waterfowl because four North American flyways pass through in Spring and Fall. *For details contact Park : Box 750, Fort Smith, NWT, XOE OPO.*

PRINCIPAL FESTIVALS

Easter	**Inuvik**	Top of the World Ski Meet
March	**Yellowknife**	Caribou Carnival
June	**Yellowknife**	Midnight Golf Tournament *(p. 236)*
June	**Yellowknife**	Folk on the Rocks
Summer	**Rotating in Western Arctic** (contact TravelArctic)	Northern Games – annual festival of traditional Inuit and Indian sports, dances, crafts, etc including the "Good Woman" contest.

PRACTICAL INFORMATION

Accommodation and Road Map. – Every year the government of the Northwest Territories publishes an **Explorers' Guide** which lists all the hotels, motels, lodges, camps, campsites in the Territories as well as much other useful information. This is available free with a road map from :

TravelArctic, Government of NWT, Yellowknife, NWT, X1A 2L9 ☎ (403) 873-7200.

Driving in the North. – What roads there are in the Territories have all-weather gravel surfaces and are continuously maintained *(precautions for driving on these surfaces p. 34)*. In summer the Mackenzie is crossed by ferry at Fort Providence and Arctic Red River (Dempster Highway), the Liard at Fort Simpson and the Peel at Fort McPherson. There are ice bridges across these rivers in winter. During the three to six week freeze-up and thaw periods (November and May), the rivers cannot be crossed. There are adequate gasoline stations in the Territories but distances between them are long so motorists should fill up at each opportunity, and be outfitted in case of emergency (tow rope, at least one spare tire, oil, fan belt, fuses, food, matches, axe to chop wood, insect repellent, water, and in winter, warm clothes and a snow shovel).

Time Zones. – The Northwest Territories span three time zones – Eastern Standard north of Québec and Ontario, Central Standard north of Manitoba, and Mountain Standard north of Alberta, Saskatchewan and British Columbia *(map p. 20)*.

Taxes. – There are no sales, hotel or restaurant taxes in the Northwest Territories.

Liquor Laws. – Liquor, wine and beer are available from government liquor stores in the larger communities, and they may be bought and consumed in licensed premises. Beer is also available from licensed hotels. The legal drinking age is 19. Some communities have voted for restrictions on liquor including prohibition of possession.

BOOKS TO READ

Canada North Now by Farley Mowat   *(McClelland and Stewart)*

Tundra - Selections from Great Accounts of Arctic Land Voyages by Farley Mowat   *(McClelland and Stewart)*

People of the Deer by Farley Mowat   *(Seal Books)*

The Land that Never Melts edited by Roger Wilson (Auyuittuq) *(Canadian Government Publishing Centre)*

The Headless Valley by Ranulph Fiennes (Nahanni)   *(Hodder and Stoughton)*

The Dangerous River by R.M. Patterson (Nahanni)   *(Gray's)*

One Woman's Arctic by Sheila Burnford   *(McClelland and Stewart)*

Nahanni Trailhead by Joanne Rohan Moore   *(Deneau)*

Access. – *Daily scheduled flights between Toronto or Montréal and Frobisher Bay ; regular service between Frobisher Bay and other communities.*

Day trips to Frobisher Bay in summer to see the midnight sun, contact TravelArctic (p. 232) for details.

Hotel accommodation in Cape Dorset, Frobisher Bay, Pangnirtung and Pond Inlet.

Baffin Island, named for British sailor **William Baffin** who explored its coasts 1615-16, is the largest, the most inhabited and the most scenically spectacular of all the Arctic islands. Its mountains rise over 2 100 m - 7 000 ft with numerous glaciers and its coasts are deeply indented with fjords. About two thirds of it lies north of the Arctic Circle and so in summer the continuous daylight causes the tundra to bloom with an infinite and changing variety of tiny flowers. Most of the inhabitants are Inuit living in a series of small settlements along the coasts. In some respects their lifestyle remains traditional *(p. 230)* although they have adopted certain southern ways (dress, housing, etc). The soapstone carvings, prints and lithographs of the Inuit of Baffin Island are world-renowned especially those of **Cape Dorset**.

The administrative centre of the island and the biggest community is **Frobisher Bay** where most of the white inhabitants live.

(by permission West Baffin Eskimo Cooperative, copyright 1975)

Caribou and Hunter by Soroseelutu

Pangnirtung★★. – Pop 839. This little community has a spectacular **site**★★ on the fjord of the same name dominated by the snowcapped mountains surrounding the Penny Ice Cap in Auyuittuq National Park. The park headquarters are located in the community *(open daily in summer, films, displays, ☎ (819) 473-8962)* and specially licensed local people will transport visitors down the fjord to the park entrance by freighter canoe when the ice in the fjord has melted *(July and August)* or by snowmobile the rest of the year. This is an impressive **trip**★ even if a visit to the park is not planned *(about 1 hr each way – warm clothing essential).*

Pangnirtung is also a good centre for studying the tundra vegetation and wildlife (birds and small mammals, and some large sea mammals in the fjord), for viewing the midnight "light" in summer (Pangnirtung is just south of the Arctic Circle so there is no sun at midnight although it never gets dark), and for buying local arts and crafts at the Inuit cooperative (specialities : woven goods, soapstone carvings).

Auyuittuq National Park★★. – Meaning the land that never melts in the Inuit language, Auyuittuq (pronounced ow-you-EE-took) is a most appropriate name for Canada's first national park north of the Arctic Circle. Fully one quarter of the park's 21 470 sq km - 8 290 sq miles is covered by the **Penny Ice Cap.** It is a stark landscape of perpetual ice, jagged mountain peaks rising over 2 000 m - 7 000 ft and glacier-scarred valleys which become deep fjords along the coast with sheer cliffs (900 m - 3 000 ft high). Only lichen survives on the rocks bared by the ice but in the valleys moss heath and a few dwarf shrubs thrive during the long hours of the Arctic summer.

Since its creation in 1972, Auyuittuq National Park has drawn climbers from all over the world to scale its rugged peaks. Hikers and campers also come for the challenge of surviving in this remote yet breathtakingly grand Arctic landscape. The most visited region of the park is **Pangnirtung Pass,** a huge U-shaped trench which stretches 96 km - 60 miles across the peninsula and rises to 390 m - 1 280 ft. It is usually ice free by late July although some years the ice never melts. It can be crossed by properly-equipped hikers who are used to rough mountain terrain and prepared to ford the frequent streams of glacial melt water. There is little shelter, constant wind and most of the going is on glacial moraine *(an average of 3 km - 2 miles an hour is maximum that can be achieved on full day's march).* However, this is a spectacular trip for those willing to make the effort.

Pond Inlet. – Pop 705. *Accompanying General Map of Canada K2.* This charming community in the north of the island overlooks the mountains of Bylot Island, summer home of thousands of snow geese, across the inlet of the same name. Soapstone and whalebone carvings can be bought in the community as well as Inuit parkas and footwear.

MACKENZIE Delta ★★

Map p. 4

Access. – *Dempster Highway from the Yukon (Dawson to Inuvik 798 km - 496 miles) - open all year except during freeze-up and thaw periods (p. 232). Few services on road. Motorists should be outfitted for emergencies (p. 232).*

Also accessible by air from Edmonton via Yellowknife, and from Whitehorse, Yukon.

The best way to appreciate the Delta is to fly over it ; charters can be arranged in Inuvik.

On leaving the Great Slave Lake, the Mackenzie is a vast and fast-moving river. It heads first west and then north for nearly 1 800 km - 1 100 miles gradually gaining size and becoming more powerful. Then suddenly 160 km - 100 miles from the sea, it shatters into a labyrinth of confused channels between which are thousands of lakes. By the time it finally reaches the **Beaufort Sea,** it is more than 100 km - 70 miles wide.

The Delta is an amazing place viewed from the air. The tangle of muddy channels which belong to the Mackenzie and to the Peel, which joins it at this point, can be distinguished from the lakes by their colour. The western edge of the Delta is clearly marked by the frequently snowcapped **Richardson Mountains,** the eastern edge by the low, humped **Caribou Hills.** Going north, it seems as though the land is gradually giving way as the areas of water become greater, then the Beaufort Sea is reached and the land ends completely. The land that exists is covered with low scrub (dwarf willow and juniper) except for areas of tundra along the coast. These shrubs turn bright yellow with the first frost *(usually late August)* making a most attractive display. The tundra itself is full of lakes and very colourful. Multihued mosses, lichens and flowers bloom in the short but light (24 hours daylight) Arctic summer.

The Delta is one of the most productive areas for wildlife in Canada's Arctic. It supports innumerable muskrats as well as beaver, mink, marten, fox, bear, moose, caribou and smaller mammals. Its channels and lakes abound with fish. White whales calve in its warm waters. The people of the Delta communities – **Inuvik, Aklavik, Fort McPherson, Arctic Red River** and **Tuktoyaktuk** survive by trapping, hunting and fishing. Today, however, a new basis for the economy of the area has been found. Under the Beaufort Sea lie huge reserves of oil and gas. Their extraction and transport to market will no doubt drastically change the region.

Inuvik. – Pop 3 147. *On Dempster Hwy ; airport ; accommodation.* Meaning place of man in the Inuit language, Inuvik lies on a large stretch of flat land beside the east channel of the Mackenzie. In 1954, the government of the Northwest Territories decided to move their administrative facilities from Aklavik, which was always being flooded. A model northern community was built and opened in 1959. Over the entire Delta the permafrost is only a few inches from the surface. This causes problems for house building as the warmth of a dwelling soon melts the ice and residents find themselves living in a swamp. The houses in Inuvik were therefore constructed on pilings, steamed into the permafrost before construction. Water, sewage and heating ducts are housed together in above-ground **utilidors** or covered corridors to stop them from freezing.

Inuvik is a thriving community. Supplies are brought in by the huge barges which sail up the Mackenzie and now by the Dempster Highway. The **Roman Catholic Church** is built in the shape of an igloo. It has a marvellously expressive **interior★** with paintings of the Stations of the Cross done by a young Inuit girl, Mona Thrasher, in 1960.

Tuktoyaktuk★. – Pop 772. *Daily flights from Inuvik ; ice road in winter ; accommodation.*
This charming little community on the shores of the Beaufort Sea is known simply as Tuk to northerners. It is the centre for the oil and gas exploration in the region and it has a Distant Early Warning (DEW) line site forming part of a chain of radar bases guarding Canada's northern frontier. It is however most famous for its **pingos.** These huge mounds of solid ice, one of nature's most curious phenomena, have been pushed out of the otherwise flat tundra by permafrost action. Covered with moss and turf, they resemble giant boils from the air. There are more than a thousand of them in the Canadian North, the vast majority located on the Tuk peninsula.

At the **Fur Garment Shop,** visitors can watch Inuit women making parkas and other items of clothing.

The accompanying General Map of Canada with its index
and the Map of Principal Sights (pp. 4–11)
will help you locate the places mentioned in these texts.

NAHANNI National Park ★★★

Maps pp. 5 - 6

This park is a wild, remote and staggeringly beautiful place in the southwest corner of the Northwest Territories. It consists of a large section of the South Nahanni River which flows through Selwyn, Mackenzie and Franklin Mountains before finally adding its waters to the Liard River, a tributary of the mighty Mackenzie. During its spectacular descent, the South Nahanni passes through majestic canyons, over an awe-inspiring waterfall twice the height of Niagara and close to a series of hot mineral springs which create around them a vegetation unusual at this latitude (between 61° and 62°N).

The Park's very inaccessibility is part of its beauty. It will never have roads and tourist facilities like other national parks. But for those willing to make the effort, one of the world's great natural glories awaits. Its universal value was internationally recognised in 1978 when it was listed by UNESCO as a world heritage site.

Land of Mystery and Legend. – Early in the 20th century, tales of placer gold lured prospectors to the valley of the South Nahanni. In 1908, the headless bodies of two of these adventurers were found. Other men disappeared without trace. Stories of fierce natives and of mythical mountain men were spread abroad... and the South Nahanni became known as a place to avoid. The mystery remains and the legends are recalled by names in the park : Deadmen Valley, Headless Range, Broken Skull River, Funeral Range, etc.

(by permission of Parks Canada)

Virginia Falls

■ SOUTH NAHANNI RIVER★★★

Access by Road and Air. – *Map p. 5-6. From British Columbia : take Alaska Highway to Fort Nelson (p. 35), Liard Highway to Fort Liard and air charter. From the Yukon : take Alaska Highway to Watson Lake (p. 36) and air charter. In the Northwest Territories : take Macken-zie Highway to Fort Simpson and air charter, or Liard Highway to Fort Liard and air charter. For details of all possibilities contact Park : Postal Bag 300, Fort Simpson, NWT, XOE ONO ; ☎ (403) 695-3151 ; or TravelArctic (p. 232).*

Access by Water. – *Various outfitters offer trips descending the river by rubber raft or outfitted canoe (equipment is flown in first). Intermediate whitewater specialists can des-cend the river in their own canoe - permission must be obtained from the Park first. There are also possibilities of ascending the river by jet boat. For details of all the above contact the Park or TravelArctic.*

Note : the following describes an ascent of the river by air or boat.

The 200 km - 125 mile excursion up the river from Nahanni Butte to Virginia Falls is one of the world's great wilderness trips. In this distance the river drops more than 120 m - 400 ft which is why canoeists generally prefer to descend it !

Soon after Nahanni Butte, the river divides into a series of channels known as the **Splits**, and passes close to a hotspring where pools of water at nearly 37 °C - 98 °F have caused ferns, chokecherries, rose bushes and flowering parsnip plants to proliferate. Then it passes through three of the largest river canyons in Canada, awesome places with immense cliffs and depths as great as 1 200 m - 3 900 ft. After the twisting 27 km - 17 miles of First Canyon, **Deadman Valley** is reached where the headless bodies were found in 1908 (p. 234). This is followed by the 34 km - 21 miles of Second Canyon and by Third Canyon where the river makes a 90° turn known as The Gate guarded by mighty Pulpit Rock.

Then, after the surging waves of Figure of Eight Rapids and a sharp bend, **Virginia Falls★★★** suddenly comes into view, the jewel of the Park and one of the North's most spectacular sights. Acres of water cascade around a central pointed rock and fall 90 m - 294 ft into the gorge below. The Albert Faille Portage can be followed around the falls (1.6 km - 1 mile). From it, a trail leads to the brink of the cataract where the river can be seen in spectacular rapids, just before it plunges over the falls.

YELLOWKNIFE ★

Map p. 6 – Pop 9 483 - Tourist Office ☎ (403) 920-4944 – *Local map p. 236*

Access. – *By Route 3 and Mackenzie River ferry (free) in summer ; ice road in winter. No road access during freeze-up and thaw periods (p. 232).*

Also accessible by air from Edmonton and Winnipeg.

The capital of the Northwest Territories lies beside Yellowknife Bay on the northern shore of the Great Slave Lake. It has a surprisingly pretty site almost completely surrounded by water and set on pink granite glacier-scarred rocks to which small trees cling. It has a modern "new town" where most of the population live and where shops and offices are located, and a charming "old town" circa 1934.

The City which sits on Gold. – Named for the copper knives traded by the local Indians and not for the colour of the metal which underlies it, Yellowknife is a very recent settlement. Its site was visited by Samuel Hearne in 1771, by Alexander Mackenzie on his epic journey to the mouth of the river which bears his name, and by John Franklin, but all were too pre-occupied with their travels to notice the gold. Prospectors en route for the Klondike 1896-99 did record some sightings but no one bothered to follow them up. It was only when pitchblende was discovered on the shores of the Great Bear Lake in 1930 that there was any interest in the rest of the region. In 1934 gold was found exposed beside Yellowknife Bay and a boom town sprang up overnight.

YELLOWKNIFE★

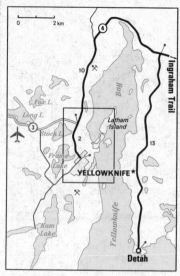

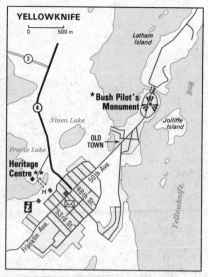

The boom did not last long, however, and the place was almost a ghost town in 1945 when new discoveries were made deep below the ground. Yellowknife is still thriving on this second boom. The mining and separating process is very expensive at the two operating gold mines but the continually rising price of the yellow metal keeps them economically viable. Yellowknife's importance was reflected in 1967 when it became the Territorial capital.

Midnight Twilight. – Yellowknife lies just north of latitude 62° and thus in summer it experiences nearly 24 hours of daylight. Every year a golf tournament is held on the weekend closest to June 21st. Teeing off commences at midnight. Among other hazards of playing golf on a course that is largely sand are the enormous black ravens (bigger than their southern cousins) that delight in making off with golf balls...

Yellowknife is also a good centre for boating, canoeing, fishing and camping. Its stores carry a fine selection of Indian and Inuit art and handicrafts.

■ **SIGHTS** *time : 1 day*

Prince of Wales Northern Heritage Centre★★. – *Entrance off Giant Mine Rd. Open daily in summer, closed Wed in winter ; snack bar in summer ; auditorium ;* ☎ *873-7551.*

This attractive museum overlooking Frame Lake is an important archaeological and ethnological research centre. It houses displays on the history of settlement in the Northwest Territories and a fine collection of Inuit sculpture. The ways of life of Dene and Inuit peoples are described as are the reasons why white settlers came to the north and the results of their having done so.

Bush Pilots' Monument★. – *Steps from Ingraham Drive in Old Town.*

This memorial, set on a rock which is the highest point in Yellowknife, honours the men who opened up the north.

From it, there is a splendid **view★** of the city, its surrounding waters and its rocky site. The red-topped tower of the Cominco gold mine dominates the skyline. The bay is a hive of activity with numerous small float planes arriving from the mining camps of the north or departing with supplies for some oil and gas exploration team. The large black ravens which are the city's emblem are frequently seen on the rocks.

From the Old Town, a causeway crosses to **Latham Island** where houses perch on rocks and on stilts above the water, where there is a Dogrib Indian settlement and views of the Giant Yellowknife gold mine.

Boat Trips. – *Cruises on Yellowknife Bay and around the islands, or anywhere on Great Slave Lake ; summer only ; contact Fred Henne, Great Slave Cruises, Box 1470, Yellowknife, NWT, XOE 1HO,* ☎ *873-2138. For other possibilities contact TravelArctic.*

These cruises enable visitors to see a little of this enormous lake (28 930 sq km – 11 170 sq miles) which is part of the Mackenzie River system and important for its fishery.

Detah ; Ingraham Trail. – These excursions by car in the vicinity of Yellowknife allow the visitor to see the landscape in this transitional area between the boreal forest and the tundra. The drive to Detah provides views of Yellowknife and its bay.

Detah. – Pop 143. *25 km - 16 miles.* This Dogrib Indian settlement has a fine **site★** on flat rocks overlooking the Great Slave Lake.

Ingraham Trail. – *64 km - 40 miles to Reid Lake.* This route skirts five lakes, a paradise for campers and canoeists.

INDEX

Montréal .... City, tourist sight or region described in the guide.
Agawa Canyon

Fraser, Simon .... Person or event described or explained in the guide.
Northwest Passage

Timmins .... Other persons, places or events mentioned in the guide.

Sask .... Province, territory or state.
NWT

Whitehorse .... National Parks or localities with National Parks.

The following abbreviations have been used :

Alta	Alberta	NS	Nova Scotia	Sask	Saskatchewan
BC	British Columbia	NWT	Northwest Territories	Yukon	Yukon
Man	Manitoba	Ont	Ontario	Wash	Washington USA
NB	New Brunswick	PEI	Prince Edward Island	Mich	Michigan USA
Nfld	Newfoundland	Que	Québec		

MANUFACTURE FRANÇAISE DES PNEUMATIQUES MICHELIN

Société en commandite par actions au capital de 700 millions de francs

Place des Carmes-Déchaux – 63 Clermont-Ferrand (France)

R.C. Clermont-Fd B 855 200 507

© Michelin et Cie, Propriétaires-Éditeurs, 1985

Dépôt légal : 1-85 - ISBN 2 06 005.161-4 – ISSN 0293-9436

Printed in France 7-84-30

Photocomposition Istra, Strasbourg - Impression Offset Aubin, Poitiers n° P 12 190

From coast
to coast...

in the city or on the highway...